Berkeley's Lasting Legacy

Berkeley's Lasting Legacy: 300 Years Later

Edited by

Timo Airaksinen and Bertil Belfrage

CAMBRIDGE
SCHOLARS
PUBLISHING

Berkeley's Lasting Legacy: 300 Years Later,
Edited by Timo Airaksinen and Bertil Belfrage

This book first published 2011

Cambridge Scholars Publishing

12 Back Chapman Street, Newcastle upon Tyne, NE6 2XX, UK

British Library Cataloguing in Publication Data
A catalogue record for this book is available from the British Library

ISBN (10): 1-4438-2726-6, ISBN (13): 978-1-4438-2726-3

CONTENTS

ABBREVIATIONS

Alciphron (Alc)	*Alciphron; or, the Minute Philosopher* (1732)
Analyst	*The Analyst; or, a Discourse Addressed to an Infidel Mathematician* (1734)
De Motu (DM)	De Motu; sive, *De Motus Principio & Natura, & de Causa Communicationis Motuum* (1721)
Notebooks (NB)	Two notebooks (*A* and *B*) published as *Philosophical Commentaries*.
Principles (P)	*A Treatise concerning the Principles of Human*
PI	Published Introduction to the *Principles*.
MI	Manuscript Introduction to the *Principles*.
Theory of Vision (TV)	*An Essay towards a New Theory of Vision* (1709)
The Theory of Vision Vindicated (TVV)	*The Theory of Vision ... Vindicated and Explained* (1732)
Three Dialogues (3D)	*Three Dialogues between Hylas and Philonous*
Siris	*Siris: A Chain of Philosophical Reflexions* (1744)
The Querist (Q)	*The Querist, containing Several Queries, Proposed to the Consideration of the Public* (1735-1737, 1750)
Works	*The Works of George Berkeley*, 9 vols, A. A. Luce and T. E. Jessop (eds), London, Nelson (1948-1957).

INTRODUCTION

George Berkeley (1685-1753) contributed to a wide range of academic disciplines; from philosophy to mathematics and empirical psychology; from theology to political economy and monetary policy. Today, he is almost exclusively known for his immaterialism, his challenging denial of matter (as this term was defined in those days). But in Berkeley's own days, his metaphysical works were either neglected or disregarded. Early on, he was famous for his contributions to moral and social philosophy. As late as the mid 1800's his psychology dominated the field. John Stuart Mill referred to it as "the Science of Man" or "the received [Berkeleian] modes of studying mental phenomena." At the same time, metaphysicians of the realist school attacked Berkeley's psychology as nothing but a vulnerable defence of idealistic metaphysics.

The result was a change of focus some 150 years ago towards either attacking or defending Berkeley's earlier forgotten immaterialism. For more than a century, Berkeley's metaphysics attracted almost all the attention, but today there is a growing interest in "the unknown Berkeley." The present volume of essays intends to meet the new interest in all of Berkeley's works, including such for a long time neglected contributions as his pioneering work of empirical psychology in the *Theory of Vision*, his contribution to economic theory in *The Querist* that inspired David Hume, Adam Smith and John Maynard Keynes, his Latin tract *De Motu* in which he anticipates modern theories in the philosophy of science, his *Passive Obedience* that has been interpreted as the first version of a utilitarian doctrine of morality, his mathematical inquiry in *The Analyst*, in which he among other things observes a slip in Isaac Newton's *Principia*, book 2, lemma 2, his *Alciphron* in which he anticipates aspects on pragmatism in moral and social philosophy, and of course the infamous *Siris*. After John Wild's *George Berkeley: A Study of His Life and Philosophy* (1936) no one has attempted to create a similar synthesis from the *Notebooks* to *Siris* along with an account of Berkeley's life and career.

In *Siris* Berkeley recommends Tar Water as a panacea and speculates about divine Trinities. He recommended tar-water because it was cheap, easy to prepare, widely available and efficient. It cools the patient down and soothes him. But most of all, it replaces strong alcohol which heats up the body and mind and destroys the person as well as the whole society.

But *Siris* is also a scientific treatise which comments on Newton, aether theory, and the nature of light. He mixes ancient philosophy, theology, physiology, physics and medicine in an intriguing manner. The renewed interest in *Siris* and also in *Alciphron*, which is evident in this volume, may well be a sign of things to come in Berkeley research.

But we also need to remember that Berkeley was a moralist who aimed at the education and eternal salvation of man. He visited America as part of his Bermuda Project and intended to build a college in Bermuda, but the British Parliament did not pay the grant as promised. The project failed. When in America 1729-1731 he stayed in Newport (now Middletown), Rhode Island, where he wrote the *Alciphron*. Through his gifts of books to Harvard and Yale and his acquaintance with (the American) Samuel Johnson he left a lasting impression on cultural life in America. In this volume, the reader will find several references to the interesting discussions between Berkeley and Johnson. Johnson later became the first president of the Anglican King's College in New York which later became Columbia University, New York. The city of Berkeley, California, was named after Berkeley.

George Berkeley has many interesting radical and challenging logical, epistemological, metaphysical and scientific ideas. Some of these have been studied very carefully and thoroughly like his immaterialism, but the full picture is still emerging and evolving. We hope that the present collection of new and previously unpublished articles by leading international scholars will mark a path towards a more adequate understanding of Berkeley and his place in intellectual history.

This new collection is published to celebrate the 300th anniversary of George Berkeley's *Principles* (1710).

The Editors are grateful to Heta Gylling, Roy Holcombe, Satu Ilta, and Birgit Strömgård for all their help.

—Timo Airaksinen and Bertil Belfrage

PART ONE:

BERKELEY'S PHILOSOPHY OF PERCEPTION

BERKELEY'S WAY TOWARDS CONSTRUCTIVISM, 1707-1709[1]

BERTIL BELFRAGE

Abstract

George Berkeley opens the *Principles* (Part I) with "a Survey of the Objects of Human Knowledge" including such ideas "as are perceiv'd by attending to the Passions and Operations of the Mind." Scholars have rejected this passage as being "philosophically impossible," not seriously meant, just a reference to John Locke's ideas of reflection, or not at all about "ideas." It is true, in a few unpublished manuscripts Berkeley used the term "ideas" for image-pictures of particular things (the Old Paradigm). But, I argue, in the *Theory of Vision* he develops a New Paradigm; and, if we follow Berkeley's advice to read his books "in the order wherein [he] published them," then his "Survey of the Objects of Human Knowledge" makes perfect sense in the light of this New Paradigm.

The Old Paradigm

Berkeley's view on perception in some of his early manuscripts is very simple.[2] God, the only active being in the world, produces perceptions in us; *we* are totally passive in perceiving. No matter, if we perceive *all* of an object or *part* of it, no matter by *what sense* or from *what perspective* we observe it; we nonetheless perceive *it*; we are certainly *not* referring to our

[1] A paper called "A Paradigm Shift in Berkeley's Philosophy 1707-1709" was published in the *Revue Philosophique* no. 1, 2010, 71-82. By arbitrary alterations the editors, Yvon Brès and Dominique Merllié, changed central passages into nonsense. Although I forbade publication, they published their version. To rectify this copyright infringement, I now publish this paper for the first time, though with a new title and without the Brès-Merllié contributions.

[2] *Notebook A* (first three fifths) (NB), "Of Infinites" and the *Manuscript Introduction* (MI).

sensations or *perceptions* of it. The relation between "real" objects and our image-pictures of them can be illustrated as follows (MI 20):[3]

(1) Objects ➔ Perceptions (= "Copies & Images" of these objects).

According to the tradition to which I oppose, "Berkeley always means by 'idea' a sensory object," and "sensory objects are essentially concrete, particular, picturable"; and he never changed his mind.[4]

Towards a New Science of Vision

I start with a general overview of Berkeley's steps towards what I take to be his new doctrine. The first step can be illustrated by an optical experiment named after Isaac Barrow. It was intended to show how we perceive distance, but it failed in a way that caught Berkeley's interest. In the experiment, an object was projected onto the subject in such a way that it looked fuzzy. Berkeley asked: How do people interpret fuzziness, when they judge about distance? In his version of the experiment, I call it "Berkeley's Experiment," he used two subjects, the one with normal eyesight, the other nearsighted. The normal-sighted person said "It is near," the nearsighted "It is not near; it is far away." I shall use the term "sensation" for what *both* of them saw (a fuzzy-looking object), and the term "perception" for what they saw, when the *one* said "I see a near-by object," the *other* "I see a far-away object." Thus in this case we have:

(2) The *same* sensations in two persons ➔ *different* perceptions.

As a non-deceiving god could not inform the one that the object is near, the other that it is *not* near in exactly the same situation, the outcome of the experiment called for an explanation. Berkeley explains it by their different experience of fuzziness: to a person with normal eyesight, an object appears fuzzy if we bring it very close to his eyes; but to a nearsighted person, distant objects look fuzzy (TV 36, 37, 39). This indicates a process, in which the perceiver interprets or judges incoming god-given data against earlier experience:

---

[3] I use clumsy arrows "➔" non-technically to illustrate what happens over a period of time. It does *not* stand either for equivalence or material implication, as Yvon Brès and Dominique Merllié insist.

[4] Editorial comment in *Works*, vol. 2, 8-9, 41n.

(3) Sensation → [- - Process - -] → Perception

How, then, does the human soul perceive? William Molyneux, for one, regarded this question "*by us unsearchable*";[5] but Berkeley had found a ticket to the field of empirical psychology, and that was the concept of mind that he developed in the early part of *Notebook A*. As known to us, he argued, "the soul" is nothing but a succession of ideas. This thesis has nothing to say about the nature of the soul, but it supplied him with a method for studying mental phenomena. I prefer to call it a Black Box Theory of Mind. We do not know what there is in the box; *all* we know is what enters the box and what comes out of it:

(4) Input (sensations) → [Black Box] → Output (perceptions)

To identify what is given, and to establish laws, by which we can predict how a person is likely to perceive an object in a given situation, Berkeley studied the causal chain from rays of light to visual perception. To carry out this task, he based his enquiry on three scientific disciplines, in modern terms: optics, physiology and psychology (TVV 37):

(5) Rays of light → Retina → Sensation → Process → Perception

Optics Physiology Black Box Psychology

In Berkeley's Experiment, for instance, the optician observed that the rays of light did not focus on the retina, which made the physiologist predict "Confusedness of Appearance." The psychologist could then forecast that the near-sighted person would perceive a far-away object, the normal-sighted one a close-by object.

In line with the Black Box Theory of Mind, Berkeley's search for significant regularities between input and output made him adopt an empiricist concept of causation in the *Theory of Vision*. Contrary to the *Principles*, the term "cause" is always used in its empirical sense in the *Theory of Vision*, never in its metaphysical sense. Accordingly, we read about such links of a causal chain as particles of the air causing effects on the rays of light, which cause effects on the retina, which cause a faint-looking sensation, and we have a psychological law saying that these kinds of events are likely to cause "an object to be thought greater" (TV 68-73). In Berkeley's psychology, the physiologist identifies the first link of

[5] Molyneux 1692, p. 106. Italics original.

unconditioned responses, such as sensations of sounds, light-and-colour, tastes, et cetera, which are not (yet) taken as sounds, colours, or tastes *of* anything. The psychologist is then supposed to investigate, by observing the last link of the chain, how these raw data are processed in the Black Box. Thus he investigates these stages of the act of perceiving:

(6) Unconditioned responses ➔ [Processes] ➔ Intelligible perceptions

One of the striking differences between the early view in (1) and the approach illustrated in (5) and (6) is that the two entities in (1), the "physical objects" and the god-given "pictures" of them, do not appear at all in (5) or (6). Ontological assumptions, he argues, are totally irrelevant to the psychology of perception:

> The Beings, ... which exist without, may indeed concern a Treatise on some *other* Science, and may *there* become a proper Subject of Inquiry. But, why they should be considered as Objects of the visive Faculty in a Treatise of Optics, I do not comprehend (TVV 19, my emphasis)

> To the absolute Nature, therefore, of outward Causes or Powers, we have nothing to say. (TVV 12)

He actually maintains that, even if his metaphysical doctrine is mistaken, then this would in no way affect his theory of vision (TVV 20). But how can a Black Box Theory of Mind help us to investigate mental states in another person's mind?

Investigating Mental States in Another Person's Mind

In the *Theory of Vision*, Berkeley returns again and again to the statement that we *can* have what he describes as an "*Idea* of [a] Passion" in another person's mind (TV 9, 10, 23, 41, 65, 94):[6]

> we see Shame or Anger, in the Looks of a Man ... for no other Reason, than barely because [certain Colours, and alterations of Countenance, which are the immediate *Object* of *Vision*] have been observ'd to accompany [Shame or Anger]: Without which Experience, we shou'd no more have taken Blushing for a Sign of Shame, than of Gladness.

This example illustrates the crucial pre-behaviouristic idea in Berkeley's Black Box Theory of Mind that we know mental states *only* by observing

[6] In this quotation from TV 65, "certain" in "certain Colours" is my gloss.

a person's voluntary or involuntary behaviour (TV 9-10).[7] What we see, when looking at a face turning red, is certainly no copy or image of the mental state in that person's mind; there is *no resemblance* between a red face and a passion. Yet, we do perceive passions, according to Berkeley, but not by sense but by a primitive form of induction.

Once we have noted the connection between red faces and a certain behaviour, the sensation of a face turning red begins to raise expectations in us (TV 23); we begin to take "Blushing for a Sign of Shame." This relation between a sign and what it signifies makes Berkeley distinguish between "two sorts of Objects apprehended by the Eye: The one, primarily and immediately, the other, secondarily and by intervention of the former" (TV 50, 54). I have referred to these two kinds of "objects" as "sensations" and "perceptions."

"Sign," as a technical term in the *Theory of Vision*, is closely connected with the concepts of "coexistence" and "suggestion." When different ideas have been "observed to go together," or to "coexist," we expect them to appear together even in the future.[8] In Berkeley's words: "Ideas, which are observed to be connected with other Ideas, come to be considered as Signs, by means whereof Things, not actually perceived by Sense, are signified or suggested to the Imagination."[9]

(7) Sensation ➔ [- - Induction/expectation - -] ➔ Perception

Berkeley illustrates this situation in one of his most quoted examples:

> Sitting in my Study I hear a Coach drive along the Streets. I look through the Casement and see it. I walk out and enter into it. Thus, common Speech wou'd incline one to think, I heard, saw, and touch'd the same Thing, viz. the Coach. It is, nevertheless, certain, the Ideas intromitted by each Sense are widely different, and distinct from each other; but having been observed constantly to go together, they are spoken of as one and the same thing. (TV 46)

When I hear a coach the sensation, that I am actually aware of, is nothing but a sound. It is my earlier experience that makes me think about those other data which normally coexist with it. But these other data are *not perceived by sense*; it is, Berkeley says, "*the Imagination*, whose Objects

---

[7] Even when Berkeley, later on, became convinced that there is a spirit in the box, he said: "Such is the Nature of *Spirit*, or that which Acts, that it cannot be of it self Perceived, but only by the Effects which it produceth" (P 27).
[8] TV 25, 55, 66, 72, 103, 110, 145.
[9] TVV 39. TV 25, 26, 28, 36, 37, 47, 50, 51, 53, 57.

they are, and which alone *perceives them*" (TVV 10, 39; TV 138-148, my emphasis). And this transition from the sensation of a sound to the perception of a coach is "So swift, and sudden, and unperceiv'd," so we are likely to make the vulgar mistake of identifying the sensation of a sound with the perception of a coach or identifying what we are actually aware of with what we expect to experience under proper circumstances. (TV 126, 145, 157)

These observations indicate that perceiving requires memory and imagination and is a mental act, which includes both induction and expectation. It can be illustrated as follows:

(8) Object(s) of sense ➔ [Mental act] ➔ Object of the imagination

The result is a surprisingly modern psychology of perception.

Berkeley's Constructivist Approach to Perception

Berkeley uses the Law of Specific Sense Responses to identify *what kind* of objects is given. It states that,

(9) If properly stimulated, each sense provides us with responses that are unique to this sense. (TV 46, 54, 129-130)

I call these sense-specific elements *pure sensibles*. They are pure in being sensations of no more than one sense. Thus by a "pure visual" I mean a sensation of *nothing but* light-and-colour, just as isolated sensations of sounds, smells or tactile experiences are "pure" audibles, olfactories, or tactuals. These basic raw data are given at time zero, "at our first Entrance into the World." At that time, "they were *not* connected in our Minds," but later on we learn to combine them into more complex units "by the slow Steps of Experience" (TV 144, my emphasis). In negative terms, the Law of Specific Sense Responses states that "the *Ideas* intromitted by each Sense are widely different, and distinct from each other" (TV 46). In other words:

(9') Responses from different senses are intrinsically different (Berkeley's term is "heterogeneous").

I refer to such more complex units, which include sensations of different senses, as *mixed sensibles* or heterogeneous units. Berkeley regarded it the main issue of his psychology to explain, how *different* raw data, or pure sensibles, become interpreted as qualities of more complex units of mixed sensibles, which are "considered *as one* thing" and "marked by *one* name" (TV 14, 35, 41, 42, 52, my emphasis). "The Solution of this Problem, in its full Extent, doth comprehend the whole Theory of Vision," he says, and adds optimistically: "Thus stating of the Matter placeth it on a new Foot, and in a different Light from all preceding Theories" (TVV 42). In (7) and (8), I illustrated the steps from sensation to perception, and in (9) I mentioned those pure sensibles that are "given," according to Berkeley. But by what laws does the mind combine these raw data into more complex units?

In *Principles* 146, we read about the "Laws of Pain and Pleasure, and the Instincts or natural Inclinations, Appetites, and Passions of Animals."[10] In the *Theory of Vision*, this law takes the form of a *Preservation Principle*:

> We regard the Objects that environ us, in proportion as they are adapted to benefit, or injure our own Bodies, and thereby, produce in our Minds the Sensations of Pleasure, or Pain ... Which Foresight, how necessary it is to the preservation of an Animal, every ones Experience can inform him. (TV 59)

This explains the direction of the process from sensation to perception. It says that,

> (10) If a person P considers a mixed sensible "as one thing," say T, in the situation S, then P expects that at least one element in T can be potentially useful (pleasant or painful) in S.

This should be understood in a very broad sense. If we run into a solid thing in full speed, such as a tree or a wall, for instance, we will be painfully aware of how useful it is to observe such things in the future. This pragmatic approach is further emphasized in the *Constructivist Thesis*:

> Every Combination of *Ideas* is consider'd as one thing by the Mind, and in token thereof, is mark'd by one Name. Now, this Naming and Combining together of *Ideas* is perfectly Arbitrary, and done by the Mind in such sort, as Experience shews it to be most convenient. Without which, our *Ideas* had never been collected into such sundry, distinct Combinations as they now are. (TV 109, 147, 153ff)

---

[10] In the *Principles*, Berkeley refers to these "never enough admir'd Laws" in an argument from design for the existence of a wise and good creator.

This is an important theme in the *Theory of Vision*. Without "the slow Steps of Experience," pure sensibles "were not connected in our Minds." And when we have learnt to use pure sensibles as signs for creating useful "Combinations of *Ideas*," then Berkeley asks us to "observe that Signs are variable and of Human Institution" (TV 144). As we read in the quotation above, the result of this "Combining together of *Ideas* is perfectly Arbitrary" in the sense that it is not necessary, which means not god-given (TV 109).[11] One important consequence is what I call the *Heterogeneity Principle*:

> (HP) If *x* is a mixed sensible, i.e. a unity of heterogeneous elements, then *x* is *not* given, but a "Combination of Ideas" made by the mind.

Several interesting consequences follow from the thesis that the mind combines ideas into units "as best suits it's own Ends and Purposes." If we "never" regard a "Combination of *Ideas*" as "one thing," unless we regard it "most convenient" in the present situation, then one consequence is the *Relativity Principle*, which says that:

> (11) If P and Q live under different conditions, with radically different background-knowledge, and P perceives *x* as "one thing" in S, then Q could very well be quite unable to perceive *x* as "one thing" in S.

Psychologists and zoologists will not be surprised at this standpoint, but philosophers will probably ask whether the faculty of perceiving is supposed to serve pragmatic purposes rather than to get at the truth? This question illustrates a fundamental difference between Berkeley's early metaphysics and his "Science of Vision." To the *Early* Berkeley, there was an immediate connection between "reality" and "truth," and the connecting link was god-given perceptions. So, at that early stage, our perceptions did provide him with indubitable "truths." But his "Science of Vision" is not about ontological truths; it is about the selective process in which animals tend to pay attention to some things, neglecting others, in the light of certain, probably inborn, pragmatic criteria. (TV 147, cp. TV 85, 87, P 146)

---

[11] For this sense of "arbitrariness," see also TV 143: "It is indeed Arbitrary that, in general, Letters of any Language represent Sounds at all; but when that is once agreed, it is not Arbitrary what Combination of Letters shall represent this or that particular Sound."

The Paradigm Shift

The Early Berkeley, on the one hand, spoke about "objects" as (1) "real" things, which (2) we are acquainted with by virtue of god-given perceptions; (3) and these perceptions represent "real" objects by resemblance.

In the *Theory of Vision*, on the other hand, (1) he is not talking about "objects" in the everyday sense of "real" things (ontological issues are irrelevant to his "Science of Vision"); (2) only such "objects" as pure sensibles are "given," whereas perceptions are end products of mental processes; (3) and these perceptions do *not* represent what they signify by likeness.

When the term "object" is used as a technical term in the one of these two contexts, its meaning is incommensurable with its use in the other context: a thesis formulated in the one cannot be translated into the language of the other.

Berkeley admits, however, that he does not always use "object" in a technical sense,[12] and that he was "betrayed thereby to say things, strictly speaking, neither true nor consistent." On the other hand, it is quite easy to follow his arguments, if we observe his method to proceed step by step, or "by degrees," as he puts it; first to formulate the problems in non-technical terms, or *outside the theory*, "gradually correcting our Judgment, and reducing it to a Philosophical Exactness" towards the end, when all entities have been properly analysed, defined, and brought *within the theory*. (TVV 35)

If a paradigm shift of the kind I have outlined can be established, then it explains the classical difficulty in understanding the opening section of the *Principles*.

The Survey of the Objects of Human Knowledge

Berkeley opens the *Principles* (Part I) as follows:

> It is evident to any one who takes a Survey of the Objects of Human Knowle[d]ge, that they are either Ideas [1] actually imprinted on the

---

[12] We read, for example, in the opening section that his design is "to shew the manner, wherein we perceive by Sight the Distance ... of *Objects*" and, accordingly, he mentions "An *Object* placed at a certain Distance from the Eye" (21); but then we read that "things placed at a Distance are not, strictly speaking, the *Object* of Sight" (46), that a "proper and immediate *Object* of Sight" is "not without the Mind" (43), and that people are prejudiced "in thinking what they see to be at a distance from them" (43).

> Senses, or else such as are [2] perceiv'd by attending to the Passions and Operations of the Mind, or lastly Ideas [3] formed by help of Memory and Imagination; either compounding, dividing, or barely representing those originally perceiv'd in the aforesaid ways. (P 1, additions in square brackets are mine.)

From the assumption that Berkeley never changed his mind it is natural to argue, as most scholars do, that the second kind of "ideas" [2] are "impossible."[13] Others maintain that he did not have his own but John Locke's "ideas of reflection" in mind.[14] The most extreme view is that "attending to the Passions and Operations of the Mind" requires looking into the Black Box to see the passions themselves and to look at the soul operating about its ideas.[15] The *only* way to "see" the passions in another person's mind is however, according to the *Theory of Vision*, by means of a systematic observation of that person's voluntary and involuntary behaviour (TV 9, 10, 23, 41, 65, 94); and "attending to" refers in this book to what we observe as empiricist psychologists, not as metaphysicians.

From a constructivist point of view, the opening sentence of the *Principles* makes perfect sense. That problem which, "in its full Extent, doth comprehend the whole Theory of Vision," is how [1] isolated, disparate pure sensibles become connected with other actual or potential sensations in the act of perceiving (TVV 42). Investigating this problem Berkeley observes, how our instinct to approach pleasure, avoiding pain, makes us [2] select and combine pure sensibles into momentary impressions, which we use as tools or principles of interacting with the surroundings.

---

[13] From the assumption that "Berkeley always means by 'idea' a sensory object," and "sensory objects are essentially concrete, particular, picturable" *Works* (2:8-9, 41n), it appears impossible to have an "idea" of "Passions and Operations of the Mind." Some scholars even argue that "such as" in Berkeley's "survey" refers to "objects" not to "ideas" (Johnston 1923, 144), but according to Alfred Klemmt "such as" does refer to "ideas" (Klemmt 1957, 122). Following Klemmt, E. J. Furlong argues that the sentence ends in a reference to "ideas ... perceived in the aforesaid ways" and, as "ways" is in the plural, it "must refer to the two previous classes specified, namely (i) 'ideas actually imprinted on the senses', and (ii) 'such as are perceived by attending to the passions and operations of the mind'." But, Furlong adds, "philosophically" Berkeley must have meant "objects," not "ideas" (Furlong 1964, 335).

[14] See A. C. Fraser (Fraser's edition of the *Works*, Oxford 1901, vol. 1, 257); Klemmt (1957, 122) and Flage (2006, 7-13).

[15] "It is clear to me that the objects we perceive 'by attending to the passions and operations of the mind' are ourselves, other finite spirits, and God," according to A. A. Luce, who concluded that "Ideas perceived by attending to the operations of the mind do not exist for Berkeley" (Luce 1945, 39f).

We use these momentary "objects of sense" as [3] signs of what we expect to perceive if we move, or if the situation changes. Thus, an "object of sense" signifies a series of potential impressions, which we consider "*as one* thing," perceive by "the Imagination," and mark "by one name" (TV 109, 147, 153ff, TVV 10, 39, my emphasis).

To sum up. At first, Berkeley regarded our perceptions as god-given pictures of "real" things:

(a) "Reality" ➔ Perceptions

In the next place, he investigated how perceptions emerge from sensations or pure sensibles:

(b) Sensations ➔ [- - ? - -] ➔ Perceptions

What we perceive as "one thing" is, according to this analysis, a "Combination of *Ideas*" created by us in a perceptual process for pragmatic purposes. Starting from this result, his new question was in the *Principles*: How do our perceptions relate to "reality"? It can be illustrated,

(c) Perceptions ➔ [- - ? - -]

but this problem falls outside the scope of the present paper.[16]

Bibliography

Belfrage, Bertil. (1992), "The Constructivism of Berkeley's *New Theory of Vision*," in Cummins and Zoeller (1992), pp. 167-186.

—. (2003), "Vers une nouvelle interprétation de la *Théorie de la vision* de Berkeley," in Berlioz (2003), pp. 159-211.

—. (2006), "The Scientific Background of George Berkeley's Idealism," in Gersh and Moran (2006), pp. 202-223.

Berkeley, George. (1987), *George Berkeley's Manuscript Introduction*. An editio diplomatica transcribed and edited with introduction and commentary by Bertil Belfrage. Doxa, Oxford.

—. (1948-1957), *The Works of George Berkeley, Bishop of Cloyne*, 9 vols, A. A. Luce and T. E. Jessop (eds), Nelson, London.

[16] I wish to express my gratitude the *Hultengrens Fond*, Lund University, for a grant that made it possible to write this paper.

—. (1871), *The Works of George Berkeley D. D.*, 4 vols, A. C. Fraser (ed.), Clarendon Press, Oxford.

Berlioz, Dominique (ed.) (2003), *Berkeley. Langage de la perception et art de voir*, Débat philosophiques. Presses Universitaires de France, Paris 2003.

Cummins, Phillip D. and Guenter Zoeller (eds.) (1992), *Minds, Ideas, and Objects: Essays on the Theory of Representation in Modern Philosophy*, North American Kant Society Studies in Philosophy, vol. 2, Ridgeview Publishing, Atascadero, Cal.

Flage, Daniel E. (2006), "Berkeley's Ideas of Reflection," *Berkeley Newsletter* 17, pp. 7-13.

Furlong, E. J. (1964), "An Ambiguity in Berkeley's *Principles*," *Philosophical Quarterly* 14, pp. 334-344.

Gersh, Stephen and Dermot Noran (eds.) (2006), *Eriugena, Berkeley, and the Idealist Tradition*, University of Notre Dame Press, Notre Dame, Indiana.

Johnston, G. A. (1923), *The Development of Berkeley's Philosophy*, Macmillan, London.

Klemmt, Alfred. (1957), "Anmerkungen," in *George Berkeley; Eine Abhandlung über die Prinzipien der menschlichen Erkenntnis*. Felix Meiner, Hamburg.

Luce, A. A. (1945), *Berkeley's Immaterialism*, Nelson, London.

Molyneux, William. (1692), *Dioptrica Nova*, Benj. Tooke, London.

BERKELEY'S NEW THEORY OF VISION: SCIENCE OR METAPHYSICS?

LUC PETERSCHMITT

Abstract

Bertil Belfrage has recently given a "new interpretation" of Berkeley's *Theory of Vision*. He opposes the view that it is a contribution to metaphysics; it is, he argues, a scientific theory comparable with physics and mechanics. I shall argue that both alternatives are mistaken: Berkeley does not present any definite theory at all in his essay on vision; it is not a contribution either to science or to metaphysics but an essay *towards* a theory that would include both scientific and metaphysical aspects. Even if the *Theory of Vision* is not a treatise on ontology or theology, and it is no doubt an empirical work, it is not a contribution exclusively to empirical psychology. Berkeley wanted to show the need for a new theory of vision. This explains why he seems to deal with both scientific and metaphysical themes at the same time.

The Principle of Autonomous Fields of Discourse[1]

Most of the time, commentators read Berkeley's *Theory of Vision* as a treatise on metaphysics: its object, its conceptual context and its consequences would be metaphysical – as A. A. Luce says, some commentators consider that it is an introduction to immaterialism.[2] Opposing this kind of reading, Bertil Belfrage has recently proposed a "new interpretation" of Berkeley's theory of vision (Belfrage 2003). He opposes the idea that Berkeley's work about vision is a contribution to metaphysics. However, at the same time, and in the same book, Margaret Atherton defends the thesis that Berkeley's theory belongs to metaphysics.

---

[1] Belfrage 2003, 159.

[2] See Luce, Introduction to the *Theory of Vision* (TV), in Berkeley, *Works*, vol. 1, 149-150.

According to her, Berkeley's intentions when he wrote his *Theory of Vision* were systematic and metaphysical, so that the *Theory of Vision* is not a piece of research about the perception of space (Atherton 2003, 137-138). Thus the question whether Berkeley's *Theory of Vision* is a part of "science" or a part of "metaphysics" arises. In this paper, my aim is to show that even if Belfrage's criticism against what he terms the "traditional interpretation" holds, it does not follow as a consequence of it that Berkeley's theory is not "metaphysical" at all. However, it does require a new interpretation of the meaning of "metaphysics" (it cannot be the sense criticised by Belfrage).

The conditions of the question have to be clarified. It can be asked only if it is possible to distinguish clearly between "science" and "metaphysics" – provided that such a distinction does not entail that the latter is not a form of knowledge. Berkeley proposes this distinction in the last sections of his De Motu. Belfrage terms this distinction the "principle of autonomous fields of discourse" (Belfrage 2003, 159-160; see DM 71-72). Berkeley clearly distinguishes three levels of discourse: physics, mechanics and metaphysics. The objects of physics are observed regularities; mechanics exists at a more theoretical level (explaining the regularities by reducing phenomena to mathematical laws); and metaphysics deals with the existence and the true nature of things. According to this principle, the question that I ask in this paper is: is the theory of vision on the same level as physics (viz. is it comparable or analogous to physics?) or is it on the same level as metaphysics? In order to answer these questions, it will be necessary to examine both the object and the method of the theory of vision.

However, it is possible to object that this principle is not that important. Indeed, Berkeley proposes it in what seems to be an occasional tract, written eleven years after he wrote the *Theory of Vision*. Reading the *Theory of Vision* in the light of this principle would be a retrospective reading. After all, it could be that Berkeley did not have this principle in mind in 1709. And this reading would give too much importance to this principle.

In fact this principle is a crucial aspect of Berkeley's thought. Even if Berkeley stated it explicitly no earlier than in 1720, it corresponds to his early thought on the relation between the sciences and metaphysics. There are notes in the *Notebooks* that show an early reflection on the relations between the sciences and philosophy (or metaphysics). Berkeley was deeply concerned about this topic from the starting point of his philosophical career. I do not intend to prove that everything is in the *Notebooks*. I just want to underline that the principle of autonomous fields of discourse is the final expression of early thoughts. If this is true, then it makes sense to read the *Theory of Vision* in the light of this principle: it was important enough to Berkeley (since he thought about it very early), and the light that it sheds on the *Theory of Vision* is not anachronistic. In his *Notebooks*, Berkeley is concerned about the relation between physics and philosophy: the former exists and the philosopher has to consider this reality[3]. He may propose new interpretations of scientific results; but his task is not and cannot be to modify these results. Berkeley declares: "My end is not to deliver Metaphysiques altogether in a General Scholastique way but in some measure to accommodate them to the Sciences, & shew how they may be usefull in Optiques, Geometry &c." (NB 207)

What does "to accommodate" mean? First, it entails that the philosopher has to prove the innocuousness of philosophy in relation to the natural sciences – "philosophy" here is to be understood in a quite broad sense. For example, Berkeley writes: "N.B. my Abstract & general Doctrines ought not to be condemn'd by the Royall Society Tis wt Their Meeting did ultimately intend. v. Sprat's History S.R." (NB 506)

There is no need for other examples. This is enough to prove that "science" exists before "philosophy." Thus, if the philosopher intends to struggle against scepticism, then he has to make sure that his philosophy is compatible with the existing science (if it is not, then this proves that the sceptics were right when they affirmed that our knowledge is not sound). However, the fact that philosophy is "accommodated" to the sciences also means that it has to be useful. This may mean: "Mem: To be eternally banishing Metaphisics &c & recalling Men to Common Sense." (NB 751)

There is something that is found in the sciences and that has nothing to do with them: a kind of metaphysics opposed to commonsense. In the context of the *Notebooks*, it is extremely difficult to assess with certainty what Berkeley meant thereby. However, one may guess that it concerns all that seems to be incredible – that is to say, all that contradicts the doctrine that Berkeley begins to elaborate in his notes. What this doctrine was

---

[3] Of course, this is true of natural sciences but not of mathematics: Berkeley does not hesitate to say that parts of mathematics, or even theorems are false – see for example NB 258: "Diagonal of particular square commensurable wth its side they both containing a certain number of M. V.," NB 263: Mem: To Enquire most diligently Concerning the Incommensurability of Diagonal & side. whether it Does not go on the supposition of unit being divisible ad infinitum, i.e of the extended thing spoken of being divisible ad infinitum (unit being nothing also V. Barrow Lect. Geom.). & so the infinite indivisibility deduc'd therefrom is a petitio principii."; and NB 264: "The Diagonal is commensurable with the Side." One may also add all the notes bearing on the calculus.

exactly does not matter here: it is enough to admit that it is a philosophical doctrine. It means that the sciences do not to deal explicitly with metaphysical themes (such as existence, causes and so on). In addition, it seems quite evident that the method that the philosopher may use to banish metaphysics is a kind of analysis of language, since "Words have ruin'd & over run all the Sciences, Law Physique Chymistry, Astrology. etc." (NB 702). This last item suggests that the metaphysics that is to be banished is conveyed by the delusion of words.

This short view[4] of Berkeley's notes tends to show that his early reflections structurally correspond to what he does in the *De Motu*. In particular, it seems that he considered that science (that is physics) is in a sense independent from metaphysics (even if the latter may be useful to the former). At least it is possible to say that there is something analogous to the principle of autonomous fields of discourse going on in the *Notebooks*. Thus, it makes sense to read the *Theory of Vision* in the light of this principle.

Moreover, this principle is a consequence of Berkeley's worry about the natural sciences. And he presents it as the received view in the *De Motu*:

> To treat of the good and great God, creator and preserver of all things, and to show how all things depend on supreme and true being, although it is the most excellent part of human knowledge, is, however, rather the province of first philosophy or metaphysics and theology than of natural philosophy which to-day is almost entirely confined to experiments and mechanics. (DM 34)

Berkeley notes that natural philosophy is limited to a certain kind of enquiry, leaving aside the theological (viz. the metaphysical) questions. This presentation is not altogether false. At least, it is a part of the programme of the Royal Academy of Sciences of Paris and of the Royal Society of London. The fellows of the Royal Society could not deal with God and human soul:

> "These two subjects, god, and the Soul, being onely forborne: In all the rest, they wander, at their pleasure."[5]

In the Royal Academy of Sciences, these subjects were not explicitly forbidden. However, they were not mentioned in the description of the tasks of the fellows: "Although each fellow has to deal mainly with all that

---

[4] For a complete study of this question, see Peterschmitt 2007, Chap. I and II.

[5] Sprat 1958, p. 83.

concerns the particular science on which he works, however all of them will be exhorted to extend their research to all that may be useful or curious in the diverse parts of Mathematics, in the diverse ways of Arts and in all that may concern anything in Natural History or belong in some sense to Physics."[6]

Implicitly the fellows of the Academy had to avoid theological questions[7]. Indeed, they did: the mentions of God are quite rare in the published memoirs. However, it is true that both Bernard le Bovier de Fontenelle and Thomas Sprat mention the possibility of dealing with natural theology. Just before the passage quoted, Sprat writes that "as to [God] they [viz. the fellows of the Royal Society] meddle no otherwise with divine things, than onely as the Power, and Wisdom and Goodness of the Creator, is display'd in the admirable order, and workmanship of the Creatures" (Sprat 1958, 82). And Fontenelle declares that "the fact that Physics leads us to some sublime thoughts about the Author of Nature is not something that should be taken as a pure curiosity of Physics [...] The true Physics rises to the point where it becomes a kind of theology" (Fontenelle 1732, XIV-XV). Both seem to admit a close link between physics and natural theology. However, it is necessary to remember that their writings had to justify the existence of the Royal Society and the Royal Academy of Sciences. Because of this apologetical aim, it is necessary to take such declarations cautiously. Indeed, the fellows of the Royal Society were charged with atheism[8]; and finally, the themes of usefulness (including the theological usefulness of physics) developed by Fontenelle are no more than *clichés* that may please the political power-

---

[6] "Règlement ordonné par le Roy pour l'Académie des Sciences," § 22, in *Histoire de l'Académie Royale des Sciences année M.DC.XCIC avec les Mémoires de Mathématiques et de Physique pour la même Année*, Paris, 1732, p. 6 (all translations from French into English are mine).

[7] This is confirmed by Bernard le Bovier de Fontenelle in his *Eloge de Malebranche*: Fontenelle emphasizes that the fact that Nicolas Malebranche was a theologian and a metaphysician was not a reason to accept him as an academician. As Fontenelle writes, as a metaphysician and as a theologian "he would have been at odds with the Académie des Sciences, which would trespass its limit recklessly in tackling theology, and which forbear metaphysics since this latter seems too much uncertain and too much disputed or at least whose usefulness does not appear clearly" (Fontenelle 1741, 108).

[8] As J. Cope and H. Whitmore note, for example, Henry Stubbes "makes the accusation that the Society is fostering a hidden atheism, basing his charge on their general sympathy with Descartes and the "mechanick" philosophy, which was popularly besmirched by its association with the terrible name of Hobbes" (Sprat 1958, Appendix B, p. 71).

that-be[9].

Then the principle set by Berkeley may be considered as descriptive of the practice in the Royal Society and the Royal Academy of Sciences. This implies that one has to take it seriously, since one of Berkeley's main aims is to secure science against the assaults of scepticism. Thus it makes sense to read the *Theory of Vision* in its light. And the question raised by Belfrage's new interpretation makes sense in its turn.

Belfrage's New Interpretation

First, I will give a short account of Belfrage's interpretation. According to him, Berkeley presents in the *Theory of Vision* an "experimental psychology" which is not a contribution to metaphysics. Belfrage gives three strong arguments in favour of his interpretation. I take these arguments to be correct, even if the conclusion drawn by Belfrage does not necessarily follow.

First, the *Theory of Vision* is not a contribution to metaphysics since Berkeley explicitly refuses ontological and theological considerations (Belfrage 2003, 173-175). He is quite clear about that point in the *The Theory of Vision Vindicated.* Berkeley restricts his discourse to the sensations whatever their cause may be. As Berkeley sees it, the problem is not to understand what the world is made of. He considers only our own ideas. In that sense, the question of the true nature of things is left aside, as well as the question of their existence[10].

This leads us to the second main argument, bearing on the conception of causality (Belfrage 2003, 175-183). Belfrage is the first to notice that in the *Theory of Vision* Berkeley uses an empirical concept of causality, as opposed to the metaphysical one (the opposition is summarized in the final sections of the *De Motu*). Berkeley always uses the notion of causality in its empirical sense in the *Theory of Vision*, whereas this is never the case in the *Principles*. The context is not the same: as the *Principles* constitutes a metaphysical book, it seems then that the *Theory of Vision* is a "scientific" one.

Last, Berkeley did not reject science, that is to say the geometrical theory of light. He contests only one point: the theory of vision is not geometrical. However, this does not mean that he criticized the whole of optics. Indeed, he uses optics several times in his theory. Even more

---

[9] See the analysis of such themes in Fontenelle's Preface to the *Histoire de l'Académie Royale des Sciences* (1699) (Mazauric 2007, 146-149).

[10] See for example TVV 20.

importantly, to Berkeley a complete theory of optics has to include the geometrical optics, as well as what could be termed a physiology of vision, and his own theory of vision.

These arguments lead Belfrage to consider that in the *Theory of Vision* Berkeley proposes a theory comparable with physics, that is to say a theory that is on the same level as physics.[11] This is the core of Belfrage's interpretation. The theory of vision describes empirical regularities, just as physics does: it is an enquiry on the way we perceive and not about what we perceive, nor its nature. According to Belfrage, it is possible to speak of an "experimental psychology of vision": Berkeley examines the psychological laws governing our perception. In a word, to Berkeley, there is a causal chain of perception (Belfrage 2003, 188-190), which ties four elements: 1. a stimulus; 2. an unconditioned answer (the consciousness of an object); 3. the background knowledge of the perceiver; 4. the conditioned answer (the object may appear more or less far way in accordance with the background knowledge). The task of the psychology of vision is to describe this chain, including the third element, which is, in Belfrage's interpretation, Berkeley's most important contribution to the psychology of vision. Indeed, this background knowledge justifies that it is a psychology: if the final answer (viz. the estimation of distance or magnitude or situation) depends on this knowledge, then the only way to know how we perceive is to build a psychology (geometry cannot take into account such parameters: they are nonsensical in a mathematical theory).

In this context, the task of the theory of vision is to describe how all the elements of perception are linked together. In particular, it seeks to know how the perceiver ties diverse "inputs" to estimate distance (visual, kinaesthetic, tactile... sensations). There is nothing metaphysical here. The method of a psychology of vision may be strictly experimental – the task of experimentation is to reveal the relations between the elements of a "perception" (in a broad sense).

A Critique of Belfrage's Interpretation

I have provided a broad sketch of Belfrage's new interpretation. Admittedly, his arguments are correct. In addition, they may confute the metaphysical interpretation of Berkeley's *Theory of Vision*. At least, they may confute a metaphysical interpretation, which amounts to reading Berkeley's theory in the context of the metaphysics of commonsense

[11] This does not mean (because it would be complete nonsense) that the theory of vision could be reduced to physics.

proposed by Reid (Belfrage 2003, 160). It is not my aim to discuss this part of Belfrage's argument – whether what he calls the traditional interpretation is truly Reidian or not (or whether it is traditional or not). I just want to show that Belfrage's conclusion should be qualified. Even if Berkeley's theory is not metaphysical in that sense, it may be metaphysical in another one. Now I will show that there are important differences between physics and Berkeley's psychology of vision. These differences entail that the psychology of vision and physics are not strictly comparable (that is to say that, according to Berkeley's principle of autonomous fields of discourse, they are not on the same level). These differences concern both the object and the method of the theory of vision.

As to the object of the theory, the question is not as clear-cut as Belfrage tends to present it. When Berkeley presents his own work on vision, he uses a vocabulary which seems to make it belong to metaphysics, according to the definition given in *De Motu*: for example, in *The Theory of Vision Vindicated*, he claims that he studies "the nature of visible things and visive faculty" (TVV 38).[12] If one has to take this vocabulary seriously, then the theory of vision, dealing with the "nature of" vision or the "nature of" the visive faculty or even (at least one time) the "nature of" visible things is a part of metaphysics. It is true that the last example is unique – it does not prove that Berkeley tries to build a complete ontology. However, this vocabulary gives us two precious indications.

On the one hand, it shows that Berkeley builds a theory of a faculty. Indeed this kind of psychology is a part of metaphysics. In the *Notebooks*, Berkeley's reflections on the soul are quite clearly metaphysical and Belfrage acknowledges that point[13]. Berkeley's starting point is metaphysical. There is no clear indication that he changed his mind between the *Notebooks* and the *Theory of Vision*. Moreover, in the *De Motu*, he clearly says that the "incorporeal things" (such as the soul) are the object of metaphysics or first philosophy.

On the other hand, Berkeley's vocabulary seems to show that he intends to examine more than empirical correlations. This is a part of his project – but it is only a part. The *Theory of Vision* tries to explain such "natures." Berkeley has in mind the thesis of the heterogeneity of sensible data: his minimal position about the "nature of" a visible object is that it is only a visible one. After all, it is not unreasonable to think that Berkeley

[12] See also TV 39, 51, 80 and TVV 16, 17, 18, 32, 43, 52, 70.

[13] In particular, he notes that Berkeley's early conception of the soul "is embedded in a religious context" (Belfrage 2007, 74). I thank B. Belfrage for bringing his paper to my attention.

had to determine the terms of the correlation before studying the correlations. However, Belfrage would answer that this argument misses the point: the question here is not the thesis of heterogeneity but rather what he calls the "law of specific sense responses" (Belfrage 2003, 207). The heterogeneity thesis concerns the thing (that is composed of different ideas); the law of specific sense responses concerns the way in which the thing is constituted by the perceiving spirit (and it includes more sensations than the thing: the estimation of distance may be grounded on kinaesthetic feelings – as the muscular sensation of the motion of the eyes, which does not belong to the thing). Nevertheless, this answer would not be complete. It supposes the specific difference between ideas (the kinaesthetic ideas are tactile ones). It is not clear that such position is a non-metaphysical one (even if everybody would admit this difference: such ideas or the parts of these ideas being the proper *sensibilia*). Indeed, this kind of question leads us back to a theory of the soul and its faculties.

As to the method now, it is not certain that psychology and physics are comparable. It is true that Berkeley's psychology is empirical. Belfrage has conclusive arguments on this point. Berkeley's method is certainly a kind of observation. However, the kind of "observation" used in psychology is not necessarily the same as the kind of "observation" used in physics. Indeed, the fact that Berkeley's psychology is empirical does not necessarily means that it is strictly experimental. Berkeley does not strictly follow the rules of the experimental essay in his theory of vision – rules that were largely accepted at the Royal Society. For instance, both Robert Boyle and Sprat stated such rules. The problem is that experiment may fail to give the outcome that is awaited. As Sprat writes:

> If the uncertainty proceeded from a constant irregularity of Nature, we had reason then to despair : but seeing it for the most part arise only for some defect or change in our progress, we should thence learn, first to correct our own miscarriages, before we cease to hope for the success. Let then the *Experiment* be often renew'd. If the same kinds, and proportions of Ingredients be us'd, and the same circumstances be punctually observ'd, the effect without question will be the same. If some little variation of any of these, has made any alteration, a judicious, and well practis'd *Trier* will soon be able to discern the cause of it; and to rectifie it, upon the next repetition. (Sprat 1958, 244)[14]

---

[14] Sprat deals with the problem of the contingency of experiments raised by Robert Boyle. For my purposes, his solution is similar enough to Boyle's one, even if both solutions are not identical. As R.-M. Sargent states it, "naturalists must not rely on single experimental results but must repeat their trials and vary circumstances of their production in order to ensure that the result could be used as reliable pieces of

Given the difficulties and contingencies of experiment, repetition and variation were the only way to establish the "matter of fact." However, this entails that the writing of the experimental essays must be as precise as possible. In particular, all the known conditions of the trials have to be described, and the results must be stated as precisely as possible (if this is not the case, then the repetition does not make any sense).

However, it is doubtful that Berkeley followed these rules in his writings about vision. This is what a careful study of the Barrow case shows. However, the case is the only piece of evidence that Belfrage exhibits to prove that Berkeley's theory of vision is experimental. First, Berkeley reinterprets Barrow's experiment in the light of his own principles. It proves that there is no real paradox (there is a paradox only for a geometrical theory of vision, which cannot account for this case). But it is only a very weak proof of his principles, because another explanation remains possible. Secondly, Berkeley presents what could be a counter experiment, which could confirm his principle and the role of the confusion of the image seen in the estimation of distance. He affirms that a purblind person would not be mistaken. However, his counter experiment cannot be performed:

> A person perfectly purblind (i.e. that could not see an object distinctly, but when placed close to his eye) would not make the same wrong judgement as others. For, to him, greater confusions constantly suggesting greater distances, he must, as he recedes from the glass, and the object grows more confused, judge it to be at a farther distance; contrary to what they do, who have had the perception of the objects growing more confused, connected with the idea of approach. (TV 37, I, 184)

The problem is that the conditions are too vague: what is a perfect purblind? What is the distance of the object? In a word, what is the degree of shortsightedness? Formally, this is a form of experimental reasoning. However, in fact, this second experiment (or, rather, counter experiment) seems to be no more than a thought experiment. Its conclusion is only expressed with a modal verb, as if Berkeley did not try it. The proof of Berkeley's experimentalism is very weak.

About this point, there is another noteworthy fact. In his *Notebooks*, Berkeley asks a very curious question about inverting glasses:

> Wt judgement would he make of uppermost & lowermost who had always

---

evidence" (Sargent 1995, 18). Moreover, Sprat writes this passage under the supervision of Oldenburg, secretary of the Royal Society: he does not express his own opinion on this point, see Hunter 1989, 68-69.

> seen thro' an inverting glass? (NB 148)

> Suppose inverting perspectives bound to ye eyes of a child, & continu'd to the years of Manhood, When he looks up or turns up his head he shall behold wt we call under. Qu: wt would he think of up & down? (NB 278)

These questions are certainly linked to the question of the inverted image on the retina. An experiment is possible. However, it is not sure that it would confirm Berkeley's position. To Berkeley, a return of upright vision should happen. However, this prediction is denied by recent research, in which none of the subjects wearing inverting glasses reports such a return (Linden *et al.* 1999, cit. in Van Cleve 2008). However, Berkeley's note remains isolated. Did Berkeley try the experiment?[15] If he did, it is possible that his theory contradicts the outcome – this would not be a proof in favour of Berkeley's experimentalism. If he did not, it could mean that the question does not really interest him. In any case, the question remains: if his psychology was experimental, why did he so completely abandon an experiment that could have been important?

Berkeley's psychology is empirical, grounded on observation. However, it does not seem that this observation is the same as in physics. This difference in method may imply that psychology and physics are not on the same level. After all, it is possible that metaphysics allows a more loose form of observation and does not require the precision of the purely experimental essay (because there are other ways or reasons to assess metaphysical tenets).

My last argument against Belfrage's interpretation is more important, since it involves the principle of autonomous fields of discourse, which justifies Belfrage's interpretation. The question bears on the relation between physics and metaphysics on the one side, and on the relation between the psychology of vision and metaphysics on the other side. If Belfrage is right in his interpretation, then there should be an analogy, and the relation should be the same. This is disputable.

In general, the relation between psychology and metaphysics is closer than the relation between physics and metaphysics. Berkeley strains the link between physics and metaphysics in two ways: he denies that physical

[15] It was possible, since William Molyneux in his *Dioptrica Nova* mentions the existence of such glasses. At least it was possible to imagine the experiment. There could have been factual reasons explaining why he did not perform the experiment – such as the fact that Berkeley could not use the glasses. But in that case, if he had been really interested, then he would certainly have complained or tried to use inverting glasses. At least, there would have been some other mentions of it in Berkeley's writings. But this is not the case.

or mechanical conclusions could be drawn from metaphysical considerations:

> But metaphysical principles and real efficient causes of the motion and existence of bodies or of corporeal attributes in no way belong to mechanics or experiment, nor throw light on them, except in so far as by being known beforehand they may serve to define the limits of physics, and in that way to remove imported difficulties and problems. (DM 41)

Secondly, and reciprocally, physics and mechanics provide neither ontology nor theology:

> To treat of the good and great God, creator and preserver of all things, and to show how all things depend on supreme and true being, although it is the most excellent part of human knowledge, is, however, rather the province of first philosophy or metaphysics and theology than of natural philosophy which to-day is almost entirely confined to experiments and mechanics. (DM 34)

The autonomy of discourses does not mean that there are no relations between discourses. For example, Berkeley proposes:

> That principle [Newton's Third Law of motion] could have been set forth in another way. For if the true nature of things, rather than abstract mathematics, be regarded, it will seem more correct to say that in attraction or percussion, the passion of bodies, rather than their action, is equal on both sides. (DM 70)

This amounts only to show that this fundamental law is compatible with immaterialism. Otherwise, Berkeley underlines that physics and mechanics provide "notable" arguments to prove and illustrate divine wisdom. However, he immediately adds that such arguments belong to theology or metaphysics: "Although it is most true that the investigation of nature everywhere supplies the higher sciences with notable arguments to illustrate and prove the wisdom, the goodness, and the power of God." (DM 34)

However, it is not certain that the relation between psychology and metaphysics is the same as the relation between physics and metaphysics. Berkeley seems to draw metaphysical conclusions from his psychology; and reciprocally, he claims to draw his theory of vision from metaphysics. The conclusion of the *Theory of Vision* is well known, but it deserves to be read carefully:

> Upon the whole, I think we may fairly conclude, that the proper objects of vision constitute an universal language of the Author of nature, whereby

> we are instructed how to regulate our actions, in order to attain those things that are necessary to the preservation and well-being of our bodies, as also to avoid whatever may be hurtful and destructive of them. It is by their information that we are principally guided in all the transactions and concerns of life. And the manner wherein they signify, and mark unto us the objects which are at a distance, is the same with that of languages and signs of human appointment, which do not suggest the things signified, by any likeness or identity of nature, but only by an habitual connexion, that experience has made us to observe between them. (TV 147)

This section is the conclusion of the *Theory of Vision*: what follows are only corollaries. Some remarks are necessary. Berkeley does not treat of the language of nature as an analogy with human language: the proper objects of vision are the way by which the Author of nature speaks to us[16]. If it is not an analogy, then this conclusion concerns the very nature of visible things, and theology. It is a metaphysical conclusion. Belfrage opposes to this reading a distinction between two analogies of language (Belfrage 2003, 204-205) – in the first, the signs are "of human institution" (TV 144): signs are considered as causes (occasions) because they suggest other ideas – this is the "scientific" (according to Belfrage) use of this analogy; in the second analogy, these signs are effects of God, and considered as such they tell us something about God (in a theological context). But in section 147, obviously, the signs are not considered as effects of God speaking; but God has instituted signs to tell us what we have to do. This mention of the language of the author of nature is more ambiguous than Belfrage admits. This conclusion gives some theological indications: if the ideas constitute a language, on the one hand, their cause is unique (if not, it would be quite difficult to understand how several causes could speak one language and produce one discourse); and it is a spirit (nature cannot be the speaker of a discourse that defines nature itself).

This conclusion is a strong one: it is possible, according to Berkeley, to argue reciprocally and deduce from it the whole theory of vision. The way from psychology to metaphysics can be followed also from metaphysics to psychology: "I shall therefore now begin with that conclusion, That Vision is the Language of the Author of Nature, from thence deducing theoremes and solutions of phænomena, and explaining the nature of visible things and the visive faculty." (TVV 38)

It is possible that this principle plays no real role in Berkeley's

---

[16] See Hamou 2003.

argumentation. It remains that Berkeley claims that it is the case. However, this claim is a direct violation of the principle of autonomous fields of discourse. To find "solutions" of phenomena is to explain them. However, physical and mechanical explanations are grounded on physical or mechanical principles only:

> The principles of experimental philosophy are properly to be called foundations and springs, not of their existence but of our knowledge of corporeal things, both knowledge by sense and knowledge by experience, foundations on which that knowledge rests and springs from which it flows. Similarly in mechanical philosophy those are to be called principles, in which the whole discipline is grounded and contained, those primary laws of motions which have been proved by experiments, elaborated by reason and rendered universal. These laws of motion are conveniently called principles, since from them are derived both general mechanical theorems and particular explanations of the phenomena." (DM 36)

If the psychology of vision is comparable to physics, one should be ready to admit that a proposition like "the proper objects of vision are a universal language of the Author of Nature" is a part of a natural science, or at least an empirical proposition. I do not find it possible; but then there is no true analogy between the psychology of vision and physics.

An Essay *towards* a New Theory of Vision: Berkeley's Theory in Context

It seems that if one has to interpret the theory of vision in the light of the principle of autonomous fields of discourse, then this theory falls in the province of metaphysics. But it is a strange metaphysics, which shares many features with empirical science – once again, Belfrage is certainly right in his criticisms of the "metaphysical" interpretations. The way in which Berkeley terms his discourse on vision indicates this oddness: the "essay" is also a "treatise"; and its content is sometimes a "science," some other times a "theory" and even a "philosophy." It is not easy to interpret this polysemy. However, it makes sense. This sense explains the ambiguity of a metaphysics, which seems to be an empirical science, or the ambiguity of an empirical science that seems to be metaphysical.

One must consider Berkeley's work in its historical context. Berkeley considers an old question about vision in the new context of the geometrical optics. This is shown by the history of "optics," as G. Simon sketches it (Simon 1996): in antiquity, geometrical optics is mainly a science of vision, with Alhazen, it becomes a science of light and vision at the same time and Descartes achieves its transformation into a science of light, by distinguishing the optical, nervous and mental moments of perception. Now, light and vision are clearly distinguished. But then, the physical and geometrical study of the former is not sufficient to explain the latter. Descartes did not ignore this field, of course. However, according to Berkeley, even if he distinguishes theory of light and theory of vision, he did not really draw the conclusion that should have been drawn: the theory of light and the theory of vision do not share their concepts and method. If the former is mathematical, the latter is not.

This explains the ambiguous status of Berkeley's theory. He has to achieve a double task: a) he has to produce a new theory; b) at the same time, he has to prove the necessity of this new theory. This double task is thus explained:

> In treating of vision, it was my purpose to consider the effects and appearances, the objects perceived by my senses, the ideas of sight as connected with those of touch; to inquire how one idea comes to suggest another belonging to a different sense, how things visible suggest things tangible, how present things suggest things remote and future, whether by likeness, by necessary connexion, by geometrical inference, or by arbitrary institution. (TVV 14)

Berkeley examines at the same time the link between ideas and the nature of this link. These two questions are different. For example, physics asks only the first, and examines which ideas are connected together. However, physics supposes that there is a link, and that it is regular: it supposes the nature of the relation. That is why, as Berkeley recalls in section 107 of the *Principles*, there is no demonstration in physics. Finally, to the philosopher of nature, it does not really matter if the ideas are connected necessarily or not. However, such a question is crucial for the "philosopher of vision": because the existence of a philosophy of vision distinct from geometrical optics and physiology depends on the answer. Reciprocally, clearing up the nature of the link between ideas is a way to examine the boundaries of the sciences, that is to say, which are the problems they can solve, and which questions they have to leave aside. One evident purpose of Berkeley's *Theory of Vision* is to prove that geometrical optics cannot explain how we see. If such a proof is given, then the necessity of a new theory is also proved. One of the roles of the *Theory of Vision* is to define the limits of geometrical optics (that is to say, to prove that it cannot be anything else than a theory of light). This is maybe why he did not say anything about inverting glasses: the Barrow case and the moon illusion are difficulties *for* geometrical optics. Thus, they are sufficient to prove that a new theory is necessary: the new theory is, as it were, called on by the geometrical theory of light, which acknowledges that it cannot explain vision. On the opposite side, the case of the inverting glasses would not have been a convincing argument: it could happen that such glasses are not a problem for geometrical optics. In a word, Berkeley exposes some difficulties for geometrical optics and shows that his own theory solves them.

It is now possible to suggest a solution to the ambiguity of the notion of "theory of vision" by distinguishing a narrow sense and a broad sense of this notion (even if this clarification is mine, and not Berkeley's). There are two kinds of "theory of vision":

> To explain how the mind or soul of man simply sees is one thing, and belongs to philosophy. To consider particles as moving in certain lines, rays of light as refracted or reflected, or crossing, or including angles, is quite another thing, and appertaineth to geometry. To account for the sense of vision by the mechanism of the eye is a third thing, which appertaineth to anatomy and experiments. (TVV 43)

In a large sense, the "science" of vision is constituted of three parts: the study of light, the study of the organ of vision and a "philosophical part," which is the theory of vision in the narrow sense. But when Berkeley begins to work on vision, the "philosophy of vision" does not exist (there is no true account of vision) – and then, to his mind, there is no real science of vision. So that Berkeley has to give room to this "philosophy" of vision, which is precisely what he does in his first book.

However, such an operation requires a definition of the sciences and their limits. This is the task of metaphysics:

> Mechanical principles and universal laws of motions or of nature, happy discoveries of the last century, treated and applied by aid of geometry, have thrown a remarkable light upon philosophy. But metaphysical principles and real efficient causes of the motion and existence of bodies or of corporeal attributes in no way belong to mechanics or experiment, nor throw light on them, except in so far as by being known beforehand they may serve to define the limits of physics, and in that way to remove imported difficulties and problems. (DM 41)

Finally, all this ambiguity is summarized in the title, which Berkeley gave to his work: he did not write a Theory of Vision, but an *Essay* which is towards a New Theory of Vision, a new theory of which he gives in his *Essay* only the essential features, waiting for the building of the complete "optics," which is now possible.[17]

Conclusion: When Science is not always Science

It is quite difficult to give a clear-cut conclusion: is Berkeley's theory of vision a part of metaphysics, or is it a science comparable to physics? The more cautious answer is: it is a part of metaphysics. If not, it violates the principle of autonomous fields of discourse. But such an answer is not completely satisfying: it is metaphysics without ontology, and with a minimal theology. Maybe one could say that it is the psychological part of metaphysics. And it is necessary to precise: it is the empirical part of the psychological part of metaphysics. This ambiguity is perhaps the reason why Berkeley termed his theory a "philosophy." It is a way not to decide its status, between science and metaphysics. The problem lies in the diverse tasks that Berkeley achieves at the same time. They make the theory of vision inseparable from the motives that led Berkeley to propose it, which were metaphysical – he had to show the limit of geometrical optics, to define a new way to account for vision as a faculty of the soul.

Of course, Berkeley's theory shares many features with the contemporary psychology of vision (even if one has to admit that it is certainly an old way for psychology). This means that Berkeley succeeded at least in achieving one of his tasks (to show the need for a new theory). So it is possible to say that Berkeley's theory belongs to philosophy also in a sense which cannot be Berkeleian. I have in mind the definition of philosophy given by John Langshaw Austin. To him, human research begins with philosophy. Sometimes, after much tumultuous debates, a part of it finds a method and then becomes a science, distinct from its origin (Austin 1962, 292-293). Finally, what is sure is that Berkeley makes the first steps towards a scientific psychology of vision – in *this* sense, it *is* philosophy.[18]

---

[17] See the conclusion of the *Theory of Vision*: "I do not design to trouble my self with drawing corollaries from the doctrine I have hitherto laid down. If it bears the test, others may, so far as they shall think convenient, employ their thoughts in extending it farther, and applying it to whatever purposes it may be subservient to" (TV 149). Berkeley does systematically study his own theory, as if his aim was not to expose a complete theory – it is not unreasonable to think that drawing corollaries, to explain new phenomena is essential to a science. If Berkeley's purpose was to establish a new science as a whole, then this "conclusion" would be quite paradoxical.

[18] I am exceedingly grateful to Camille Peterschmitt, who helped me to write this paper in English; Samuel Rickless read and corrected earlier drafts of this paper.

Bibliography

Atherton, Margaret. (2003), "Apprendre à voir: les enseignements de la *Défense de la Théorie de la Vision*," in Berlioz (2003), pp. 135-157.

Austin, John L. (1962), "Discussion," *Cahiers de Royaumont*, pp. 282-304.

Belfrage, Bertil. (2003), "Vers une nouvelle interprétation de la Nouvelle Théorie de la Vision," in Berlioz (2003), pp. 159-211.

—. (2007), "Berkeley's Four Concepts of the Soul," in Daniel (2007), pp. 172-187.

Berkeley, George. (1948-1857), *The Works of George Berkeley*, 9 vols, A. A. Luce and T. E. Jessop (eds), Nelson, London.

Berlioz, Dominique. (ed.) (2003), *Berkeley, Langage de la perception et art de voir*, PUF, Paris.

Van Cleve, James. (2008), "Berkeley vs. Reid on Three Puzzles of Vision" (International Berkeley Conference, Newport RI, June 2008).

Daniel, Stephen H. (ed.) (2007), *Reexamining Berkeley's Philosophy*, University of Toronto Press, Toronto.

Fontenelle, Bernard le Bovier de. (1732), "Préface sur l'utilité des mathématiques," in *Histoire de l'Académie Royale des Sciences année M.DC.XCIC avec les Mémoires de Mathématiques et de Physique pour la même Année*, Paris.

—. (1741), "Eloge de Malebranche," in *Histoire de l'Académie Royale des Sciences année M.DCC.XV avec les Mémoires de Mathématiques et de Physique pour la même Année*, Paris.

Hamou, Philippe. (2003) "Sens et fonction du modèle linguistique dans la Nouvelle Théorie de la Vision," in Berlioz (2003), pp. 47-78.

Hunter, Michael M. (1989), *Establishing the New Science: The Experience of the Early Royal Society*, Boydell Press, Woolbridge.

Linden, D. E. J. et al. (1999), "The Myth of Upright Vision: A Psychophysical and Functional Imaging Study of Adaptation to Inverting Spectacles," *Perception* 28, pp. 469-491.

Mazauric, Simone. (2007), *Fontenelle et l'invention de l'histoire des sciences à l'aube des Lumières*, Fayard, Paris.

Peterschmitt, Luc. (2005), *Sciences de la nature et philosophie dans la pensée de George Berkeley*, Atelier National de Reproduction des Thèses, Lille (see also http://documents.univ-lille3.fr/files/pub/www/recherche/theses/PETERSCHIMITT_LUC/html/these.html).

Last but not least, Bertil Belfrage considerably helped me to make my ideas and arguments more precise. This paper owes him all that is sound.

Sargent, Rose-Mary. (1995), *The Diffident Naturalist. Robert Boyle and the Philosophy of Experiment*, The University of Chicago Press, Chicago and London.

Simon, Gérard. (1996), "Kepler ou les leçons d'un contre-exemple en épistémologie," in *Sciences et savoirs aux XVIe et XVIIe siècles*, Presses Universitaires du Septentrion, Villeneuve d'Ascq.

Sprat, Thomas. (1958), *History of the Royal Society* [1667], ed. with critical apparatus by J. I. Cope and H. W. Jones, Washington University Studies, Saint-Louis, Miss.

ANALYSIS IN BERKELEY'S *THEORY OF VISION*

DANIEL E. FLAGE

> It is to be noted that, in considering the theory is in the synthetical method of delivering science or truth already found, we proceed in an inverted order, the conclusions in the analysis being assumed as principles in the synthesis. (TVV 38)

Abstract

In Section 38 of the *Theory of Vision Vindicated*, George Berkeley claims he had used the method of analysis throughout the *Theory of Vision*. What does that mean? I first show that "analysis" denoted a fairly well-defined method in the early modern period: it was regularly described as a method of discovery. Then I show that the discussion of distance perception in the *Theory of Vision* exemplifies the method of analysis and may be seen as a modification of a non-geometrical account of distance vision in René Descartes' *Optics*.

Analysis

In this section I show that the early moderns recognized a method of inquiry known as the "method of analysis."[1] I begin with Descartes' allusions to his use of analysis in the *Meditations*. Since Descartes claimed that analysis was the method of the ancient geometer Pappus of Alexandria, I look briefly at Pappus' remarks on the methods of analysis and synthesis in the "Treasury of Analysis." This will provide a general account of the method. I then turn to the account given by the Port Royal logicians, showing that their *Art of Thinking* reflects the same procedure

[1] As we shall see, this method was also known as the method of discovery, the method of resolution, and the regressive method. I am certainly not the first to examine this distinction within the context of Berkeley's work. See, for example, Turbane 1970, 28-53. See also Pappas 1983, 571-585, particularly 581-584; cf. Stoneham 2002, 121.

and objectives that are exemplified in Pappus, as do Isaac Newton's remarks in the *Optics*. While the evidence might be insufficient to show that Berkeley derived an understanding of the method of analysis from any one of these philosophers, the prevalence of uniform accounts of analysis is sufficient to show that the expression, "the method of analysis," was part of the intellectual *milieu* of the early eighteenth century and that one can reasonably assume that Berkeley understood it in the same way.

The meanings of words change. Since Immanuel Kant's work, the notions of analysis and synthesis have been patterned primarily on the analysis and synthesis of concepts: when one analyzes, one takes concepts apart, and when one synthesizes, one puts concepts together.[2] But before Kant, the analytic/synthetic distinction often marked a distinction between two methods of inquiry.[3] Synthesis is the geometric method of Euclid's *Elements*: it is the deduction of theorems from axioms, postulates, and definitions. Analysis is the "geometric method" that allows one to discover those axioms, postulates and definitions.

When the authors of the Second Objections to Descartes' *Meditations* suggested that "it would be worthwhile if you set out the entire argument in geometrical fashion, starting from a number of definitions, postulates and axioms,"[4] Descartes distinguished between the methods of analysis and synthesis. Both methods agree regarding order, viz., "The items which are put forward first must be known entirely without the aid of what comes later; and the remaining items must be arranged in such a way that their demonstration depends solely on what has gone before."[5] The demonstration is by analysis or synthesis. The latter was requested by the authors of the Objections; the former was used throughout the *Meditations*.[6] Of analysis, Descartes wrote:

> Analysis shows the true way by means of which the thing in question was

---

[2] This is not to say that Kant was the first philosopher to use the terms in this way. Thomas Reid likened conceptual analysis to abstraction: analysis involves taking concepts apart. See Reid 1969, 428-429, 479, 485-489. As Reid notes, this notion of conceptual analysis is analogous to chemical analysis, which involves the division of compounds into their simpler parts.

[3] Kant himself recognized the methodological distinction. See Kant 1977, 21n; Kant 1974, §§117-118, p. 149; see also Hegel 1975, §§227-288, pp. 285-286. Indeed, Kant said that the *Prolegomena* "is sketched out after an analytical method, while the *Critique* itself had to be executed in synthetical style" (Kant 1977, 8).

[4] Second Objections, in Descartes 1984-1985, 2:92.

[5] Descartes 1984-1985, 2:110.

[6] Descartes 1984-1985, 2:111.

> discovered methodically and as it were *a priori*, so that if the reader is willing to follow it and give sufficient attention to all points, he will make the thing his own and understand it just as perfectly as if he had discovered it for himself. But this method contains nothing to compel belief in an argumentative or inattentive reader; for if he fails to attend even to the smallest point, he will not see the necessity of the conclusion. Moreover there are many truths which – although it is vital to be aware of them – this method often scarcely mentions, since they are transparently clear to anyone who gives them his attention.[7]

Analysis is contraposed to synthesis. While synthesis begins with definitions, axioms, and postulates,[8] in analysis one seeks what is given in synthesis. In *Descartes*' works, analysis is a very general method; it is found equally in metaphysics[9] and geometry.[10] It is a search for explanatory principles: in geometry it is the search for axioms, postulates, and definitions, as well as solutions to specific problems; in the natural sciences it is the search for natural laws; in metaphysics it is the search for first principles. If, as some have argued, the method of analysis is identified with Descartes' method,[11] it is applicable to any subject-matter. As Descartes notes in the *Discourse*, the method he uses is doubly explanatory:

> For I take my reasonings to be so closely interconnected that just as the last are proved by the first, which are their causes, so the first are proved by the last, which are their effects. It must not be supposed that I am here committing the fallacy that the logicians call 'arguing in a circle'. For as experience makes most of these effects quite certain, the causes from which I deduce them serve not so much to prove them as to explain them; indeed, quite to the contrary, it is the causes which are proved by the effects. And I have called them 'suppositions' [hypotheses] simply to make it known that I think I can deduce them from the primary truths I have expounded above.[12]

But even if analysis and the Cartesian method are identical, this gives us relatively little insight into the method, since Descartes seems to have followed the ancient geometers in treating analysis as a sacred mystery.[13]

---

[7] Descartes 1984-1985, 2:110.

[8] Descartes 1984-1985, 2:111; should one have any question that such was Descartes' notion of synthesis, see the proofs at the end of the Second Replies.

[9] Descartes 1984-1985, 2:110.

[10] See Descartes 1952, 6-9.

[11] See Flage and Bonnen 1999; Hintikka 1978.

[12] Descartes 1984-1985, 1:150.

[13] On Descartes on the ancients, see Descartes 1984-1985, 2:111; of his own

How then, might we obtain more insight into the presumed method of analysis? Descartes regularly identified it with the method assumed by the ancient geometers, particularly Pappus.[14] So, by looking at Pappus' methodological remarks, we might gain some insight into the method of analysis.[15] Pappus described analysis as follows:

> Now analysis is the way from what is sought – as if it were admitted – through its concomitants [the usual translation reads: consequences] in order to something admitted in synthesis. For in analysis we suppose that which is sought to be already done, and we inquire from what it results, and again what is the antecedent of the latter, until we on our backward way light upon something already known and being first in order. And we call such a method analysis, as being a solution backwards. In synthesis, on the other hand, we suppose that which was reached last in analysis to be already done, and arranging in their natural order as consequences the former antecedents and linking them one with another, we arrive at the construction of the thing sought. ... In the theoretical kind we suppose the thing sought as being and as true, and then we pass through its concomitants [consequences] in order, as though they were true and existent by hypothesis, to something admitted; then, if that which is admitted be true, the thing sought is true, too, and the proof will be the reverse of the analysis.[16]

---

method, he said in the *Discourse*, "My present aim, then, is not to teach the method which everyone must follow in order to direct his reason correctly, but only to reveal how I have tried to direct my own" (Descartes 1984-1985, 1:112); cf. the remark following the double-explanatory passage quoted above: "I have deliberately avoided carrying out these deductions in order to prevent certain ingenious persons from taking the opportunity to construct, on what they believe to be my principles, some extravagant philosophy for which I shall be blamed" (Descartes 1984-1985, 1:150). As is widely recognized, Descartes' four rules of method (Descartes 1984-1985, 1:120) are compatible with any number of distinct methods of inquiry.

[14] See *Rules for the Direction of the Mind*, Descartes 1984-1985, 1:18-19; Dedicatory Letter for the *Meditations*, Descartes 1984-1985, 2:5.

[15] In some form, the method of analysis can be traced back to at least Aristotle's *Prior Analytics* and *Posterior Analytics*, if not to Plato. As John Herman Randall has shown, discussions of analytic method(s) were not uncommon during the middle ages and renaissance. Even those of a more Aristotelian inclination were at one with the geometers such as Pappus insofar as they held, for example, that in searching for a cause from an effect, the effect must be known to us, even if the cause is prior. See Randall 1940.

[16] From Pappus, "The Treasury of Analysis," quoted in Hintikka and Remes 1974, 8-9.

Notice that for Pappus, as for Descartes (and Berkeley, TVV 38), analysis and synthesis are mirror images of one another. Analysis is a search for general principles that would explain a certain phenomenon; in Pappus' case it is a geometrical phenomenon. The *proof* of the analysis is in the actual explanation; in Pappus' case it is the deduction of the phenomenon from the geometrical principles. Notice, analysis is fundamentally a method of discovery: that which is sought is a general (explanatory) principle.[17]

While a deduction of a phenomenon from general principles might be a necessary condition for an adequate analysis, it certainly cannot be a sufficient condition. Individual explanations are cheap: if there are no theoretical constrains, virtually anything will count as an explanation. "Why didn't my car start this morning? The gods of General Motors were frowning upon me, and whenever the gods of General Motors frown upon me, my car doesn't start" might count as an explanation, but it is certainly not an adequate explanation: the explanans are, at best, unverifiable. If one takes Pappusian geometrical analysis as one's paradigm – as Descartes certainly did – one can infer at least some of the properties that are assumed by an adequate analysis. The analyses of individual phenomena are parts of a larger system: the same principles that will allow one to infer or explain the properties of a triangle should also allow one to infer or explain the properties of any other plane figure. Insofar as the explanatory principles form a system, they must be internally consistent. Insofar as they are to have practical applications, for example, the construction of a figure with a determinate area, the consequences drawn from the principles (predictions) must be consistent with one's observations. The possibility of providing an explanation, as well as internal and external consistency were generally recognized as necessary conditions for the adequacy of an explanatory system even by those who were not explicit proponents of the *method* of analysis. For example, Robert Boyle listed the following as "The Requisites of a *Good Hypothesis*":

> 1. That it be Intelligible.
> 2. That it Contain nothing Impossible or manifestly False.
> 3. That it Suppose not any thing that is either Unintelligible, impossible or Absurd.
> 4. That it be Consistent with it self.
> 5. That it be fit & Sufficient to Explicate [explain] the *Phaenomena*, especially the Chief.

[17] In the Second Replies, Descartes also suggests analysis is or reflects a method of discovery (Descartes 1984-1985, 2:110).

> 6. That it be at least Consistent with the rest of the *Phaenomena* it particularly relates to, & do not Contradict any other known Phaenomena of Nature, or manifest Physical Truth.[18]

With the possible exception of the first and the allusion to unintelligibility in the third,[19] Pappus as a builder of a system of geometry would seem to grant each of these, as he would grant the fourth of Boyle's "Qualities and Conditions of an *Excellent Hypothesis*, predictability based upon the principles discovered:

> 4. That it enable a skilfull Naturalist to Foretell Future *Phaenomena*, by their Congruity or Incongruity to it: and especially the Events of which Expts are aptly derived to Examine it; as Things that ought or ought not be Consequent to it.[20]

While these might be necessary conditions for the adequacy of a hypothesis, they are not sufficient conditions. There are various additional conditions that tend to indicate that a hypothesis is true or probably true. Descartes held that at least the highest principles are known by the natural light (self-evident), although such a move seems unavailable to Berkeley.[21] When deciding among conflicting theoretical explanations, considerations of parsimony often were taken to play a role.[22] Descartes[23] and Berkeley[24]

---

[18] Boyle 1979, 119. That Boyle's notion of "analysis" was properly chemical analysis may be seen by perusing the other papers in the collection.

[19] The notion of intelligibility is somewhat obscure. As far as I can tell, there is nothing explicit in Pappus' account that requires the intelligibility of the explanans, although one would be surprised if Pappus were not committed to at least the *presumption* of intelligibility. *Berkeley*, of course, was clearly committed to the intelligibility principle, as is clear from his discussion of abstraction in the Introduction to the *Principles*. Indeed, he contends that the commitment to abstract ideas both hides actual unintelligibility and impossibility. For example, Berkeley held that the paradoxes that arise from the notion of the infinite divisibility of a finite line shows that the notion of a mathematical point is unintelligible. See Berkeley NB 21 and 21a, 322, 877; P 123-128; 3D 258.

[20] Boyle 1979, 119. Berkeley, of course, was strongly committed to the use of natural laws to predict events. See P 30-32, 62.

[21] Berkeley might have held that natural laws are necessary truths, but coming to knowledge of these truths is not a simple matter of self-evidence. See Flage 2009.

[22] Boyle included "2. That it be the Simplest of all the Good ones we are able to frame, at lest Containing nothing tht is Superfluous or Impertinent" among "The Qualities & Conditions of an *Excellent Hypothesis*," Boyle 1979, 119.

[23] Letter to Regis, January 1642, in Descartes 1991, 205; the *Meteorology*, Descartes 1984-1985, 1:187n2; cf. remarks in the *Optics*, Descartes 1984-1985,

almost certainly take parsimony to be a factor involved in deciding among theoretical explanations.[25]

So, one might ask whether Berkeley developed an understanding of analysis from Pappus or Descartes. The answer in both cases seems to be "No." There is no evidence that Berkeley read Pappus.[26] While Berkeley was clearly familiar with Descartes' *Meditations* as well as at least parts of the Objections and Replies,[27] Descartes' discussions of the method of analysis are so conceptually thin that it is unlikely that Berkeley gleaned his understanding of the method from Descartes. Nonetheless, since Berkeley's remark in *Theory of Vision Vindicated*, that "I observed a certain known method, wherein, from false and popular suppositions, men do often arrive at truth" (TVV 38) seems to echo Descartes' remark in the *Optics* that "In this I am imitating the astronomers, whose assumptions are almost all false or uncertain, but who nevertheless draw many very true and certain consequences from them because they are related to various observations they have made,"[28] there is reason to believe that Berkeley took his analytic method to be comparable to that Descartes used in the *Optics*. If Descartes himself was not the source of Berkeley's understanding of the method of analysis, there were ample accounts of analysis from which Berkeley could have drawn.

One of the most widely-read logic books of the early eighteenth century was Antoine Arnauld and Pierre Nicole's *Logic or the Art of Thinking* (*Port-Royal Logic*). Their discussion of analysis is drawn largely from Descartes' *Rules for the Direction of the Mind*, even though Descartes never explicitly identifies his method there with the method of

---

1:153-154, 165, *Principles of Philosophy*, Part 2, §43, Descartes 1984-1985, 1:243-244.

[24] In the discussion of abstract ideas (PI 11-12) the fact that Berkeley provides an account of the meaning of general terms that *does not* require Lockean abstract ideas suggests a commitment to parsimony, as does his discussion of occasionalism in 3D 220; cf. P 151 and NB 637.

[25] The quality of the explanation was commonly taken the mark of a strong hypothesis. Ideally, there would be only one hypothesis that would explain the phenomenon. One finds this among Boyle's the Qualities & Conditions of an *Excellent Hypothesis*: "3. That it be the only Hypothesis that Can explicate [explain] the *Phaenomena*, or at least that it does explicate them so well" (Boyle 1979, 119). Kant claimed it must be the *only* hypothesis that will explain the phenomenon, Kant 1977, p. 21n.

[26] This is based on an electronic scan of the *Works*.

[27] See NB 784, 785, 790, 794-799, 805, 818, 845. Berkeley provides no explicit references to the discussion of analysis in the Second Replies.

[28] Descartes 1984-1985, 1:152-153.

analysis. Analysis is the explicit topic of Part 4, Chapter 2 of the *Port-Royal Logic*.

The discussion of analysis or resolution is constructed largely in contrast to the method of synthesis or composition. The latter is based on definitions and self-evident principles.[29] Analysis is the search for those definitions and general principles.[30] The paradigm of analysis is geometrical analysis, which is a search for the basic elements of geometry.[31] Another type of analysis is the search for causes from effects.[32] The focus in analysis is typically narrow: it is concerned with a specific issue rather than an entire body of science.[33] One of the examples of analysis that Arnauld and Nicole discuss is "the figure of a Tantalus which, when set on a column in the middle of a vase in the posture of a man who is bending over to drink, can never do it because the water may easily raise in the vase up to his mouth, but flows out as soon as it reaches his lips, without leaving the vase."[34] This can be explained by a siphon. Another is "the secret of the water drinker who appeared in Paris nearly twenty years ago, and how, by spitting water from his mouth, he could fill five or six different glasses with different colored water at the same time."[35] It is probable that the difference in color is explained by coloring that was placed in the bottom of each glass.[36] Analysis "differs from the method of composition [synthesis] in that these known truths are taken not from more general things as is done in the method of instruction [synthesis]. Thus, in the example we presented, we did not begin by establishing these general maxims: that no substance perishes, properly speaking; that what is called destruction is only a dissolution of parts; that therefore what has no parts cannot be destroyed, etc. Instead we rose by stages to these general maxims."[37]

Analysis is comparable to climbing up a mountain from a valley; synthesis is comparable to climbing down a mountain to a valley.[38]

---

[29] Arnauld and Nicole 1996, 239; cf. Descartes 1984-1985, 2:110-111.
[30] Cf. Descartes 1984-1985, 2:110.
[31] Arnauld and Nicole 1996, 238.
[32] Arnauld and Nicole 1996, 234; cf. Descartes 1984-1985, 1:50.
[33] Arnauld and Nicole 1996, 234.
[34] Arnauld and Nicole 1996, 235.
[35] Arnauld and Nicole 1996, 236.
[36] Arnauld and Nicole 1996, 236. They also discuss the riddle of the Sphinx, which is resolved by the clarification of ideas (Arnauld and Nicole 1996, 235).
[37] Arnauld and Nicole 1996, 237.
[38] Arnauld and Nicole 1996, 237-8.

Conceptually, analysis is a search for higher principles.[39] Again one might ask, was it from the *Port-Royal Logic* that Berkeley derived his understanding of the method of analysis? Again, there is no hard evidence that he was familiar with the work.[40] And again, this hardly means that Berkeley's understanding of the method of analysis differed from that presented there.[41]

Berkeley might have derived at least part of his understanding of the method of analysis from Newton. In *Optics*, Book III, Part I, Newton

---

[39] Some might object that I have presented a very selective reading of the *Port-Royal* discussion of analysis. I plead guilty, but I believe my reading is justified. The discussion of analysis in the *Port-Royal Logic* (Arnauld and Nicole 1996, 233-239) combines remarks on analysis with more general problem-solving techniques. Insofar as the paradigm of synthesis is Euclidean geometry and analysis is contrasted with it in terms of the direction of inquiry, one can infer that analysis is a search for general principles (see Arnauld and Nicole 1996, 238 on analysis in geometry). But Arnauld and Nicole's discussion also includes more general issues. For example, the discussion closes with Descartes' list of the four rules of method in the *Discourse*, which "may be useful for guarding against error when we try to find the truth in the human sciences, although in fact, they are general enough for all kinds of methods, and not specific to analysis alone" (Arnauld and Nicole 1996, 238). Similarly, it is a rule that applies to any method that "we should practice proceeding from what is better known to what is less well known. For there is no true method which could dispense with this rule" (Arnauld and Nicole 1996, 237). Hence, while Arnauld and Nicole introduce four kinds of reasoning regarding things – effect to cause, cause to effect, part to whole, and whole and some part to another part (Arnauld and Nicole 1996, 234; cf. Descartes 1984-1985, 1:53) – it is unclear that reasoning from cause to effect and whole to part fit the general the paradigm of analysis: they seem to be concerned with synthesis. What *is* clear is that at least one role of analysis is the search for general explanatory principles. In geometrical analysis, for example, one begins with an assumption taken as true (what would be a theorem), and one searches for more general principles upon which the assumption rests. "If in this examination they arrive at some clear truth from which the assumption follows necessarily, they conclude that the assumption is true. Then starting over from the end point [the general principle], they demonstrate it by the other method which is called *composition* [synthesis]" (Arnauld and Nicole 1996, 238). Insofar as Berkeley uses analysis in the *Theory of Vision*, it can only be understood as a search for general principles – natural laws – that explain a phenomenon.

[40] This claim is based on an electronic scan of Berkeley's *Works* for "Arnauld," "Port Royal," and "Port Royale."

[41] Malebranche also alludes to the method of analysis, but since all of Malebranche's allusions to analysis are in mathematical contexts, we may pass over in silence the question whether Berkeley derived his understanding of analysis from Malebranche. See Malebranche 1980, 209, 435-436, 483, 753.

writes:

> As in Mathematics, so in Natural Philosophy, the Investigation of difficult things by the Method of Analysis, ought ever to precede the Method of Composition. This Analysis consists in making Experiments and Observations, and the drawing general conclusions from them by Induction, and admitting no Objections against the Conclusions, but such as are taken from Experiments, or other certain Truths. For Hypotheses are not to be regarded in experimental Philosophy. And although the arguing from Experiments and Observations by Induction be no Demonstration of general Conclusions; yet it is the best way of arguing which the Nature of Things admits of, and may be looked upon as so much the stronger, by how much the Induction is more general. And if no Exception occur from Phænomena, the Conclusion may be pronounced generally. But if at any time afterwards any Exception shall occur from Experiments, it may then begin to be pronounced with such exceptions as occur. By this way of Analysis we may proceed from Compounds to Ingredients, and from Motions to the Forces producing them; and in general, from Effects to their Causes, and from particular Causes to more general ones, till the Argument end in the most general. This is the Method of Analysis: And the Synthesis consists in assuming the Causes discover'd and establish'd as Principles, and them explaining the Phænomena proceeding from them, and proving the Explanations.[42]

We should notice that Newton's account of the method of analysis is wholly consistent with that we have constructed based upon the examinations of Pappus, Descartes, and Arnauld and Nicole. Analysis is a search for general explanatory principles. These principles are of successively greater degrees of generality as the analysis proceeds. Newton places a greater emphasis on experiment and observation than is explicitly found in Descartes,[43] but the method is the same insofar as it is a search for general principles that can be used in explanation and that it stands in contradistinction to synthesis. That Berkeley shares Newton's greater emphasis and inductive generalization is clear from his remark in *Principles*, Part I, section 50, where, in reply to the materialistic hypothesis, Berkeley writes, "that there is not any one *phenomenon* explained on that

---

[42] Newton 1952, 404-405; cf. Newton's "Rules of Reasoning in Philosophy," in Newton 1966, 2:398-400.

[43] Cartesian sciences, however, are not without an emphasis on careful observation, as is clear from Discourse Three of the *Optics*. Flage and Bonnen have gone so far as to argue that a principal objective of the *Meditations* was at to show the scope and limits of observational knowledge in the Cartesian sciences. See Flage and Bonnen 1999, 251.

supposition, which may not as well be explained without it, as might easily be made appear by an induction of particulars. To explain the *phenomena*, is all one as to shew, why upon such and such occasions we are affected with such and such ideas." As is clear from the *Theory of Vision* as well as *Principles*, Part I, sections 30-31, the "principles" sought are natural laws, general descriptions that reflect the correlations among ideas of the same and different sorts.

One might cite further instances of philosophers who draw the distinction between the analytic and synthetic methods along the same lines,[44] but this discussion is sufficient to show that the distinction between the analytic method as a search for general principles and the synthetic method as a axiomatic system based upon those general principles was part of the intellectual *milieu* of the early eighteenth century. Thus, while one may not be able to point to a particular philosopher who explicitly influenced Berkeley's claim that the *Theory of Vision*, as a search for general explanatory principles, proceeds by the method of analysis, his contemporaries would not have found such a remark puzzling.[45]

Analysis in the *Theory of Vision*

But what evidence is there that Berkeley employed the method of analysis in the *Theory of Vision*? If he practices analysis, then we should find an emphasis on explanation. But as we noted above, the fact that a hypothesis will explain a phenomenon can be no more than a necessary condition for its acceptability. When operating within the context of an ongoing theoretical discussion, theoretical parsimony can play a role in deciding among rival hypotheses, as can empirical evidence for the explanatory laws and evidence that the laws actually explain the phenomena. The last might be particularly poignant when dealing with aspects of human behavior, such as the judgment of distance.

In this section I show that Berkeley's account of distance perception is a

[44] The distinction was already in the intellectual air at the time of Descartes. In Galileo's *Dialogue Concerning the Two Chief World Systems* (Galilei 1967, 51) Salviati alludes to the method of analysis, and describes it in much the same way as one finds throughout the period. Francis Hutcheson (Hutcheson 2006, 54) and Isaac Watts (Watts 1996, 330-333) provide brief discussions of analysis in their logic books.

[45] The method of analysis is still with us, although the nomenclature has changed. It is not unlike what Charles Sanders Peirce called "abduction" (see "Abduction and Induction," in Peirce 1940, 150-156), and what more recent philosophers call "argument to the best explanation" (see, for example, Lipton 1991).

critical reformulation of a Cartesian account of distance perception. I show that Berkeley criticizes the geometric account of visual perception in terms of (1) the lack of evidence for the alleged geometrical judgment, (2) the inconsistency of the geometrical explanation with the facts regarding judgment of distance, and (3) its failure to explain the correct phenomena. Since the geometrical account as *part* of the Cartesian account of visual perception fails to adequately explain visual perception, it ought to be rejected. Since the nongeometrical part of the Cartesian account – at least once adequately overhauled – will explain the phenomenon of distance vision, it should be accepted on grounds of parsimony as well. And since it can be expanded to cover the whole of vision, it is also preferable to the geometric account on grounds of generality.

At the beginning of the eighteenth century, accounts of vision were provided within the context of theories of optics. Optics, since the time of Johannes Kepler, was dominated by geometrical description. It is well-known that Descartes, like most of the optical theorists of the time, placed his principal explanatory emphasis on natural geometrical calculations when explaining vision. What might be less known is that he presented a second account of distance perception in the *Optics*, an account which might be a progenitor of Berkeley's account.

In his chapter "Vision" (Discourse Six), after explaining distance perception by an appeal to triangulation,[46] Descartes writes:

> We have yet another way of perceiving distance, namely by the distinctness or indistinctness of the shape seen, together with the strength or weakness of the light. Thus, if we gaze fixedly towards X [referring to his figure], the rays coming from objects 10 and 12 do not converge so exactly upon R or T, at the back of our eye, as they would if these objects were at points V and Y. From this we see that they are farther from us, or nearer to us, than X. Then, the light coming from object 10 to our eye is stronger than it would be if that object were near V, and from this we judge it to be nearer; and the light coming from object 12 is weaker than it would be if it were near Y, and so we judge it to be farther away. Finally, we may already have from another source an image of an object's size, or its position, or the distinctness of its shape and its colours, or merely the strength of the light coming from it; and this may enable us to imagine its distance, if not actually to see it. For example, when we observe from afar some body we are used to seeing close at hand, we judge its distance much better than we would if its size were less well known to us. If we are looking at a mountain lit up by sunlight beyond a forest covered in shadow, it is solely the position of the forest that makes us judge it the nearer. And when we look at two ships out at sea, one smaller

[46] Descartes 1984-1985, 1:170.

> than the other but proportionately nearer so that they appear equal in size, we can use the difference in their shapes and colours, and in the light they send to us, to judge which is the more distant.[47]

Let us call this an empirical theory of vision. Notice that Berkeley virtually parrots this account of vision:

> I find it also acknowledged, that the estimate we make of the distance of objects considerably remote, is rather an act of judgment grounded on experience, than of sense. For example, when I perceive a great number of intermediate objects, such as houses, fields, rivers, and the like, which I have experienced to take up a considerable space, I thence form a judgment or conclusion, that the object I see beyond them is at a great distance. Again, when an object appears faint and small, which at a near distance I have experienced to make a vigorous and large appearance, I instantly conclude it to be far off: And this, 'tis evident, is the result of experience; without which, from the faintness and littleness I should not have inferred any thing concerning the distance of objects. (TV 3)[48]

When one has had previous experience regarding the sizes of objects, the apparent relative size of perceived objects allows one to infer at least their relative positions. Descartes' account also anticipates Berkeley's later account of the correlations between faintness and distance and magnitude.

Notice that even for Descartes the geometrical account of vision is contraposed to this empirical theory. Descartes seemed to assume that both accounts would explain one's judgments of distance. But the presence of two theories also raises several questions. (1) Will both theories explain judgments of distance? (2) If so, are there theoretical grounds for preferring one theory to the other? (3) If both will not explain judgments of distance, will the remaining theory or some modification thereof explain judgments of distance?

To answer those questions, Berkeley begins by making clear the differences between the two theories. The geometrical theory of binocular vision assumes a triangle with the object perceived at its apex: the object is closer insofar as the angle is more obtuse; it is farther insofar as the angle is more acute. There are necessary connections between the angles and distance: this allows one to calculate distance by triangulation (TV 4 and 5). In the case or monocular vision, distance increases as the several rays reaching the pupil approach parallel (TV 6-7). In both these cases, there is

---

[47] Descartes 1984-1985, 1:170-172.

[48] See also TV 28.

a necessary connection between distance and the basis for knowing it.[49] In contrast, on the empirical method there is merely a correlation among ideas. These correlations are contingent (TV 5).

Berkeley argues, that *any* case of mediate perception is a case of perceiving one idea by means of another, and if one perceives B mediately by perceiving A, A must be perceived in order to perceive B (TV 9-10). For example, one perceives that John is embarrassed by perceiving that his face is red (cf. TV 10). Both the geometrical and empirical theories of distance perception are mediate theories of perception. So, in both cases there must be an idea immediately perceived in order to mediately perceive distance.

Berkeley's first criticism of the geometrical theory is that there is not the immediate idea that provides the basis for mediate perception. "But those lines and angles, by means whereof some men pretend to explain the perception of distance, are themselves not at all perceived, nor are they in truth ever thought of by those unskilful in optics" (TV 12). If one cannot perceive the lines and the angles that provide the basis for the geometric calculation, then one cannot infer the distance. So, even if the inference itself were completely unconscious,[50] the inability to know the basis entails that the geometrical theory is defective. (TV 13)

Does Berkeley take this to be a fatal flaw of the geometric theory? He almost certainly did, yet he did *not* deem this the most fundamental problem with the geometric theory. As one might expect in one following the method of analysis, the most serious problem is that "though we should grant the real existence of those optic angles, &c., and that it was possible for the mind to perceive them; yet these principles would not be found sufficient to explain the phænomena of distance." (TV 15)

Before showing why the geometrical theory fails to explain, however, Berkeley begins his discussion of the empirical theory. Here it is all a matter of correlation of ideas. In binocular vision, Berkeley grants the geometer that the dispositions of the pupils change with distance. These changes in the dispositions of the eyes are accompanied by kinesthetic sensations, and it is these sensations that are correlated with different distances (TV 16). By the regular correlation of sensations, the mind develops an associative habit: one "sees" distance by way of the kinesthetic sensations of the eyes focusing on an object (TV 17). Similarly, with respect

---

[49] As Margaret Atherton notices, Cartesian theories of vision do *not* require that one be conscious of the geometrical calculations involved in perceiving distance, and, therefore, they do not require that the theory be empirically testable. See Atherton 1990, 80.

[50] See Descartes 1984-1985, 1:170, Malebranche 1980, 46-47.

to monocular vision, there is a correlation between distance and the degree of confusedness of the idea, the repetition of which yields an associative habit (TV 21-22). In both cases, one might be unaware of the long-established habit, but it differs from the geometric theory insofar as it is testable. By attending to one's ideas, one can discover *that* there is a correlation among various kinds of ideas in judging distance. There is no comparable evidence for the geometrical theory, a point Berkeley takes in support of his own account. As he remarked:

> I know it is a received opinion, that by altering the disposition of the eyes, the mind perceives whether the angle of the optic axes, or the lateral angles comprehended between the interval of the eyes and the optic axes, are made greater or lesser; and that accordingly by a kind of natural geometry, it judges the point of their intersection to be nearer, or farther off. But that this is not true, I am convinced by my own experience, since I am not conscious that I make any such use of the perception I have by the turn of my eyes. And for me to make those judgments, and draw those conclusions from it, without knowing that I do so, seems altogether incomprehensible. (TV 19)

Notice, here Berkeley's objection to the geometrical theory is not the absence of an angular basis for drawing the geometric inference; here it is the absence of evidence that the inference occurs. So, even if one were to grant that the geometric theory would explain the judgment of distance *if* the inference occurred, the absence of any evidence that the inference occurs casts further doubt on it: in contradistinction to the empirical theory, there are no grounds for testing the geometric theory.

But this is not the end of the criticism of the geometric theory of distance perception. There are cases in which it seems utterly incredible to claim that judgments of distance are based upon calculation. Notice the remarks in TV 24:

> What seems to have misled the writers of optics in this matter is, that they imagine men judge of distance, as they do of a conclusion in mathematics; betwixt which and the premises it is indeed absolutely requisite there be an apparent, necessary connexion: But it is far otherwise, in the sudden judgments men make of distance. We are not to think, that brutes and children, or even grown reasonable men, whenever they perceive an object to approach, or depart from them, do it by virtue of geometry and demonstration.

Calculating takes time. Judgments of distance are almost instantaneous. So, there is reason to believe the geometrical theory is false. It becomes virtually incredible when applied to "brutes and children." To suggest that children who have no formal training in mathematics are implicitly involved in sometimes intricate calculations to determine distances seems incredible. Brute beasts raise different worries. Animals act as if they make judgments of distance. But no one – least of all a Cartesian, who takes animals to be merely complex machines[51] – would attribute intricate powers of calculation to animals. So, Berkeley might well claim that the geometric theory cannot explain distance judgments by children and beasts, although the phenomena are easily explained on his empirical theory of the association of ideas.

Nor is this the end of problems for the geometric theory. As Isaac Barrow and many geometric theorists recognized, the geometric theory fails when there is a difference between actual distance and apparent distance. The problem is that on the geometrical account of monocular vision, if the rays of light are parallel when they reach the eye, the object seen should appear distant, but if the rays of light are reflected or refracted, the apparent distance of the object is less than the actual distance: the geometrical model does not allow for a distinction between the apparent and the actual distance. Berkeley's account in terms of the confusion of appearance – nearer objects appear more confused (blurry) than distant objects – explains the appearance. Berkeley's account does more than this. If all judgment of distance is a function of the correlation of ideas – visual ideas to tactual ideas (TV 45) – his account can accommodate differences in visual acuity. While those with normal vision will find an increase in confusion as an object approaches the eye, the nearsighted person will find less confusion as the object approaches the eye (TV 37). This implies that while there are general correlations between the degrees of confusion and (tactual) distance, the precise correlations are learned by individuals.[52]

So what has Berkeley shown? He has pointed to shortcomings of the geometrical theory vis-à-vis his own empirical theory. Insofar as the geometrical theory is inferential, it must be based upon the observation of lines and angles that provide the basis for the inference. No such lines and angles are available to experience. If they were available to experience, then to claim that there is an inference, there should be some experience of it. There is no experience of an inference. If there were an inference, it would be fairly complex, even though it is made by infants and brute

---

[51] See Descartes 1984-1985, 1:139-141. One is left with the impression that the young Berkeley was not opposed to an occasional argument with *ad hominem* force. See also TV 125.

[52] Notice Berkeley appeals to optical accounts to explain the differences in degrees of confusion, TV 36.

beasts. But even if there were an experience of an inference from some experiential basis, the results of the theory are not uniformly correct. In particular, the Barrovian case shows that a distinction must be drawn between the actual distance from an object from the object's apparent distance, a distinction that cannot be accommodated by the geometrical theory.

Berkeley's empirical theory faces no such problems. The ideas of sight and touch that are correlated are both available to the senses. The repeated joint experience of the two kinds of ideas explains how a habit of association is formed, which, in turn, explains why one moves from an idea of sight to an idea of touch (cf. TV 28). It also explains the judgments of apparent distance that proved problematic in the Barrovian case, and how there can be individual variants in correct judgments of distance perception. Further, if Descartes took the empirical theory to be part of a single theory of which the geometrical was another part,[53] the empirical theory alone is also preferable on grounds of parsimony.

But the virtues of the empirical theory do not stop here. The empirical theory is broader and will explain more phenomena than the geometrical theory. Not only does it solve the puzzle posed by the Barrovian case, Berkeley goes on to show that it provides an answer to the moon illusion and the puzzle of the inverted image on the retina. Indeed, insofar as it accounts for perception in terms of correlation of ideas (natural laws), it is the basis for Berkeley's general account of the distinction between imagination and reality on the basis of natural laws (P 30-33, 36, 62).[54] The empirical theory is extremely fruitful.

Conclusions

Thus we have seen that Berkeley's claim that the *Theory of Vision* proceeds by the method of analysis is reasonable. We have seen that the methods of analysis and synthesis were widely discussed in the late seventeenth and early eighteenth centuries. The method of analysis is fundamentally a method that seeks explanatory principles. We found this exemplified in the *Theory of Vision*, where Berkeley takes the optical theory (or theories) of Descartes' *Optics*, shows that a carefully honed empirical theory of distance perception more plausibly explains distance perception than the

[53] Cf. Descartes 1984-1985, 1:170-173.

[54] While the Berkeley of the *Theory of Vision* seems to write as if the objects of touch are external (TV 45, 64, 77, 78, 82, 88, 99, 111, 117 and 165), I believe the more significant point is that the account of the lawful correlation of different kinds of ideas was developed into his account of real objects.

much touted geometrical theory. Further, it is a fruitful theory insofar as it provides solutions to the moon illusion and the problem of inverted retinal images, and ultimately explains how the perception of ordinary objects occurs.

Bibliography

Arnauld, Antoine and Pierre Nicole. (1996), *Logic or the Art of Thinking*, tr. J. V. Buroker, Cambridge Texts in the History of Philosophy, Cambridge University Press, Cambridge.

Atherton, Margaret. (1990), *Berkeley's Revolution in Vision*, Cornell University Press, Ithaca.

Berkeley, George. (1948-1957), *The Works of George Berkeley*, 9 vols, A. A. Luce and T. E. Jessop (eds), London, Nelson.

Boyle, Robert. (1979), *Selected Philosophical Papers of Robert Boyle*, M. A. Stuart (ed.), Philosophical Classics, Manchester University Press, Manchester.

Descartes, René. (1952), *The Geometry of René Descartes*, tr. D. E. Smith and M. L, Latham, Open Court, La Salle, IL.

—. (1984-1985), *The Philosophical Writings of Descartes*, 2 volumes, tr. J. Cottingham, R. Stoothoff, and D. Murdoch, Cambridge University Press, Cambridge.

—. (1991), *The Philosophical Writings of Descartes: The Correspondence*, tr. J. Cottingham, R. Stoothoff, D. Murdoch, and A. Kenny, Cambridge University Press, Cambridge.

Flage, Daniel E. (2009), "Berkeley's Contingent Necessities," *Philosophia* 37, pp. 361-372.

Flage, Daniel E. and Clarence A. Bonnen. (1999), *Descartes and Method: A Search for Method is Meditations*, Routledge, London.

Galilei, Galileo. (1967), *Dialogue Concerning the Two Chief World Systems*, tr. S. Drake, 2nd revised edition, University of California Press, Berkeley.

Hegel, Georg Wilhelm. (1975), *Hegel's Logic: Being Part One of the Encyclopaedia of the Philosophical Sciences*, tr. William Wallace, foreword J. N. Findlay, Clarendon Press, Oxford.

Hintikka, Jaakko. (1978), "A Discourse on Descartes' Method," in Hooker (1978), pp. 74-88.

Hintikka, Jaakko and Unto Remes. (1974), *The Method of Analysis: Its Geometrical Origin and Its General Significance*, Boston Studies in the Philosophy of Science, vol. 25, Reidel, Dordrecht.

Hooker, Michael (ed.) (1978), *Descartes: Critical and Interpretive Essays*,

Johns Hopkins University Press, Baltimore.

Hutcheson, Francis. (2006), *Logic, Metaphysics, and the Sociability of Mankind*, James Moore and Michael Silverthorne (eds), Liberty Fund, Indianapolis.

Kant, Immanuel. (1974), *Logic*, tr. R. Hartman and W. Schwartz, Library of Liberal Arts, Bobbs-Merrill, Indianapolis.

—. (1977), *Prolegomena to Any Future Metaphysics*, tr. Paul Carus revised J. W. Ellington, Hackett, Indianapolis.

Lipton, Peter. (1991), *Inference to the Best Explanation*, Routledge, London.

Malebranche, Nicholas. (1980), *The Search After Truth*, tr. T. Lennon and P. J. Olscamp, and *Elucidations of the Search After Truth*, tr. T. Lennon, Ohio State University Press, Columbus.

Newton, Isaac. (1952), *Optics, or A Treatise of the Reflections, Refractions, Inflections & Colours of Light*, based on the 4th edition London [1730], Dover, New York.

—. (1966), *Mathematical Principles: Of Natural Philosophy and His System of the World*, 2 volumes, tr. A. Mott, revised F. Cajori, University of California Press, Berkeley.

Pappas, George S. (1983), "Adversary Metaphysics," *Philosophy Research Archives* 9, pp. 571-585.

Peirce, Charles Sanders. (1940), *Philosophical Writings of Peirce*, Justus Buchler (ed.), Dover, New York.

Randall, John Hermann. (1940), "The Development of Scientific Method in the School of Padua," *Journal of the History of Ideas* 1, pp. 177-206.

Reid, Thomas. (1969), *Essays on the Intellectual Powers of Man*, introduction B. A. Brody, M.I.T. Press, Cambridge.

Stoneham, Tom. (2002), *Berkeley's World: An Examination of the Three Dialogues*, Oxford University Press, Oxford.

Turbane, Colin, M. (1970), *The Myth of Metaphor*, University of South Carolina Press, Columbia.

Watts, Isaac. (1996), *Logic, or The Right Use of Reason in the Inquiry After Truth with a Variety of Rules to Guard Against Error in the Affairs of Religion and Human Life, as well as the Sciences* [1724], Soli Deo Gloria Publications, Morgan, PA.

BERKELEY AND THE TIME-GAP ARGUMENT

MYKOLAS DRUNGA

Abstract

Berkeley doesn't use the Time-Gap Argument, as Leibniz does, to prove either that we immediately see only ideas or that we see physical objects mediately. It may be doubted whether he was even aware of the time-gap problem that gives rise to the argument. But certain passages in the *Three Dialogues* and elsewhere suggest that Berkeley would have had cogent answers to anyone who claimed that this argument, construed as being in aid of the conclusion that we only perceive ideas, is unsound. Discussing points made by Bertil Belfrage, Len Carrier, John Foster, A. C. Grayling, Howard Robinson, A. D. Smith, Tom Stoneham, and Colin Turbayne, I try to show that the Time-Gap Argument can be expanded into a strong argument for Berkeleian Idealism. I also indicate how the latter provides a solution to J. J. Valberg's "puzzle of experience" and disarms James Cornman's argument in *Perception, Common Sense, and Science* that Berkeley, too, faces a time-gap problem.

Introduction

It is one of the main theses of a quite brilliant philosophical book recently written on visual perception – *The Problem of Perception* by A. D. Smith – that "Direct Realism ... cannot be shown to be" false "by reflecting on the nature of perception."[1] In aid of this, Smith extensively and carefully discusses the Argument from Illusion and the Argument from Hallucination, and attempts to show that they do not pose insuperable threats to (a certain sort of) Direct Realism. However, he says very little about the Time-Gap Argument, which Bertrand Russell,[2] C. D. Broad,[3]

---

[1] Smith 2002, 5-6.

[2] Russell 1927, 132-143, 144-150; Russell 1948, 172-173, 203-209.

[3] Broad 1947, 120-124.

James Cornman,[4] and a few other philosophers believe does effectively refute (that very sort of) Direct Realism.

In this paper I will try to make this belief plausible. I will do so with the help of George Berkeley who, I shall argue, is both (1) useful for the defense of a crucial premise in this argument and (2) himself in need not only of its conclusion but also of the way it has been reached, in order to reinforce his own case for a rather idiosyncratic view – that very special (and different) brand of Direct Realism combined with Idealism that he alludes to towards the end of the *Three Dialogues*:

> My endeavors tend only to unite and place in a clearer light that truth, which was before shared between the vulgar and the philosophers: the former being of opinion, that *those things they immediately perceive are the real things*; and the latter, that *the things immediately perceived, are ideas which exist only in the mind*. Which two notions put together, do in effect constitute the substance of what I advance. (3D 262)

The first of these "notions" is a Direct Realism that is distinct from the Direct Realism discussed by Smith. The latter combines (1) an epistemological component, the view that we "directly perceive the physical world," with (2) a metaphysical component, the view "that the physical world has an existence that is not in any way dependent upon its being 'cognized' – that is, perceived or thought about." Smith goes on to say that according to Direct Realism's metaphysical component, "[t]he physical world is not, as it is usually put, dependent on 'consciousness,' at least not finite consciousness." This gives us a Realism that "is opposed to Idealism: the view that whatever seems to be physical is either reducible to, or at least supervenient upon, cognitive states of consciousness."[5]

Berkeley's Direct Realism, too, has an epistemological component, and it is the same as that of the Direct Realism discussed by Smith; but its metaphysical component is just the opposite. The metaphysical component of Berkeley's Direct Realism is captured in the second "notion" that he mentions, which, of course, implies Idealism as characterized by Smith. Thus we may call Berkeley's Direct Realism Idealist, and Smith's Direct Realism Non-Idealist.

Smith, as I said, is rather terse about the Time-Gap Argument, and Berkeley doesn't use it all. I think that Berkeley could and should have used it if only for the reason of making things even easier for himself –

---

[4] Cornman 1971, 221-224; Cornman 1975, 243-246.

[5] Smith 2002, 1-2.

and other defenders of Idealist Direct Realism – than he thought they already were.

And Berkeley did think they were *quite* easy; we need only recall what he says in the *Principles* (P 6): "Some truths are so near and obvious to the mind, that a man need only open his eyes to see them." The eyes and the seeing here are metaphorical, of course, but what Berkeley wants to say is that the truths in question don't need any elaborate arguments on their behalf; it's almost enough just to state them, as he forthwith proceeds to do with one of them, which he calls "important": "to wit, that all the choir of heaven and furniture of the earth, in a word all those bodies which compose the mighty frame of the world, have not any subsistence, without a mind, that their being is to be perceived or known; that consequently so long as they are not actually perceived by me, or do not exist in my mind or that of any other created spirit, they must either have no existence at all, or else subsist in the mind of some eternal spirit: it being perfectly unintelligible and involving all the absurdity of abstraction, to attribute to attribute to any single part of them an existence independent of a spirit."

Now, of course, this 'important' truth so obvious to Berkeley was very hard to see for very many if not most other philosophers, then and now; instead, what they found it absolutely easy to do is just what Berkeley claimed in the same section of the *Principles* to be utterly impossible; that is, to "separate" in their "own thoughts the being of a sensible thing from its being perceived."

Hence, these philosophers needed to see good arguments for Idealist Direct Realism, since they thought that Berkeley provided either none at all or very unconvincing ones. I don't think they're by and large right; but to the extent they are, the Time-Gap Argument might help remedy the deficiency at least somewhat.

Leibniz's Argument

The first philosopher to state and use the Time-Gap Argument (henceforward, TGA) was, as far as I know, Gottfried Wilhelm Leibniz, in his *New Essays on Human Understanding*. He did so in the context of claims (by Philalethes, a spokesman for John Locke) that "the ideas which are received by sensation are often altered by the judgment of the mind in grown people" and that "we substitute the cause of the image for what actually appears to us, and confound judging with seeing." Assenting to this, Leibniz (in the guise of Theophilus) says that when "we are deceived by a painting our judgments are doubly in error. First, we substitute the cause for the effect, and believe that we immediately see the thing that causes the image. For strictly we see only the image, and are affected only by rays of light. Since rays of light need time – however little – to reach us, it is possible that the object should be destroyed during the interval and no longer exists when the light reaches the eye; and something which no longer exists cannot be the present object of our sight. Secondly, we are further deceived when we substitute one cause for another and believe that what comes merely from a flat painting actually comes from a body."[6]

It is, of course, just the first deception that concerns us here, and it is in the course of describing it that Leibniz succinctly lays out the version of TGA just stated. Its conclusion – that we immediately see only the image and not the thing that causes the image – is one that Berkeley, although he didn't use the argument, no doubt would have accepted, if only because he thought that the image, in strict parlance, is caused by God and we can't see God.

Let's restate this Leibnizian argument in terms of an example that Berkeley uses:

1. Suppose I behold a picture of Julius Caesar by candle-light.
2. Since rays of light need time to reach me, it is possible that the picture should be destroyed during the interval and no longer exist when the light reaches my eye.
3. Now suppose that this picture actually has been destroyed during this interval.
4. But something that no longer exists cannot be the present object of my sight.
5. Therefore, what I immediately see when I behold the picture of Julius Caesar is not the picture itself but something else, its image, which is both like the picture and has been caused by it.

Is this an argument that Berkeley could or would have used? *First* of all, even though the notion of cause employed in it is *not* the notion of "proper active efficient cause" which is central to his metaphysics and is employed by him in the *Principles* and the *Three Dialogues*, it is the notion of "second corporeal causes" that he mentions in Sec. 71 of *De Motu* and also in his 1729 letter to Samuel Johnson, where he refers to such causes as "occasional causes" and claims this notion is "requisite in the best physics."[7]

In other words, it is precisely the notion to whose existence and

---

[6] Leibniz 1982, 134-135.

[7] *Works,* vol. 2, 279-280. Berkeley also mentions "second causes" (very disparagingly) in P 32.

importance for George Berkeley Bertil Belfrage[8] has done so much to call our attention, a notion which is also deftly handled by A. C. Grayling in his elegant exposition of Berkeley's arguments as moving at three levels: (1) that of "the basic data of sensory experience"; (2) that of "ordinary thought and talk about everyday experience and its objects"; and (3) the "metaphysical level, which provides the ultimate framework of explanation for levels 1 and 2."[9] Thus on this count (involving the notion of "cause"), the preceding imaginary argument cannot be disqualified from being one that Berkeley could have used.

Second, if Berkeley had wanted to use TGA as an argument for Idealist Direct Realism, it would have had to be metaphysical, using the strict and philosophical notion of "proper active efficient cause." Therefore, Berkeley

---

[8] See Belfrage 1992, 2003 and 2005. Indeed, Belfrage's highlighting (a) of three "lights," "branches," or disciplines in Berkeley's "science of vision"; of (b) three "fields of discourse" ("physics" [descriptive science], "mechanics" [theoretical science], "metaphysics" [first philosophy]) in Berkeley's thought as a whole, and of (c) three "stages" in a person's experience–conditioned passage from being "totally inexperienced" to becoming a "fully trained" perceiver (with correspondingly three distinct senses of "to see") is different from, yet resonates with, Grayling's distinction of three "levels" (see next note). Whereas Grayling thinks that Berkeley's philosophy is essentially unified even if tension-filled (a main aspect of which tension shows up in his treatment of causality), Belfrage appears to believe that this unity ("integrat[ing] his scientific and metaphysical texts") has not as yet been conclusively established.

[9] Grayling 1986, 22 *et passim*. It is instructive to compare Belfrage's structuring of Berkeley's thought (in terms of fields of discourse) with Grayling's (in terms of levels of argumentation). According to Belfrage, Berkeley "distinguishes between three fields of discourse," physics, mechanics, and metaphysics, "which study *different* kinds of objects, establish *different* kinds of laws, and presume *different* conceptions of causality." Now all of the objects talked about in Berkeley's third field of discourse according to Belfrage are also talked about at Berkeley's third level of argumentation according to Grayling – they all concern metaphysics. But, for Grayling, this third level is much more inclusive; it includes all the other objects talked about by Berkeley, for metaphysics ties everything together by "provid[ing] the utimate framework of explanation for levels 1 and 2." Hence, the metaphysical level also includes the objects talked about in Berkeley's first and second field of discourse (i.e., physics and mechanics) as distinguished by Belfrage; but in doing so it, according to Grayling, gives their ultimate explanation in terms of a concept of causality that is "strict and speculative" and "philosophic," as opposed to one that is "vulgar," empirical, and established by "use" or "custom." So Grayling has Berkeley using two concepts of causality where Belfrage has him using three, but two of Belfrage's are covered by one of Grayling's.

would not have used this argument, appealing as it does only to second corporeal causes, to make a metaphysical point.

On the other hand, and *third*, could he have used it to prove a point in the psychology of vision – the same point that Leibniz makes, i.e., that in seeing Julius Caesar's picture I immediately see only its causal effect, not it itself?

Other, later philosophers who have used TGA did go on to argue that even though I see the effect immediately or directly, I see the picture itself indirectly. Berkeley could not and did not argue this. But even if an appeal to second corporeal causes is perfectly acceptable in the psychology of vision, I think – and this is my *fourth* point – that Berkeley would definitely *not* have used TGA, *as just formulated*, for the following reason.

To see this, let's go back once more to the Leibniz version, where he is saying that we see something all right and believe it's the picture we see – but it *can't* be the picture because *it* has been destroyed, so what we see is something *very much like* it (otherwise we wouldn't think we still *see* it), and that is the image. We may presume that Leibniz would have known that light travels at such a high finite velocity and that the distance between any picture and human eyes is so small that the picture's destruction one or two nanoseconds after light-rays had left it is something we could not *consciously* notice.

Since, however, he famously had a doctrine of unconscious perception, this would not have impeded Leibniz from making a meaningful distinction between our seeing the picture and our seeing its image. So Leibniz would probably have claimed, in defense of his time-gap argument (and here I state this defense in the words of Howard Robinson who wrote them without explicit reference to Leibniz), "that the fact that we cannot discriminate very small time intervals is simply irrelevant. Whether or not I can discriminate such an interval, I do in fact perceive" the picture as it was some minuscule part "of a second ago; and it could, conceivably, have changed in some perceptible respect just in that time, so that by the time I in fact perceive it it is different from how I perceive it to be."[10]

Speaking for himself now, Robinson goes on to say that "the response to this defence [of the time-gap argument] would be that it misses the point." This, I think, is exactly what Berkeley would have said. Although it is a matter of controversy whether he countenanced insensible corpuscles, he certainly did not believe there could be insensible perceptions. So he would not have used this version of TGA to show anything, much less that

[10] Robinson 1994, 83.

we only see a picture-like thing that is caused by the picture rather than the picture itself.

Berkeleian Arguments

For Berkeley TGA could only get off the ground if we knew, on independent grounds, that a certain visible object had ceased to exist at time t and yet an intuitively appreciable moment later we still seemed to see it, i.e., it appeared to us as though it were still there. That's why Berkeley, if he had used TGA, would have stated it in terms of seeing a star, the sun, or even the moon. Let us, therefore, construct a TGA for Berkeley in terms of seeing the sun. And let us put it at a place where it might naturally have occurred. That could be late in the *First Dialogue*, somewhere after Hylas suggests "there are two kinds of objects, the one perceived immediately, which are likewise called *ideas*; the other are real things or external objects perceived by the mediation of ideas, which are their images and representations."(3D 203) This is a statement of the Representative, or Indirect, Realism that Philonous is concerned to refute, and a *Berkeleian* TGA would do that nicely.

Let's recall that the main purpose of TGA is usually to refute Non-Idealist *Direct* Realism. Those who endorse TGA then usually go on to prove *Indirect* Realism rather than refute it. But it's also possible instead to go on to try to prove *Idealist* Direct Realism. This would require a Berkeleian TGA, which aims to refute *both* Non-Idealist Direct Realism and Indirect Realism. The best way to lay out this argument, though, is to start with what Hylas might say to refute Non-Idealist Direct Realism and to prove Indirect Realism:

> 1. Suppose I look at what I take to be the sun.
> 2. Since rays of light from the sun need about eight minutes' time to reach me, it is possible that the sun should be destroyed during that interval and no longer exist when its light reaches my eye.
> 3. Now suppose that the sun actually has been destroyed during this interval.
> 4. But something that no longer exists cannot be the present object of my sight.
>
> *Therefore,*
>
> 5. What I immediately see when I look at the sun is not the sun itself, which so long as it exists exists without the mind, but something else which never exists without the mind, which is an image or representation of the sun, and which has been caused by the sun.

So far this is only an argument against Non-Idealist Direct Realism and for

Indirect Realism in one case; arguing for Indirect Realism in general would involve showing that in all cases where the sun (or any other object) is not destroyed but continues to exist, a perceiver would both immediately see the image of the sun (or other object) and mediately see the sun (or other object) itself. For non-fictional philosophers, this usually means having recourse to a Continuity Argument.

Philonous, of course, cannot accept this conclusion, but Hylas's argument seems to be valid with no false premises. So how might Philonous answer it? He might say, first, that what strictly follows from premises (1)-(4) is not (5) but something weaker, something without the explicit mind-independence claim about the sun and without the explicit mind-dependence claim about the image and also without the causal claim: (5') What I immediately see when I look at the sun is not the sun itself but something else which is an image or representation of the sun.

That the sun is mind-independent and that the image is mind-dependent are further claims needing additional premises for their derivation. But even (5') is something that Philonous would not accept for a variety of reasons, one of which is implied by his question, "... directing your open eyes toward yonder part of the heaven, can you avoid seeing the sun?" (3D 196)

Still, since (5') seems to have been validly derived from true premises, how can Philonous *avoid* it? Consistently with Berkeley's principles he can do so only by claiming that the term "sun" in the argument is not univocal and that the sun which has emitted the light-rays that reach my eyes and which has been destroyed while the rays were travelling is not the sun that, as premise (1) has it, I take myself to be looking at when looking "toward yonder part of the heaven."

What I see, therefore, is the *visible sun* the existence of which Berkeley implies in his works on vision (and which Grayling would assign to level 1). But what is the sun that has emitted the light-rays and has since been destroyed? Remembering that we have not only the Berkeley who speaks strictly and philosophically but also the one who speaks with the vulgar,[11] we claim this sun is precisely the sun in the "common vulgar sense" of, say, *Notebooks* 724, the sun of Grayling's level 2. This is the ordinary, causally active physical sun which at level 3 is replaced by Berkeley (according to Grayling) with an inactive, mind-dependent collection of ideas caused by God. – Now let us recapitulate, and then continue and complete, the argument entirely from Berkeley's point of view:

[11] See end of note 9.

1. Suppose I look at what I take to be the sun.
2. Since rays of light from the sun, according to the physicists, need about eight minutes' time to reach me, it is possible that the sun should be destroyed during that interval and no longer exist when its light reaches my eye.
3. Now just suppose that the sun actually has been destroyed during this interval.
4. But something that no longer exists can't be something that I now immediately see.
5. Yet I do see something immediately that I take to be the sun.
Therefore,
6. What I immediately see is a visible sun, not the sun of physics that I suppose to have been destroyed.
7. But I immediately see only one visible sun and nothing else having a "conformity or resemblance to it"; only one dazzlingly bright thing in the heavens rather than two.
8. And in addition to an immediately seen visible sun I do not mediately see anything other resembling it.
Therefore,
9. Indirect or representative realism is false.
10. This visible sun, though perhaps secondarily caused by the sun of physics, has, like all things, strictly and truly been caused by God.
11. But a visible sun is a collection of, or a "fiction of our own brain" constructed from, ideas of color, light, and figure.
12. This collection of, or this "fiction of our own brain" constructed from, ideas either exists without the mind or within the mind.
13. If it exists without the mind, then it could radically change without my noticing it.
14. But this collection of, or this "fiction of our own brain" constructed from, ideas could not radically change without my noticing it.
Therefore,
15. The visible sun I see exists within the mind.
16. Even if the sun of physics had not been destroyed (as in reality it never has been and most likely never will be in human life-time), I still would be immediately seeing a visible sun only – for exactly the reason mentioned in (7).
17. Suppose that the sun of physics has not been destroyed, i.e., that (3) is false.
18. Then in the very act of immediately seeing a visible sun I am also perceiving, whether immediately or mediately, the undestroyed sun of physics, which is a larger collection of ideas of which the visible sun is a part.
Therefore,
19. Whenever I see the visible sun I perceive a larger collection of ideas, some of which I perceive immediately.
20. But what is true of perceiving the visible sun is true, mutatis mutandis,

of perceiving any sensible object whatsoever;
Therefore,
21. All sensible objects are ideas or collections of ideas which exist only in the mind. QED.

This, then, is a Berkeleian TGA. Why didn't Berkeley use something like it? Probably because he didn't think he needed to: its conclusion – that we immediately see only ideas in the mind and not any things "behind them" – was obvious to him and he thought he already had sufficient arguments for it, without any help in the form of a TGA (which most likely didn't even occur to him).

Some Modern Objections

Since at least the beginning of the 20th century, however, the situation has been radically different. Not only has this conclusion not been obvious to most philosophers, but some of them have doubted whether there are such things as ideas at all, even under their modern appellations of "sense-data," "sense-impressions," "sensa," and so forth. Hence there was a need to bring forth arguments for their existence if you believed in them. And TGA was one of those arguments. Most philosophers criticized it for its premise (4) Something that no longer exists can't be something that I now immediately *see* because this entails that any object of direct awareness exists at the *time* of the awareness. Call this the *simultaeneity-requirement* on perception and distinguish it from the *existence-requirement*, which is simply that the object of direct awareness exist at some time or other. According to Smith, for example, the simultaneity-requirement can be rejected "without absurdity."[12] But can it?

Many philosophers share Smith's view on this issue but many others do not. The latter have a strong intuition that the notion of direct perceptual awareness of something in the past just doesn't make any sense. Clearly, the point can rationally be decided only by argument. Therefore, let me, following Howard Robinson,[13] set out an argument for this premise as follows: (1) The direct perceptual awareness of a star, for example, is a psychological state that has content. (2) The content of a psychological state is what (in whole or in part) constitutes that state, what (in whole or in part) makes it the state that it is. (3) What constitutes the direct perceptual awareness of a star, what makes it the state that it is, is, in part, the star one is directly perceptually aware of. (4) Anything which (in

[12] Personal communication.
[13] Here I am restating and amplifying an argument given in Robinson 1994, 81.

whole or in part) constitutes something else must exist at the same time as, or overlap in time with, the thing which it wholly or partly constitutes. (5) Therefore, the content of a direct perceptual awareness of a star cannot cease to exist at an earlier time than the direct perceptual awareness of which it is the content.

In comments to me in an e-mail exchange, John Foster has objected to (4) on the grounds that it isn't "obvious that anything which partly constitutes something else must exist at the same time as, or overlap in time, this other thing," and anyway, that my claim would be taken by the Direct Realist as begging the question. In answer to my question, "If 'this other thing' exists from time *t* onwards to time *t+1*, then how can the thing that partly constitutes it (and thereby is a part of it) exist entirely before time t?," Foster replied by saying that the Direct Realist "won't think that the earlier object is part of the later perceptual episode, but only that the perceptual state (type-state) which that episode realizes is a state of being aware of that earlier item, *and so a state that could not be realized if that item did not exist* (my emphasis). It is only in this sense that he will take the earlier item to be partly constitutive of the later perception."

What would Berkeley say about this?

Perceivings and Perceived Objects

At *Principles*, section 5 he says that "it is impossible for me to conceive in my thoughts any sensible thing or object distinct from the sensation or perception of it." This, plus the statement in the first edition that "in truth the object and the sensation are the same thing and cannot, therefore, be abstracted from each other"[14] and the *Notebooks* 585 entry "wherein I pray you does the perception of white differ from white" all suggest a principle that S. A. Grave and Colin Turbayne have called the *Identity Principle*; but Grayling thinks that this label is "wholly misleading," since Berkeley, according to Grayling, is not committed "to the view that ideas are *identical* with perceivings of them."[15]

If that *were* Berkeley's view, the conclusion that if a thing is perceived at a certain time then it must exist at that time would readily follow. But that's *not* his view, according to Grayling: Berkeley is not claiming "that a particular idea is to be identified with a particular perceiving of it, for the non-identity of states of awareness and their contents is a thesis already well entrenched as the view that, from the finitary viewpoint, ideas, at any

[14] Quoted in Turbayne 1982, 299.
[15] Grayling 1986, 169-170.

rate those that constitute real things, are not dependent for their existence on any particular finite perceiving of them. What it means not to be able to 'conceive apart' any 'sensible thing or object distinct from the sensation or perception of it' (P 5) is therefore far from a claim that the idea and the perception of it are numerically the same thing, but rather that an idea is always and essentially an *idea perceived*, and perception is always and essentially the *perception of ideas*."[16]

So the question is as follows: For Berkeley, are sensations and their objects merely non-abstractable one from the other, as Grayling claims, or actually numerically identical, as Turbayne claims? I think that this specific objection to Turbayne's reading misfires. When Grayling says that "from the finitary viewpoint" ideas that constitute real things "are not dependent for their existence on any particular finite perceiving of them," this is true, of course, if "dependent" means "causally dependent" (and in this context it cannot mean anything else). Now, for Berkeley, all ideas are particular and of particulars, and my idea of the visible sun can be like yours and a lot of other finite observers', yet all of these ideas are in some way ontologically dependent on God (a point not only not denied, but positively emphasized, by Grayling). Which way that is, scholars dispute about: does God Himself perceive ideas like those of finite observers; or does He have a "volitional policy" vis-à-vis finite observers, and if so, how does that work? But none of this in the least implies "the non-identity of states of awareness [particular perceivings] and their contents [particular ideas perceived]," as Grayling contends. On the contrary, the non-dependence of any particular idea's existence on any particular finite perceiving of it seems to be perfectly compatible with any particular perceiving of it being numerically identical with that particular idea's being perceived; just as this identity claim is compatible with Grayling's own, weaker reading of Berkeley "that an idea is always and essentially an *idea perceived*, and perception is always and essentially the *perception of ideas*."

Still, I think Grayling is absolutely correct in thinking there is something wrong with the view (whether Berkeley held it or not) "that a particular idea is to be identified with a particular perceiving of it." I will discuss this important point a bit later; first I briefly want to take up another thought of Grayling's, namely, that there are a lot of examples of distinct items that are related by mutual non-abstractability. In his words, "[e]very process-product relation, for example, is of this kind; bread and

[16] *ibidem*, 171.

the baking of it, a picture and the painting of it, are cases in point."[17] Obviously, the loaf of bread cannot exist before it has been baked nor can the baking of it come after it, the loaf, has ceased to exist. But is the perception of a thing a process-product relation?

According to Belfrage, that's exactly what it is in Berkeley's *Theory of Vision*, where he "analyzes the perceiving *process*, not the *end-product*, so-called 'sensible things', which play a crucial part in the *Principles*."[18] In Grayling's view, "the natural model for Berkeley's account of perception" is neither the process-product model nor even the act-object model "because finite minds are passive in perceiving real ideas, which are input from an independent external source. Their passivity is embedded in activity, however, in the sense that to receive an idea involves having, say, to turn one's eye or sniff at a rose (3D 196). But although to this extent perception of real ideas involves activity, the content of a particular state of awareness is not produced by an act of will, as in the case of ideas of imagination, but is 'somewhat consequent' to eye-turnings and sniffings (ibid.), and therefore to be distinguished from them (3D, 197)."[19]

The best model, Grayling implies, is, therefore, the "state-content model"; and it is just in terms of such a model that last section's Robinsonian argument (for the premise that if I see something now then it must exist now) has been formulated.

If Turbayne's interpretation of the "Identity Principle" in *Principles*, section 5 is correct, i.e., if the thing immediately seen is *identical* with the seeing of it, then, of course, it just follows that if I see something now it must exist now. The problem here is not only that if someone doesn't already accept the simultaneity-requirement he might be even less inclined to accept *this* as a reason for it, but also, and more importantly, that *this* is just dead wrong. A thing, whatever it is, can no more be identical with the seeing of it than a horse can be identical with the kicking of it. A headache, of course, is identical with the feeling of it; but this in no way warrants the claim that this pain (this headache, this feeling of it) is identical with the head that aches. The headache is only *like* the head in that both are mind-dependent.

Tom Stoneham argues forcefully in this connection that Berkeley is best understood as adhering to the subject-object model of perception, to be distinguished from the act-object model (which, according to Stoneham, is better called the "subject-act-object model" to reveal all its elements). In addition to these two, there are three more models relevant to Berkeley:

---

[17] *ibidem*, 172.
[18] Belfrage 2005, 217.
[19] Grayling 1986, 173.

the adverbial model; the Representative Theory's subject-object-object model, which Berkeley tries to refute; and the intentional model, which he never explicitly discusses.

The subject-object model, dubbed SMP (The Simplest Model of Perception), is introduced by Stoneham in the context of "the debate about whether Berkeley holds an act-object model of perception or an adverbial model"; according to the latter the distinction between act and object collapses. As Stoneham writes, "It is standardly assumed that if this distinction collapses, we are left with just the act, the perceiving, and consequently the difference between seeing red and seeing green must be the difference between seeing redly and seeing greenly. But a collapse can go either way: the object could collapse into the act or the act into the object. SMP holds that we do not have a duality of act and object, but merely an object (and a subject, of course, but the identity and properties of the subject are irrelevant to the content of the perception, to what is perceived). This alternative is obscured by the universal assumption that if *S* perceives *O*, then there is a (mental) event which is a perceiving of *O* by *S*. SMP simply denies this: when *S* perceives *O*, *S* and *O* exist, and they stand in a relation, namely perceiving, but their standing in this relation is neither constituted nor enabled by any concurrent event or occurrence in *S*."[20]

Their standing in this relation is a state. That state, though (obviously) not constituted or enabled by any (other) event or occurrence in *S*, is trivially constituted by itself, by *S*'s perceiving *O*; and it exists as much as *S* and *O* do. There being this state of perceiving makes SMP a case of the state-content model (where content = object) preferred by Grayling (again, it might be more perspicuous to call it the "subject-state-content model").

Thus SMP is committed to maintaining that when *S* perceives *O* there is a subject of perceiving, a relation of perceiving, and an object or content perceived. Now every model of perception except the adverbial one must agree that there is between *S* and *O* a relation of perceiving. Thus it is clear that SMP is incompatible with Turbaynes's account of Berkeley, according to which the perceiving and the perceived are the same (unless the perceptual relation between *S* and *O* is not *S*'s perceiving of *O*; or that perceptual relation is identity; or there is no perceptual relation between *S* and *O* at all. But all three options are absurd.) This is another thing wrong with Turbayne's reading, assuming that SMP really is Berkeley's "default account of perception," as Stoneham claims (correctly, in my opinion).

On Stoneham's account of Berkeley, if *S*'s perceiving of *O* is realized

[20] Stoneham, 2002, 54-55.

at time t, then obviously *S* must exist at t; but doesn't the same go for *O*? I would say so, but some philosophers (e.g., John Foster) claim it is logically possible for a perceptual relation to obtain now between a currently existing S and a past item *O*. I will return to this issue shortly (in the next section).

If *Grayling's* interpretation of *Principles*, section 5 in terms of non-abstractibility is correct (something very likely given the failure of Turbayne's), then we do not get from *that alone* the conclusion that if I see something immediately now it must exist now. It could have existed earlier: what I immediately see now is something that existed earlier and was then also immediately perceived, of course; but not necessarily by me.

However, if perceiving is a process-product relationship, as Grayling has Berkeley allowing "for ideas of imagination and for all God's ideas" and Belfrage has Berkeley allowing for all human ideas that constitute sensible objects, then of course the object seen cannot *cease to be before* the seeing of it, but must *come to be* some time *during* the seeing of it (most likely, *toward, or at, the end* of it). And very often, the object endures after its production. Thus at least Belfrage's Berkeley supports the premise we need.[21]

Further Berkeleian Defense of Simultaneity

John Foster, as we saw, is one philosopher who says he lacks the intuition that perception and perceived must at least be partly simultaneous. He also claims that insisting on this requirement would mean begging the question against the Non-Idealist Direct Realist.

But why can't we take a hard line here and say the simultaneity-requirement is so obvious that it's the Non-Idealist Direct Realist who's begging the question against both the Indirect Realist and the Idealist Direct Realist? If the speed of light had been infinite, or as long as its finitude had not dawned on people, nobody would have questioned the simultaneity requirement on perceivings and perceived items in the first place. I think that this is how Berkeley would have seen things. And here's my argument.

---

[21] Belfrage thinks (correctly, I believe) that, for Berkeley, sensible objects can be viewed as constructions out of, among other things, "raw data" of "light and color." On this level, according to Belfrage, Turbayne's Identity Principle for Berkeley applies, so that seeing a color is not distinct from the color seen. Cf. Belfrage 1992, 23. Since Turbayne is probably wrong, more argument must be given for (Berkeley's accepting) the simultaneity-requirement, which I do in the next section.

In *Three Dialogues* 238, when Hylas brings up the oar with one end in the water and asks Philonous how a man can be mistaken in thinking it crooked, Philonous gives a long reply, from which it is evident that Berkeley did take the simultaneity-requirement to be achingly self-evident, so much so that he neglected to spell it out explicitly. (This is in line with Robert J. Fogelin's observation that "Berkeley's grounds for committing himself to idealism involve a direct appeal to *intuitions* concerning the nature of things we encounter in experience."[22] I quote each of Philonous's sentences and follow it with my elaboration of what I take to be Berkeley's relevant intuition:

Philonous: "*He is not mistaken with regard to the ideas he actually perceives; but in the inferences he makes from his present perceptions.*" What are they, these present perceptions? The perceivings he now has, or the ideas he now perceives? For Berkeley these presuppose each other. In the realm of ideas, every perceiving is of an idea; and every idea is actually perceived. The man's present perceptions include both his perceivings and the ideas he perceives, about which, Berkeley emphatically tells us, he cannot be mistaken. His perceptions are not just his states of perceiving; they also contain the *objects* of perceiving, what he actually perceives; and it can't be the case that he is at present perceiving something and that thing be not present but past; the perceiving and the perceived both occur at present, that is, now.

Philonous: "*Thus in the case of the oar, what he immediately perceives by sight is certainly crooked; and so far he is in the right.*" The perceived thing is, not was, crooked. It could have been, but needn't have been, crooked before; but now, at the time of perception, it certainly is crooked.

Philonous: "*But if he thence conclude, that upon taking the oar out of the water he shall perceive the same crookedness; or that it would affect his touch, as crooked things are wont to do: in that he is mistaken.*" So if he takes the oar out of the water, in the immediate future, he will perceive not crookedness but straightness; now, not having taken the oar out of the water yet, he sees crookedness and would, if he touched the oar now, feel straightness; but upon taking the oar out he would both feel and see straightness (or, more precisely, feel tangible straightness and see visible straightness).

Philonous: "*In like manner, if he shall conclude from what he perceives in one station, that, in case he advances towards the moon or tower, he should still be affected with the like ideas, he is mistaken.*" Each perceiving at a station has its own distinct perceived object at that station;

[22] Fogelin, 2001, 42.

a station is a place, and at each place a moving man perceives an idea at least numerically different from the previous one. The perceived object is at the same time as the perceiving but not at the same place in physical space, since the man is moving toward the moon or tower. But, of course, in the final metaphysical synthesis, that is, at Grayling's level 3, the stations and the perceived objects are at the same metaphorical places in God's mind and in any number of finite minds.

Philonous: "*But his mistake lies not in what he perceives immediately, and at present (it being a manifest contradiction to suppose he should err in respect of that) but in the wrong judgment he makes concerning the ideas he apprehends to be connected with those immediately perceived: or, concerning the ideas that, from what he perceives at present, he imagines would be perceived in other circumstances.*" "What he perceives at present," is mentioned twice – this refers both to the time of the perception and to the time of the *what*, the content, of the perception – these times are the same. And this is something he can't be mistaken about.

Philonous: "*The case is the same with regard to the Copernican system. We do not here perceive any motion of the earth: but it were erroneous thence to conclude, that, in case we were placed at as great a distance from that as we are now from the other planets, we should not then perceive its motion.*" We do not here and now see the vanishing of the sun or the explosion of a star; but because we know the Laws of Nature which, as Berkeley says at *Principles* section 105, "extend our prospect beyond what is present, and near to us, and enable us to make very probable conjectures, touching things that may have happened at very great distances of time and place, as well as to predict things to come," we know that if we had been placed sufficiently close to the sun or that star, we would at once have seen the vanishing or the explosion; but here and now, of course, we only see the sun's shining or the star's twinkling. Moreover, by the same Laws of Nature, we know that if it were possible (which it isn't) to travel now, instantaneously, closer to (say, within ten million km of) where the vanished physical sun used to be, we wouldn't see any visible sun anymore, not even the much greater one we'd see if the sun were still there.

Conclusion

Let me end by briefly discussing two contemporary philosophers who accept the simultaneity-requirement but stand in different relations to Berkeley's philosophy. They are stumped by questions to which Berkeley's idealism has an answer.

J. J. Valberg, in his *The Puzzle of Experience*, presents an amended and highly simplified TGA, which, he thinks, gives rise to an insoluble puzzle. Suppose that after the light-rays have left an external object, God eliminates that object but lets the light-rays reach our eyes and set in motion the usual cortical processes so that everything in our experience remains the same. What we then see is not, of course, the external object, which has been eliminated, but a sense-datum, an internal object, which exists only in so far as it is perceived. That's what we are forced to conclude philosophically, because of the TGA, which is irrefutable and which exploits, most fundamentally, the "potential irrelevance" of the external thing to our experience. On the other hand, says Valberg, it's just obvious that external objects do exist; one need only be open to how things are in one's experience. So what we have is an irresolvable antinomy, which he calls "the puzzle of experience."[23]

But, I think, Berkeleian idealism does solve this puzzle. For according to it, it isn't the object itself that causes my experience of it through any activity in my visual cortex, but God Himself who directly causes all external objects and all our experiences of them under certain appropriate circumstances. Hence, external things are actually (not just potentially) irrelevant to our experience. That's exactly what the Berkeleian TGA leading to Idealism shows; it shows that all perceivable things are internal, but not that all things are internal: perceivers (including God) are all external with respect to each other. Valberg, of course, doesn't believe that Berkeleian idealism can be proven, and that's why his puzzle stays a puzzle, for him.

James Cornman holds that Berkeleian idealism or "phenomenalism is plausible enough to be one of the leading contenders for the most reasonable theory of perception and the external world"[24], but he thinks that it faces an objection from the time gap as revealed by the following argument: "If Berkeleian phenomenalism is true, then someone, s, sees a star at time t, if and only if at t he senses a sensum that is in the group of sensa which is identical with the star. But if at t someone senses a sensum that is in a group of sensa which is identical with a star, then the group and, therefore, the star exists at t. But just as some stars exist unseen, some stars are seen at times they do not exist. Therefore Berkeleian phenomenalism is false. It seems that a Berkeleian has at most two ways to counter this argument: he can either deny that some things are seen when they do not

---

[23] Valberg 1992, 3-66.

[24] Cornman 1975, 208-209.

exist, or deny that every sensum sensed when an external object is perceived is in the group of sensa that is identical with the object."[25]

This is absolutely right, and what our Berkeleian does is take the first alternative – he denies that some things are seen when they do not exist. He says that all things are seen when and only when they exist (if not by finite beings, then by God) and that what I see when I see something in the case of the no-longer existent (because exploded) star is its light. More exactly, since "star" is ambiguous as between "tangible star," "visible star," and "physical star," what no longer exist (and therefore can no longer be felt or otherwise observed) are the *tangible star* and the *physical star*; but the *visible star* still exists; it is seen; and it is nothing but a speck of light. That, by the way, is what we human beings always see in the way of physical stars, even when they're not exploded and still exist: in all cases we see just pinpricks of twinkling yellowish light – "visible stars" that have been emitted or caused ("vulgarly" speaking) by the "physical stars."

As L. S. Carrier has said, "this saves what is correct in Berkeley."[26] Carrier is another Non-Idealist Direct Realist who accepts the simultaneity-requirement but, because of his deep Australian Materialist convictions, cannot follow Berkeley all (or even much of) the way. Still, by taking the TGA as proving that we always see light he plays directly into Berkeley's hands. He stops where he does because he thinks (a) light is physical and (b) physical things do not depend on being perceived. But Berkeley would have no trouble accepting (a); he only denies (b), and his arguments for that denial are familiar and controversial. In the imagined Berkeleian TGA, some of them would come as support for premises (7), (8), (10), (11), (13), (14), (18), (19), and (20). I hope I have said enough to show that had Berkeley deployed his arguments against (b) in the course of presenting and defending something like the TGA, i.e., had he used TGA as a scaffold or framework for all his relevant arguments, his case for Idealist Direct Realism would have been even stronger and more perspicuous. In any event, the perceptual time-gap is an ace in the hole for any metaphysics in the vicinity of Berkeley.[27]

---

[25] *ibidem*, 353-354.

[26] Carrier 1969, 271.

[27] Special thanks to Bertil Belfrage and Tom Stoneham for their comments and help extended to me before, during, and after the 2007 Helsinki Berkeley Conference at which I presented an early version of this paper.

Bibliography

Belfrage, Bertil. (1992), "The Constructivism of Berkeley's New Theory of Vision," in Cummins and Zoeller (1992), pp. 167-186.

—. (2003), "Towards a New Interpretation of Berkeley's *Theory of Vision*" (in French), in Berlioz (2003), pp. 159-211.

—. (2006), "The Scientific Background of Berkeley's Idealism," in Gersch and Moran (2006), pp. 202-223.

Berkeley, George. (1948-1957), *The Works of George Berkeley*, 9 vols, A. A. Luce and T. E. Jessop (eds), Nelson, London.

Berlioz, D. (ed.) (2005) *Berkeley: language de la perception et art de voir*, Presses Universitires de France, Paris.

Broad, C. D. (1947), "Professor Marc-Wogau's *Theorie der Sinnesdaten*," *Mind* 56, pp. 120-124.

Carrier, L. S. (1969), "The Time-Gap Argument," *Australasian Journal of Philosophy* 47, pp. 263-272.

Cornman, James. (1971), *Materialism and Sensation*, Yale University Press, New Haven and London.

—. (1975), *Perception, Common Sense, and Science*, Yale University Press, New Haven and London.

Cummins P. and Guenter Zoeller (eds.) (1992), *Minds, Ideas, and Objects: Essays on the Theory of Representation in Modern Philosophy*, North American Kant Society Studies in Philosophy 2, Ridgeview, Atascadero, Calif.

Fogelin, Robert J. (2001), *Berkeley and the Principles of Human Knowledge*, Routledge, London and New York.

Gersh, Stephen and Dermot Moran (eds) (2006), *Eriugena, Berkeley and the Idealist Tradition*, Notre Dame University Press, Notre Dame.

Grayling, A. C. (1986), *Berkeley: The Central Arguments*. Open Court, La Salle, Illinois.

Leibniz, G. W. (1982), *New Essays on Human Understanding*, Cambridge University Press.

Robinson, Howard. (1994), *Perception*, Routledge, London and New York.

Russell, Bertrand. (1948), *Human Knowledge: Its Scope and Limits*, Simon and Schuster, New York.

—. (1927), *An Outline of Philosophy*, W. W. Norton, New York.

Smith, A. D. (2002), *The Problem of Perception*, Harvard University Press, Cambridge, Mass.

Stoneham, Tom. (2002), *Berkeley's World: An Examination of the Three Dialogues*, Oxford University Press, Oxford.

Turbayne Colin, M. (1982), "Lending a Hand to Philonous: The Berkeley, Plato, Aristotle Connection," in Turbayne (1982), pp. 295-310.

—. (ed.) (1982), *Berkeley: Critical and Interpretive Essays*, University of Minnesota Press, Minneapolis.

Valberg, J. J. (1992), *The Puzzle of Experience*, Clarendon Press, Oxford.

PART TWO:

BERKELEY'S NATURAL PHILOSOPHY

Two Berkelian Arguments about the Nature of Space

Howard Robinson

Abstract

I consider two arguments about the nature of space that occur in George Berkeley which I think are not sufficiently discussed. The first concerns the phenomenology of space, the second its physics. The first is the "mite" argument and the second concerns Isaac Newton's two thought experiments about absolute space, the "bucket" thought experiment and the "balls" thought experiment. The former suggests that there is no such thing as objective size. Berkeley's position is more confusing on the second experiment, but I argue that the clash between absolutist and relationist spatial intuitions can be reconciled only by an idealist approach to space.

Mites, Men, and Objective Space

Berkeley states his argument as follows:

> PHILONOUS. A mite must, therefore, be supposed to see his own foot, and things equal or even less than it, as bodies of some considerable dimension; though at the same time they appear to you scarcely discernable, or at best as so many visible points.
> HYLAS. I cannot deny it.
> PHILONOUS. And to creatures less than the mite they will seem yet larger.
> HYLAS. They will.
> PHILONOUS. Insomuch that what you can hardly discern, will to another extremely minute animal appear as some huge mountain.
> HYLAS. All this I grant.
> PHILONOUS. Can one and the same thing be at the same time in itself of different dimensions?
> HYLAS. That were absurd to imagine.
> PHILONOUS. But from what you have laid down it follows, that both the

> extension by you perceived, and that perceived by the mite itself, as likewise all those perceived by lesser animals, are each of them the true extension of the mite's foot, that is to say, by your own principles you are led into an absurdity. (3D 188-189)

Unfortunately, taken in its context, the force of the argument is ambiguous. At this point in the *First Dialogue* Philonous is arguing that the sensible qualities that we directly perceive exist in our minds, not in the external world. This hypothesis is ambiguous between the claim that *the instances that we directly perceive* of those sensible qualities are in our minds and *those sensible qualities per se* exist only in our minds. Because he confuses these claims, Philonous conflates arguments which refute naive or direct realism – like the argument from illusion – with arguments that refute realism in general, that is, including representative realism. This is a confusion which Hylas notices, and draws to Philonous's attention, only later in the dialogue. The argument *can* be interpreted, therefore, as no more than a version of the argument from illusion and as establishing, if successful, no more than that the instances of spatiality of which we are directly aware exist only in our minds. But I think the argument can also be deployed for the more ambitious purpose of showing that *the very idea of space itself* cannot be separated from experience. In the case of this particular argument, that is, Berkeley's failure to distinguish between representational and naive realism does not prevent the argument from having the full force intended. On this interpretation, the argument is meant to show the impossibility of mind-independent space by arguing that *determinacy of spatial magnitude* is mind-dependent.

If one adds the premise that space, like anything else, must be determinate to be real, it would follow that space could not be real without the mind. The argument, therefore, on this interpretation, is that because things look bigger to a mite than to a human and there is no clear sense in which one of them perceives the "right" size, then there is no fact about the size and, therefore, no such thing as real or objective size, and so no such thing as mind-independent spatial dimensions. The contrast with the normal "argument from illusion" is that, in other cases of that argument, there are standard procedures or conventions which stipulate which appearance is, or is nearest to, the accurate representation of the object. So we know how to determine which appearances of the shape of an object should be deemed to present its real shape: it is the "head on" view that presents it the shape that it is, and other apparent shapes are deemed to be "views from an angle." Similarly, we can work out what are to be taken as the "standard conditions" that show an object in its true colour, and what are the conditions in which we would say that it, for example, is white but looks yellow. The force of the "mite" argument by contrast, is that, having fixed, by these sorts of means, what the "real shape" of an object is, there are not, and could not be, any means of fixing what the "real size" is. And that "real size" is as essential as "real shape" to the objective existence of spatial properties.

The first objection to this argument that springs naturally to mind is that we can use measurement to pick out real size and that, irrespective of how it looks to mite or man, an object will have a specific measurable size; for example, it will be two inches long. But this will achieve nothing unless we can give objectivity to units of measurement, and an inch is a long distance to a mite and a small one to a human, so in agreeing that an object is two inches long the mite and the man have only an illusion of agreement. There is agreement on the relative sizes of the object and an inch on a ruler, but no agreement about the absolute size of either. It seems that subjects of radically different sizes can agree on the *relative* sizes of objects, but not on their intrinsic dimensions.

One natural response to this is to argue that size is a relative matter and agreeing on the relative dimensions of things is agreeing on their actual dimensions. Man and mite agree about the relative proportions of all things and that is all that is involved in agreeing about their sizes. The matter cannot be solved quite so simply, however. It can be proved that a purely formal definition of space, in terms, say, of Cartesian co-ordinates and axes, is not a complete representation of the nature of space.[1] As well as such formal features, there must be something intuitive and qualitative, like the way that extension presents itself experientially in vision. But it is in respect of such a qualitative feature that things look many times larger to the mite: relative sizes are preserved, and the same geometry applies, but the qualitative interpretations of dimensions differ in intrinsic magnitude. If such an interpretation is essential to any real space, as I have claimed it is, then the problem remains.

The following worry might arise at this point. If there can be two phenomenal spaces that differ only in their intrinsic magnitudes, and if the kind of qualitative element that makes this possible is essential also to any real space, then should it not be possible for there to be two physical worlds that differ only in their intrinsic magnitudes: more exactly, should not the suggestion that everything in the world might double in size, by dint of the doubling of the intrinsic qualitative element, without any alteration in the geometry, also make sense? But this suggestion is generally rejected as vacuous. One might reject the accusation of

[1] Foster shows this in 1982, 73-88.

vacuousness on the grounds that it is verificationist, but it is interesting to note that an idealist is in a better position to accommodate the intuition that everything could not double in size than is the realist. For the idealist, the physical world in which things cannot all double in size – as they can when one moves from a human world to a mite's – is an abstraction created by measurement from the various worlds of experience, which are the ultimate constituents of reality. The qualitative element of space falls out as irrelevant in such an abstract projection of the formal features of experience. – The argument can be summarised more formally as follows:

1. There is more to our conception of physical space than can be captured purely formally.
2. The only thing this non-formal element could be is something qualitative concerning the intrinsic nature of extension.
Therefore,
3. There is a qualitative element concerning the intrinsic nature of extension in our conception of physical space.
4. The only source for acquiring anything of this sort is sense-experience, by which we get an intuitive grasp on certain qualities.
Therefore,
5. There is an intuitive grasp on the intrinsic nature of extension, and, hence, of space, which is gained through sense-experience.
6. For any extension to be real it must have a determinate metric - that is, things in it must have determinate sizes.
Therefore,
7. If the quality of extension grasped intuitively through sense experience is identical with the intrinsic qualitative nature of real physical space, objects possessing such extension must have determinate sizes.
8. Berkeley's example of the mite shows that the quality of size grasped intuitively through sense-experience is observer-relative.
9. There could be no principled reason for thinking that the human or the mite had grasped the real size - the real degree of extension - of the physical objects in question.
Therefore,
10. Berkeley's example of the mite shows that there is no determinate size, and, therefore, no determinate degree of extension, attaching to the intuitive component in extension, considered as a property of physical bodies.
Therefore,
11. The intuitive quality of extension is not physically real.
Therefore,
12. Physical space (which needs intuitive extension) is not real.

This argument could perhaps be rejected by detecting an ambiguity in the notion of "our conception of physical space," which occurs in line 3. This expression might have a more and a less psychological sense. Because space cannot be purely formal, when we imagine it there must be a non-formal, qualitative element in how we imagine it to be. Perhaps this imagined feature, however, bears no qualitative resemblance to the quality space possesses intrinsically. For some empiricists it was almost a common-place that the way space actually is is neither like the way it looks, nor the way it (that is, in this case, the extension of objects) feels. The argument would then only prove that no space qualitatively like our visual space - or, probably, by parity of argument, any other sensory space - can be physically real.. So though step 11 is correct in its assertion that the quality of extension *as we intuit it* is not physically real, we cannot conclude that no space with a qualitative element could be physically real; we just cannot know what the qualitative element is.

This reply is not convincing, however. Although the intrinsic quality of space may not be the same quality as that presented in any of our senses, it must be something directly analogous to such qualities, for they are the only model we have from which to understand monadic qualities. Any such quality must be the kind of thing that could, in principle, be the object of *some* possible sense or other. I can imagine no reason why it should not, therefore, be possible that something similar to what applies to the perception of mite and man should apply to it.

This reading of the "mite" argument enables one to connect it to two of Berkeley's more discussed arguments. Berkeley argues that "an idea can be like nothing but an idea." This can be interpreted as saying that monadic qualities are essentially mental, because they are essentially features of sensations. I have argued elsewhere that this is a plausible argument, and, if it is, then the attempt to give qualitative content to a mind-independent space must fail.[2] The other argument with which it connects is Berkeley's claim that we cannot conceive of primary qualities without secondary qualities. As the "new science" claimed that this was how the world was really constructed, this was intended to undermine scientific realism. It is natural to read this argument as depending on Berkeley's attack on abstract ideas. It then moves in two steps: (i) it is impossible to conceive that which one cannot image; (ii) it is impossible to image primary without secondary qualities. If one rejects the attack on abstract ideas, one will abandon (i). It is possible, however, to reconstruct the argument in a different way. Most, if not all, primary qualities have a spatial element. If space, for reasons that are nothing to do with abstract ideas, cannot be conceived without a qualitative element, and if such

[2] I argue this in Berkeley 1996, xiv-xvi.

elements are essentially experiential, then, given that nothing experiential lacks some secondary quality, then no primary quality will be conceivable as really existing without some secondary. I do not want to suggest that this is how Berkeley intended his claim that secondary qualities cannot be conceived without primary be defended - he was, indeed, relying on the attack on abstract ideas – but I think it is useful to see how closely the "mite" argument, the doctrine that nothing can be like an idea but an idea, and the interdependence of primary and secondary qualities, are connected.

The argument that I would like to have made more plausible is, therefore, the following. Any real space requires a qualitative filling, and qualities of the appropriate kind have absolute extent, independent of relational features. But once abstracted from the phenomenal context, the attribution of absolute extent becomes arbitrary in a way that shows that such qualitative notions do not really belong outside the experiential. This shows that our notion of physical space is a hybrid, of the abstract-cum-relational and the qualitative, of a sort that is operationally sound, but which cannot be taken realistically.

Newton's Thought-experiments and Absolute Space

The "bucket experiment" is one of two thought experiments that Newton employed to show that space was absolute not relative. Imagine a bucket containing water and suspended by a rope. Now imagine the bucket spinning – say turning it until the rope becomes tense and letting it go. At first the bucket will turn leaving the water stationary, but, as a result of friction, the water will start to turn with the bucket, until it is fully turning with the bucket and so stationary with respect to it. Centrifugal force will make the water higher at the edge, with a trough in the middle. Now suppose that the bucket is the only thing in the physical universe. It will not be spinning with respect to anything, but, as the state of the water shows, it is spinning. Hence it is moving through absolute, not relative, space. In the other thought experiment we imagine two metal spheres joined by a taught rope. If the spheres begin to spin round each other tension increases in the rope. If they are alone in the physical universe, they are not moving with respect to anything, yet the increased tension shows they are moving, hence they, too, are moving in absolute space.

As far as I am aware, no-one has answered these arguments satisfactorily. Berkeley seems to miss the point. He summarizes his view of motion as follows:

> For to denominate a body moved, it is requisite, first, that it changes its distance or situation with regard to some other body: and secondly, that the

> force or action occasioning the change be applied to it. If either of these be wanting, I do not think that agreeably to the sense of mankind, or the propriety of language, a body can be said to be in motion. (P 115)

> As to what is said of the centrifugal force, [namely] that it doth not at all belong to circular relative motion: I do not see how this follows from the experiment which is brought to prove it ... For the water in the vessel, at that time at which it is said to have the greatest relative circular motion, hath, I think, no motion at all (P 114).

Berkeley's version of relativism is interesting in itself. He adds the second condition, that the moving object is the subject of a force, so that he can say that when he walks down the street, though he and the pavement are in relative motion, he is moving and the pavement is stationary (P 113). He concludes that it follows that the water in the bucket is initially stationary, so we do not have here a case of relative motion. This is doubly mistaken. First, it is a case of relative motion if the one that is moving is the bucket, not the water. Second, and more important, the interesting case is where the water has "caught up" with the bucket and is moving with it in a centrifugal way. Supposing the bucket and the water to be the only things in the universe, they are moving relative to nothing, but, as the efforts of the water to climb the sides of the bucket show, are in motion. The power of this example is that, at the initial stages, the water and the bucket are moving relative to each other. The relativist cannot, therefore, use the simple blocking move of saying that a lone bucket cannot spin, because there is no distinction between its orientation and the orientation of space. It originally spins in a way that is acceptable to the relativist. The water in the bucket continues to move relatively to the bucket, though increasingly slowly, until the process is complete and it is moving with the bucket, pressed up against its side. Then there is no relative motion, but there are the physical effects of motion.

Ernst Mach showed a better grasp of the issue, but did not provide a convincing response. He claimed that we do not know that these phenomena would occur in an otherwise empty universe, as we cannot test such a claim. So, if there was nothing else in the universe, then perhaps the water would never rise up the sides of a lone bucket and we would never have grounds for saying that it was spinning. This strongly verificationist approach is not convincing because the centrifugal force is not deemed to be caused by the gravitational pull of other bodies, so their absence should not lead to the water's remaining flat, according to the principles of physics. (The same consideration applies to the tension in the rope in the other example.) Berkeley concludes his discussion by saying:

> From what hath been said it follows that the philosophic consideration of motion doth not imply the being of an *absolute space*, distinct from that which is perceived by sense, and related to bodies: which that it cannot exist without the mind, is clear upon the same principles, that demonstrates the like of all other objects of sense. (P 116)

Berkeley here seems to me to confuse two different things. He confuses denying that there is any absolute space outside the mind with denying that a single body could move in a way that was not relative to any other body. He conflates these two because he accepts Newton's claim that if a body moved without there being any other body for it to be moving in relation to, then it must be moving in an absolute space. This is, indeed, a correct inference if one takes physical space as existing independently of mind, for then motion which is not relative to another body must be, if it exists at all, absolute, and if it occurs in a mind-independent space, that space must possess absolute positions. But Berkeley does not accept such a mind-independent space, and he has the option of allowing that a lone object could rotate *with respect to the viewpoint of a mind*. In fact, Berkeley can turn Newton's thought-experiments to his own advantage by using them to show that there is no adequate account of mind-independent physical space. The experiments show that the relational view is defective; as I argued against Mach, physical theory seems to require that the lone bucket should spin and the balls rotate. *Provided* that there is something wrong with the absolutist notion, then it would seem that there is no adequate conception of mind-independent space, either relationist or absolute.[3]

The point which should have appealed to Berkeley is that the notion of the rotation of a single objects round its own axis makes clear sense in a visual or phenomenal field. So, without absolute space, only by reference to what it would be experientially like can the phenomena Newton cites make sense. If absolute space is a defective conception then space must be a construct from experience. This seems appropriate, for, if one asks oneself why, intuitively, it seems to make sense that a lone object in a universe might rotate, the answer is that one could imagine what it would look like. Similarly, one might argue that purely phenomenal visual space allows rotation of unique objects - a lone after-image could rotate - and our intuitive notion of physical space is based mainly on our grasp of visual space. Notice that these things do not seem

[3] Notice that the relativist cannot explain the motion of the lone objects by reference to a relationship to other *possible* objects, for to say that it would be moving relative to *something at p* presupposes an independent identity of that point, and so falls back into absolutism.

to be rotating with respect to one's *body* but simply with respect to one's *viewpoint*. This fact gives, I think, Berkeley the materials for replying that Newton's thought experiments show that his "absolute motion" requires not an absolute, mind-independent space, but a space possessing features essentially derived from its experiential roots, but it does so only if the conception of absolute space is independently defective.

But is the notion of absolute, mind-independent space, demonstrably defective? Berkeley says "that [space] cannot exist without the mind, is clear upon the same principles, that demonstrate the like of all other objects of sense." (P 116). But appeal to these other considerations would undermine the point of the present argument, which is to extract an independent argument for an idealist approach to space. The traditional objections rest on the fact that absolutism means that the universe could have happened in any of an infinite number of different places without this making any empirical difference. Leibnitz thought this objectionable because it meant that God lacked a sufficient reason to put it in one place rather than another. Verificationists think that the absence of empirical difference means that the hypothesis must be vacuous. It may well be, however, that one subscribes neither to the principle of sufficient reason, nor to verificationism. What, then, is wrong with absolute space? Now one may be tempted to argue that though verificationism is not true across the board, there is something fishy in the idea that the very same universe could have happened in a different location: such an idea fails to do justice to the way in which physical space is bound up with the physical world, as part of the same system. This could be true of space, even if space were not *simply* the relation between its occupants. – The argument which I have been suggesting so far runs like this:

1. If physical space is mind-independently real, then it is either absolute, as Newton thought, or it is relational, as Leibniz and Berkeley thought.
2. Newton's thought experiments show that it is not relational, and the considerations just mentioned strongly suggest that it is not absolute.
Therefore,
3. Space is not mind-independently real.
4. A conception of space that ties it essentially to its perceivability from our viewpoint would accommodate the correct intuitions of both parties: that is, it would accommodate the rotatability of lone objects, whilst tying the identity of spatial points to their role in accommodating the empirical world.
Therefore,
5. An idealist approach to space seems to be the best way of preserving our intuitions.

This, I think, is an appealing argument provided that the first premise is correct in its claim that absolutism and relationism, as conceived in the debate over Newton's bucket, represent the only realist options. Unfortunately for my idealist strategy, it is possible that Einsteinian space constitutes another option. The space-time of relativity endows space with physical properties, unlike the pure receptacle of Newton's theory, but does not seem to collapse space into relational properties of its occupants.[4] It is, indeed, comparable with the ether. In Albert Einstein's own words: "physical space and ether are only different terms for the same thing; fields are physical states of space."[5] Thus space is non-reducible, but physically influenced by its occupants:

> Einstein restricts the label "absolute" to a specifically "causal" sense, in that this "space" conditions the behaviour of ponderable bodies without in turn being influenced by them. It is in this sense that Einstein emphasizes the nonabsolute character of the aether of general relativity . . .[6]

It seems that as well as the two options that I originally considered, there is also the possibility of conceiving of space as a medium for objects, itself endowed with physical properties: it is rather like the ether, except that, obviously, no further question of its location in space can be raised (as, in general, it was not actually raised in the case of the ether). Space is, thereby, essentially tied to the objects that occupy it, and there is no question of the universe as a whole being located in a different place.

I seem to face a dilemma in my attempt to use Newton's thought-experiments to support idealism. If Einstein's space can accept Newton's conclusions, then there is a conception of physical space, other than the rejected form of absolutism, which can accommodate the phenomena. If, on the other hand, Einstein cannot accommodate Newton's bucket, then I, in defending Newton, appear to be saying that Einstein's theory of space is false, and this seems rather reckless. What follows is very tentative.

How does Einstein's theory stand on Newton's argument? This, in turn, depends on how the special and the general theories stand with regard to the "bucket" thought-experiment. I think I am correct in saying that there is no agreement on this. Whether the special theory of relativity allows motion round an axis for an object in a single object universe must depend on whether such a universe allows the existence of an inertial frame by reference to which such motion could be deemed to occur. As far

---

[4] See the fascinating article, Rynasiewicz, 1996.

[5] Quoted by Rynasiewicz 1996, 288. It is originally from Einstein 1934, 274.

[6] Rynasiewicz 1996, 297-8.

as I can see, it could not, for, without ascribing independent identity to points, there are insufficient references by which to set up all the co-ordinates required. A bucket is asymmetrical from top to bottom, and this establishes an axis, but nothing other than points distinguish the different parts on the symmetrical circumferences. (It might be thought that one could pick out individual atoms on the rim of the bucket, but this will not do, for they move as the bucket rotates – if it does – and so do not establish an independent axis.) In comparing, in a concessionary spirit, relativistic space with the ether, Einstein said:

> As to the mechanical nature of the Lorentzian aether, it may be said of it, in a somewhat playful spirit, that immobility is the only mechanical property of which it has not been deprived by Hendrik Lorentz. It may be added that the whole change in the conception of the ether which the special theory of relativity brought about, consisted in taking away from the ether its last mechanical quality, namely its immobility.[7]

In other words, Lorentz's ether is rather like Newton's space, in being a fixed frame of reference, and nothing else; and Einstein's space is like that ether, except that, apart from the relations of objects in it, it determines no location, and so has lost the properties of a Newtonian space.

The fact that, at the beginning of the rotation, the water moves with respect to the bucket might be taken to suggest that relativity can accommodate the later stages by allowing for the temporal dimension of space-*time*. This might suggest that the General Theory fairs better than the Special in accommodating the buckets, for the General Theory is a theory of space-time and not just of space. On the other hand, this might seem rather contrived, for, as the water catches up with the bucket, what happens is that the two inertial frames collapse into each other, and the original difference becomes irrelevant. Perhaps one could argue that Einsteinian space is devised for a world with a plurality of objects: it is, after all, about their relativities. If there were only one object, or, if you deem the water and the bucket to be at least two, if there were only objects operating insufficiently independently, space could not exhibit Einsteinian characteristics. But what would such a space be like; in particular, would the bucket spin and the water climb the sides? If space were physically real, then this question should have an answer, which it does not seem to have. It should have an answer because there would seem to be no reason why God, or bizarrely improbable accident, should not have created it. But if physical space were ideal, that is, existed as a form of organisation for

[7] Einstein 1922, 10-11: quoted in Rynasiewicz 1996, 296.

human (and perhaps other) experience, and if this thought experiment abstracts from any context which could be empirically genuine, then there need be no fact about the matter. We can *imagine*, say, visually, a world with a single rotating bucket: but it is not a physical world in which we could ever be physically located. It is not an option for which a theory of space designed to deal with a world which could ever be our physical environment need cope.

Bibliography

Berkeley, George. (1948-1957), *The Works of George Berkeley*, 9. vols, A. A. Luce and T. E. Jessop (eds), Nelson, London.

Berkeley, George. (1996), *Principles of Human Knowledge* and *Three Dialogues between Hylas and Philonous*, Howard Robinson (ed.), Oxford World's Classics, Oxford University Press, Oxford.

Einstein, Albert. (1922), "Ether and the Theory of Relativity," in his *Sidelights on Relativity*, Methuen, London.

Einstein, Albert. (1934), "The Problem of Space, Ether, and the Field in Physics," in his *The World As I See It*, Covici-Friede, New York.

Foster, John. (1982). *The Case for Idealism*, Routledge, London.

Rynasiewicz, Robert. (1996), "Absolute versus Relational Space-Time: An Outmoded Debate?," *Journal of Philosophy* 93, 279-306.

LIGHT AND CAUSALITY IN *SIRIS*

TIMO AIRAKSINEN

> Since heat takes its origin from light, it is an infinite heat, an infinitely beneficial heat in the infinite good. . . The more radiant His light, the more unknown it is naturally to the intellect; the more vehement His heat, the more certain so to speak it is to the will.
> —Marsilio Ficino[1]

Abstract

George Berkeley's *Siris* (1744) has been a neglected work, for many reasons. Some of them are good and some bad. The book is difficult to decipher, mainly because of its ancient metaphysics. He talks about the world as an animal or plant. He speculates about man as a microcosm which is analogous to the universe as a macrocosm. He recommends tar-water as a universal medicine. This was understandable in his own time. But *Siris* is also a Newtonian treatise which both criticizes and develops important physical and chemical theories. Berkeley's own contribution is formulated in terms of light and fire. I study these arguments in detail. It is also clear that *Siris* is no longer an immaterialist treatise. The doctrine of ideas is not so important to him any more. However, he never changed his doctrine of causality. I analyze several versions of it. This looks like his lasting main contribution to the philosophy of science. And causality is also theologically crucial, as I try to show. We must keep in mind the fact that Berkeley might have been interested in the contemporary science, but he insisted that science must ultimately be ruled by religion. Science is never an autonomous or sovereign field of human enterprise.

Introduction

My purpose in this paper is first to review and explain all those causality-like relations Berkeley introduces and discusses and then ask how the last

[1] Ficino 2006, 239.

one, *light*, as God's causal instrument, works. Why is it introduced at all? Why is light needed in his mature philosophy of science? What is its true nature? What does it mean to say that it is a divine instrument? These are the main questions. The point is that to Berkeley light is a crucially important *explanans* of all the various and novel terrestrial phenomena he now observes around him. His conception of natural phenomena changes and expands after he starts thinking about tar water and reads Sir Isaac Newton's *Opticks* and its speculative, ground-breaking Queries. I emphasize Newton's influence and leave the speculations on tar water and its beneficial medical effects on the side.[2]

Every student of *Siris* must ask the question: how has Berkeley's philosophical outlook changed since the early days of the *Principles* (1710), which made him so (in)famous? T. E. Jessop, the latest editor of *Siris*, says that not much has changed.[3] I disagree. To me it is obvious that, for instance, immaterialism does not matter much to a mature Berkeley. The visual atoms no longer look stable and evident to him. He may hint at them in *Siris* but that is all (S 251). The possibility of ideas in the mind is preserved, but the philosophical context is now that of Cartesian dualism of mind and matter, or mind and something like matter, or mind and corpuscles. In a strange way, Berkeley never accepts matter, but when he dismisses, however implicitly, his theory of ideas, it is difficult to say what is left. Small particles or corpuscles are material in the sense that they obey the laws of physics, but in the ontological sense of the word "matter" they may be ambiguous (see S 225).

Causality, not ideas, was Berkeley's major contribution to philosophy. Ideas are needed when mechanistic causality is first criticized, and this is a key role of ideas in immaterialist philosophy. But in *Siris*, he needs another way to characterize causality when immaterialism no longer interests him. Yet he never changed his theory of God's agency as efficient cause. Ideas may be obsolete in 1744, but God's powers remain. To change the theory of causality would have been fatal to his whole philosophical outlook, much more so than the rejection of immaterialism and the external world consisting of ideas. God's causal role has the right type of metaphysical and even theological consequences. So, how does one restore the causal role of God in the new world, in which corpuscles rather than ideas figure? Some classes of particles are invisible, as *Siris* says, so that the rule of ideas must end now. Here light, which is "invisible and imperceptible to all our senses" (S 169), enters the inquiry.

---

[2] On Tar Water, see Airaksinen 2006. – Newton 1730/2003 (*Opticks*).

[3] Jessop in *Works*, vol. 5, 12.

Seven Types of Causality

Berkeley distinguishes between at least seven different types of causality in different places and phases of his works. Only one of them is true and real causality, as I said above. The rest are instances of other types of causality, which mean metaphysically superfluous but scientifically understandable ascriptions of causal relations to varying physical contexts. We can call this Berkeley's Metaphysical Error Theory of Causality: most types of causality, which philosophers have detected and identified, are metaphysically false.

Here, a word of warning is needed. Berkeley emphasizes that only agent causality is real and true causality. At the same time, there is no need to deny that the other types of causality constitute useful and understandable ways of understanding how the physical world functions. The problem of causality is, therefore, ambiguous: metaphysical considerations are different from those of science and everyday life. Berkeley, himself, is conscious of this problem. He writes to Johnson about causality: "Cause is taken in different senses. A proper active efficient cause I can conceive none but spirit; nor any action, strictly speaking, but where there is will. But this doth not hinder the allowing occasional causes (which are in truth but signs), and more is not requisite in the best physics, i.e., the mechanical philosophy." (*Works*, vol. 2, 280). This expresses Berkeley's attitude towards the problems of causality as clearly as possible.[4]

In order to understand what this means, let us review the various types of causality. The first one is, of course, Berkeley's early theory of mental expectations (ME theory), according to which we see a cloud and, therefore, expect rain as if the cloud were an efficient cause of rain or "[t]he fire which I see is not the cause of the pain I suffer upon my approaching it, but the mark that forewarns me of it." (P 65). When we pull the trigger of a gun, we mentally prepare for a gunshot. In both cases, we need to make certain preparations when we expect the causal effect. In case of rain, we take an umbrella. In the case of a gunshot, we stiffen our body, as we know that the gun kicks back. All this is very useful, says Berkeley, otherwise we must suffer. Now there is no need to suffer as we learn how to prepare ourselves for such events as rain and a gun kicking back. God is benevolent, and he allows us to learn about these things by

---

[4] Bertil Belfrage mentions Berkeley's three different fields of discourse, or physics, mechanics, and metaphysics, which all utilize a different conception of causality. It is true that agent causality is the only true causality in metaphysics but "at the purely descriptive level 'a moving body is the cause of the motion of another'." (Belfrage 2003)

keeping such causal contexts regular enough so that learning may take place. Notice that we tend to think we can predict events on this basis, but can we explain them? Perhaps we need to answer in the negative: our expectations do not explain rain or the recoil of the gun. For this reason, alone, we may say that the mental expectation theory is not a true theory of efficient causality.

Such every-day causal contexts are, in a sense, truncated, because we seldom observe anything we might want to call a cause. If I drop a glass bowl and it shatters on the floor, what is the cause of its destruction? What is the mark or sign, which forewarns me of the breakage? We see it falling, but the fall is not a cause. If it is a copper pan, we do not expect it to break. It just bounces off the floor. In fact, we seldom perceive a clear-cut cause. Berkeley is right. When we drop a glass bowl, we correctly expect it to break, and that is all. When I touch a red-hot iron, I expect to burn my finger, but again, the hot iron is only a relevant sign. We really do not know what the cause is, although we say that the red-hot iron burns. The iron is not the cause we want to find. Nevertheless, all these relevant mental expectations are useful.

The second theory is that of causal laws (CL theory), which is to say that we now move from psychology to science. Of course, Berkeley realizes that science plays with something called the laws of nature. These seem to be objective regularities between events of which the earlier one can be called cause and the latter one effect. Moreover, such laws may well explain the success of the ME theory: "Now the set of rules or established methods, wherein the mind we depend on excites in us the ideas of sense, are called the Laws of Nature . . ." (P 30). In other words, some expectations are based on the laws of nature, and if such laws are interpreted causally, we have a new candidate for the theory of causality. Moreover, the laws are valid independently of the existence or success of our psychological expectations. The laws of nature are in God's mind.

But as we know, this view of causality is suspicious. Regularities are just that, rules and regularities, and they have nothing to do with efficient causality as such. Things happen according to the laws of nature, not because of them. Yet, popular thinking and vulgar science assign a causally efficient role to the temporarily earlier event. At a more sophisticated level, we have contexts like gravity. We say that the laws of gravity explain how a material object behaves when it (say) falls down to the Earth. Notice that these laws allow us to predict events, but explanations are still missing. (Of course one may refer to something like an early version of the Covering Law Model of explanations: the applicability of natural laws explains phenomena.)

Third, we have causal mechanisms (CM theory), which may both predict and explain: "he [God] will act agreeably to the rules of mechanism, by him for wise ends established and maintained in the Creation" (P 62). A mechanism allows us to predict, but by describing a mechanism, we can also say why we can predict. This is to explain something.

Berkeley has much to say against mechanisms and mechanistic explanations in science. He has so much to say that many of his readers and commentators have thought that he rejects them all. Moreover, this seems to make him an enemy of mechanistic natural philosophers like René Descartes and Newton (*A Defense of Free-thinking in Mathematics, Works*, vol. 4, 2). It is true that Berkeley rejects Descartes' physics in *Siris*, but he does not reject Newton in spite of what he might say against him in his earlier writings.

On the contrary, *Siris* testifies how Newton's *Opticks* has opened the Bishop's eyes to the complexity of scientific phenomena and the real intractability of mechanisms. Yet, it is true that in many places he argues against the use of mechanism in causal explanations. Causal mechanisms do not explain anything, he says. When clockwork moves the hands of a clock driven by a pendulum or a spring, everything we are able to say about it accounts as a mere description of events. In this sense, mechanistic language for Berkeley is redundant. The mechanism, itself, has no causal powers or virtues; it does not explain. It only describes. Yet it is useful: "though the fabrication of all those parts and organs be not absolutely necessary to the producing any effect, yet it is necessary to the producing of things in a constant, regular way, according to the Laws of Nature." (P 62)

Many types of visible and invisible, natural and artificial mechanisms exist (TV 43; Alc VII 16). Clockworks regulate time. Gunlocks bring about explosions inside the barrel and so on. Nevertheless, the major scientific problem is gravity. Gravity depends on an invisible or theoretical mechanism or at least it has been said to. The particles of aether group around a material object in such a way that it becomes weighty and tends to fall down towards the center of the Earth. According to this view, gravity explains the accelerating motion of matter towards the Earth (Newton), but yet gravitational mechanism, itself, should be described and explained. It is now an *explanandum*. Here we meet the modern aether hypothesis, which Berkeley discusses at length in *Siris*.[5] He rejects Descartes' and Newton's explanations of gravity in terms of aether particles, but he also rejects the aether hypothesis itself in *Siris*. Aether

[5] See the discussion on Newton, aether, and gravity in Airaksinen 2010.

does not exist. (S 226, 227). Berkeley calls light/fire aether, but his light is different from Newton's aether; hence Berkeley can say that aether does not exist.

Gravitational laws are causal laws in the sense of the CL theory. Gravity is also a causal mechanism, which should be explained in the sense that this particular mechanism is described. We want to know how it works. The result is a particular application of the CM theory. These theories are familiar to all the readers of Berkeley. The following theory is different.

The fourth theory of pseudo-causality or the fourth form of the causal Error Theory is that of occult and specific causes (OS theory).[6] Berkeley says in *Siris* that many causes are occult and specific. What does he mean by this new thesis? He writes: "For although the general known laws of motion are to be deemed mechanical, yet peculiar motions of the insensible parts, and peculiar properties depending thereon, are occult and specific." (S 239). I take "occult" to mean (a special kind of) unperceivability and "specific" those phenomena whose appearance, changes, and behavior cannot be captured by law-like propositions. Occult things do not make sense as objects of perception, and specific changes cannot be predicted.

A gap seems to open up between the first three theories of causality and OS. This gap is created by the fact that the first three theories are metaphysically erroneous – there was never any question about it. But the fourth OS is not self-evidently within the scope of the Error Theory. On the contrary, Berkeley speaks of it as if he accepted it. Here is a possible reason for this anomaly: the three earlier theories were all variants of one and the same idea, regularity of nature, which means that benevolent God speaks to us by means of His marks and signs and tells us how He arranges the future events. They are based on the divine Language of Nature. OS is different.

We are able to predict phenomena and thus avoid pain and harm. We can avoid harm and profit from our foreknowledge. But the OS theory changes this. All the laws, regularities, and correct expectations are denied from us. They are occult, or as I said, they are forever beyond human perception and knowledge. They are specific, which means "not captured by means of law-like statements." Within OS, phenomena are unique, so to speak. Now, the world is more unpredictable and stranger than ever. Events occur in an apparently random order so that we cannot mentally handle them, but there are some causes, which make them that way. The hypothesis of such causes is not erroneous in the old and familiar sense discussed in the *Principles*. Berkeley seems to say that the action of light

[6] See Hutchison 1982.

allows us to understand occult and specific causes. These causes depend "on the good pleasure of the Creator" via light. (S 238)

Before explaining the causal theory of light (L theory), I must clarify the OS theory. In his *Opticks*, Newton gives a long and bewilderingly varied list of phenomena, which should be explained in the future.[7] Many of these have systematic interest to science: what are the causes and explanations of putrefaction, fermentation, gravity, various types of attraction and repulsion, magnetism, and electricity? All these present new problems to science and require new methods and theories. Newton challenges his reader: "Let him also tell me how," and Berkeley evidently wants to take up the challenge and answer some of his questions, however sketchily he may be able to do so – and he does it in terms of light. Why is a fly able to walk on water? Both Newton and Berkeley mention this same problem. Berkeley says it has not been explained (S 235; *Opticks* 396). This is indeed a specific problem.

So, the OS theory says that a large variety of phenomena and types of phenomena exist, which are not uniformly connected by means of the laws of nature. They are specific in this sense. They are not covered by any law-like regularity, which allows us to make accurate predictions and utilize them in practice. We know that glowworms emit light, as Newton says, but we have no idea what causes this phenomenon. Both Newton and Berkeley mention the whitecap waves in a storm, which emit light (S 195; *Opticks* Qu. 8). Newton describes many puzzling effects of electricity. Magnetism is an enigma as well. Some pieces of iron and loadstone attract or reject similar objects in an unpredictable manner. Such causes are occult and specific for Newton as well. Here, Berkeley follows Newton closely, as can be seen by comparing the examples he gives. Many of them are taken directly from the *Opticks*, for example the fly. Sometimes Berkeley refers to *Opticks*, like in the case of Newton's claim that red-hot iron is fire (S 221; *Opticks* Qu. 9). Berkeley rejects this idea.

Berkeley must make an important strategic choice. He has read Newton's *Opticks* and he agrees with its author that a large number of strange occult types of phenomena should be explained scientifically. Yet, the standard methods and theories of science look hopelessly inadequate. How would one begin to study magnetism if this requires a description of magnetic mechanisms and their associated scientific laws? Berkeley's OS

---

[7] *Opticks* Qu. 8 and 31. These lists seem to have changed the way Berkeley thought about the physical world. He repeats many examples and questions given by Newton. The world appears immensely complex to him now. As a consequence, the language of ideas cannot describe it in any comprehensive manner.

theory shows us that he has rejected such a standard approach and has decided to aim at something else.

This is why he calls the relevant causes occult and specific. These two words mean that some phenomena cannot be explained by means of law-like statements. In that sense, OS is a negative theory and a transition point on the way to Berkeley's final formulation of causality, independently of the Error Theory. This formulation is in terms of the effects of light. Light is everywhere as *Opticks* Qu. 8 shows. Bodies emit light in all kinds of conditions. Berkeley's choice is to leave all the old methods behind and reach for something new. Therefore, *Siris* has its own claim to novelty. He hopes that his new theory can rescue him from all the problems, which crop up with the old and false theories of causality. All of them are philosophically erroneous anyway, no matter how attractive they may be to common sense and a naive scientific mind set.

Agent Causality

In order to understand Berkeley's methodological new way, we must first make a detour to his own valid theory of causality. This is the theory that God is a causally efficient agent (G theory), and all changes in the world can and must be explained on this unique metaphysical basis: modern philosophers "will have God alone to be the immediate efficient cause of all things." (P 53). Newton agrees in *Opticks* (Qu. 31). Notice, however, how short and simple such explanations are ("X happened because God wanted so") and how such explanations are asymmetric and impotent in relation to predictions. God is free, and thus, we can never predict on the basis of a given successful explanation, which is always available to us. We can always explain event X by saying that God wanted it, but on the basis of this fact alone, we cannot predict it. This kind of knowledge is practically useless. The wrong theory of causality is useful but the correct theory is useless. The situation is (almost) paradoxical.

Causal explanations are usually symmetric. What we can explain, we can predict as well and the other way around. In Berkeley's case, we know the cause of X, which is God, but this fact does not allow us to predict anything. This is a strange theory of causality. It is also strange that we know the cause of every X without doing any X-related research: God brought it about. This is an *a priori* theory whose explanations are empty and predictions impossible. (Of course we can predict X on the basis of the ME, CL, and CM theories, but not on the basis of the G theory.) The G theory is just a metaphysical construction without any epistemic import. The Error Theory covers all the epistemic, practically useful cases.

Before we go on to the role of light in the causal explanations of the world, the method of the causal influence of God must be specified. In immaterialist contexts, the following can be said. God wants me to see, for example, a black cloud, which is raining, and therefore, I perceive the same thing, a cloud.[8] God's act of will brings about this idea in my mind. This is easy to understand. Man, himself, can create new ideas in his mind by means of his faculty of imagination. God does the same, except that men who live under God's power receive these images or archetypes of ideas, as Berkeley sometimes calls them (e.g. P 9). Moreover, it all happens directly. God needs no instruments or other mediating factors when he imprints the ideas as he effects of His will into the feeble mind of man.

However, it is not easy to see where exactly causality is located in this picture. God brings to my mind the idea of a trigger, then the idea of a finger pulling the trigger, and finally that of a loud shot. This is still a series of events, which are all connected in a law-like manner. The same can be said of all the changes in the world. The new twist here is merely that God imprints the relevant ideas to my mind – but where is His causal role located then? I can see no causality here except something, which is covered by the Error Theory of causality described above. Obviously, the only causal role, which God has in the immaterialist world, is that of an agent who creates ideas for man to recognize and comprehend. Then he provides us two different sets of ideas, which are related in a law-like manner, namely, black cloud and rain. But where is causality now?

The locus on causality has been changed. Think again of a black cloud and rain. The question was: is the cloud the cause of rain? Berkeley answers in the negative. Then he says that God puts the idea of a cloud and the idea of rain into one's mind, but this is another thing. In the physical world, causality means a connection between the cloud and rain. But in reality, God causally brings about some ideas for us to think about. If causality is a horizontal relation, G theory treats causality as a vertical relation, as I explained above. A black cloud means rain and a red-hot iron means blisters. We (wrongly) see a causal relation between these signs. My point is that because God is the (metaphysical) cause of rain and the blisters, the cloud and the iron, as apparent causes, are irrelevant. They just happen to be there. We can think as follows: God brings about both the hot

[8] Luce and Jessop preach: "and unless one takes the Berkeleian world of sense and spirit as 'in God', as Malebranche saw all things 'in God', the Berkeleian philosophy is nonsense" (*Works*, vol. 9, 12). This must be an exaggeration when we think of God as a genuine causal agent. Obviously cause and effect must be independent of each other.

iron and the blister, but now there is no connection between the iron and the blister. Therefore, the G theory and the CL theory speak of different things when they speak of causality. True causality is a vertical view. Nevertheless, all that happens in our world takes place because God decided to bring it about and not something else. This is for Berkeley a plain and simple metaphysical truth. Ideas cannot act as causes, but God can. God is free and omnipotent, and therefore, no changes may happen without his will. Sometimes he actively wills these changes, and sometimes he just permits them to happen.

When God permits a change to happen in the world, he obviously allows for another real causal factor to step in. How is this possible? If God does not do it, how can it take place? Of course, there is no natural physical causality (see above), and therefore, there must exist another non-natural causal factor, which is able to bring about the phenomena God just allows to emerge. This is the finite human mind and its causally efficient will (H theory). Does this mean that as many causal agents exist in the world as there are human beings, plus one? This question is difficult to answer, because Berkeley says that there is only one causal agency, God, but then the human mind is free and causally efficient as well. It "governs and actuates this mundane system . . .; as it is in the microcosm with limited power and skill by the human mind." (S 154). We are able to sin, for example, and this requires freedom. God does not sin, we do. And in order to sin, we need to bring about changes in the world in such a manner that God is not responsible for them. All minds are active, and this entails their causal function and virtue (Alc VII 20, Crito).

I bypass the problem concerning the comparison of man's and God's causal powers here. They are different for the following reason. God's will is both the necessary and sufficient condition of causal change. Only man's will is a necessary condition of change. It is never sufficient alone. That is why Berkeley calls it limited. God's will is the limit. Man needs God's permission or otherwise nothing happens. Only God can work alone, according to Berkeley's logic, but some changes are brought about by man's active will – when God is quiet. Hence, two slightly different types of agent causality exist.

Here is a question. I raise my hand (I imprint this visual idea to my mind). I lower my hand quickly and it breaks a glass panel. Why can I not put in my mind the (non-imaginary) idea of a broken panel without the two intermediate steps? Could God do so? Certainly, God can do it. Why can I not do it? The answer must be related to the causal structure of the world, which is independent of my will. Berkeley's answer would possibly be by saying that God does not allow me to do all of what He, himself, might do. These restrictions must be part of what I mean by causality in the Error Theory. We notice that there is a certain order of events in the world itself, which seems to be unavoidable and unalterable from our human point of view. We humans must play by God's rules.

The Nature of Light

Light in *Siris* is Berkeley's new creation, or actually, we should talk about light/fire/aether/spirit as one single entity. Berkeley denies the existence of aether, of course; thus we are left with light/fire/spirit (see Appendix 1 below). It is difficult to understand why Berkeley wants to talk about aether if he also denies its existence, at least in the sense in which it was understood by Descartes and Newton. One possible explanation is, of course, that the ancient authors whom Berkeley quotes so often speak about aether, and Berkeley wants to keep close to them.

Fire is the same entity as light, but light has priority over fire because we have a Newtonian theory of light. Fire is then Berkeley's addition to this context: light carries fire, although he is not the first to say so. Experiments with burning glasses show that light is fire. Hence he tends to speak about fire when he emphasizes the effects created by or by means of light. For instance, "No eye could ever hitherto discern, and no sense perceive, the animal spirit in a human body, otherwise than from its effects. The same may be said of pure fire, or the spirit of the universe, which is perceived only by means of some other bodies, on which it operates, or with which it is joined." (S 159). When Berkeley discusses Newton's theories and the relevant corpuscular theories, he prefers "light."

The Bishop in his *Siris* says, both, that light/fire is a "mighty agent" and it is God's instrument (L theory), in other words, a secondary or "inferior instrumental cause." (S 158, 154). The basic idea is simple. A hammer in hand is an instrumental and secondary cause when one drives in a nail. First, I will provide a brief summary of my argument and then go into its details. The basic L theory is indeed simple, but its ramifications lead to some questions, which are as difficult as any other in *Siris*.

In L theory, light is a hail of minimal corpuscles like small material bullets from the Sun, exactly as Newton says. Light is invisible to man, meaning that light particles cannot be seen or otherwise perceived. (S 159). We can perceive light and fire only through its effects, and we can perceive heat, which co-exists with fire. Berkeley repeatedly emphasizes that light cannot be seen and its particles are invisible. The debate concerning the exact interpretation of this claim is complicated.[9] Perhaps some powerful technology such as microscopes could reveal the light particles or some angel-like creatures can see them. One can also say that light cannot be seen because we see by means of light. To see light would be like an eye seeing itself. But Berkeley, himself, does not use this kind of an argument.

Berkeley himself says that light particles are invisible, and this is what we have to accept. [10] It is, of course, a radical step to maintain that some corpuscles cannot be perceived. Therefore, they are not ideas. This is to say that either matter exists independently of ideas or corpuscles are not material. Berkeley does not use the word "matter" in the context of light/fire. Instead, he uses words like "corporeal." In other words, the particles or corpuscles are corporeal entities, which seem to entail that they are not soul-like; they can as well be called material. Once again Berkeley relies on systematic ambiguity as a rhetorical device.

Light particles are corpuscular and corporeal entities, which is a highly interesting claim in *Siris*. Light/fire particles obey all the laws of nature just like any other "material" entity does. (S 162). If we could perceive the particles of light, which we cannot, we could also form rational and functional expectations of their motion and effects according to causal laws (cf. ME and CL theories). But we cannot perceive them directly by sense. Light, when it is understood in this Newtonian manner, has one more property, which is useful for Berkeley, that is, it can form a natural mechanism (cf. CM theory). *Prima facie* it can work like aether works for Descartes and Newton. Thus, it may explain gravity and perhaps even the mysteries of putrefaction, fermentation, and magnetism, certainly not just now but when science progresses. Light as fire does not only illuminate the world, also changes it. Light does not change the world only gradually but abruptly and even violently (S 170; cf. *Opticks* Qu. 31, 379). For instance, fermentation is a gradual process. Extreme heat is a very powerful cause but in explosions we witness light and fire together, and the results can be dramatic. Innocent light is turned in Berkeley's hands into a "mighty agent" which is fit for the Lord's service. Light as fire has its violent side as well.

---

[9] See Airaksinen 2008. This paper reviews much of the earlier discussion on *Siris*.

[10] Alc IV 4: "ALCIPHRON. I do not perceive them [animal spirits] immediately by any of my senses. I am nevertheless persuaded of their existence, because I can collect it from their effects and operations. They are the messengers, which, running to and fro in the nerves, preserve a communication between the soul and outward objects." In *Siris* animal spirits are light/fire. In this way the world according to immaterialism starts breaking down (Alc IV 4).

Newton's prism scatters light and shows us its multicolored spectrum. This rose is red because light makes it red. Grass is green because light makes it green. Light, as fire is also responsible for many other things such as, for instance, flavors and odors in plants (S 162). Light can do this because its corpuscles are so varied; in other words, because light is complex, it can causally bring about many varied things.[11] Light is multi-functional because it is multi-propertied. A most important feature of light is that it is infinitely variable, unlike Newton's simple aether whose constitution is uniform.

Light is also the fastest and most elastic type of matter, but yet it is able to sit and wait in large caverns: "The eye by long use comes to see even in the darkest cavern" (S 368). Light exists in dark places, which is said to explain the fact that some people and animals can see in darkness. (Perhaps he means the ideas of imagination or hallucinations?) How can light stand still in darkness? This is what fire and heat are able to do. Therefore, fast and elastic light whose motion is restricted and stopped is a very strange thing, indeed.

The Ultimate Theory of Causality: Light and Fire

The L theory in *Siris* is the seventh causal theory presented by Berkeley. It is only mentioned and developed in this last book of his. I said above that light is causally responsible for many phenomena; from the redness and smell of roses to the violent eruption of gases. What kind of causality is this? When we try to answer this question, we enter Berkeley's newly discovered fantasyland of metaphysics. He was reluctant to enter it, unlike many other philosophers. Even in *Siris*, the main sources he wants to use are scientists like Homberg and Newton, but he also consults a wide variety of ancient sources.[12] He likes Platonists and the Stoics, but all Ancient doctrines are of interest to him if they are not openly materialist and atheistic. He had time to read in Cloyne, and now he utilizes his knowledge of ancient learning.

He is a religious man who wants to defend and promote the Christian faith against freethinkers and all the new trends of thought, which promote

---

[11] Notice that Newton's experiments with prisms show that white light has its typical, complex constitution. Berkeley infers from this that "fire contains parts of different kinds" (S 162). This is possible only if light is fire. Newton observes the affinity between non-culinary fire and light (*Opticks* Qu. 28).

[12] See Principe 2001. The basic affinities between Berkeley and Homberg are obvious. The use of burning glasses is especially interesting. Also, the richness of new chemical phenomena needs to be emphasized.

hidden atheism. One obvious threat is science itself or natural philosophy, which is able to explain more and more without mentioning God. Perhaps God is no longer needed? Science expands and progresses and may soon claim the monopoly of natural knowledge. Its mode of thought, scientific ideology, seems to be, if not atheistic, at least non-religious. Science does not need religion and faith to explain the natural world. On the contrary, it pushes God aside and leaves Him alone to be worshipped only in special places at special times. Berkeley, himself, has already gone far in this direction. He has flirted with Newton's mechanistic explanations of gravity and some other forms of attraction. He has accepted many contemporary physiological doctrines such as, for instance, the heart as a mechanical pump (William Harvey) as well as producer of hot blood and thin animal spirits, which animate living animals and men (Descartes). (S 32, 241; also Alc IV 5, V 35). He never mentions Harvey and, moreover, he subscribes with equal enthusiasm to the two different and actually mutually incompatible theories of the function of heart.

He has introduced the term "animal spirit" into his own natural philosophy. He used to identify spirit, mind, and soul, but he cannot do so any more. The term "spirit" has been divided into two parts: first the soul-like substance, which is the opposite of matter and then spirits, which are animal spirits. These are corpuscular entities and, thus, something like matter, and Berkeley identifies that type of spirit with light and fire, which is understood as very fine particles. That is why we now need to write light/spirit. Animal spirits come from heated hot blood and they appear to be a kind of lively vapor, which fills the tube like nerves. They are "darting through the nerves" (S 87, 166). This kind of new science must have been a frightening prospect to Berkeley whose religious beliefs are pushed further and further from the center of useful and valid learning and knowledge. Berkeley must have been sensitive to such a crucially important theological issue. He still believes that he is right, of course, but he may also feel a need to say more about God's role in this possibly godless new world of natural philosophy.

It is necessary to know something about the ancient philosophy in *Siris*, or otherwise, the L theory may look too strange. It must be understood in its context. Now, the physical world is a macrocosm and man is a microcosm. (S 43). Strong analogical connections exist between these two entities.[13] Most importantly, both are living beings, which is to say that the whole world, the macrocosm, and not only man, the microcosm, is a living being. This is a well-known ancient thesis, which is

[13] Walmsley 1990, Ch. 12.

as old as philosophy itself. Democritus and many others supported such a view, although Berkeley believes that Democritus did not accept this view.[14] (S 273). Anyway, Berkeley promotes this type of cosmic and global animism. He never says directly and openly that he believes it. He only says that such ancient views exist and that they may be plausible to a degree. They may contain a kernel of truth. But, even such a cautious approach is enough for Berkeley. His L theory gets off the ground. He is able to communicate his new views to his readers.

Light is actually light/fire/aether/spirit – a complex thing. Light is a corpuscular entity and so is spirit, which is understood as animal spirits, of course. We may then proceed deeper into the foundations of the L theory. Berkeley's crucial metaphysical invention, which makes the L theory possible, is as follows: animal spirits animate the living body of men and animals (microcosm) just like light animates the living body of the whole world (macrocosm). This precious analogy depends, of course, on the identity of light and spirit. Animal spirits allow man to know, move, feel and breed, which is what we mean by being alive. The world is alive, too. Light makes trees grow, and it keeps the whole atmosphere moving as it creates tar, which nourishes man's body and mind and keeps him healthy and vigorous. Fire is needed to keep things moist and warm, which are preconditions of life.

Siris is also a biological and physiological book, which focuses on life on earth and its causes. And when we say that a macrocosm is alive because it is animated by light understood analogically as its animal spirits, we see that Berkeley's speculations about light and fire as an *explanans* in natural philosophy (physics) are of secondary importance in *Siris*, considering its major results and grand design. One of the main themes of the book is the life of an organism, as it should be, because *Siris* starts from tar water and proceeds to explain its beneficial effects. The problems of gravity, electricity, and magnetism are secondary in this context. The main point is that the whole universe is alive, and that is why it is able to support life on earth.

Tar is the supreme expression of this animistic principle, and tar water brings life to all people who bother to take notice and drink it. Tar water is good for the body and mind alike. This is a significant point. What nourishes the body is good for the mind as well: "But the calm cheerfulness arising from this water of health (as it may be justly called) is permanent." (S 66). In this sense, body and mind cannot be anything like opposites.

[14] Democritus 1968, Fragment 34. On microcosm, see for instance Timmermann, Jardine, and Banham 2006.

They live together even if they do not die together. Yet, a healthy mind requires a healthy body.

The next step towards the understanding of the L theory follows. Man thinks, imagines, moves, and acts by mediation of his animal spirits. Man's mind is able and willing to command those animal spirits, which flow in his nerve tubes performing the necessary functions, which result in thinking, imagining, moving, and acting. This is according to the H theory of causality, according to which the human mind has its own (limited) causal capabilities. He can change the world according to the acts of his free will. This means that the man's mind commands the animal spirits, which move in the nerves ever eager to do the work, which is entrusted to them.

Animal spirits are the secondary or inferior instrumental causes. If man's mind is able to change causally the configuration and motion of his animal spirits, and it must be in order to be able to act, these animal spirits are instrumental in bringing about the necessary bodily changes, which then appear as, say, bodily motions. This is to say that animal spirits are instrumental or secondary causes. They are not active in any sense; the human mind is. They are just minimally small particles, which move inside the small nerve tubes, but they are necessary for the body to move and act. But the mind or spirit must move the (material) animal spirits first.

Now, we enter the hallowed grounds of the G theory of causality. The G theory tells us how causality works. Only God can change the world freely. The old version of this was formulated in terms of ideas; the new version requires light/fire. God does not imprint the ideas of the changing world into the mind of man directly but he uses light. This is to say that He activates the animal spirits, or light, and in this way changes the world according to His free and omnipotent will. This is the essence of the new L theory, which is an extension of the original G theory and also an analogue of the epistemically prior H theory.

Metaphysically speaking, the L theory must be the primary one, but epistemologically we need to consider the H theory first. This order of thinking makes it easier to understand the L theory, which may, otherwise, look quite mysterious – which, however, it is not. The L theory is simple and easy to understand if we keep in mind the idea of the living macrocosm and the vital, animating function and virtue of light/fire, which constantly flows through it. Light changes the world; animal spirits change the body. Therefore L and H are analogous theories.

Again, we see how important the ancient learning is to Berkeley and *Siris*. (S 298). Berkeley may say that these doctrines are mentioned by him quite tentatively. Yet, his new contribution, the metaphysics of science in the L theory, rests firmly on a strikingly old and odd ancient view of the world as an animal. The world is, indeed, an animal if this is not just an empty metaphor or a figure of speech. Although, it is also clear that the L theory of causality cannot, as such, be taken literally, but because it should be taken seriously, the animistic theory of the macrocosm must also be taken in a similar vein to a certain degree, of course. Our language may not express its main point accurately, but light not only illuminates the world, it also animates and changes it like animal spirits do. They allow man to see, live, and move. The same point can be made of the whole universe. Everything is alive.

Light as a Divine Instrument

Why does the omnipotent God use instruments in order to realize His free will? Why does He just not do it, if he is capable of doing so? Why would he violate the canon of Occam's razor? Of course, God can command the world directly. Perhaps, he could do it even without pantheism? Berkeley rejects pantheism because he wants to promote a personal, theistic God. Philosophically speaking, Berkeley is now, according to *Siris*, locked in a world, which is different from what we meet in the *Principles* and the *Three Dialogues*. The immaterialist universe is only a fleeting memory in *Siris*. It is mentioned here and there but utilized nowhere. Therefore, all direct influences of God on the world are also a thing in the past. God needs to now do more than just put ideas in man's mind.

As I explained above, in the immaterialist world of ideas and spirits, it is easy to figure out how God changes the human world of ideas directly. He dreams of things and we humans dream along with him. Then, His benevolence allows us to make sense of the world and even to predict its changes, which is useful indeed (ME theory). The early theories of pseudo-causality, which are covered by the Error Theory, are formed on this very basis. But, in his new world in *Siris*, and perhaps already in *Alciphron* (1732), written in America, it sounds philosophically heavy handed and uninformative just to say that God changes the world. To say that food nourishes, alcohol kills, and tar water heals, is informative. If we say, instead, that God nourishes and God heals, we give no information. We need and want to know more than what God's role is in the world. We desire more detailed information about what is now called the instrumental causes if we hope to get good nourishment and medication and be successful in life. I criticize the G theory above. Now we see how Berkeley tries to fix if by means of his new L theory of causality.

How does one explain alcohol and its bad effects on us? Certainly, we cannot say that God kills people when we mean that alcohol kills. People drink freely, and they kill themselves by means of alcohol. We need to know that alcohol makes man hot and is, therefore, unhealthy, while tar water cools and soothes and is, therefore, healthy. We talk all the time about God's instruments, and we need to know what we are talking about. God's benevolence dictates that we, indeed, get information about such instrumental causes. When this happens, we can guide our lives in the correct direction and, thus, realize God's plans. This is good. Without knowledge of the instruments, we could not do this. Therefore, God uses instruments.

What I said above is supported by the text of *Siris*. Berkeley, himself, gives his readers this explanation why God needs crutches: "The mind of man acts by an instrument necessarily. The ... Mind presiding in the world, acts by an instrument freely. Without instrumental and second causes there could be no regular course of nature. And without a regular course, nature could never be understood; mankind must always be at a loss, not knowing what to expect, or how to govern themselves, or direct their actions for the obtaining of any end." (S 160). This is strange and unconvincing, because we can never see light, fire or spirits, and thus, they give us no information about what will happen next in the sense of the ME and CL theories of causality. The main point is this: to see a black cloud makes it easy to forecast rain; but it is not the point of the L theory of causality to allow us to infer something from antecedent signs. We are no longer discussing ME or CL theories. We discuss light as the instrument of God's and man's will. We need to know how light changes the world, especially in the occult and specific cases (OS theory).

In his *Principles*, Berkeley says that the ME theory of causality, even if it is false, allows us to predict what God will do next, and this ability is very useful to us. But, that early model is too simple – thus, the need for the OS theory – and they are then replaced in *Siris* by the more complicated and sophisticated L theory. But, of course, both the L and the ME theories are grounded on the G theory.

Also notice that the L theory may be interpreted as a novel CM theory but never as a new CL theory. The point is simple. Light can be taken as a new mechanism, which replaces Descartes' and Newton's aether (and can, therefore, be called light/aether). When light brings about dramatic changes in the world, it looks like a mechanistic (false) cause in the CM theory: "And this animated heterogeneous fire should seem a more adequate cause, whereby to explain the phenomena of nature, than one uniform aethereal medium." (S 229). Aether forms explanatory mechanisms as Newton thinks, but light/fire does it better according to Berkeley. Two difficulties emerge here with the first one being less serious than the second one. First, it is difficult to see how light changes the world as it is described in physics. I mentioned this problem above, so I do not return to it now. Light is also fire, and fire is heat. So, light/heat is able to do great things, but can it do all the things? It can heal, but how does it bring about rain? Second, because *Siris* is largely a physiological and biological book, which describes a living universe, it is unlikely that Berkeley would find many actual similarities between the L theory and the CM theory.

When tar water heals the sick Bishop, the explanation of this cannot be given in terms of a mechanism. Here, we have an organic and holistic event according to Berkeley himself. The disease influences both the body and the mind. A person cannot be cured by changing the way some single localized mechanism works. A good example is alcohol –Berkeley hates it– as it destroys the whole human being and even society. Again, we are talking about a holistic and organic state of affairs.

We must keep in mind the fact that the principal reason why Berkeley designs the L theory to account for the changes in the world according to God's will is that it allows him to cope with the scientific enigmas of the OS theory. Putrefaction, fermentation, gravity, attraction, electricity, and magnetism exemplify some new fields of phenomena, whose causal explanations are exceedingly difficult, as I already said. The L theory is custom made to cope with these new and strange scientific problems. Light has many properties, and it can create an infinity of different effects. Therefore, the L theory is needed. But notice that such new phenomena cannot be explained on the basis of scientific laws like the CL theory does. The new phenomena and their causes are occult and specific, which I take to mean that they are beyond any descriptions by means of law-like statements. Instead, we need to study light and fire in order to understand them. If we do that, the knowledge of instrumental causes becomes useful to mankind. We can study light, and this is the good news, because the particles of light obey the laws of nature. Because these particles are invisible, they can be known by their effects only, but they can be known, and this is the main thing.

Why then would Berkeley mystify light and his new L theory? Many readers of *Siris* have thought and said that light, itself is a spiritual agent and not only light/spirit in the corpuscular sense of the term.[15] It is easy to misread *Siris* here, as Berkeley calls light "a mighty agent" and an "active principle." (See Appendix 2 below). He seems to say that light is somehow

[15] See Airaksinen 2008.

divine and has some soul-like powers and virtues. Of course, this is impossible if light is just a shower of corpuscles from a source of light, for example the sun.

The Ambiguity of Light

To make sense of Berkeley's problem concerning the ambiguous nature of light and its possible function as an instrumental/active cause and a "mighty agent," we may argue as follows:

> Ideas are self-evidently passive, and thus, they cannot be real causes.
> Light is invisible, and therefore, it cannot be a collection of ideas.
> Therefore, it is not impossible that light acts as a real cause or is active.
> *Hence:*
> Light is corporeal, and thus, a corporeal entity can be active.

This argument shows that light can be a real causal factor even if ideas cannot be. It all depends on whether Berkeley still supports the theory of ideas. But, it is difficult to understand how invisible light could be an idea. Light creates ideas only when it reveals itself in its effects. Also notice that the acceptance of the argument above shows how difficult it is for Berkeley to reject ideas if he wants to protect the G theory of causality. The reason for this is that the rejection of ideas may open the door for the wrong types of causal virtues and powers. It is difficult to believe that matter could be active.

Lisa Downing argues as follows: light/fire/aether/spirit possesses "qualities of a sensible kind," like size, shape, weight etc., and therefore it can be imagined and understood in the same way as ideas.[16] This means that light is passive and cannot act as a real cause. Therefore, one should be able to imagine a real particle with all its properties, otherwise it is an abstraction. As it seems to me, we have too little information about light particles to call them real things in the immaterialist sense of the term. For instance, what is the color of such a particle? Berkeley says that these particles are not uniform, but on the contrary, they have a large number of different properties – what kind of properties? How can one tell? We can form some kind of idea about them, but it is an incomplete and rudimentary picture. Perhaps, among such innumerable physical properties, occult, known and unknown, imagined and unimaginable, some causal powers and virtues lie buried? Light/fire is called an occult entity (S 210).

---

[16] Downing 2005, 250-251.

Downing's reading is attractive, but she rather purposefully truncates the text. "Occult" is a key term here.

I must confess that I do not have any convincing solution to the problem concerning the nature of light/fire, however obvious and central this notion is. Berkeley is so fascinated by his new pet theory L that he exaggerates its virtues. Somehow, he has a hard time following his own logic when he postulates a fully corpuscular and naturalistic theory of light. Then he expands it to cover fire as well. Next, he introduces its connection to animal spirits. He even flirts with the aether theory, which he wants to reject. In this way, he gets a new monster notion of light/fire/aether/spirit. He makes light serve so many different functions that he feels he can add some more, and then he starts speaking of light as an agent and active principle. He also calls light an instrumental and secondary cause, which makes sense from the point of view of his metaphysical outlook in *Siris*. Finally, he says that light is pure or the purest thing in the world, and this rhetorical insight makes light suitable as God's own instrument. (S 171, 179, 182, 211). Moreover, light is needed because "[t]here is an instinct or tendency of the mind upwards, which sheweth a natural endeavour to recover and raise ourselves from our present sensual and low condition into a state of light, order, and purity." (S 302). Light's purity makes it heavenly. Purity attracts the pure. Thus, light in the L theory is a fundamentally ambiguous notion. Any attempt to disambiguate it leads to the distortion of Berkeley's philosophy in *Siris*.

When Berkeley calls light and fire a mighty agent and an active principle, one may also say that light behaves as if it were divine itself, which is a certain kind of extension of God or God's hand. This conceptual move allows its reader to appreciate the ultimate destiny of philosophy in *Siris*, namely, the possible accusation that Berkeley's new theory L collapses into Cartesianism and is marred by its dualistic mind/body problem. How is man supposed to move his animal spirits if mind is mind and animal spirits are mere small corpuscles? It is a kind of miracle if man's will can move matter-like things directly. We cannot do it, and we know it. How does God move light particles, which function as the animal spirits of the living macrocosmic animal? This is a problem. Berkeley hints at his own solution, for instance, in S 86: animal spirit "nearly touches the soul" (cf. S 163). There is no dualism.

We have two problems with light. First, how does light work when it changes the world, for instance, in connection with putrefaction of animal bodies? We know that it does not work like a mechanism, but that is all. Somehow, it brings about all those occult and specific effects. Second, how does the immaterial mind influence the corpuscles of light? Mind and matter are in some kind of a causal contact here.

One of the problems concerning *Siris* comes down to the basic question of simple Cartesian dualism of mind and matter: how are mind and matter causally connected? It is both disappointing and sad if Berkeley's philosophical progress should end up with this banal *cul-de-sac*. His immaterialism avoids it beautifully, but when in his old age Berkeley comes to admit the existence of such a world, which is not just a concoction of ideas, the Cartesian problem starts haunting him. If one reads *Siris* in immaterialist terms, these problems can be avoided. Berkeley keeps this very alternative open by means of some sketchy remarks in that direction, and as I said above, I do not find them convincing.

However, if light is divine, or if it is part of God, the problem does not arise. All is well and those deadly philosophical questions are avoidable. Theologically speaking, Jesus Christ is the light who illuminates the world, as he is man and god at the same time. Perhaps, we should follow this lead, which we find in the end of *Siris*. Nothing else is needed but a minor concession to the effect that light has its double nature. If it does, then light is corpuscular and divine at the same time. It is an instrumental and secondary cause in the sense of the L theory, but it is also an element of the G theory (and of course the H theory). Light is "an intellectual and artificial fire" (S 277) and "living fire" (S 281).

It is not necessary to go so far as saying that light is divine and that God is actually present in light. According to that exaggerated view, God works in light and not by means of light. What we need to say is that God works by means of light – Berkeley says so. Although, he also says that light is an agent, which is certainly hard to accept. Perhaps light is ambiguous as to its nature in a more robust sense than merely, "it is as-if light were divine."

Of course, we might think that light is so pure, subtle, fast, elastic, and special in many other ways that it brings to us maximal information from God, and this information is so complete that light, itself, starts resembling God. If we knew light fully, we would get very close to God, indeed. Perhaps this is what Berkeley thinks. An extra benefit of this type of argument is that it gets rid of the Cartesian mind/body problem. If light is divine in any sense, whatever that sense is, we need not worry about the Cartesian trap. From the scientific point of view, light is corpuscular. From the epistemological point of view, the information, which is stored in light is divinely comprehensive. From the metaphysical point of view, light has its special relation to the nature of God.

Let us consider the following final argument. Suppose light is material and corpuscular in the sense that it follows the normal laws of nature, as we know them from the CL theory. Berkeley says that properties of light and the L theory can be used to explain the world and its changes. In that case, what does causally explain the typical behavior of light, itself? Does the CL theory give an account of the behavior of light particles in terms of the behavior of light particles? Light would behave as it does because of light, which behaves as it behaves because of light, and so on ad *infinitum*. This is not possible.

This problem of self-reference and auto-explanation casts a dark shadow over the robust thesis, which says that light is just material particles, which obey the laws of physics. Berkeley did not recognize this difficulty. He missed it. Then the robust, Newtonian theory of light is in trouble. But perhaps the truth is not so simple. Perhaps, light has its divine aspect, as Berkeley also suggests, and this entails agency. If light has an aspect of agency in it, then it is active and does not need to be explained in terms of the laws of nature (although it follows the laws of nature). An agent is free; therefore a reference to light can be used in all natural explanations without creating any circularity.

All of this is incredible. This Newtonian robust theory looks attractive, which means that we must reject Berkeley's dreamland philosophy of active light. Should we really do so is the deepest possible question directed to modern Berkeley scholars. Are we sure that Berkeley's metaphysics in *Siris* does not have a hidden point? At least David Berman thinks so,[17] and I agree with him. Why do we not call it an esoteric work? And, what is the point? It is the alleged special relation between God and light, his messenger, the "aethereal seminary" (S 282). Nothing exists without the mind, and this applies to light/fire/spirit as well. (S 354)

In the robust Newtonian perspective, light is just small scale matter, but Berkeley did not think he needed to be loyal to Newton to the bitter end. What is true, however, is that he failed to formulate a convincing view concerning light as an agent and active principle. Therefore, we must try to understand what he might have wanted to say and not only what he actually said.

Conclusion

I have summarized Berkeley's main argument, which can be found in that part of *Siris*, which concerns the philosophy of science and its metaphysics. He says in *Siris* that man is a microcosm and the world a macrocosm. Both of them are living creatures who are animated by animal spirits. Man's

[17] In private discussion, Dublin, summer 2009.

animal spirits are formed by light particles, which hot blood in the heart emits. They animate him. The world is animated by light, or light/fire/aether/spirit. As we see, light is also spirit, and this means that the light of the universe, or the macrocosm, also acts like animal spirits.

Now, Berkeley accepts only agent causality, as we know. Man is able to bring about changes in the world by means of his will, which uses animal spirits as its tools, or instrumental and secondary causes. There is no problem here. God uses in an analogous fashion light/spirit as His instrumental cause in order to bring about changes in the world. He is able to move and change the man too, and he changes when His illuminating light works on him.

This is the way Berkeley introduces light as a special type of causality. Then we must discuss the question of whether light is just an instrumental cause, or does it have an active role as well? This is a difficult problem of interpretation because Berkeley says, both, that light is a corpuscular entity and that it is an active agent. The robust interpretation rejects the activity interpretation. But, it is not necessary to accept the robust view as such.

The account of causality in *Siris* leads us from the philosophy of science to metaphysics. It is influenced by Berkeley's ancient scholarship, which he now trusts, more or less, unconditionally. Much of what he says cannot be taken seriously, but at least the idea of the living macrocosm is crucial to him. Is this too fantastic, it is difficult to say. Perhaps it is. And certainly, Berkeley was already quite old-fashioned and reactionary in 1744 when *Siris* was published. This did not prevent the book from being a great success unlike, for instance, the radical and progressive *Principles*. *Siris* was widely read. However, *Siris* is a demanding book to read and comprehend. It does not have much structure, only numbered paragraphs, and the text is often repetitive, circular, or elliptic. Yet, I am convinced that, ultimately, *Siris* makes sense and forms a coherent, if hidden, argument. A good example is the explanation of how light works as an instrumental cause in the hands of your Lord Almighty.[18]

[18] My thanks are due to Dr. Bertil Belfrage (Lund) and Mr. Ville Paukkonen (Helsinki) for their many critical comments, and to Dr. Manu J. Vuorio (Turku) and my friend Roy Holcombe, MSc, (Texas) for all their help.

Appendix 1

This is a list of terms used in *Siris* to characterize light/fire. The list is not complete, and it also contains terms, which are used in an ancient historical context, and which are, therefore, suspicious. But it is a good tool for the reader of *Siris*. The numbers refer to numbered paragraphs in *Siris*:

Sun's light, S 32
solar emanations 43
(fire is acid) 128
aether, fire, or spirit 151
aether, or pure invisible fire 152
pure fire, or the spirit of the universe 159
aethereal fire or light 164
pure fire, aether, or substance of light 169
pure elementary invisible fire 190
aethereal fire 199
pure flame 203
occult light 210
an intellectual and artificial fire 277
aethereal seminary 282

solar fire 37
light 110
pure aether, fire, or spirit 150
aether 151
pure spirit or invisible fire 157
pure aether or invisible fire 162
aethereal substance or fire 166
tunicle of the soul 171
luciform aethereal vehicle 171 fine
celestial aether 181
real actual fire 198
(fire is sulphur 202)
occult fire or spirit 210
aethereal fiery spirit 216
living fire 281

Appendix 2: Documentation

1. Newton's Prism: "… the experiment of a prism, which separating the heterogeneous rays of light, alters the colour of any object; and will cause the whitest to appear of a deep blue or red to the naked eye." (3D 186). And in *Siris*:

S 165. "Blue, red, yellow, and other colours have been discovered by Sir Isaac Newton to depend on the parted rays or particles of light. And, in like manner, a particular odour or flavour seemeth to depend on peculiar particles of light or fire (Sect. 40); as appears from heat's being necessary to all vegetation whatsoever, and from the extreme minuteness and volatility of those vegetable souls or forms, flying off from the subjects without any sensible diminution of their weight. These particles, blended in one common ocean, should seem to conceal the distinct forms, but, parted and attracted by proper subjects, disclose or produce them; as the particles of light, which, when separated, form distinct colours, being blended are lost in one uniform appearance."

2. The Problem of Mechanistic Explanation: S 132. "Homberg, nevertheless, holds in general that acids are shaped like daggers, and alkalies like sheaths, and that, moving in the same liquor, the daggers run into the sheaths fitted to receive them with such violence as to raise that effervescence observed in the mixture of acids and alkalies. But it seems very difficult to conceive how or why the mere configuration of daggers and sheaths floating in the same liquor should cause the former to rush with such vehemence, and direct their points so aptly into the latter, any more than a parcel of spigots and fossets floating together in the same water should rush one into the other."

3. "A Mighty Agent": S 158. "There is no effect in nature great, marvellous, or terrible but proceeds from fire, that diffused and active principle, which, at the same time that it shakes the earth and heavens, will enter, divide, and dissolve the smallest, closest, and most compacted bodies. In remote cavities of the earth it remains quiet, till perhaps an accidental spark, from the collision of one stone against another, kindles an exhalation that gives birth to an earthquake or tempest, which splits mountains or overturns cities. This same fire stands unseen in the focus of a burning glass, till subjects for it to act upon come in its way, when it is found to melt, calcine, or vitrify the hardest bodies."

4. There Is No Aether: S 226. "It doth not seem necessary, from the phenomena, to suppose any medium more active and subtle than light or fire. Light being allowed to move at the rate of about ten millions of miles in a minute, what occasion is there to conceive another medium of still smaller and more moveable parts? Light or fire seems the same with aether. So the ancients understood, and so the Greek word implies. It pervades all things (Sect. 157), is everywhere present. And this same subtle medium, according to its various quantities, motions, and determinations, sheweth itself in different effects or appearances, and is aether, light, or fire."

5. A Paradox: S 213. "The vivifying luminous aether exists in all places, even the darkest caverns; as is evident from hence, that many animals see in those dark places, and that fire may be kindled in them by the collision or attrition of bodies. It is also known that certain persons have fits of seeing in the dark. Tiberius was said to have had this faculty or distemper. I myself knew an ingenious man who had experienced it several times in himself." (Also S 368)

6. Corporeal Light: S 207. "But it is now well known that light moves; that its motion is not instantaneous; that it is capable of condensation, rarefaction, and collision; that it can be mixed with other bodies, enter their composition, and increase their weight (Sects. 169, 192, 193). All which seems sufficiently to overthrow those arguments of Ficinus, and shew light to be corporeal."

Bibliography

Airaksinen, Timo. (2006), "The Chain and the Animal: Idealism in Berkeley's *Siris*," in Gersh and Moran (2006), pp. 224-243.

—. (2008), "The Path of Fire: The Meaning and Interpretation of Berkeley's *Siris*," in Daniel (2008), pp. 261-281.

—. (2010), "Berkeley and Newton on Gravity in *Siris*," in Parigi (2010), pp. 87-106.

Belfrage, Bertil. (2003), "Vers une nouvelle interprétation de la *Théorie de la vision*," in Berlioz (2003), pp. 159-211.

Berkeley, George. (1948-1957), *The Works of George Berkeley*, 9 vols, A. A. Luce and T. E. Jessop (eds), Nelson, London.

Berlioz, D. (ed.) (2003), *Berkeley. Langage de la perception et art de voir.* Débats philosophiques, Presses Universitaires de France, Paris.

Daniel, S. H. (ed.) (2008), *New Interpretations of Berkeley's Thought*, Humanity Books, Amherst.

Democritus. (1968), in W. Capelle (tr. and ed.), *Die Vorsokratiker: Die Fragmente und Quellenberichte*, Alfred Kröner Verlag, Stuttgart.

Downing, Lisa. (2005), "Berkeley's Philosophy of Science," in Winkler (2005), pp. 230-265.

Ficino, Marsilio. (2006), *Platonic Theology* vol. 6, M. J. Allen (tr.), Harvard University Press, Cambridge, MA.

Gersh S. and D. Moran (eds) (2006), *Eriugena, Berkeley, and the Idealist Tradition*, Notre Dame University Press, Notre Dame.

Hutchison, Keith. (1982), "What Happened to Occult Qualities in the Scientific Revolution?" ISIS 73, pp. 233-253.

Lüthy, C., J. E. Murdoch, and W. R. Newman (eds) (2001), *Late Medieval and Early Modern Corpuscular Matter Theories*, Brill, Leiden.

Newton, I. (1730/2003), *Opticks*, Prometheus Books, Amherst.

Parigi S. (ed.) (2010), *George Berkeley: Religion and Science in the Age of Enlightenment*, International Archives of the History of Ideas, Springer, Berlin.

Principe, L. M. (2001), "Wilhelm Homberg: Chymical Corpuscularianism and Chrysopoeia in the Early Eighteen Century," in Lüthy, Murdoch, and Newman (2001), pp. 535-556.

Timmermann, A., N. Jardine, and D. Banham (eds) (2006), *The Body as Instrument*, Latin Therapy Group, HPS Department, Cambridge: "The World on a String" and "Kepler and the Earthly Soul Detector."

Walmsley, P. (2001), *The Rhetoric of Berkeley's Philosophy*, Cambridge University Press, Cambridge.

Winkler, K. P. (ed.) (2005), *The Cambridge Companion to Berkeley*, Cambridge University Press, Cambridge.

PART THREE:

BERKELEY IN CONTEXT

STOICISM IN BERKELEY'S PHILOSOPHY

STEPHEN H. DANIEL

Abstract

Commentators have not said much regarding Berkeley and Stoicism. Even when they do, they generally limit their remarks to Berkeley's *Siris* (1744) where he invokes characteristically Stoic themes about the World Soul, "seminal reasons," and the animating fire of the universe. The Stoic heritage of other Berkeleian doctrines (e.g., about mind or the semiotic character of nature) is seldom recognized, and when it is, little is made of it in explaining his other doctrines (e.g., immaterialism). None of this is surprising, considering how Stoics are considered arch-materialists and determinists. My aim is to suggest that our understanding of Berkeley's philosophy is improved significantly by acknowledging its underlying Stoic character. I argue that Berkeley proposes not only a semantic ontology based on assumptions of Stoic logic but also a doctrine in which perceptions or ideas are intelligible precisely because they are always embedded in the propositions of a discourse or language.

Introduction

It is not unusual to find references to Stoic themes in accounts of Rene Descartes' ethics or Baruch Spinoza's treatment of freedom and determinism. Indeed, one has to look no further than G. W. Leibniz to see how Descartes and Spinoza are understood as "new Stoics."[1] Recent studies have highlighted how Thomas Hobbes, Leibniz, John Locke, A. A. Cooper (third Earl of Shaftesbury), and Joseph Butler also appropriate tenets of Stoicism – especially as developed in the Neo-Stoicism of Justus Lipsius (1547-1606).[2] In Hobbes's case, the Stoic contribution is most explicit when he appeals to Lipsius to show that the Stoic concept of fate

---

[1] Leibniz 1677-80, 282-283. Cf. Miller 2003, 126-35; Rutherford 2004, 178; Rutherford 2001, 138-164; James 1993, 289-316; and Kristeller 1984, 1-7.

[2] See Long 2003, 9-17, 27-28, and Moreau 1999b, 23-25.

is consistent with the Christian doctrine that God is the necessary cause of all things.[3] Locke and Shaftesbury appeal to Stoic ideas in developing their doctrines of virtue; and Leibniz endorses the Stoic view that human beings attain happiness by acting in accord with the rationally ordered cosmos.[4]

Regarding Berkeley and Stoicism, commentators have not said much. Even when they do, they generally limit their remarks to Berkeley's *Siris* where he invokes characteristically Stoic themes about the World Soul, "seminal reasons," and the animating fire or ether of the universe.[5] The Stoic heritage of other Berkeleian doctrines (e.g., about mind or the semiotic character of nature) is seldom recognized; and when it is, little is typically made of it in explaining features of his thought (such as immaterialism) for which he is most well known.[6]

Recently, however, Jeffrey Barnouw has argued that Berkeley's theory of signs parallels the Stoic treatment of how things in the cosmos are related.[7] And Geneviève Brykman has proposed that Berkeley's account of human freedom is similar to that of the Stoics, Shaftesbury, and even Spinoza, in that "for all these thinkers, liberty is connected with the comprehensive knowledge and understanding of nature."[8] Such interpretations are problematic, however, considering how the Stoics are commonly portrayed as extreme materialists and determinists – neither of which views Berkeley endorses.

My aim here is to indicate how the common portrait of Stoicism fails to acknowledge certain features that appear in Berkeley's philosophy as well. Even though those features are not typically emphasized in popular accounts of Stoicism, they are crucial for showing how other Stoic doctrines are related to one another. By recognizing how they function in Stoic thought, we are better prepared to see not only how Berkeley adopts Stoic ideas but also how disparate aspects of his philosophy – from its earliest expressions about mathematics and the epistemology of vision to the metaphysics and cosmology of *Siris* – can be understood as more unified than has previously been noted.

---

[3] See Hobbes 1656, 242-243. Cf. Kassler 1991, 54-55.

[4] Cf. Mitsis 2003, 45-61; Rutherford 2003, 62-89; and Forman 2008, 206-211.

[5] Cf. Moked, 126-127; Leduc-Fayette 1997, 414, 419; and Jacob 1991, 115. Berkeley, *Siris*, 153, 159, 161, 166, 169, 172, 177, 229, 273, 276-279, 323-324.

[6] Cf. Bracken 1974, 137.

[7] See Barnouw 2008, 170-172.

[8] Brykman 2008, 243-244.

Stoic Immaterialism

Our attending to Stoic themes in Berkeley's philosophy has the reflexive effect of making us reconsider aspects of Stoicism (e.g., materialism, determinism) that seem to conflict with Berkeley's views. This reconsideration is important because, as Anthony Long argues, the medieval assimilation of Stoic doctrines in Christian ethics and theology blurs the profound differences between Stoicism and Christian thought.[9] In particular, Stoic teachings on perception, the passions, morality, and providence are recast by medieval thinkers in Platonic and Aristotelian terms and divorced from the distinctive logical and metaphysical contexts in which those teachings are inextricably grounded for their intelligibility. So in the effort to Christianize Stoicism, medieval thinkers gloss over differences between Stoic and Platonic/Aristotelian ways of thinking. And it is this gloss that produces the standard understanding of Stoicism that seems so contrary to Berkeley's immaterialism.

The appearance of Stoic themes in Berkeley's philosophy invites us to reconsider not only (a) how Stoicism allows for (and even requires) recognition of immaterial realities and freedom but also (b) how his Christianity accommodates the view expressed by the Stoic poet Aratus and repeated by St Paul, that in God we "live, and move, and have our being" (Acts 17:28). The key to this latter point lies in noting how Berkeley's emphasis on the discursive character of nature and his rejection of abstract ideas depend on his appeal to a form of Stoic metaphysics (and the propositional logic underlying it) rather than the metaphysics and predicate logic found in the Platonic/Aristotelian strategies appropriated by most of his contemporaries.

Typically the default way of treating Berkeley's metaphysics and logic is to claim that he at least starts with a version of Cartesian, Malebranchean, or Lockean metaphysics that is based on the kind of predicate logic proposed in the *Port Royal Logic* and popularized by Locke. The problem with such a strategy is that it does not explain – nor does it attempt to explain – why Berkeley would adopt three doctrines that unite his thought: (1) The proper objects of perception constitute a divine language (which is what we learn from Berkeley's works on vision and *Alciphron*); (2) that divine language is structured to enhance human well-being (about which we learn in the *Principles*, the *Three Dialogues*, and *De Motu*); and (3) the positing of objects within such a law-governed framework can be understood, epistemologically, as the perception of

[9] Long 2003, 8.

things by which they exist and are known to exist (*Principles* and *Three Dialogues*), and metaphysically, as products of an ethereal fire that providentially orders the cosmos (about which we learn in *Siris*).

If the "traditional" way of explaining Berkeley's philosophy fails to provide an account that can accommodate all of these points in all of his writings – or worse, explains their variety by dismissing his remarks as merely metaphorical, contradictory, or instances of his changing his mind – that should tell us there is something wrong with the traditional approach and that we need to look elsewhere for an interpretive framework to discern the unity in his thought. That framework, I suggest, can be found in Stoicism.

Indeed, not only does Berkeley propose a semantic ontology based on the assumptions that inform Stoic logic, but he also insists on a doctrine in which perceptions or ideas (what the Stoics call presentations, *phantasiai*) always appear embedded in an aboriginal *logos*, and that that is what Berkeley means when he claims that reality is a *discourse* or *language*. By describing sensations as presentations initially intelligible only in terms of linguistic structures, the Stoics and Berkeley thus reveal how sensations are experienced as always already framed in propositions in terms of which they are intelligible.[10] Accordingly, because the strategies that guide Stoic and Berkeleian ethics and epistemology depend on a logic and a metaphysics that are inherently linguistic, they are significantly different from those developed by other contemporary thinkers.

In particular, when framed in Platonic and Aristotelian terms, Stoic doctrines always appear to be beside the point. The same result occurs if we attempt to frame Berkeley's views in terms of Cartesian or Lockean filters that do not take seriously Berkeley's semantic ontology. So to wean ourselves away from the Platonic and Aristotelian preconceptions in logic and metaphysics that underlie the Cartesian and Lockean accounts often used to "explain" Berkeley, we need to know how the logic of the Stoics (and Berkeley) portrays all experiences as ineradicably linguistic. Furthermore, we need to understand how Berkeley's immaterialistic metaphysics is also compatible with Stoic metaphysics. This latter challenge is especially daunting, considering how Stoics are often portrayed as claiming that everything that exists is material. One of my aims, therefore, is to show that that portrayal needs to be qualified in such a substantive way that it loses any polemical punch it might have had when raised as an objection to a proposed Stoic–Berkeley connection.

We need to begin, then, with Stoic logic (or what the Stoics call

---

[10] See Imbert 1980, 185-186. Also see Daniel 2008b, 41-48, 52-53.

dialectics). Dialectics is the art of the discursive practices in terms of which all things are discernible and relatable. Since discursive practices identify what it means for something to be intelligible, the art of dialectics forms the basis or rationale for all ontological, epistemological, and affective identity and relations. It thus identifies the natural vocabulary, semantics, and syntax by which the universe of things is made accessible for experience, thought, and practical engagement. So in addition to being the *art* of rational discourse, dialectics is also the *science* of the real nature of things, because all determinate, intelligible things exist and can be thought only in virtue of the discursive *logos* or *ratio* (or for Berkeley, the divine language) in which they are originally identified as entities.[11]

That is why the Stoics claim that dialectics is concerned primarily with the incorporeal events that are expressed in and as propositions. It is also why (as Susanne Bobzien puts it), "Stoic logic is in its core a propositional logic," for no term is intelligible apart from its being presented in a proposition.[12] Furthermore, the things with which we are presented (*phantasiai*) are perceived and related to one another hypothetically, conjunctively, or disjunctively in virtue of utterances (*lekta*) that establish the limits or boundaries of those things and the propositional structures on which all inferences about those things are based.[13] Because the propositional placement by which a thing becomes a thing is not itself a thing – just as the limit of a thing is not itself a thing but rather the act by which something becomes that thing – the lekta expressed by these events do not exist but rather "subsist."[14] *Lekta* are thus the incorporeal propositions that enable perceptions to be objects of rational assent.[15] "They" have no discernible identity apart from their being the active principles by which the things they identify come into existence. Or in more explicitly Berkeleian terms: thinking (i.e., perceiving, willing) consists in being the act whereby certain things become identified and related to one another.[16] Accordingly, the pattern or set of actions we describe as a mind is only reflexively and derivatively said to exist in virtue of the body or bodies it is said to perceive.

The doctrine of the lekton is the most obvious indication that the Stoics definitely do not adopt a metaphysics that is exclusively materialistic. Indeed, the Stoics conclude that minds are material only in the sense that

---

[11] See Long 1974, 121-122; and Long 1971b, 84. Cf. Neuchelmans 1980, 182-184.
[12] Bobzien 2003, 85. Also see Mates 1961, 2.
[13] Imbert 1980, 182-188, 191, 211.
[14] See White 2003, 150; Long 1971b, 97; and Deleuze 1990, 4-5, 19, 21.
[15] See Frede 1999, 307, and Annas 1992, 76-77.
[16] Cf. Daniel 2004, 165; and Daniel 2008b, 212-223.

they do not exist (or more properly, "subsist") apart from their activities of specifying bodies in relations. Berkeley reverses this insight by arguing that if the existence of bodies depends on the immaterial activity of positing the limits and relations whereby objects of perception are identified, then bodies must be understood in immaterial terms. Both the Stoics and Berkeley agree, however, that minds and bodies cannot exist or be conceived apart from one another. Regardless of whether one calls this a form of materialism or immaterialism, what is significant is how Berkeley agrees with the Stoics in rejecting the attempt to treat minds and bodies as abstractions. To be sure, Berkeley rejects all forms of materialism in which determinate bodies are said to exist independently of mind, or in which minds and mental activities are considered as epiphenomena of independently existing bodies. But such a description does not characterize the Stoic account of mind either, in that it ignores how (for the Stoics as well as Berkeley) incorporeal acts determine the identities and relations of bodies as elements in a system of signs.

The Inherent Linguisticality of Existence

No doubt, the Stoic focus on the discursive, linguistic rationale of the universe is often misunderstood in the predicate logic of substantialist metaphysics either as a substitution of rhetoric for metaphysics or as a metaphorical guide for understanding ontological relations. So Chrysippus' paradoxical remark "If you say 'chariot', a chariot passes through your lips" is typically cited in such a view as a confusion of mention and use. The question of how to defend the initial ontological distinction of things, ideas, and words is seldom asked; and if it is, answers are frequently couched in terms that attempt to disavow their communicative heritage.

In the Stoic mentality, though, everything is intelligible in virtue of signifier–signified relations. All reality is understood as inherently semiotic and comprises, as Berkeley puts it, a natural language of signs (TV 144, 147; TVV 40).[17] For the Stoics, a natural sign is not a word or an idea that refers to some thing apart from itself; for if that were the case, then both sign and referent would be intelligible apart from their being related by the signifying event.[18] Instead, a sign – or more properly, a signifier – has meaning to the extent that it is a function within a network of propositions. No thing exists or can be conceived apart from that network, because the determination of a thing as one thing rather than another depends on its

[17] Cf. Verbeke 1991, 19-20.
[18] See Todorov 1982, 19-23.

place in that network. Such a placement requires that the thing have a case ending and appear in propositions that make explicit the mood and tense of the verbs that associate it with other things. From this perspective, any attempt to describe a metaphysics that is not inherently linguistic is bound to fail.[19]

This is not to say that Stoic semiotics (or Berkeleian ontology) is a version of linguistic idealism. For to think in terms of idealism, we would have to assume that the distinction between mind and matter can be made without acknowledging the unavoidably linguistic conditions in terms of which such an assumption is made. If anything, the self-conscious focus on what is most immediate in experience accounts, in part, for why Stoicism is often treated as a materialist philosophy. And when understood in terms of the substantialist metaphysics or predicational logic of Plato, Aristotle, Descartes, or Locke, Stoic doctrines about the materiality of truth or the reality of only the present seem to contradict the claim that meanings and the acts by which they are determined (*lekta*) are immaterial. But, as Gilles Deleuze notes, the Stoics avoid such apparent contradictions by focusing on the events that inscribe the surface of experience.[20] Beyond that surface, nothing can exist or be known, because even to allude to a beyond is to invoke a concept intelligible only in terms of discursive differentiations.

Here, even the distinctions between word and object, or linguistic surface and referent, are functions of the sensual expressions in terms of which things are identified and differentiated. In what Deleuze refers to as this *logic of sense*, "everything that happens and everything that is said happens on the surface," for there is nothing other than the immediate events that introduce sense.[21] The Stoics discover sense by recognizing how events establish the conditions by which propositions become intelligible (i.e., conditioned). Because events are themselves unconditioned, there is no "sense" of an event: as Deleuze says, "the event is sense itself and belongs essentially to language."[22] The event by which an expression becomes meaningful or significant is not linguistic in the sense of being distinct from the proposition that expresses either it or the mental state of the pronouncer or the state of affairs denoted by the proposition. Rather, the proposition, its intentionality, and its object are all intelligible only in terms of the event.

Berkeley's contemporary, Étienne Bonnot de Condillac, puts it this

---

[19] See Deleuze 1990, 8-9, 22; Long 1974, 125.
[20] See Deleuze 1990, 105, 132-133.
[21] See Deleuze 1990, 19, 21, 34, 132.
[22] Deleuze 1990, 22; also see 181-184.

way: even to refer to sensual actions or gestures as expressions of a language is already to appeal to a language in terms of which the distinction of world, thought, and language is itself intelligible.[23] This meta-language – for Berkeley, this divine speech – is the unconditioned expression of the events that establish the conditions for intelligibility. So in the matrix of events that form that aboriginal language, the differentiation of objects, ideas, and words is not simply accepted as an ontological given. Instead, existence or being is understood as intelligible only as a function of the structure of the determinations (or *logos*) of this discourse. In this logic of propositions, the ontological, epistemological, semantic, and affective features that identify, distinguish, and relate things in the universe (and thus allow things to make sense) are themselves recognized as intelligible only as functions in what the Stoics and Berkeley refer to as the book of nature or language of God.

For the Stoics, then, the event in which a proposition is expressed – that is, the expression itself – identifies things in relation to one another, thus making language and the states of affairs denoted by language meaningful. Since propositional terms are intelligible only in virtue of their associations with other terms in propositions, their juxtapositions are most properly expressed as apprehensions ("this A is B"), hypotheticals ("if A, then B"), conjunctions ("A and B"), or disjunctions ("A or B"). But because everything in the universe is intelligible only in terms of such associations, everything can legitimately be considered a function of a conditional expression (that is, as either a signifier or that which is signified). In this way, a sign is the antecedent that always and necessarily refers to the consequent of a conditional proposition. [24] Even though the antecedent is presupposed as the means for determining the sense of the consequent, it does not *cause* the consequent; rather, it situates the consequent in a domain of discursive exchange.

By specifying logical (antecedent–consequent) relations through determinate declensions and conjugations, the Stoic wise man thus unites what is expressed with what is meant. His pronouncements about the world of causal relations are infallible, in that his pronouncements articulate the ordered structure of reality.[25] His pronouncements are not "true" (as if there is some other standard on which they can be evaluated) as much as they are truth itself. He cannot be wrong, because error is possible only where there is an ontological discrepancy between what is

---

[23] See Daniel 1990, 195-202; and Derrida 1980, 59-65.

[24] Cf. Verbeke 1991, 21; Mates 1961, 13n; Gould 1970, 75-82; Deleuze 1990, 69; Kneale and Kneale 1962, 141; and Ebert 1987, 85.

[25] See Long 1974, 130; Long 1971b, 102; Watson 1966, 42-43, 58.

said and what is meant. Since complete *lekta* are meaningful in virtue of their being propositionally expressed, they cannot be other than *what is the case*. That is, their case or tense is their fate. Only by being made determinate (by fate) can they provide the standard on which derivative, predicational thinking is judged as true or false.

In this sense, the expressed associations of things with one another in space, time, and experience seem (as Berkeley points out) completely arbitrary and (as the Stoics note) a matter of fate (Alc IV.7; IV.10).[26] The language of nature they inscribe identifies a thing as intelligible in virtue of its place within that matrix of differentiation. But since a thing has a determinate identity only as a function of the discourse that defines intelligibility, it (along with everything else) cannot be anything other than what it is. It thus discloses a divine rationale or order. That order (*logos*) is intelligibility itself, or simply mind. "Minds" (in the plural) are the means by which the ontological identification of things is manifested in propositional judgments.[27] Through such judgments, minds express the differentiation and association of things in the cosmos, but they cannot account for their own differentiation. That is, they cannot account for the strategies by which they originally become intelligible: in short, they cannot account for mind itself.

This insight is crucial for understanding how, for the Stoics and Berkeley alike, individual minds can be free. To the extent that we see the things we experience as parts of a divinely orchestrated harmony, we act according to reason and are not led astray by our passions. In this respect, we aspire to emulate the Stoic sage – not in the sense that we passively accept fate, but in the sense that with more familiarity with the workings of nature, we affirm our roles as parts of God's plan that there be certain, determinate sequences of experiences whereby things are differentiated and associated. We thus contribute to the on-going creation of the world.

This is why, for the Stoics, mind is not simply another thing that exists in the universe. Rather, it is the intelligibility of all things, the invisible fire (the *pneuma*) that differentiates and permeates all parts of the cosmos.[28] It is the semantic and syntactic order of relations in which all things are united in a "universal sympathy" and on which divination and astrological reasoning is based. Berkeley picks up on this theme, commenting that "Providence or Mind was supposed by [the Stoics] to be

---

[26] See Deleuze 1990, 34.

[27] See Deleuze 1990, 176; Graeser 1978, 98; Long 1971b, 102; and Lloyd 1978, 237.

[28] See Lapidge 1978, 163-170; Hahm 1977, 158-168; Long 1974, 154; and Cléret 1999, 67.

immediately resident or present in fire, to dwell therein, and to act thereby" (*Siris* 172; see also 177). Mind is the intellectual fire that differentiates all things (*Siris* 190) and connects all things (*Siris* 192) in a wise and provident manner (*Siris* 272). Berkeley concludes, therefore, that it is wrong to think then that the Stoics thought of this fire in a corporeal way, just as it is wrong to think that the Stoics confused mind with the system of sensible objects or described God as corporeal (*Siris* 323-324).

Berkeley has no problem, then, in saying that the "vegetative soul or vital spirit of the world" expressed in the aether or fire that accounts for all motion and change is corporeal, because in his view (and the view of the Stoics) the principle of the motion or change of any determinate body must itself be considered corporeal (*Siris* 152). But that does not mean that the principle by which those bodies become determinate is itself corporeal, for that would require yet another principle to account for its being determinate. Berkeley precludes such an endless regress by acknowledging that, even though the motions or changes that identify a body as this or that body must themselves be identified in corporeal terms, the principle by which those motions or changes themselves come about is not corporeal.

To ask for the cause of this or that body is thus to ask for a specific cause of this or that body. Likewise, to ask for the cause of the multiplicity of bodies in the universe is to ask for the specific cause of such multiplicity. In a Neoplatonic account, this differentiation would be explained in terms a prior differentiation of the ideas of such bodies (e.g., as archetypes in the mind of God). But such an account simply delays the question of how divine ideas or archetypes are differentiated in the first place; or worse, it subordinates the differentiation of divine ideas to the differentiation of bodies without explaining how bodies are initially differentiated.[29]

Berkeley thus appropriates the Stoic strategy for God's immanence in the world by distinguishing the cause of corporeal differentiation (viz., the Stoic *pneuma* or "aethereal spirit") from the Mind that activates it (*Siris* 258). This is what prompts Berkeley to insist (contra Leibniz) that even though the force that accounts for the differentiations and motions of bodies is mind, the actual differentiations and movements by which bodies are differentiated and related are corporeal (DM 16-18, 20, 34, 42).[30] We see the bodies and their interactions, but we do not see the boundaries by

---

[29] Being caught up in the study of the secondary-cause workings of nature can also lead our thoughts away from the "governing spirit whose will constitutes the Laws of Nature" (P 32).

[30] Cf. Daniel 2007b, 174-175.

which those bodies are *those* bodies, or the motions by which *those* interactions occur. Nonetheless, those bodies have limits and do interact, and for Berkeley the only way to explain this is in terms of something that is literally aethereal, namely, the Stoics' invisible elementary fire of the cosmos.

My conclusion, then, is that we can think of Berkeley's discussion of the aethereal fire in *Siris* in a way that is consistent with his earlier doctrines about mind and bodies by understanding those remarks in their distinctly Stoic context. In that context, the limits and relations of bodies are corporeal even though they are invisible; for if we were able to see them, we would see them only in terms of the limits and relations by which *they* are differentiated. To push the principles of such differentiation back into the mind of God (as divine ideas or archetypes) is merely to shift the location of the problem; for then, the issue turns to how God's ideas are differentiated (which, of course, raises another bugbear of Berkeley scholarship, namely, the relation of God's ideas to our ideas).[31] Thankfully, the Stoic strategy of portraying individual minds as expressions of God's benevolent will that there be coordinated sequences of perceptions avoids that problem altogether.

Bibliography

Algra, K., J. Barnes, J. Mansfeld, and M. Schofield (eds.) (1999), *The Cambridge History of Hellenistic Philosophy*, Cambridge University Press, Cambridge.

Annas, Julia. (1992), *Hellenistic Philosophy of Mind*, University of California Press, Berkeley.

Ariew, Roger and Daniel Garber (eds.) (1989), *G. W. Leibniz: Philosophical Essays*, Hackett, Indianapolis.

Berkeley, George. (1948-1957), *The Works of George Berkeley*, 9 vols, A. A. Luce and T. E. Jessop (eds), London, Nelson.

Barnouw, Jeffrey. (2008), "The Two Motives Behind Berkeley's Expressly Unmotivated Signs: Sure Preception and Personal Providence," in Daniel (2008a), pp. 145-177.

Bobzien, Susanne. (2003), "Logic" in Inwood (2003), pp. 85-123.

Bracken, Harry M. (1974), *Berkeley*, St. Martin's Press, New York.

Brown, S. and P. Phemister (eds.) (2007), *Leibniz and the English-Speaking World*, Springer, Dordrecht.

[31] See Daniel 2001a, 239-258.

Brykman, Geneviève. (2008), "On Human Liberty in Berkeley's *Alciphron* VII," in Daniel (2008a), pp. 231-246.

Charles, Sébastien (ed.) (2004), *Science et épistémologie selon Berkeley*, Presses de l'Université Laval, Quebec.

Cléret, Nathalie. (1999), "Paracelse, l'alchimie et les stoïciens: Quelques aspects des conceptions stoïciens et paracelsienne du feu," in Moreau (1999a), pp. 65-76.

Daniel, Stephen H. (1990), *Myth and Modern Philosophy*, Temple University Press, Philadelphia.

—. (2001a), "Berkeley's Christian Neoplatonism, Archetypes, and Divine Ideas," *Journal of the History of Philosophy* 39, pp. 239-258.

—. (2004), "Les limites de la philosophie naturelle de Berkeley," in Charles (2004), pp. 163-170.

—. (ed.) (2007a), *Reexamining Berkeley's Philosophy*, University of Toronto Press, Toronto.

—. (2007b), "The Harmony of the Leibniz-Berkeley Juxtaposition," in Brown and Phemister (2007), pp. 163-180.

—. (ed.) (2008a), *New Interpretations of Berkeley's Thought*, Humanity Books, Amherst, NY.

—. (2008b), "Berkeley's Stoic Notion of Spiritual Substance," in Daniel (2008a), 203-230.

Deleuze, Gilles. (1990), *The Logic of Sense*, C. V. Boundas (ed.), M. Lester and C. Stivale (trs.), Columbia University Press, New York.

Derrida, Jacques. (1980), *The Archeology of the Frivolous: Reading Condillac*, J. P. Leavey, Jr. (tr.), Duquesne University Press, Pittsburgh.

Ebert, Theodor. (1987), "The Origin of the Stoic Theory of Signs in Sextus Empiricus," *Oxford Studies in Ancient Philosophy* 5, pp. 83-126.

Forman, David. (2008), "Free Will and the Freedom of the Sage in Leibniz and the Stoics," *History of Philosophy Quarterly* 25, pp. 203-219.

Frede, Michael. (1999), "Stoic epistemology," in Algra et al. (1999), pp. 295-322.

Gaukroger, Stephen (ed.) (1991), *The Uses of Antiquity: The Scientific Revolution and the Classical Tradition*, Kluwer, Boston.

Gould, Josiah B. (1970), *The Philosophy of Chrysippus*, State University of New York Press, Albany.

Graeser, Andreas. (1978), "The Stoic Theory of Meaning," in Rist (1978), pp. 77-100.

Hahm, David E. (1977), *The Origins of Stoic Cosmology*, Ohio State University Press, Columbus.

Hobbes, Thomas. (1656), *The Questions concerning Liberty, Necessity,*

and Chance, in Molesworth (1839-1845), vol. 5.
Imbert, Claude. (1980), "Stoic Logic and Alexandrian Poetics," in Schofield *et al.* (1980), pp. 182-216.
Inwood, Brad (ed.) (2003), *The Cambridge Companion to the Stoics*, Cambridge University Press, New York.
Jacob, Alexander. (1991), "The Neoplatonic Conception of Nature in More, Cudworth, and Berkeley," in Gaukroger (1991), pp. 101-122.
James, Susan. (1993), "Spinoza the Stoic," in Sorrell (1993), pp. 289-316.
Kassler, Jamie C. (1991), "The Paradox of Power: Hobbes and Stoic Naturalism," in Gaukroger (1991), pp. 53-78.
Kneale, William C. and Martha Kneale. (1962), *The Development of Logic*, Clarendon Press, Oxford.
Kremer, Elmar J. and M. J. Latzer (eds.) (2001), *The Problem of Evil in Early Modern Philosophy*, University of Toronto Press, Toronto.
Kristeller, Paul O. (1984), "Stoic and Neoplatonic Sources of Spinoza's *Ethics," History of European Ideas* 5, pp. 1-15.
Lapidge, Michael. (1978), "Stoic Cosmology," in Rist (1978), pp. 161-185.
Leduc-Fayette, Denise. (1997), "Qu'est que 'parler aux yeux'? Berkeley et le 'langage optique'," *Revue philosophique de la France et l'étranger* 122, pp. 409-427.
Leibniz, G. W. (1677-80), "Two Sects of Naturalists," in Ariew and Garber (1989), pp. 281-284.
Lloyd, A. C. (1978), "Emotion and Decision in Stoic Psychology," in Rist (1978), pp. 233-246.
Long, A. A. (ed.) (1971a), *Problems in Stoicism*, Athlone Press, London.
—. (1971b), "Language and Thought in Stoicism," in Long (1971a), pp. 75-113.
—. (1974), *Hellenistic Philosophy: Stoics, Epicureans, Sceptics*, Charles Scribner's Sons, New York.
—. (2003), "Stoicism in the Philosophical Tradition: Spinoza, Lipsius, Butler," in Miller and Inwood (2003), pp. 7-29.
Mates, Benson. (1961), *Stoic Logic*, University of California Press, Berkeley.
Miller, Jon. (2003), "Stoics, Grotius, and Spinoza on Moral Deliberation," in Miller and Inwood (2003), pp. 116-140.
Miller, Jon and Brad Inwood (eds.) (2003), *Hellenistic and Early Modern Philosophy*, Cambridge University Press, New York.
Mitsis, Phillip. (2003), "Locke's *Offices*," in Miller and Inwood (2003), pp. 45-61.
Moked, Gabriel. (1988), *Particles and Ideas: Bishop Berkeley's*

Corpuscular Philosophy, Clarendon Press, Oxford.

Molesworth, William (ed.) (1839-1945), *The English Works of Thomas Hobbes*, 11 vols, John Bohn, London.

Moreau, Pierre-François (ed.) (1999a), *Le Stoïcisme au XVIe et au XVIIe Siècle: Le retour des philosophies antiques à l'Age classique*, Albin Michel, Paris.

Moreau, Pierre-François. (1999b), "Les trois étapes du stoïcisme moderne," in Moreau (1999a), pp. 11-27.

Neuchelmans, Gabriel. (1980), *Late-Scholastic and Humanist Theories of the Proposition*, North Holland, Amsterdam.

Osler, Margaret J. (ed.) (1991), *Atoms, Pneuma, and Tranquility: Epicurean and Stoic Themes in European Thought*, Cambridge University Press, New York.

Rist, John M. (ed.) (1978), *The Stoics*, University of California Press, Berkeley.

Rutherford, Donald. (2001), "Leibniz and the Stoics: The Consolations of Theodicy," in Kremer and Latzer (2001), pp. 138-164.

—. (2003), "*Patience sans Espérance*: Leibniz's Critique of Stoicism," in Miller and Inwood (2003), pp. 62-89.

—. (2004), "On the Happy Life: Descartes vis-à-vis Seneca," in Strange and Zupko (2004), pp. 177-197.

Schofield, M., M. Burnyeat, and J. Barnes (eds.) (1980), *Doubt and Dogmatism*, Clarendon Press, Oxford.

Sorrell, Tom (ed.) (1993), *The Rise of Modern Philosophy*, Clarendon Press, Oxford.

Steven K. Strange, K. Steven, and J. Zupko (eds.) (2004), *Stoicism: Traditions and Transformations*, Cambridge University Press, New York.

Todorov, Tzvetan. (1982), *Theories of the Symbol*, Catherine Porter (tr.), Cornell University Press, Ithaca, NY.

Verbeke, Gerard. (1991), "Ethics and Logic in Stoicism," in Osler (1991), pp. 11-24.

Watson, Gerard. (1966), *The Stoic Theory of Knowledge*, Queen's University Press, Belfast.

White, Michael J. (2003), "Stoic Natural Philosophy (Physics and Cosmology)," in Inwood (2003), pp. 124-152.

ABSTRACTION: BERKELEY AGAINST LOCKE

TALIA MAE BETTCHER

Abstract

In this paper, I argue Berkeley's critique of abstract generalizing involves the view that, *pace* Locke, general terms are not univocal, but analogical. Berkeley's position is motivated by the insight that Locke's theory of meaning fails to accommodate the general names of simple ideas.

Preliminaries

It is not uncommon for commentators to argue that Berkeley misunderstands John Locke's views about abstraction; the case has been made in several different ways. This paper is a partial defense of Berkeley's critique of Locke. At the *Introduction to the Principles* (PI 10), Berkeley distinguishes between abstraction as generalization from particulars (attacked at PI 8-9) and as the "singling out" of properties which are blended with others (attacked at PI 7). For the limited purposes of this paper, I focus mainly on the former. While this may seem to be of limited consequences with respect to Berkeley's views about abstraction more generally, we will nonetheless find ourselves better positioned to understand Berkeley's views about the significance of general terms. Moreover, even though this does not constitute an exhaustive account of Berkeley's anti-abstractionism, the fact that the anti-abstractionist attack in the *Principles* Introduction is the longest and most detailed, an understanding of how Berkeley attempts to disarm his most important opponent therein will afford new insights into Berkeley's general rejection of abstract ideas.

Locke is clear that the process of abstraction involves generalization: "This is called ABSTRACTION, whereby *Ideas* taken from particular Beings, become general Representatives of all of the same kind . . ." (E.

2.11.9, 159).[1] However, abstraction, for Locke, not only involves generalizing from particulars, but also generalization from universal, abstract ideas themselves. In this way, one can move from the abstract ideas of man and horse to the idea of animal; then from animal and plant to *vivens* (or living thing); then from living and non-living to body; then from body and spirit to substance; then finally from substance and accident to being or thing itself (E. 3.3.9, 412). In light of this distinction, I will speak of "universalisation" from particular ideas and "categorical ascension" from universal ones.

In his account of abstraction, Locke first discusses a simple idea; he speaks of the white today observed in chalk, while yesterday observed in milk (E. 2.11.9, 159). When it first comes into the senses, this simple idea is connected with other ideas. The mind then considers the idea of white alone, thereby making it a universal representative of all the same kind. Since the idea of white is already simple, there is nothing to leave out of *it*. Rather one universalizes by leaving out all relevant but extrinsic features which are not included within the starting, simple idea itself.

With respect to complex ideas, Locke's account of universalisation is slightly different. Rather than simply considering a complex idea of a particular human being in isolation from extrinsic features, abstraction requires several particular complex ideas from which one then leaves out the differences and retains the similarities. Thus, one moves from the particular ideas of Peter, Paul, and James to the universal idea of man in general. Locke provides a similar account of categorical ascension from universal ideas as well – when these ideas are complex. This, again, involves taking several universal, complex ideas and leaving out differences and retaining similarities. Thus Locke writes:

> . . . this whole *mystery* of *Genera* and *Species* ... is nothing else but abstract *Ideas*, more or less comprehensive, with names annexed to them. In all which, this is constant and unvariable, That every more general term, stands for such an *Idea*, as is but a part of any of those contained under it. (E. 3.3.9, 412)

Now at PI 10, Berkeley departs from Locke by distinguishing between abstraction *as generalization from particulars* (attacked at PI 8-9) and as the *"singling out" of properties* which are blended with others (attacked at PI 7). He writes:

---

[1] Locke 1957. Citations of *An Essay concerning Human Understanding* (E) refer to book, part, section and page.

> But I deny that I can abstract one from another, or conceive separately, those qualities which it is impossible should exist so separated; or that I can frame a general notion by abstracting from particulars in the manner aforesaid. Which two last are the proper acceptations of *abstraction.* (PI 10)

Yet this "abstract singling" appears to be the very sort of abstraction involved in the Lockean universalisation of simple ideas; it involves considering one simple idea to the exclusion of all others.[2] The question, of course, is why, for Berkeley, the idea of a colour, isolated from all other ideas, is not a universal idea to which the various particular instances conform. Notice that at §8, Berkeley speaks of generalizing from particular extensions, and *particular* colours (such as red and blue). This suggests that the abstraction Berkeley has in mind here is not, in his estimation, a form of categorical ascension at all, but rather a form of universalisation. In other words, it would seem that for Berkeley determinate colours are themselves particulars. This would explain why considering such colours in isolation would be insufficient to universalize them. The question, now, of course, is why Berkeley views ideas of determinate colours as particulars, while Locke views them as universals which represent the various different tropes thereof as individuated by time, place, and substance. While this is an important question, it is not one that I will have the opportunity to examine in great depth in this paper.[3]

---

[2] However, I think that "considering" is also broader than abstraction (i.e., generalization) for Locke.

[3] There is a well known controversy in Aristotelian scholarship that may help clarify. In the *Categories*, Aristotle recognizes particulars that are not substances. For example, the genus colour is said of the species white, and both are said of the particular white. In the traditional interpretation, the particular white is a trope (i.e., a specific instance of white) individuated by the substance in which it inheres. According to a dissenting view, first defended by G. E. L. Owen (Owen 1965), the particular white is a *shade* of white (rather than a trope). As such, it is a universal insofar as it inheres in many things. However, it is a particular insofar as it is not "said of anything" in the way that white and colour are said of it. Now it may be that for Berkeley, colours are particulars in this sense. It is worth noting that Locke himself explicitly universalizes white from particular tropes of white. Consequently, Berkeley may be rejecting this type of generalization. In previous work, I have argued that Berkeley denies that there is a fact of the matter how to individuate sensible ideas per finite perceiver, per perceptual intermittence, and per temporal passage; the only non-trivial way to individuate is by qualitative difference. If this is right, then it is little wonder Berkeley does not take universalisation from tropes seriously, since the very distinction between tropes and universal is in this case merely verbal. See Bettcher 2007, 88-95.

Instead, I want to observe that Berkeley never appears to recognize categorical ascension as a form of abstraction in the way that Locke does. Instead of considering the alleged abstraction from the universal ideas of man and horse to the idea of animal, his account of higher forms of generalization is also characterized in terms of universalisation. He writes: "the mind leaving out those parts which are peculiar to men, and retaining those only which are common to all the living creatures, frameth the idea of *animal*, which abstracts not only from all particular men, but also all birds, beasts, fishes, and insects." (PI 9)

His strategy makes sense. Locke's account allows that one could yield the idea of animal by universalizing from all particular ideas of animals just as one could by categorically ascending from the universal ideas of man, horse, dog, and the like. However, if universalisation is impossible, then so is the sort of categorical ascension Locke imagines, since there are no abstracted universals from which to ascend. In attacking one, Berkeley thereby undermines the other.

Now note that abstract singling, discussed at §7, (and which for Locke is implicated in the universalisation of simple ideas) appears to have become an issue for Berkeley *after* he had already formulated an attack on what he recognizes as generalization from particulars. His *Manuscript Introduction* to the *Principles* (written 1708 or earlier) criticizes only the latter kind of abstraction; no mention of *abstract singling* is made at all.[4] Here he describes abstract ideas as:

> Ideas which equally represent the Particulars of any Sort, & are made by the Mind which observing that the Individuals of each Kind agree in some things, & differ in others, takes out & singles from the rest, that which is common to all, making thereof one Abstract, General Idea; Which contains all those Ideas wherein the Particulars of that Kind agree ... (MI 7, 67)

This suggests Berkeley omits any discussion of abstract singling, since the procedure here described clearly only applies in the case of complex ideas. Consequently, it may be the case that Berkeley has independent grounds for wanting to reject what he sees as *abstract generalization from particulars* (i.e. universalisation).

My primary aim, at any rate, is to understand Berkeley's reasons for rejecting Lockean abstraction independently of his ultimate, subsequently developed views about "abstract singling." I argue that, regardless of the validity of singling out simple ideas, Locke does not and cannot provide an account of categorical ascension from simple ideas, that this failure

[4] Belfrage 1987 (MI).

afflicts his account of universalisation from complex ideas, and that the exploitation of this is one of Berkeley's main arguments against Locke's account.

Berkeley's Failure

Two different accounts of abstraction have been discussed in the literature, and it seems to matter which model Locke holds, and which model Berkeley takes Locke to hold. In what I shall call *division*, one is supposed to conceive of the abstracted feature separated from the features that are left out; viz, one is supposed to conceive of a feature existing separated from the rest. Thus, one would conceive of colour as somehow existing without any determinate shade of colour. By contrast, in the case of *consideration*, one only attends to certain features without attending to the others. Thus, one might think of colour without thinking of any determinate colour.

The charge against Berkeley is that he wrongly takes Locke to advocate a *division* account of abstraction. In this view, Berkeley's concern is that Locke is attempting to conceive of something that is impossible. For it is impossible that there exists an indeterminate colour, and so it seems impossible to conceive of such a thing. If this is what is required by Lockean abstraction (taken as *division*), then such abstraction clearly fails and Berkeley is right. However – at least this is how the charge goes, drawing on the work of John Mackie and others – Locke actually endorses consideration, not division.[5] Ironically, Berkeley goes on to employ abstract consideration himself as if it were his own discovery.[6]

There are, however, several difficulties with this story. One preliminary inconvenience is the fact that this distinction between division and consideration was long recognized. Thomas Aquinas himself drew the distinction:

> Abstraction may occur in two ways: First, by way of composition and division, as when we understand that one thing does not exist in some other, or that it is separate from it. Secondly, by way of simple and absolute consideration, as when we understand one thing without considering the other. . . [7]

---

[5] For this type of criticism, see Winkler 1989, 39-43. For further discussion of this issue, See Pappas 2000, 73-79. See also Jesseph 1993, 27-31. For this reading of Locke see Mackie 1976, 107-112.

[6] Winkler 1989, 42.

[7] Aquinas 1947-1948, IQ. 85, A. 2, c.

If this distinction was well known, one is hard pressed to see how Berkeley could have seen his critique of Lockean division as a serious attack on abstraction more generally. Certainly, it wouldn't have touched the Thomistic notion of "consideration" (which Berkeley, according to the story, goes on to adopt himself as if it were his own invention).

A more serious difficulty with the view is its simple failure to heed the fact Berkeley and Locke offer different accounts of how general terms receive meaning. If Berkeley and Locke are in agreement about abstraction as consideration, then why are their semantic views so different?

For Locke abstraction is deeply connected to his account of how terms become general – the term is made to stand for an abstract idea. This abstract idea effectively constitutes the meaning of the term. By contrast, Berkeley denies that general terms have one precise, settled idea: "Whereas, in truth, there is no such thing as one precise and definite signification annexed to any general name, they all signifying indifferently a great number of particular ideas" (PI 18). If Berkeley mistakenly rejects what he takes to be Lockean division, only to replace it with consideration, why does consideration play no evident role in his semantic account of general terms?

In the first edition of the *Principles* (PI 16) Berkeley appeals to a form of consideration in describing how one might yield general knowledge of triangles without there being an abstract, general idea of it. He explains that while the idea of a particular triangle may be used in the proof (as a diagram), none of its particularities are used in the actual demonstration. In the 1734 edition he adds, suggesting that what follows is given content by this preceding discussion: "And here it must be acknowledged that a man may consider a figure merely as triangular, without attending to the particular qualities of the angles, or relations of the sides." However the consideration that Berkeley endorses plays no noticeable role whatsoever in the difference between his semantic account of general terms and the account of Locke. If it did play an important role, would he not simply say that the meaning of a general term "human" can be given content by the idea of a particular human where only certain aspects of it are attended to? In such a view, Berkeley would allow for general ideas that provide content to general terms. For he would simply be under the false impression that while Locke attempted to divide ideas one from the other, he himself admitted only consideration. This is not the semantic account Berkeley offers.

To be sure, in the *Principles* Introduction, Berkeley does allow that particular ideas can become general. However, the mechanism by which they become general is not identified by Berkeley as consideration. Rather, it is the fact that particular ideas come to represent all such particular ideas in the same way that the idea of the general term itself comes to represent such terms (PI 12). Consideration plays an important role with respect to these general ideas. For they are commonly used in demonstrations – and so no particularities of the idea are mentioned in order to secure general knowledge. But – and this is the most important point – the general idea plays absolutely no role in Berkeley's *semantic* account of general terms. The general idea does not give the general term its content. Indeed, the way in which an idea becomes general is the same way a term becomes general (namely, semantic representation); so any appeal to a general idea in the semantic account of general terms would be redundant at best.

Moreover, as Belfrage has brought to our attention, the status of general ideas in the development of Berkeley's thought is actually quite problematic.[8] For in the *Manuscript Introduction*, it appears Berkeley does not allow for such general ideas at all. His business is to reject abstract, general ideas – "ideas which equally represent the particulars of any sort" (MI 7). For Berkeley, the only way in which an idea can represent another idea is through resemblance, unlike the case of linguistic representation between word and idea which does not require such resemblance (MI 19). It is precisely because he denies that an idea can represent in any way besides resemblance, that Berkeley then goes on to deny that any one idea can represent all ideas of the same sort equally. Notably, in this earlier version, Berkeley already allows that particular ideas can be used in diagrams for demonstrative purposes and that the demonstration only involves considering the relevant features while omitting the particularities. He does not allow, however, that this particular idea can serve as a general idea, since at this point he does not extend the possibility of linguistic representation to ideas themselves.

Locke, General Terms, and Abstraction

While Locke introduces his account of abstraction in Book II, it is especially useful to consider the role it plays in his account of general terms (in Book III). Since for Locke, all categorematic terms require ideas annexed to them in order to count as significant, Locke requires that a general term receive its significance by being "made the sign" for a general idea. Unfortunately, it's not clear how "constant and unvariable" Locke's semantic account is, despite his own brag to that effect.

Apply his account to categorical ascension from universalized simple

[8] See Belfrage 1987, *Editor's Commentary.*

ideas. The difficulty is this: If universal simple ideas (or qualities) are *simple*, then there is nothing to *leave out*. Consider the idea of blue and the idea of red. The two ideas *differ* from each other. But to omit them would be to omit *all ideas* entirely. There would therefore be nothing left to supply the general term "colour" with content. If so, Locke's account of the significance of general terms *fails* with respect to simple ideas of the same kind. And the argument can be pressed.

For how does one generalize from two different shades of white? Given the ideas are both simple, there is nothing to leave out without leaving *everything* out and thereby draining the term "white" of any content. Locke's view is that different shades of white are different "modifications" of the same simple idea of white (E. 2.18.4, 224). The view applies to sounds, tastes, and smells, as well. "In general it may be observed," he writes, "that those *simple Modes, which are considered but as different degrees of the same simple* Idea; though they are in themselves many of them very distinct *Ideas*; *yet have ordinarily no distinct Names*, nor are much taken notice of, as distinct *Ideas*, where the difference is but very small between them." (E. 2.18.6, 224-225)

Yet Locke's position is strained. According to his overall position, simple modes are supposed to be complex ideas which are built up out of simple ideas – either as *variations* of the same simple idea or as different combinations of the same simple idea. However, in the case of colours, sounds, odours, tastes, and the like, these *variations* are not so much complex ideas, as simple ideas themselves to which the same name has been applied. For example, Locke recognizes *scarlet* as a simple idea (E 3.4.11, 425), nonetheless it is a variation of red. "Sweet" is applied to a host of different fragrances – as that of a rose, a violet, and the like (E. 2.4.2, 122). This means that in the case of secondary qualities, what are called simple modes (i.e., complex ideas) are not complex ideas at all. Rather, a secondary quality term has been applied to cover a range of distinct simple ideas which resemble each other imperfectly.

The view is especially interesting because it is also a departure from his overarching view about general terms. There is no abstract idea of white which is yielded by leaving out the differences between the shades and retaining only what is similar. This is because the initial ideas are simple, and so to leave out anything is to leave out everything. This means that it would be more correct to speak of the universalisation of specific shades of white from particular instantiations, rather than the universalisation of white itself. No categorical ascension is possible at all from these universal simple ideas of shades, since there is nothing to leave out.

Unfortunately, Locke's account of modes of simple ideas can't help him with colours that are noticeably different from each other (such as blue, white, and red), and so the same type of account is not available to him with respect to the general term "colour." Locke himself is conscious of the difficulty. He writes:

> This farther may be observed, concerning *simple Ideas*, and their Names, that they *have but few Ascents in linea prædicamentali*, (as they call it,) *from the lowest Species, to the summum Genus*. The reason whereof is, that the lowest Species being but one simple *Idea*, nothing can be left out of it, that so the difference being taken away, it may agree with some other thing in one *Idea* common to them both ... There is nothing can be left out of the *Idea* of White and Red, to make them agree in one common appearance, and so have one general name ... (E. 3.5.16, 427-428)

Here Locke explicitly admits the problem of categorical ascension with respect to simple ideas. Locke's solution to this problem is to say the term "colour" "denotes only the way they [the ideas of white, blue, red] get into the Mind," namely by sight (ibid, 428). This obviously involves sacrificing his account of how general terms acquire significance once again. Moreover, there are deep concerns about the adequacy of this account.

In the first place, it's unclear just what exactly Locke means. *Prima facie*, it would seem that in his proposed view "colour" can be *defined* in terms of the way in which an idea enters the mind. If so, the idea of colour is not simple.[9] Indeed, it would appear that a blind man could understand the definition of "colour" as "qualities perceived by the eyes," without ever having even seen a colour at all. That said, Locke then goes on to say "For when *White*, *Red*, and *Yellow*, are all comprehended under the *Genus* or name *Colour*, it signifies no more, but such *Ideas*, as are produced in the Mind only by the Sight . . ." (E. 3.4.16, 428). This suggests, instead, that the term simply ranges over all of the ideas that enter into the mind through sight – in which case it begins to look a lot like Berkeley's own account. Either way, Locke's account of general terms in the case of simple idea seems to fail.

Berkeley Against Locke

A strong case can be made that one of Berkeley's main arguments against Locke involves precisely an exploitation of the failure of Locke to account for (or rather allow for) categorical ascension from simple ideas, and

[9] Since in this very chapter, Locke argues that simple ideas *cannot be defined.*

consequently the failure of his official account of general terms with respect to simple ideas. At §8 of the Introduction, Berkeley writes: "So likewise the mind by leaving out of the particular colours perceived by sense, that which distinguishes them one from another, and retaining that only which is common to all, makes an idea of colour in abstract which is neither red, nor blue, nor white, nor any other determinate colour." This is plainly a form of abstraction that Locke himself admits impossible. Given that Locke *agrees* with Berkeley that such abstraction is impossible, one might worry that Berkeley is attacking a position that Locke does not hold (perhaps because he has misread him). However, given the differences we have already noted, it is more probable that this is a deliberate attempt on Berkeley's part to pervert Locke's position. His claim that abstraction from white, blue and red is impossible (a claim explicitly *accepted* by Locke) points to the failure of Locke's account of general terms with respect to names of simple ideas.

Now notice that at §9, Berkeley turns to the type of generalization Locke discusses in his overall account of general terms (categorical ascension from complex ideas). Here Berkeley at each stage of generalization insists that possession of a determinate colour, shape, size, and the like are part of the complex ideas in question.[10] But if it is true that colour is part of the idea of man, and we cannot form the abstract idea of colour, then the idea formed of man itself cannot be one that is formed abstracted from a determinate colour. But if so, how is this an *abstraction* at all?

This is not an issue that Locke considers. Categorical ascension to the idea of animal involves leaving out some of the ideas in the complex idea of man, the complex idea of horse, and so forth; and retaining those ideas which are similar. Berkeley's point, however, is that the ideas which are retained ought to include the idea of colour, shape, and the like. And the problem is that there is no abstract idea of indeterminate colour, and so the abstract idea of an animal must involve a determinate colour – which is absurd.

It is worth noting that in Berkeley's *Manuscript Introduction*, there is

---

[10] I think there is something correct about Jonathan Dancy's account of Berkeley's anti-abstractionism. According to him, Berkeley insists that having a colour (and so forth) must be part of complex abstract ideas, such as the abstract of human being. Yet the idea of colour in general must be strictly determinable (not determined). Yet this is an (abstract) idea which Berkeley takes to be impossible. See Dancy 1987, 27-29. What has not been noticed is the fact that Locke would actually agree with Berkeley that no abstract idea of colour is possible in the first place, since there is nothing to leave out of any simple idea of some determinate colour.

only the equivalent of his attack at PI 9. However, Berkeley again explicitly presses the point that the general idea of man would need to include an abstract, general idea of colour, extension, shape and the like. And the problem, once again, concerns the dubious status of such simple ideas derived, somehow, from categorical ascension from simple ideas themselves. The cruciality of this point comes out later at MI 18 where the final stratum reads:

> Now I would fain know, why a Word may not be made to comprehend a great number of particular things in it's Signification, without the help of a General Idea. Is it not possible to give the name Colour to black, white & red & c. without having first made that strange &, to me, Incomprehensible Idea of Colour in abstract?

One of the important changes from the earlier strata is precisely that instead of talking about applying the name "man" to Peter, James, and John, Berkeley talks about colours. The shift from compound to simple idea is hardly inconsequential.

Division and Consideration Revisited

In my interpretation, both Berkeley and Locke *agree* that in the case of determinate colours, one cannot generalize by leaving out differences and retaining similarities: there is nothing to retain, once the differences are discarded. This seems to suggest that Locke endorses a form of division. For if Locke believed in consideration, wouldn't he simply solve the problem of categorically ascending from determinate colours by claiming that one attends to the fact that an object has colour without attending to the determinate colour itself?[11] The issue is not so straightforward, and it is worth pausing to reflect more deeply on the respective views endorsed by Locke and Berkeley. The strongest evidence that Locke endorses consideration is his discussion of spatial parts that cannot be separated. Here he distinguishes a "partial consideration" from a "Separation or Division." One example he gives of the former is that one may consider mobility in Body without considering extension (despite the fact that mobility cannot exist without extension) (E. 2.12.13, 172-3).

Now if Locke really believes that we merely consider motion without considering extension, one might wonder how he can speak of two distinct ideas – one of motion, the other of extension – both of which are simple.

[11] For this point see George Pappas 2000, 77. Also Tom Stoneham uses this as a criticism of Dancy's account of Berkeley's argument (Stoneham 2002, 230).

Shouldn't there be only one idea which is then considered in different ways? It seems that, for Locke, these simple ideas are in many cases objects of partial consideration. Locke suggests as much in his discussion of abstraction when he refers to general notions as nothing but "abstract and partial *Ideas* of more complex ones" (E. 3.3.9, 412, my underline). This is why Locke can allow that distinct simple ideas have necessary connections between them. "'Tis true, Solidity cannot exist without Extension, neither can Scarlet-Colour exist without Extension; but this hinders not, but that they are distinct *Ideas*" (E. 2.13.11, 172). This is important, because it enables us to see how, while recognized by Locke, consideration is not itself denominated a form of abstraction. Rather abstraction (as generalization) presupposes the existence of partial ideas which are then either considered or not.

Now let's take the simple ideas of blue, red, and white. One may not consider merely colour in general without considering the differences. If one could, there would be an additional idea involved over and above those of blue, red, and white; namely, the partial idea of colour itself. That Locke rejects such a possibility is clear from the fact that there is no conceivable room for it in his theory. If the idea of red is simple, then it will be connected to the idea of colour in the same way that it is connected to the idea of some extension, motion, and so forth. But it seems wrong to suppose that the ideas of red and colour are related in such a way. Rather, one thinks that the idea of colour ought to be *part of* the idea of red. However, that would mean the idea of red is not simple after all.

Nor is Locke's denial that consideration can help us categorically ascend from universal simple ideas an unreasonable or arbitrary position.[12] If we can consider colour without considering determinate colour (such as blue), then we ought to allow for two distinct partial considerations. Why? Insofar as one considers colour without considering blue specifically, there appears to be something left out that one might have considered – namely the blue. But if we have two distinct partial considerations, then it ought to

[12] According to George Pappas, Locke is only successful against Berkeleian criticism if the selective attention he endorses is propositional (i.e. noticing that an object has property P without noticing that an object has property Q). He cannot endorse *de re* conceiving which involves simply non-propositionally perceiving one property without perceiving the other (Pappas 2000, 77-78). While I think there are difficulties with attributing this propositional model to Locke, I will simply observe that in my understanding, Locke is indeed claiming that shape and colour, and motion and extension are targets of *de re* consideration. The point is that, even if we accept this as possible, there are independent grounds for denying this in the case of categorical ascension from simple ideas.

be possible to consider the blue without considering the colour; yet this is surely impossible since the blue simply is a colour. The only other possibility is to deny that such considering involves two distinct partial considerations. But if so, how is it one ignores something in one's preliminary act of considering? And if one doesn't ignore anything at all, in what way does this count as *considering* in the first place?

What this means is that Berkeley's argument against Locke is effective, regardless of the latter's commitment to mental consideration. To rehearse the argument: Locke himself recognizes that categorical ascension from universal simple ideas is impossible. Consequently he is forced to provide a different account of general terms in the case of simple ideas. However, a complex idea such as a man, for example, must include an idea such as of colour in general. Since the latter is impossible, in light of Locke's own account of the term "colour" as applying to all ideas that enter by sight, it would appear that rather than one (abstract) idea of man, there are multiple ideas of differently coloured men. In short: There is no abstract idea of man at all. Instead, we have been left with Berkeley's own account of general terms.

Berkeley Against Abstract Extension

One of the difficulties with my preceding interpretation is that it only appears to work in the case of secondary qualities. Locke has quite different (and fairly complicated) views about extension, figure, and motion. Yet Berkeley also mentions these in his critique of Locke. At §8, he considers the formation of an abstract idea of extension from particular extensions and an abstract idea of motion from particular motions. Like colour, both of these features are harkened back to at §9. There he also mentions stature, shape, and figure as if they, too, were especially problematic. My interpretation is only plausible if I can point to similar difficulties with these other features as well. Since Locke's view on the primary qualities is fairly complex, I will content myself with a brief discussion of his views about extension.

The first thing to notice is that just as Berkeley misrepresents Locke as endorsing abstraction from determinate colours at §8, Berkeley likewise misrepresents Locke on the issue of extension (which Locke ultimately calls "expansion" or "space"). According to Berkeley, there is supposed to be an abstraction from particular extensions, to a most general abstract idea which has left out whether the extension concerns line, surface or solid and also any particular figure or magnitude. This view misrepresents Locke, however, since according to him, space is particular and the term "space" or "expansion" is not general to begin with. Moreover, our idea of expansion (i.e., space) is a simple idea which arrives through the senses. Thus when we see a particular distance between two coloured bodies, we thereby receive the simple idea of space. However, space may be "considered" (Locke writes) in various different ways (as one-dimensional distance, as three-dimensional "capacity"). And each different distance is a different *modification of space*. Correspondingly, each idea of each different distance is a *simple mode of space*. Thus the idea of a foot or a yard is "made up only of Space" (E. 2.13.4, 167). As such, it is a *complex idea*. Similarly, complex geometrical figures are produced through this "consideration" of the simple idea of expansion – thus we have ideas of triangles and the like (E.2.13.6, 169).

Unlike Locke's account of variations on secondary qualities, this account nicely captures what he presumably means in recognizing simple modes (variations) of simple ideas as somehow *complex*. Locke, again, appeals to this activity of "consideration." Here, however, the issue is not that one "considers" a simple idea without considering another to which it is connected (as one might consider motion or scarlet without considering extension), rather space itself is one simple idea and the various different simple modes of it are but "partial considerations" (or modifications) of that simple idea.

Here is the difficulty. It appears the perception of particular distances and the like is the canonical way in which the simple idea of expansion enters the senses, it only ever makes it into the understanding *as a simple mode*. Yet there is no mental operation one can perform to somehow extract the simple idea of expansion itself from the various simple modes. One cannot consider expansion itself without considering the specifics of the simple mode. On the contrary, a simple mode is nothing but an idea of expansion itself considered in a specific way: To leave out the simple mode would be to leave out the expansion itself. To be sure, one might consider expansion in a different way. But the question now is whether one can have an idea of expansion without considering it in some specific way. If one could, I suppose one might speak of abstraction (although it would be fairly different from the kind that Locke describes). However, it's pretty difficult to imagine what a failure to consider expansion in any way at all might amount to, and it's downright impossible to consider expansion in a way but not any one particular way.

Besides, Locke himself doesn't seem to recognize this as a possibility. Instead, he says that "extension" (which at this point in his argument he is using in the way that he will ultimately use "expansion") is a term usually applied to space "in what manner soever considered" (E. 2.13.3, 167).

Rather than applying in cases of no consideration (or no specific consideration), it applies in *all* cases of consideration. This makes sense, since in all cases the idea is nothing but space (or expansion) itself considered in some particular way or other. This does, however, result in a fairly important problem: No "naked" simple idea can be affixed to the term "expansion" in order to determine its meaning. Rather, it would seem that *any* of the multiple simple modes of extension will do. However, we are now well on our way to Berkeley's own account of the meaning of general terms. For rather than deriving its significance from one fixed simple idea of expansion, it would derive its significance from any of a range of simple modes. I should add that, curiously, when Locke comes to examine how general terms get their meaning in Book III he omits any discussion whatsoever of simple modes and any discussion of expansion, space, or extension at all. In my opinion, the absence is hardly a surprise.

Theories of Meaning

In my reading of Berkeley, it is clear why his semantic account of general terms must be different from Locke's. Any attempt to abstract from the ideas of Peter, Paul, and James, will yield an idea which includes the partial idea of colour. In order for Locke's semantic account to work, this idea of colour must be an idea of colour in general, rather than an idea of some determinate colour. But this is where Locke's own account of general terms breaks down. In his own admission, there is no such abstract idea of colour in general; categorical ascension from simple ideas is impossible; so an alternative semantic account is needed. If this is right, Locke's semantic account of general terms must also fail for complex ideas as well: Instead of one abstract idea of man (which includes the abstract idea of colour), Locke is left with many ideas of men (with differing ideas of colour). It is little wonder, then, that Berkeley's own account of the meaning of general terms in some ways picks up on Locke's unheralded accounts of meaning when his "constant and unvariable" account of general terms had broken down in the case of simple ideas.

To put this in proper context, recall Berkeley himself is interested to attack what he regards as universalisation from particulars. He sees determinate colours as, in some sense, particulars. He rejects the possibility of universalisation (which for Locke is accommodated in the same way as categorical ascension in the case of complex ideas), because in the case of determinate colours no such ascension appears possible at all: There is nothing left to leave out anymore; we seem to have reached the highest categorical level. But the failure to universalize from particular simple ideas such as colours means that any attempt to universalize from a particular complex ideas will likewise fail.

Now a natural reading of Berkeley's account of meaning is that it is *extensional*, where the significance of a given general term is determined by the several individuals to which the term itself applies.[13] Yet rather than saying that a general term has one meaning (constituted by the entire extension), Berkeley may be saying that the term does not have one single meaning at all, but rather multiple meanings (as many meanings as correspond to the particular ideas themselves). This need not suggest that general terms are *equivocal* in the strong sense that the term "bank" is equivocal. Rather, terms can have multiple senses that although different, are also related to each other. For example, Aquinas recognizes that the term "health" can be applied to an animal, urine, and food *analogously*.[14] Food is not healthy as a dog is healthy. Yet, the healthiness of the food is deeply connected to the healthiness of the dog. Another example is provided by Descartes, who denies that the term "substance" applies to God and finite minds and bodies *univocally*.[15] In denying this, he does not mean to suggest that it applies entirely equivocally. Rather, "substance" is taken to apply to God simply in a stricter, more proper sense. The point is that if one allows for *analogous predication*, then there is as Aquinas explains, a mean between univocity and pure equivocation.[16]

Still, it seems somewhat extreme that Berkeley should have maintained such a thesis with respect to all general terms. So the view that a general term's single signification is constituted by the extension may seem more attractive. However, a good case can be made that Berkeley does endorse this analogical view of general terms. Begin by noticing that in the Introduction itself, Berkeley explicitly denies that general terms have "one precise, definite signification" (PI 18). On the face of it, this seems to be a straightforward rejection of the view that general terms are univocal. However, one might point out that in an extensional account of meaning, because the extension is often in flux owing to the creation and destruction of objects, the extension itself may not be precise or settled. The remainder of the passage goes against such an alternative interpretation.

First, Berkeley points to the error of his opponents that each general

[13] For an example of this widely accepted account, see Flage 1987, 94-132, esp. 98.

[14] Aquinas 1947-1948, I Q 13, A 5; Aristotle 1984, *Metaphysics* IV, 2 (1003a 34ff.).

[15] Descartes 1984, Part One, § 52, vol. 1, p. 230.

[16] Ibid.

term has "one only precise and settled signification." This leads them to postulate abstract ideas which "constitute the true and only immediate signification of each general name." Berkeley then considers the objection that since every name has a definition, it is thereby "restrained to one certain signification." He responds by pointing to the fact that the definition (of a triangle, say) does not specify whether the triangle is big or small, black or white, and so forth. He then concludes: "'Tis one thing for to keep a name constantly to the same definition, and another to make it stand everywhere for the same idea: the one is necessary, the other useless and impracticable." The overall context surely makes much more sense in the interpretation that Berkeley is affirming that that general terms are analogical. The definitions themselves, of course, will involve further terms that will likewise be analogical.

More evidence for this interpretation can be found in the *Manuscript Introduction.* At §31, after denying that general terms have a precise and settled signification, Berkeley writes: "Whereas there is in Truth a *Diversity of significations* in every general Name whatsoever" (my italics). More tellingly, in the original stratum of the text, Berkeley had written ". . .there is in Truth an *Homonymy* . . ." (my italics). This is surely evidence that Berkeley means to deny the univocity of general terms, and the fact that "homonymy" is ultimately lined out suggests that Berkeley wanted something weaker than pure equivocation that still denied univocity. Thus he speaks of a "Diversity of significations."

My interpretation fits well with the specific Lockean difficulties that Berkeley is attempting to address. Despite the fact that there appears to be some resemblance between two shades of blue, there is no one common thing which can be considered to the exclusion of the differences. According to Locke, simple ideas and their names, "*have but few Ascents in linea prædicamentali,* (as they call it,) *from the lowest Species, to the summum Genus.*" Yet for many Scholastics being itself, above substance, quality, quantity and the other predicaments, was not considered a genus. In this case, analogical predication was invoked to avoid the problem. According to Cardinal Cajetan, for example:

> Things which give rise to *univocation* are similar to one another in the sense that the foundation of similitude in one has exactly the same nature as the foundation of similitude in the other. Thus the notion of one contains in itself nothing which the notion of the other does not contain. In this way, the foundation of univocal similitude in both extremes abstracts equally from the extremes themselves. (Cajatan 1959, 33)

He continues, "Hence no matter in what extreme animality, which is the foundation of similitude, is considered absolutely, say, in a man or a lion, it will be found to abstract equally from its subject and not to include in one extreme anything which it does not include in the other." Yet "substance, quantity, quality, etc. do not have in their quiddities anything which can be abstracted in the way just mentioned, say entity, for there is nothing else above substantiality; consequently there cannot be any substantial univocation between them." (Cajatan 1959, 34)

This seems to be precisely the difficulty that Locke's own account faces. There is nothing above the red, blue, and white which can be abstracted. And with respect to shades of blue, while there may be some kind of similitude, nothing is found in one that is found (at least equally) in the other. How is categorical ascension possible? It is worth noting, then, that Berkeley's explicit target in the *Manuscript Introduction* are abstract ideas which "equally represent the Particulars of any Sort" (MI 7). He goes on to explain:

> They [ideas] are not thought to Represent them [things] otherwise than as they resemble them. Whence it follows, that an Idea is not capable of representing indifferently any Thing whatsoever it being limited by the likeness it beares to some particular Thing, to represent it rather than any other ... I cannot frame an Idea of Man, which shall equally represent & correspond to each particular of the Sort of Creature, that may possibly exist. (MI 20)

Even though Berkeley ultimately comes to allow for the possibility of general ideas which represent all particulars equally it remains true that this representation is not secured through equal similitude. But it is equal similitude which is important in securing univocity.

It is plausible that Locke himself rejects the notion of analogical predication altogether. Although Walter Ott has provided some evidence in favour of this view,[17] I think the best argument for it can be found in one of Locke's reasons for rejecting a robust positive idea of substance in general. Locke constructs a dilemma between the following two possibilities. First, he considers the possibility that God, finite spirit, and body are all substances in the same sense. For Locke, this means there must be only one idea (which is shared by the three). It also means that all three substances must share the same nature: ". . . That God, Spirits, and Body, agreeing in the same common nature of *Substance*; differ not any otherwise than in a bare different modification of that *Substance*; as a Tree and a Pebble, being in the same sense Body, and agreeing in the common

[17] Ott 1997, 56.

nature of Body . . ." (E. 2.13.18, 174), which Locke takes to be repugnant. Second, he considers the possibility that the three are called "substance" in different significations (and that there are three different ideas). One problem with this possibility, according to Locke is the danger of equivocation; he recommends that different words be used for each idea to avoid confusion. The second problem is that one might now arbitrarily add other ideas to these three, thus proliferating the confusion.

The first option clearly involves an insistence that the word "substance" be used univocally since he takes the three to belong to the same genus. And it also seems pretty clear that Locke has pure (non-analogical) equivocation in mind in the second option. After all, only pure equivocation would require distinct names to avoid confusion. And analogical predication is non-arbitrary, but based upon relations of similitude. One could hardly add new ideas willy-nilly, did Locke have analogical predication in mind. Since this is intended as an exhaustive dilemma, we must conclude that Locke does not take analogical predication as a serious option. By contrast, Berkeley denies that general terms must have "one precise, definite signification." In doing so, he is prepared to admit that a term may signify a variety of different, but related and imperfectly similar ideas. In doing so, he can offer a solution in the face of the failure of Locke's own semantic account of general terms; it requires denying the univocity of general terms.

Final Thoughts

So we now understand one of Berkeley's most important arguments against Lockean abstract generalizing. Regardless of whether one believes in mental consideration or even simple ideas themselves, simple ideas cannot yield further abstract ideas through categorical ascension, since there is nothing to be left out of them: There is at most one partial idea there to be considered. However complex ideas must include abstract simple ideas – for example the idea of man must include the idea of colour which must itself be abstract. The solution recognized by Berkeley is to allow for the view that general terms do not have one fixed signification, but rather many significations which are related to each other through relations of resemblance. This requires accepting analogical predication, however, a view which Locke seems to explicitly disavow.

The interpretation sheds light on Berkeley's understanding of kinds or sorts. Members of a kind are actually analogates - related to each other through similitude in different degrees. Such a view is notably suggested by remarks Berkeley makes in the *Theory of Vision*. For example, in denying that tangible and visible ideas are of the same kind, Berkeley remarks, ". . . it must be acknowledged the visible square is fitter than the visible circle to represent the tangible square, but then it is not because it is liker, or more of a species with it" (TV 142). In a typical view of course, species membership is not something that ought to come in degrees. But Berkeley is here admitting that similitude comes in degrees and that similitude itself constitutes species membership. He continues by identifying likeness with analogy. Thus he says that we "imagine a likeness or an analogy between the immediate objects of sight and touch." (TV 145)

To be sure, one needs to know, in greater detail, just what Berkeley's account involves. Analogy is a complicated affair, theorized by the Scholastics in many different ways. And consider the puzzle how the general term "colour" can signify both black and white. While shades of blue may share some imperfect resemblance, one wants to say that black and white don't look alike at all. How then is there any analogy? Worse, how can sounds and colours have any similitude, if they can't possibly resemble each other at all? What can be like a colour but a colour, and a sound a sound? But then how is it that they alike ideas? Such questions are very deep, and in my view strike at the heart of Berkeley's ontology. Such issues, however, are also beyond the scope of this paper which is only a first stab at Berkeley's account of abstraction.[18]

Bibliography

Aquinas, Thomas. (1947-1948), *Summa Theologica*, Fathers of the English Dominican Province (tr.), rev. ed., Benziger Brothers, New York.

Aristotle. (1963) *Aristotle's Categories and De Interpretatione*, J. L. Ackrill (tr.), Clarendon Press, Oxford.

—. (1984), *The Complete Works of Aristotle*, W. D. Ross (ed.), 12 vols, Oxford, 1938-1952, revised by J. Barnes, 2 vols, Princeton University Press, Princeton.

Belfrage, Bertil. (1987), *George Berkeley's Manuscript Introduction: An Edition Diplomatica Transcribed and Edited with Introduction and Commentary by Bertil Belfrage*, Doxa, Oxford.

Berkeley, George. (1948-1957), *The Works of George Berkeley*, 9 vols, A. A. Luce and T. E. Jessop (eds), Nelson, London.

---

[18] Thanks to Susan Forrest for her comments as well as her constant support and encouragement.

Bettcher, Talia Mae. (2007), *Berkeley's Philosophy of Spirit: Consciousness, Ontology, and the Elusive Subject*, Continuum Press, London.

Cajetan, Thomas de Vio. (1959), *The Analogy of Names and The Concept of Being*, 2nd ed., Edward A. Bushinski with Henry J. Koren (tr.), Duquesne University, Pittsburgh.

Dancy, Jonathan. (1987), *Berkeley: An Introduction*, Blackwell, Oxford.

Descartes, Rene. (1984), *Principles of Philosophy,* in *The Philosophical Writings of Descartes*, 2 volumes, J. , Robert Stroothoff and D. Murdoch (tr.), Cambridge University Press, Cambridge.

Flage, Daniel E. (1987), *Berkeley's Doctrine of Notions: A Reconstruction Based on His Theory of Meaning*, Croom Helm, London.

Jesseph, Douglas M. (1993), *Berkeley's Philosophy of Mathematics*, Chicago University Press, Chicago, 1993.

Locke, John. (1975), *An Essay concerning Human Understanding*, P. H. Nidditch (ed.), Clarendon Press, Oxford.

Mackie, J. L. (1976), *Problems from Locke*, Oxford University Press, Oxford.

Ott, Walter. (1997), "Locke and the Scholastics on Theological Discourse," *Locke Newsletter* 28, pp. 51-66.

Owen. G. E. L. (1965), "Inherence," *Phronesis* 10, pp. 97-105.

Pappas, George. (2000), *Berkeley's Thought*, Cornell University Press, Ithaca.

Stoneham, Tom. (2002), *Berkeley's World*, Oxford University Press, Oxford.

Winkler, Kenneth P. (1989), *Berkeley: An Interpretation*, Oxford University Press, Oxford.

DID HUME READ BERKELEY'S *THE QUERIST*?

GEORGE CAFFENTZIS

> Whether, if there was a wall of brass a thousand cubits high round this kingdom, our natives might not nevertheless live cleanly and comfortably, till the land, and reap the fruit of it.
> —The Querist, 134

> But as any body of water may be raised above the level of the surrounding element, if the former has no communication with the latter; so in money, if the communication be cut off, by any material or physical impediment, (for all laws alone are ineffectual) there may in such a case, be a very great inequality of money…We need not have recourse to a physical attraction, in order to explain the necessity of this operation. There is a moral attraction, arising from the interest and passions of men, which is full as potent and infallible.
> —David Hume, *Political Discourses*[1]

Abstract

In this paper I will answer two questions concerning the relation between Berkeley's and Hume's philosophies of money: (1) Did Hume read Berkeley's *The Querist*? and (2) How much did reading *The Querist* affect Hume's monetary philosophy? I will answer the first with an affirmative and the second with a qualified "Substantially." To answer these questions I deploy a term from the methodology of determining authorial and textual relations: "influence."

Canon Construction: Philosophy and Money

Philosophers practice a form of ancestor worship (and denigration) that constitutes its own sub-discipline: the History of Philosophy. In this Philosophy is not unique, most disciplines have their own version of valuation of past performance that is often called in cultural studies "canon

[1] Hume 1987, 312-313.

construction" or "the invention of tradition" or the creation of an "imagined community." The struggles around a discipline's canon construction, its invention of tradition and its sense of imagined community – or its mythic meta-narrative of origin and development, if you will – is a territory thick with the intersections of powers and knowledge that Marxists, sociologists of knowledge and post-structural theorists have studied intensely since the late 1960s. Inevitably, however, for philosophy this "sacred," hence bloodied, disciplinary territory is especially self-reflective and contested.

Certainly a major result of 19th and early 20th century philosophical canon construction has been the manufacture of the much refined and retold story of the "British Empiricists": John Locke, George Berkeley, and David Hume. According to this narrative, Locke begins philosophy's turn to Experience as the source of knowledge, Berkeley radicalizes the turn, and Hume leads the philosophy of Experience to a chilling skeptical dead-end that awaits its transcendental transformation in Germany.

Like it or not, the trio and their tragicomic story appear together as implacably as the stone figures on Mount Rushmore. The structure of an untold number of introductions to philosophy, historical surveys, philosophy department curricula, and final exams rely on the rubric, "British Empiricists," and texts from the three philosophers set in a row. Such a long-lasting construction has attracted its share of skeptics anxious to deconstruct the unity of three figures who, historically and culturally, were quite distinct. After all, what made an 17th century English imperial bureaucrat, an early 18th century Anglo-Irish clergyman, and a mid-18th century Scottish man of letters all "British" and "empiricists" to boot? Many have taken both attributions to task when applied to one or another of the trio. We know that while Hume might accept being called a "North Briton," he was anxious to distinguish himself from the Scotophobic English. Who can forget Hume's letter to his close friend George Eliot in 1764 where he writes:

> I do not believe there is one Englishman in fifty, who, if he heard that I broke my Neck to night, would not be rejoic'd with it. Some hate me because I am not a Tory, some because I am not a Whig, some because I am not a Christian, and all because I am a Scotsman. Can you seriously talk of my continuing an Englishman? Am I, or are you, an Englishman? Will they allow us to be so?[2]

Also, was Locke truly an empiricist? After all, he argued that moral and mathematical knowledge were rooted in definitions and reasonable deductions

---

[2] Mossner 1980, 637.

and he borrowed heavily from Descartes' Meditations. Similar objections and reservations can be easily multiplied.

In fact, as Michael Ayers pointed out more than twenty years ago, the "establishment" view of the relationship among the three philosophers (and especially that between Berkeley and Hume) is paradoxically contrary to the "traditional canon."[3] There is "a tendency on the part of some to see nothing good, 'interesting,' or even true in the old way of looking at things [concerning Berkeley's 'influence' on Hume]. The anti-traditional stance has itself become a rather long-standing orthodoxy with a spurious air of innovation."[4]

Indeed, for a period of time there was even a genuine debate as to whether Hume read Berkeley at all! It began with Richard Popkin claiming that "It is highly questionable whether Hume ever read Berkeley, or derived any views from him" in a review of a history of modern philosophy written by George Boas.[5] Phillip Weiner and Ernest Mossner responded to Popkin's provocative question in defense of the traditional view, though in a decidedly circumspect way.[6] Popkin's view seemed to be moving with the tide of non-conformity of the time until 1964 when he learned of a scholarly discovery in Cracow: a 1737 letter from the young David Hume to his friend Michael Ramsey where Hume urged his friend to read among other works, "the Principles of Human Knowledge by Dr. Berkeley" in preparation to examining his performance.[7] But even this discovery did not settle the question, of course, since Popkin's admission, "So, Berkeley did read Hume," was mitigated by the supplement,"...but not much." The discussion as to how much evidence of Berkeley's views and words could be found in Hume's *Treatise* and *Inquiries* continued through the 1960s and early 1970s.[8] This debate was punctuated again by the discovery (this time unauthenticated) of an earlier letter of Hume's to Michael Ramsey stating – in 1734, long before the completion of the *Treatise* – that he was in Rheims where he had access to Abbe Noel-Antoine Pluche's library where "It is my Pleasure to read over again today Locke's Essays and the Principles of Human Knowledge by Dr. Berkeley."[9] But the debate continued, of course, on the matter.

Ayers, in an attempt to correct Popkin's overwrought perspective,

---

[3] Ayers 1984, 304.
[4] Ayers 1984, 304.
[5] Popkin 1959, 71.
[6] Weiner 1959 and Mossner 1959.
[7] Popkin 1964.
[8] Cf., Conroy 1969 and Hall 1970.
[9] Morrisroe Jr. 1973, 314-315; Mossner 1980, 97.

argues that Berkeley's philosophy obviously "influenced" Hume's *Treatise*. He discusses two such areas of influence (among many other possibilities) – (1) in Hume's discussion of Space and Time and (2) in Hume's discussion of substance where Ayers finds Berkeley's work "influentially" present, even though there is no direct reference to Berkeley's texts.[10] Ayers implies that there are many other areas in Hume's work where similar arguments can be made. Indeed, there is no point in counting direct references in Hume's philosophical work to determine the source of an "influence." For example, in the *Treatise* there are no direct references to Descartes, six to Spinoza, two to Hobbes, none to Leibniz, four to Locke, one to Malebranche, and one to Berkeley.[11] But these references in a four hundred-page book hardly can give a fair assessment of a philosophic ancestor's influence on Hume's thought.

The process of canon formation in the Philosophy of Money, for good or ill, is in an early stage compared with Philosophy proper. In this paper I will deal with a small, but important sub-region of the territory. For a set of questions similar to the ones cited above concerning Philosophy can be posed for the "British Empiricists'" Philosophy of Money, in general, and for Berkeley's relationship to Hume in particular. For example, to paraphrase the earlier debate on whether Hume "read" Berkeley's major philosophical works (especially the *Principles*): did Hume read Berkeley's *The Querist*?

This paper's first aim is to answer this question as best I can (since, of course, "reading" is such a subtly ambiguous word), and in so doing contribute to the discussion of canon formation of the Philosophy of Money. To perform this task I will utilize a term that is in common use in literary theory: "influence." It is problematic. "Influence" is deployed in the history of philosophy in a rather offhanded way while it carries with it an immense, untheorized historical baggage from astrology (the effluvia from the stars affecting human behavior) to medicine (e.g., "influenza") to physics (as an electromagnetic "action at a distance"). Therefore its use in the history of philosophy is vague and indecisive, especially when we wish to answer the metric question: how much did philosophy X influence philosopher Y? I will use "influence" to demarcate a terrain of social causation, personal motivation, and political strategy that will be anchored by David Hume qua author of the 1752 *Political Discourses*.

[10] Ayers 1984, 306-323.
[11] Hume 2000.

Evidence of Influence

The first bit of evidence to note in determining whether the reading of Berkeley's *The Querist* influenced Hume in the writing of the *Political Discourses* is that Hume never directly refers to Berkeley or to *The Querist* in *Political Discourses*, Hume's main contribution to monetary theory and policy. Is this conclusive evidence that Hume never read *The Querist*? No, simply because the rules of scholarly reference in the eighteenth century did not require that an author publicly specify the text that s/he was consciously "influenced" by (for an extensive study of Adam Smith's unacknowledged "borrowing" or even "plagiarism" see Rashid's work).[12]The very legal concept of an author who owns a text was only beginning to be formed one or two generations before Hume. He became the first (some might claim, last as well!) major philosopher writing in English at least who was able to support himself and grow rich on the basis of selling his writings to book publishers.

Aside from "Of the Populousness of Ancient Nations" and *History of England*, Hume made very few direct, named references in his writing. In the "economic" essays of *Political Discourses*, he made a number of references to participants in the French discourse on political economy (e.g., Melon, Dutot, Paris de Verney, and Vauban), but Hume rarely mentions similar writers in English. I believe that only Mandeville, Swift, Gee, Hutcheson, and Temple would qualify. Although they were important figures in the development of monetary theory in the English language, there are many eminent late 17th and 18th century names that are missing. Where are the references to Petty, Locke, Child, Davedant, Law, Barbon, North, and Vanderlint as well as to Berkeley? Are we to believe that Hume, ever the bibliophile, did not peruse the work of these important figures, whose books and pamphlets were available in the bookshops and libraries of Edinburgh and London, in preparation for his mature work on money and commerce published in his 41st year? Did not Hume, for example, peruse Locke's monetary writings when he made reference to the 1696 "recoinage"?[13]

In fact, we have good evidence that Hume did read many of the important authors in the literature that he did not openly refer to in *Political Discourses*. The evidence comes from the early memoranda that Hume made while reading during the period 1729-1740, a period when he was writing the *Treatise* and the first volume of the *Essays*. The bulk of

[12] Rashid 1990.

[13] Hume 1987, 288.

the memoranda deal with readings from what we would today call the social sciences. Hume clearly read widely in the French literature on politics and commerce, but he also notes a number of English writers that he does not refer to in the *Political Discourses* like Sir Josiah Child and Charles Davenant. Even more important for the question of this paper, the young Hume studied John Law's *Money and Trade Considered, with a Proposal for Supplying the Nation* [i.e., Scotland] *with Money* and Arthur Dobb's *An Essay on the Trade and Improvement of Ireland*, showing that he was already considering the particular problems of what we now might call "underdeveloped" economies (or "poor countries" then), including the two that were tied to the largest economy of the day (for Scotland and Ireland were a bit like Canada and Mexico today).[14]

Moreover, we know that Hume self-consciously repressed the increasingly "modern" practice of using footnotes even in his historical works (much less his essays "moral, political and literary"). Seven years after he finished the *Political Discourses* he regretted his past (mal)practice, at least with respect to his historical works. Horace Walpole chided Hume for his lack of notes in his *History of England*. In his reply to Walpole Hume apologized for "my negligence in not quoting my authorities," and claimed that it would have "cost no trouble" for him to have added "the references on the margin.")[15]

Hume's excuse was stylistic. He claimed to follow the model of the Renaissance historians "Matchiavel, Fra Paolo, Davila, Bentivoglio" who in turn mirrored the footnoteless classical tradition. But Hume conceded that the use of footnotes "was more modern than their time, and having been once introduc'd, ought to be follow'd by every writer."[16] In fact, it was only with the formation of the initial "intellectual property regime" of the 18th century that the issue of quotation and attribution becomes increasingly vital as the author and work begin to have legal status. Indeed, a short time after receiving Walpole's nudge, Hume spent the winter months 1760 at a "very laborious, but not unentertaining Occupation ... adding the Authorities to the Volumes of the Stuarts."[17]

Hume never revised the *Treatise* in a similar way, of course, because it was never reprinted during his lifetime. However, the "economic" essays in the *Political Discourses* were reprinted and revised many times. They were originally almost footnoteless (with the sole exception of "Of the Populousness of Ancient Nations") and remained so throughout his life.

---

[14] Mossner 1948.

[15] Quoted in Grafton 1997, 190.

[16] Quoted in Grafton 1997, 191.

[17] Quoted in Mossner 1980, 401.

Why is it that he never "added the Authorities" in the essays?

Perhaps it had to do with the nature of the essay that Hume described in his self-reflexive essay "On Essay-Writing" (that was only included in the first 1742 edition of *Essays, Moral and Political*).[18] Hume, in an extended analogy, compared himself as an essay writer to "a Kind of Resident or Ambassador from the Dominions of Learning to those of Conversation; and shall think it my constant Duty to promote a good Correspondence betwixt these two States, which have so great a Dependence on each other."[19] Such an ambassador would hesitate to bring heavily freighted and lengthily deferred internal commentary and textual evidence as part of his "traffic" betwixt the learned and conversible. The footnote, which is introduced to make explicit the commerce among texts, decenters the essay and adds a weight that is antithetical to its goal of deriving its "Materials" from "Conversation and common Life."[20] In other words, a genuine scrupulousness in footnoting might make the essay reader look upon Hume's work as originating in the land of Learned alone, with harmful consequences to his income before the publication of the *History of England*. This might especially be a source of concern since Hume, in continuing his "allusion," calls "Women of Sense and Education" the "Sovereigns of the Empire of Conversation."[21] These rulers might be especially impatient with "the dull labors of Pedants and Commentators" who had made the footnote their weapon of choice.

Hume's anxiety to respect the essay genre might explain the lack of reference to *The Querist*. But there is evidence that Hume *could* have read and been influenced by *The Querist* as part of his preparation for writing *Political Discourses*. This possibility is due to *The Querist's* publication dates and locales. It was published anonymously in three parts, one part each in 1735, 1736, and 1737 in both Dublin and London. Hume was living in London from September 1737 until the end of 1738, correcting and preparing his *Treatise* for publication. He might have seen it at that time. Then a revised version of *The Querist* that carried Berkeley's name was published in 1750 in four editions, three in Dublin and one in London. In 1751 *The Querist* was published once again in London and then in Glasgow.[22] The publication of six editions of a book in two years means that it had created quite a "buzz" in the not-so United Kingdom. If Hume missed *The Querist* in its original 1735-1737 publication, he could hardly

---

[18] Hume 1987, 533-544.
[19] Hume 1987, 535.
[20] Hume 1987, 535.
[21] Hume 1987, 535-536.
[22] Johnston 1970, vi-vii.

have missed it in 1750 and 1751, the period he was composing and preparing *Political Discourses* for publication. Moreover, in this second chance for *The Querist*, with Berkeley plainly named as the author, Hume would hardly not have been curious to know what "a great philosopher" who has "disputed the receiv'd opinion" on abstract ideas had to say about exactly the issues he was writing about: money, commerce, and public credit.

There is further support for this hypothesis in the Hume Library. *The Querist* was definitely in this collection.[23] The book appears to have been the 1751 Glasgow edition and was, interestingly enough, bound together with *The Manual of Epictetus*. It was not identical to the 1735-1737 edition, because many of the detailed queries concerning the actual running of the National Bank that Berkeley suggested (to evade the fate of Law's Banque Royale) were redacted in this edition (for a book that presents both the original 1735-37 edition and the later one, though in a somewhat confusing way, see Johnston's edition of *The Querist*).[24] It definitely posed a subtle but strong anti-Lockean, anti-metallist, pro-paper money position and proposed a National Bank that would manage the new paper currency.

We are not sure, of course, *when* Hume actually acquired this edition of *The Querist*, or, indeed, whether David Hume's nephew, Baron Hume, added it to the library after his uncle's death. Or *The Querist* could have been a very late arrival to the library, entirely inconsequential to Hume during the composition of *Political Discourses*. But this evidence certainly increases the probability that Hume took *The Querist* into account in writing his "economic" essays in the late 1740s and early 1750s.

Although we should remember that even if Berkeley's *The Querist* was not in Hume's library that would by no means have precluded his study of the quizzical text. After all, a review of the pre-1777 publications (that theoretically could have been acquired by David Hume) in the general field of political economy (as indicated by the authors appearing in the table of contents of Terence Hutchison's *Before Adam Smith*) reveal that Hume possessed books written by only 15 of 57 authors listed.[25] The authors whose books he possessed included, beside Berkeley, Graunt, Davenant, Locke, Mandeville, Law, Cantillon, Montesquieu, Farbonnais, Galiani, Mirabeau, Beccaria, Morellet, Ferguson, and, of course, Smith. But the authors missing are also important. They include Petty, Child, Barbon, North, Boisguilbert, Vanderlint, Franklin, Francis Hutcheson,

[23] Norton and Norton 1996, 75.
[24] See Johnston 1970.
[25] Hutchison 1988.

Melon, Quesnay, Mercier, Verri, Turgot, Steuart, among others.

However, Hume definitely had access to other libraries besides his own in France, in London and in Scotland. This was especially true of the Advocates Library in Edinburgh. Long before he became its Keeper in 1752, he was able to borrow from the 30,000-volume library through the courtesy of lawyer friends. He most likely would have had ample opportunity to borrow *The Querist* from there, if he had not purchased his own copy before the publication of *Political Discourses*. The present National Library of Scotland (which received all the non-legal books of the Advocates Library in the early 20th century) has four editions of *The Querist* published in 1750 (London), 1751 (Glasgow), 1751 (London again), and 1752 (Dublin). There is a good chance that at least one of these editions would have entered the library during Hume's preparation of the *Political Discourses*. But if Hume were acquainted with the original 1735-1737 edition of *The Querist*, it would not have been as a reader in the Advocates Library, since the library apparently has no record of it.

Why would Hume read *The Querist*?

Now that we have established the possibility, or even the likelihood of Hume's reading *The Querist* on the basis of contextual evidence, let us look at the reasons *why* and *how* Hume might have read it. We need to take these motivations into account, since we are not in possession of evidence like Hume's decisive letters to Michael Ramsey that definitively answered the question "Did Hume read Berkeley at all?" affirmatively.[26] As far as I know, there is no comparable letter or memorandum that would make it possible to go from *whether* Hume read *The Querist* to *how* did Hume read *The Querist*. We must rely here on contextual evidence.

The textual evidence that Hume did read (and could have been influenced by) *The Querist* is strong, but it is not overwhelming. In this I take a position in opposition to Joseph Johnston who claimed that "Hume must have read *The Querist*, but it is impossible to say for certain whether he was consciously influenced by it or not."[27] Johnston took this position because he believed that "essential elements in Berkeley's monetary philosophy failed to penetrate the mind of Hume" and that Hume was a "retrograde" monetary thinker whose "instinct, if not his reason" attached considerable importance of the precious metals.[28] What a barrage on

[26] Mossner 1980, 97, 104.
[27] Johnston 1970, 85.
[28] Johnston 1970, 85-87.

Hume: thickheaded, passé, and atavistic! This is not the Hume that we know. Somehow Johnston sees the subtle thinker of our contemporary studies as an arch reactionary in the monetary field because Hume is a "theoretical" metallist (in Schumpeter's terminology) whose influence on Smith "impoverished" monetary theory until the rise of Keynes.

However, Johnston's identification of Hume as a thoroughgoing metallist is mistaken, though Hume clearly argued for "the French road" from the 1720 bubble.[29] For the French government, capitalists and aristocracy revalorized gold and silver coinage as their money vehicle of choice after their collective "fling" on the rue Quincampoix. Hume's reasons for this choice were not based upon an ontological preference for specie. Once that assumption is undermined, the effect of Johnston's barrage is blunted. Hume might not have been so thickheaded as to block the penetration of Berkeley's monetary philosophy in his mind, he might not have been so passé as to advocate for a totally metallic currency, finally, he might not have been so atavistic as to deny the plain evidence that paper currency was "the wave of the future."

A more complex assessment than that provided by Johnston—Hume simply couldn't understand Berkeley—is necessary in order for us to explain the differences between Hume's and Berkeley's philosophies of money and their conflicting monetary policies.

The main contextual evidence for Berkeley's "influence" on the *Political Discourses* is rooted in the similarities between Hume and his circle's challenges in the Scotland of the early 1750s with the situation Berkeley and his circle faced in the Ireland of the 1730s. Berkeley had to both find ways to "excite the industry" of the native Irish (as he called the disenfranchised Catholic population) and to not provoke the mercantilist police of the London-dominated state.[30] The Scottish Enlightenment circle had a similar problematic that they shared with their Anglo-Irish counterparts. For they had in the Scottish Highlands a recalcitrant, and at times rebellious, population that had not been integrated into the commercial society of the Lowlands and of England. This population was not, as in the case of the "Irish natives," politically catatonic at the time. The Highlanders were positively aggressive and had invaded England a number of times within memory. They had to be "civilized" (or exterminated or "cleared") in order for the Lowland Scots to have any claim to the power of being the citizens of a world empire.[31] In fact, the interest this similarity might generate among the reading public could have

[29] Caffentzis 2001 and 2008.
[30] Caffentzis 2000.
[31] Caffentzis 1996 and 2005.

been the reason why the revised editions of *The Querist* published in the early 1750s were all accompanied with *A Word to the Wise*, a remarkable public statement addressed to the "Catholic clergy of Ireland" urging them to call on their laity to increase their work effort and to scrutinize their sanitary habits.

Money had an important role to play in this process of "civilizing" the Highlands according to Hume.[32] Consequently, the efforts of the Anglo-Irish "improving" intelligentsia to use money to motivate those outside of the money economy to come into it would have been important to understand. Since Berkeley and his circle in Ireland made that their primary task and since this task was most forcefully expressed in *The Querist*, there is good reason to believe that Hume found it imperative to reflect on Berkeley's quizzical suggestions.

Others in the Scottish Enlightenment were definitely students of *The Querist*. A most prominent one for us was Robert Wallace, Hume's opponent in the "populousness of ancient nations" debate. He criticized Hume's strictures against "paper credit" and directly referred to *The Querist* in his *Characteristics of the Present Political State of Great Britain* (1758) where he suggested that "a poor but growing country stood in need of paper money and credit to boost her economy."[33] In fact, Wallace urged that *The Querist* be "perused by every lover of this country and of mankind."[34]

In this regard, it should be remembered that Wallace was a member of the Rankenian Club, a group of faculty and students of divinity and law, which met in the 1720s and 1730s to discuss the "New Philosophy" with special reference to the work of George Berkeley. They carried on a correspondence with the then Dean of Derry concerning his philosophy and they earned his high regard. It was claimed that Berkeley had said, "no persons understood his system better than this set of young gentlemen in North Britain."[35] Berkeley invited the Rankenians to join him on his venture to found a "utopian" college to educate together American Indians' and colonists' sons in the Bermudas. He was so persuasive that one of their number, John Smibert, did follow Berkeley "westward." The young Hume's teachers at the university included a number of Rankenians including, of course, Newton's major expositor at the time, Colin Maclaurin. Hume, then, definitely imbibed some of Berkeley's thought (including his moral and political concerns) in Edinburgh, since there was

---

[32] Caffentzis 1996, 2001, and 2005.
[33] Hont 1983, 290.
[34] Quoted in Hont 1983: 290.
[35] Mossner 1980, 48.

likely no other place where his work was so well received.[36]

Hume in the *Treatise* had to confront the *Principles* or the *Three Dialogues* exactly because he learned so much from the "God-appointed Berkeley," as W. B. Yates called him. But he had to take his distance with care. He could hardly have written, "I am Berkeley *without* God." In fact, he separated himself so slyly that two hundred years later some of his most sophisticated readers could be wondering, "Did Hume read Berkeley?" Hume also had to confront the Berkeley of *The Querist*, again *because* though he shared so much of (or was influenced by) Berkeley's conception of money, he at the same time drew contrary conclusions, again for problematic reasons (both logical and political). Wallace clearly understood this ambivalence in and potential weakness of Hume's position. In pitting Berkeley against Hume, Wallace inevitably evoked the direct connection between Berkeley's *The Querist* and the bugbear of Scottish economics: John Law. Just as Hume does not refer to *The Querist*, he doesn't refer to Law's *Money and Trade Considered* (even though from the early memoranda we have definitive evidence that he did read that work, as noted above).

Let us consider what concepts of money Hume could have learned from or might have been confirmed by Berkeley's *The Querist*. Hume shared with Berkeley the view that gold and silver do not function as money due to their "intrinsic value." This commonality is deeply rooted in the one affinity with Berkeley that Hume openly admitted to in the *Treatise*: the radical rejection of abstract ideas. This involved not only in the rejection of a contradictory, vague abstract idea that is supposed to subsume a set of contradictory predicates (a view that Berkeley attributes to Locke). But Berkeley, during his second conceptual revolution in the early 1730s, widened his rejection of abstract ideas to a rejection of ideas that "naturally" represented others, since there were no special ideas of X that "naturally" represent all X ideas because they have the "essential" properties of X, i.e., they are self-reflexive. Thus, according to this view, a gold coin can "naturally" represent monetary value because it is valuable, whereas paper notes cannot. Berkeley rejected such a view when he made algebra, not geometry, his model of signification in his mathematical writings.[37] Just as the number two can be represented by both "2" and the letter "x" in the equation 7-x=5, so too geometric lines need not be represented by geometric lines. This revolution had a profound effect on Hume who was a close student of Berkeley's critique of both abstract ideas

[36] Davie 1965.

[37] Cf. Caffentzis 2000, 252-263 and Caffentzis 2007.

and analysis. To the point that he paraphrases Berkeley's understanding of abstract or general ideas as "all general ideas are nothing but particular ones, annex'd to a certain term, which gives them a more extensive signification, and makes them recal upon occasion other individuals, which are similar to them."[38] The "annexing" process is, as the word implies, an arbitrary one, while the "recal" is "a kind of magical faculty in the soul…inexplicable by the utmost efforts of human understanding."[39] This combination of the magical and the arbitrary liberated Hume (with Berkeley's help) from a rigid similitude or homology between signifier and signified.

Once Berkeley leaped over this semantic hurdle, the path to a critique of theoretical metallism became evident. Hume shared not only his critique of abstract ideas, but also the rejection of theoretical metallism. Both use rather similar, but complex metaphors to express this shared functionalist notion of money. Berkeley, for example, queries:

> Q 34. Provided the wheels move, whether it is not the same thing, as to the effect of the machine, be this done by the force of wind, or water, or animals?[40]

Berkeley clearly sees money's relation to force or power as crucial. Money for Berkeley must both excite and regulate power, otherwise it is nothing. That is why he follows Q34 with Q 35:

> Q 35. Whether power to command the industry of others be not real wealth? And whether money be not in truth tickets or tokens for conveying and recording such power, and whether it be of great consequence what materials the tickets are made of?[41]

Berkeley's metaphor is complex, because there are three powers that must be distinguished – (1) the power to "convey and regulate" a power y [R(y)], (2) the power of command over x [M(x)] and (3) the power of industry and work (I) – and the third replaces the first in the metaphor. Money is, in this symbolism, R(M(I)), and the point is that just as a machine will be moved by a variety of natural forces (I) – wind, water, animals – so too the material used for R might vary as well – paper, brass, gold, shell. Of course, there is an important lacuna in the set of forces Berkeley listed: non-natural human labor power, but that is because it is

---

[38] Hume 2000, 17.
[39] Hume 2000, 21.
[40] Johnston 1970, 127.
[41] Johnston 1970, 127.

that problematic power that makes the metaphorical wheels of industry turn.

Hume takes a similar stance before the great metaphorical machine of the economy as Berkeley does in the first sentences of "Of Money":

> Money is not, properly speaking, one of the subjects of commerce; but only the instrument which men have agreed upon to facilitate the exchange of one commodity for another. It is none of the wheels of trade: It is the oil which renders the motion of the wheels more smooth and easy.[42]

Hume makes the "same points" as Berkeley – (1) money is not the object of commerce, the "wheels," and (2) there are alternative forms of money whose consequences can only be judged by their results, "the motion of the wheels"– but in a subtly different way. Hume sees money as a lubricant of economic motion, not a power that might drive it. Money facilitates movement, it does not originate or excite it. Moreover, not all oils are the same. Whale oil, olive oil and walnut oil have different lubricating properties and capacities. It might indeed be "of great consequence" to the machine what kind of oil is used "in" it, especially since a lubricant is not outside of the machine it lubricates (in the way that the motive power is outside of the machine it animates).

The subtle differences between Berkeley and Hume multiply in considering these two passages. Hume is insistent from the very beginning on the conventional aspects of money, whereas Berkeley does not tell us about how the "tickets or tokens" originate. In fact, they were usually "issued" by a company in a region to pay its workers or to facilitate in "making small change" for its customers. Returning to the beginning of *The Querist* we find not a set of men agreeing "to facilitate the exchange of one commodity for another," but a "wise" and "well-governed" State concerned "to encourage industry in its members," and therefore concerned about money, as the querist asks:

> Q 5. Whether money be not only so far useful, as it stirreth up industry, enabling men mutually to participate the fruits of each other's labor?[43]

These differences explode when we consider the conflicting monetary strategies Berkeley proposed for Ireland and Hume for Scotland. Indeed, it is *because* of these conflicts that Hume would have been driven to read and study *The Querist*. They are most clearly presented in two essays –"Of

---

[42] Hume 1987, 281.
[43] Johnston 1970, 125.

Money" and "Of the Balance of Trade." In "Of the Balance of Trade" Hume refutes the querist's suggestion that is vividly projected by the metaphor of "a wall of brass" in the first epigraph of this paper. Indeed, the "wall of brass" referred to in Berkeley's query is directly answered by Hume's "hydraulic" model of money and trade. Hume questions the very possibility of creating such an impermeable barrier between, say, Ireland or Scotland from the English economy, for to do so would force the state to fight against the force of "moral attraction, arising from the interest and passions of men, which is full as potent and infallible" which was as subtle but as powerful as the force of gravity in the natural realm. The only way that such an economic and monetary delinking can take place is through physical distance or geological separation that did not exist in this case. Moreover, such a "wall of brass" would attempt to block the main way a "poor country" can change its situation: the use of cheap wages to undercut the trade advantage of richer countries.

Interestingly enough, Hume harshly criticizes Berkeley's mentor, Dean Jonathan Swift, and his *A Short View of the State of Ireland* (1727-1728) in the original 1752 versions of "Of the Balance of Trade." He identifies Swift as "An author, who has more humour than knowledge, more taste than judgment, and more spleen, prejudice, and passion than any of these qualities."[44] Indeed, this characterization was so harsh Hume left it out of all future editions of the *Essays*. Swift predicted in *A Short View* the dramatic decline of gold and silver coin in Ireland in a few years time due to an imbalance of trade with England and was skeptical of any effort to have the country "trade" itself out of its predicament. In fact, it was in the late 1720s that Swift wrote *A Modest Proposal* suggesting that Irish parents exploit their "comparative advantage" in Irish children by offering them up to discerning British diners. Swift's favored approach out of this dilemma was one that we would now call "import substitution." It was an economic policy both Berkeley and Swift shared, although Berkeley chose what he thought to be a less confrontational strategy.

In the face of such "spleen, prejudice, and passion," Hume pointed out that if Swift were correct, then "in the course of 30 years [sic] [the currency] is absolutely nothing."[45] However, by the early 1750s Ireland had not become totally destitute. On the contrary, there was a noticeable "advance of riches" due, if contemporary research on Irish economic history is correct, to increased trade.[46] Consequently, Swift's (and Berkeley's) effort at "import substitution" was hardly the path to Ireland's

---

[44] Hume 1987, 633.
[45] Hume 1987, 311.
[46] Cullen 1972.

(and Scotland's) transformation from poor to modestly rich countries.

In "Of the Balance of Trade" Hume also attacks the method Berkeley proposed to create the "brass wall": a paper currency issued by a National Bank. He uses his hydraulic model to argue that paper money literally "drives out" specie (in accordance to Gresham's Law):

> I scarcely know any method of sinking money below its level, but those institutions of banks, funds, and paper-credit, which are so much practiced in this kingdom. These render paper equivalent to money, circulate it throughout the whole state, make it supply the place of gold and silver, raise proportionably the price of labor and commodities, and by that means either banish a great part of those precious metals, or prevent their farther encrease. What can be more short-sighted than our reasoning on this head?[47]

In the end, then, Berkeley's "reasoning" will inevitably make Ireland or Scotland, if either country took up the Querist's recommendations, unable to enter into world trade with dreaded consequences, according to Hume.

The other essay directly in conflict with Berkeley's policy recommendations is "Of Money" where Hume again invokes and attacks Berkeley's and Law's proposals for the founding of a National Bank (of Ireland and Scotland, respectively) that would regulate the issuing of "paper-credit" money that is "so generally esteemed advantageous to every nation."[48] Hume rejects this "paper" path to increasing the amount of money in a nation, since it will lead to set of "inconveniences": (1) it will "encreas[e] money beyond its natural proportion to labour and commodities" leading to higher prices of labor and provisions, (2) foreigners will not accept the "counterfeit money" whose value "any great disorder in the state will reduce to nothing." Hume recognizes the advantages of paper money for the rich who find it dangerous to transport large quantities of specie. He specifically mentions the private bankers of Dublin who provide such a service, and who perhaps, along with Law's Banque Royale, were practical models for Berkeley's suggestions. But he finds any Bank that did not "lock up all the money it received" (like the one that Berkeley suggested) dangerous to the nation, since it tended to create "counterfeit money."

Hume's critique of Berkeley's monetary strategy was not based on Berkeley's ontological rejection of "intrinsic value" (or "theoretical metallism"), but on semantic and practical considerations. He argued in a

[47] Hume 1987, 316.
[48] Hume 1987, 284.

utilitarian fashion that in fact "paper credit" money, when one examines its actual and potential use, just like public credit in general, one "will find no comparison between the ill and the good which result from them."[49]

I conclude that Hume's decision not to directly refer to Berkeley's *The Querist* was sign of its influence on *Political Discourses*, not of its lack of effect. His critical reference to Swift's *A Short View* (and his positive reference to Swift's maxim: "in the arithmetic of the customs, two and two make not four, but often make only one") as well as the description of the Dublin private bankers made it clear to the philosophical politician, the ideal reader of *Political Discourses*, that he was cognizant of and had taken into account the theoretical and practical monetary situation in Ireland.[50] And, to be so in 1752 required familiarity with the suggestions of *The Querist*.

Bibliography

Ayers, Michael. (1984), "Berkeley and Hume: A Question of Influence," in Rorty *et al.* (1984), pp. 303-327.

Caffentzis, C. G. (1996), "The Scottish Origin of Civilization," in Federici (1996), pp. 13-36.

—. (2000), *Exciting the Industry of Mankind: George Berkeley's Philosophy of Money*, Kluwer, Dordecht.

—. (2001), "Hume, Money, and Civilization; or, Why was Hume a Metallist?" *Hume Studies* 27, pp. 301-335.

—. (2005), "Civilizing the Highlands: Hume, Money and the Annexing Act," *Historical Reflections* 31, pp. 169-194.

—. (2008), "Fiction or Counterfeit? David Hume's Interpretations of Paper and Metallic Money," in Wennerlind and Schabas (2008), pp. 146-167.

Conroy, Grapham P. (1969), "Did Hume Really Follow Berkeley?" *Philosophy* 44, pp. 238-242.

Cullen, L. M. (1972), *The Economic History of Ireland Since 1660*, Batesford, London.

Davie, G. E. (1965), "Berkeley's Impact on Scottish Philosophers," *Philosophy* 40, pp. 222-234.

Federici, Silvia. (ed.) (1996), *Enduring Western Civilization*, Praeger, Westport, CT.

Grafton, Anthony. (1997), *The Footnote: A Curious History*, Harvard

[49] Hume 1987, 354.

[50] Hume 1987, 324.

University Press, Cambridge, Ma.

Hall, Roland. (1970), "Yes, Hume Did Use Berkeley," *Philosophy* 45, pp. 152-153.

Hont, Istvan. (1983), "The 'Rich Country-Poor Country' Debate in Scottish Classical Political Economy," in Hont and Ignatieff (1983), pp. 271-315.

Hont, I. and M. Ignatieff (eds.) (1983), *Wealth and Virtue: The Shaping of Politcal Economy in the Scottish Enlightenment*, Cambridge University Press, Cambridge.

Hume, David. (1987), *Essays Moral, Political, and Literary*, Revised Edition, E. F. Miller (ed.), Liberty Fund, Indianapolis.

—. (2000), *A Treatise of Human Nature*, D. F.Norton and M. J. Norton (eds), Oxford University Press, Oxford.

Hutchison, Terence. (1988), *Before Adam Smith: The Emergence of Political Economy*, 1662-1776, Basil Blackwell, Oxford

Johnston, Joseph. (1970), *Bishop Berkeley's Querist in Historical Perspective*, Dundalgan Press, Dundalk.

Morrisroe Jr., Michael. (1973), "Did Hume Read Berkeley? A Conclusive Answer," *Philological Quarterly* 52, pp. 310-315.

Mossner, Ernest Campbell. (1948), "Hume's Early Memoranda, 1729-1740: The Complete Text," *Journal of the History of Ideas* 9, pp. 492-518.

Mossner, E. C. (1959), "Did Hume Ever Read Berkeley? A Rejoiner to Professor Popkin," *Journal of Philosophy* 56, pp. 992-95.

—. (1980), *The Life of David Hume*, 2nd Edition, Oxford University Press, Oxford.

Norton, David Fate and Mary J. Norton. (1996), *The David Hume Library*, Edinburgh Bibliographical Society, Edinburgh.

Popkin, Richard H. (1959), "Did Hume Ever Read Berkeley?" *The Journal of Philosophy* 56, pp. 535-545.

—. (1964), "So, Hume did Read Berkeley," *The Journal of Philosophy* 61, pp. 773-778.

Rashid, Salim. (1990), "Adam Smith's Acknowledgments: Neo-Plagiarism and the Wealth of Nations," *The Journal of Libertarian Studies* IX, pp. 1-24.

Rorty, Richard, J. B. Schneewind, and Q. Skinner (eds.) (1984), *Philosophy in History: Essays in the Historiography of Philosophy*, Cambridge University Press, Cambridge

Weiner, Philip. (1959), "Did Hume Ever Read Berkeley?" *Journal of Philosophy* 56, pp. 533-535.

Wennerlind, Carl and M. Schabas (eds.) (2008) *David Hume's Political Economy*, Routledge, London.

LEIBNIZ AND BERKELEY ON BODY

CHARLES J. MCCRACKEN

Abstract

There is a *prima facie* similarity between Leibniz's and Berkeley's conceptions of *body*: both held that all substances are perceivers, that there are no extended substances, and that the bodies we perceive are not substances but rather "phenomena" (Leibniz) or "ideas" (Berkeley). But there are important differences between their views about bodies. This paper seeks to show where their conceptions are alike and where they differ. The central difference between their views is that for Leibniz bodies are the *appearance* of something substantial albeit unextended, whereas for Berkeley what we perceive by sense are not "appearances" at all, but simply ideas that God causes in our minds. This difference is examined in detail as are some other notable differences between their conceptions of body. The paper concludes that Leibniz's notion of body allows for a more satisfactory account of the nature of non-human organisms than Berkeley's ontology can offer.

Introduction

Late in his life, the elderly G. W. Leibniz read the young George Berkeley's recently published *Principles of Human Knowledge*. On the last page of his copy of that work, Leibniz wrote this comment:

> Much in this is right and agrees with my way of thinking. But it is paradoxically expressed. We need not say that matter is nothing, but it suffices that we say it is a phenomenon, like the rainbow – not a substance, but what results from substances, and that space is no more real than time, space being nothing other than the order of coexisting things [*ordinem coexistentiarum*], as time is the order of successively existing things [*ordinem subexistentiarum*]. True substances are monads or perceivers. But the author should have pressed on, to an infinity of monads from which all things are constituted, and to their pre-established harmony. He wrongly, or at least needlessly, rejects abstract ideas,

> restricts ideas to images, and scorns the subtleties of arithmetic and geometry. Worst of all, he rejects the division of extension to infinity, even if he might rightly reject infinitesimal quantities.[1]

The focus of this paper will be Leibniz's account of body and matter, and where his views and Berkeley's about these topics agree and where they differ.[2] Several things make giving an account of Leibniz's opinions about body and matter difficult. One is that Leibniz's opinions about these topics changed over the many years during which he wrote out his views. A second is that Leibniz would on occasion accommodate his use of terms to the usage of others, and that is sometimes true of "body" and "matter." Thus in his correspondence with Antoine Arnauld he sometimes uses "body" in the sense it had for a Cartesian, and in his *New Essays on Human Understanding* he sometimes accommodates his use of the term to how John Locke used it. And third, in some places – above all in his correspondence with the Jesuit Bartholomew Des Bosses – Leibniz deliberately introduced modifications into his account of corporeal substance because he wanted to show how a modified version of his theory could accommodate the dogma of transubstantiation. It isn't surprising, hence, that Leibniz scholars have not always agreed on how to interpret his doctrine of body.[3] I shall here make no attempt to set out the possible changes that Leibniz's views about body and matter underwent, nor shall I look at how others have interpreted his theory of body. Instead, I limit myself to setting out what I take to be his mature doctrine of body and matter, and to comparing it with Berkeley's.

Leibniz on "Matter"

Although Leibniz says that much in Berkeley's *Principles* is right, he cautions that we need not deny that matter exists, but say only that matter is a phenomenon, analogous to the rainbow – "not a substance, but what results from substances." Now here, as we can see from his analogy with the rainbow, Leibniz is using *phenomenon*, as he often did, to refer to how something appears to perceivers – without perceivers there would be no *phenomena*, in this sense of the term. And this might suggest that the

---

[1] In McCracken and Tipton 2000, 191-192.

[2] For other discussions of Leibniz and Berkeley, see Kabitz 1932; MacIntosh 1970-1971; Robinet 1983; Wilson 1987; and Adams 1994, 224-228.

[3] For differing accounts of that doctrine, see Furth 1972; Broad 1975, 88-92; Loeb 1981, chap. 7; Garber 1985; Jolley 1986; Hartz 1992; Adams 1994, pt. iii; Rutherford 1994, 65-90; Rutherford 1995, chap. 10; and Rutherford 2008.

distance between Leibniz and Berkeley is less than Leibniz thought, for certainly Berkeley did not deny the existence of bodies, if by "bodies" we understand the things we perceive by our senses. In his notebooks, Berkeley wrote, "I am certain of that which Malbranch seems to doubt of. viz the existence of Bodies." (NB 686a) And in the *Principles*, he stressed that he believed in the *rerum natura*: "That the things I see with mine eyes and touch with my hands do exist, really exist, I make not the least question." (P 34-37) He did not deny their existence, but instead insisted that their existence depends on their being perceived, something Leibniz himself held to be true of the extended, figured, moving objects we perceive by sense.

Did Leibniz then overlook Berkeley's own insistence that bodies – understood as phenomena that present themselves to perceivers – exist? Did he not notice that Berkeley was willing even to grant the existence of "corporeal substance," provided that term was rightly construed? (P 37) I don't think so. There are important differences here between the two thinkers.[4] For Leibniz, extended things (the bodies finite perceivers actually perceive) are the appearance of something substantial, the appearance of corporeal substances, whereas Berkeley was intent on denying that there is anything "behind" the "ideas" we perceive, anything that they are the "appearances" of.

So, we may note, at the outset, this important difference between the two thinkers: for Berkeley "ideas" are not representatives of something different from ideas – something that is not an "idea" (though he grants that an idea is sometimes the sign of another *idea*, e.g., the red poker I see is a sign of the heat I will feel if I put my hand near it). But for Leibniz the extended things we perceive by our senses are how corporeal substances appear to finite perceivers. Those corporeal substances are not themselves extended, yet to perceivers like us they appear to be extended. So we must look at Leibniz's doctrine of corporeal substances; and to understand that doctrine, we must begin by looking at his doctrine of simple substances (or monads, as he came, in his later period, to call them), for simple substances are what corporeal (that is, composite) substances are composed of. In doing so, we will come on two important notions of matter that Leibniz employs: the "primary matter" of monads, and the "secondary matter" or "body" of corporeal substances. This will let us see some ways in which Leibniz's doctrine (though not his vocabulary) agrees with Berkeley's – allowing Leibniz to say that much in Berkeley's *Principles*

[4] Leibniz's letters to de Volder are helpful for the light they cast on Leibniz's subsequent remarks on Berkeley. See especially his letter of 30 June 1704, in Leibniz 1989, 178-181.

"is right and agrees with my way of thinking," while we will see other ways in which his doctrine differs markedly from Berkeley's.

Leibniz on "Simple Substances"

For Leibniz, the basic existents must be simple, indivisible substances, for what is composite is divisible into its constituents, but that division cannot go on to infinity: it must terminate in things that are indivisible. That is why, according to Leibniz, there cannot be *extended* substances, for what is extended always admits of further division, *ad infinitum*, and hence can never have the true unity that must characterize substances.[5] So extended things must be phenomena, or how things appear to perceivers, and Descartes erred in believing extension a substance. This is one reason Leibniz had for saying that Berkeley's greatest error was to deny the infinite divisibility of extension: for infinite divisibility is precisely what proves that matter, taken in the usual sense of something extended, cannot be a substance.[6]

But what kind of thing is simple and indivisible – that is, what kind of thing can be a substance? Leibniz (like Descartes before him, and Berkeley after[7]) held that in the reflective experience we have of our own minds, we discover something indivisible. The mind itself, thus, provides the model of simple substances: they are either minds or things like minds, in the sense that they are perceivers.[8] "There is nothing in things," Leibniz wrote in an oft-quoted passage from a letter to Burcher de Volder, "but simple substances, and in them, perception and appetite."[9]

Although monads are indivisible substances, every monad is a center of force, according to Leibniz, and in every finite monad its "primitive active force" can be distinguished from its "primitive passive force" (God being the only substance in which there is nothing passive). These are not *parts* of the monad – what is simple is *a fortiori* without parts; but the

---

[5] Leibniz 1969, 454.

[6] Berkeley denied both infinite divisibility of extension and infinitesimal quantities (P 123-132). While Leibniz thought the denial of infinite divisibility a cardinal sin, he granted that Berkeley might "rightly reject infinitesimal quantities," and indeed Leibniz himself later said "I consider infinitesimal quantities to be useful fictions." Leibniz 1989, 230.

[7] Descartes, *Meditations* VI and Berkeley P 146.

[8] Leibniz 1969, 454.

[9] Leibniz 1989, 181. Leibniz uses "minds" for beings that *reason*; hence not all simple substances are minds, in his strict sense, but they are all "mind-like," for they are all perceivers.

mind can (by "abstraction") distinguish one of these forces from the other. Leibniz calls the primitive active force the "primitive entelechy" or "substantial form" of the monad, the primitive passive force its "primary matter."[10] He chooses these terms because he is seeking to rehabilitate, and at the same time radically modify, the Aristotelian concept of a substance as something having form and matter. (The fact that in his time matter was regularly held to be passive would have given him added reason to use *matter* as the name for what is passive in a substance.) How distant his notion of substance is, however, from the Aristotelian-Scholastic notion is shown when he analyzes these forces as *kinds of perception*: "We attribute *action* to a monad insofar as it has distinct perceptions, and *passion*, insofar as it has confused perceptions."[11]

Berkeley would certainly have been unhappy here with the Scholastic jargon of "substantial form" and "prime matter" (cf. P 11), but he would not disagree with the notion that we can distinguish something active and something passive in finite perceivers. Thus, in the *Three Dialogues* he has Philonous tell Hylas that the mind "is to be accounted active in its perceptions, so far forth as volition is included in them," as for example when I pick a flower, put it to my nose, and inhale; but when I then experience a certain smell, "this is independent of my will, and therein I am altogether passive."[12] So Berkeley would not have objected to Leibniz's claim that there is passivity in monads – that is, in perceiving substances – but only to his use of "primary matter" as the name for it.

Leibniz on "Corporeal Substances"

Although all that exists, for Leibniz, is finally reducible to monads or *simple* substances, with their perceptions and appetitions (where by "appetition" or "appetite" Leibniz means an internal principle in a perceiver that brings about the transition from one perception to the next),[13] monads enter into combinations from which result *composite* substances (or, as Leibniz usually calls them, "corporeal substances") that

---

[10] Leibniz 1989, 176-177. In this letter to de Volder, Leibniz gives an especially clear delineation of the chief components of his ontology – the simple substance or monad, made up of primitive entelechy and primary matter, and the composite or corporeal substance, with a dominant monad as its soul and secondary matter as its body.

[11] Leibniz 1714a, sec. 49; Leibniz 1981, 210.

[12] 3D, 196. "That the soul of man is passive as well as active, I make no doubt," he later wrote to Samuel Johnson of Connecticut (Berkeley, *Works*, vol. 2, 293).

[13] Leibniz 1714a, sec. 15; and Leibniz 1989, 181.

appear to us as extended things. In conceiving these composite substances, Leibniz again makes use of the Aristotelian-Scholastic notion of substance, distinguishing in the composite its "substantial form" or "soul" from its "secondary matter" or "body" (though here again Leibniz's notion of substance is markedly different from Aristotle's). All of the constituents of a composite or corporeal substance are monads: the *body* or *secondary matter* of that composite is an aggregation of (infinitely many) monads that are united because "dominated" by a single monad, while that "dominant" monad is the composite substance's *soul* or *substantial form.*[14]

The aggregation of monads that constitutes the secondary matter or body of a corporeal substance has no intrinsic unity when considered apart from that corporeal substance. When so considered, secondary matter is merely an accidental collection of monads (an aggregation *per accidens*), and such unity as it may appear to have belongs only to the phenomenal realm and is a result of perceivers' adopting (often unconsciously) a convention of viewing it as "one thing," in the way that we may look on a pile of rocks or a flock of sheep as "one pile" or "one flock." "For, in a word, body does not have true unity; it is only an *aggregate*, what the schools call one *per accidens*, an assemblage like a flock; its unity arises from our perception. It is a *being of reason*, or rather, of *imagination, a phenomenon*."[15] Of course, each of the monads in that aggregation has unity, but there is nothing that can provide unity to the aggregate itself when it is considered apart from its "soul" or "substantial form" – that is, from the dominant monad that provides unity as such (unity *per se*) to the corporeal substance.[16] (Some phenomena are, for Leibniz, appearances of *merely* accidental aggregations of monads that have no substantial form.[17] That seems to be his view of most of the inanimate objects we perceive, in contrast to plants, animals, and human beings, which are how genuine corporeal substances appear to us.)

Now it is important to grasp that the aggregation of monads in the corporeal substance is not a *spatial* arrangement: the aggregated monads do not occupy space and so are not joined together by being spatially contiguous with or spatially related to one another.[18] The monads in the aggregate are real and indivisible unities, whereas space is a continuum, an "ideal" thing (that is, a mental thing) that cannot be composed of irreducible unities. Thus Leibniz told de Volder that "in real things,

[14] Leibniz 1989, 167.
[15] Leibniz 1989, 263, see also 167 and 227, and Leibniz 1969, 456, sec. 11.
[16] Leibniz 1989, 147, 175, 289-290.
[17] Leibniz 1969, 365.
[18] Leibniz 1989, 199.

namely, in bodies, the parts [i.e., the monads] are not indefinite (as they are in space, a mental thing)."[19] Instead, spatial arrangement is the order in which simultaneous aggregations of monads (and indeed aggregations of corporeal substances) appear to perceivers. And for the same reason, corporeal substances are not extended things, for that would imply that they occupy space; nor do they have the various properties that modify extended things (size, shape, mobility, and so forth). Extension, figure, and motion are again ways that corporeal substances *appear* to perceivers.[20] Thus, "properly speaking, matter isn't composed of constitutive unities [monads] but results from them, since matter, that is, extended mass [*massa*] is only a phenomenon grounded in things, like a rainbow or a parhelion, and all reality belongs only to unities."[21] Hence, whether we use *matter* as the Cartesians did, for what is extended, or as Leibniz did when speaking of the *secondary matter* of corporeal substances, matter is, as he insisted in his comments on Berkeley, not nothing: It is either the appearance of being extended that corporeal substances make to perceivers or the secondary matter that constitutes the bodies of those substances.

But how, in the corporeal substance, does the "dominant monad" or soul give unity to that aggregation of "dominated" monads that is its body? In Leibniz's answer to this question, there can be no question of real relations holding among the monads of the composite, for Leibniz's monads are famously "windowless" – that is, none of their properties are the result of an external influence exerted on them by other monads (except for the influence that God, as their creator, has on all monads); thus there is no real bond uniting the monads.[22] (It is true that Leibniz introduced a real "substantial bond" [*vinculum substantiale*] in his letters to Des Bosses, but I think the view held by a number of Leibniz scholars is right: Leibniz was there trying to show a way in which his ontology could be modified to make it acceptable to a believer in the Roman Catholic doctrine of transubstantiation, without himself embracing that modification; as a Lutheran, Leibniz did not believe in transubstantiation, so had no personal reason to accommodate it in his system.[23]) But if there are no real causal relations among the monads that form a composite substance, how can the monad that is the "soul" of that composite

[19] Leibniz 1989, 178.

[20] Leibniz 1989, 184-185, note 239; 203.

[21] Leibniz 1989, 179.

[22] Leibniz 1989, 147-149.

[23] In January 1710, Leibniz wrote to Des Bosses that a substantial bond was not needed by "those of us who reject transubstantiation." Leibniz 1875-1890, v. 2, 399.

"dominate" the monads that form its "body"? Leibniz's answer is given wholly in terms of perception, which is unsurprising, since there is nothing in composite substances but monads, and nothing in monads but perceptions and appetitions. In particular, although every finite monad perceives – albeit confusedly – all other monads that exist, the dominant monad in a corporeal substance perceives the monads that form its own body more distinctly than it perceives all other monads, and indeed it "represents the whole universe by representing this body, which belongs to it in a particular way."[24]

Now the perceptions of each monad in the composite at a given time are correlated in a harmonious way, pre-established by God, with the perceptions of that monad at other times, and with the perceptions of other monads; it is in this harmonious correlation of the monads' perceptions that the phenomenal world of matter and motion finds its foundation. "Matter and motion are not substances or things as much as they are the phenomena of perceivers, the reality of which is situated in the harmony of the perceivers with themselves (at different times) and with other perceivers."[25] Here again, of course, the perceptions of the monads are not the result of any real causal interaction among monads, but are perceptions that God, in creating each monad, has programmed, as it were, into that monad; and it is the appetitions in each monad that call those perceptions forth in an order (the "law of the series") that God has determined in creating the monads and that assures the harmony of the perceptions of all monads.[26]

It is this harmonious congruence of the perceptions of all the dominated monads composing the body of a corporeal substance that allows the dominant monad to give unity to that substance – indeed, what that unity consists in is the dominant monad's distinct perception of the harmonious congruence of the dominated monads' perceptions.[27] Thus a Leibnizian corporeal substance depends necessarily on perception in a twofold way: (1) each member of the aggregate that composes the body of a corporeal substance is a perceiver and has perceptions that are harmoniously correlated with those of the other members of the aggregate; and (2) the unity of the corporeal substance results from the dominant monad's distinct perception of the monads it dominates. Of course the *existence* of the dominated monads does not depend on those monads being perceived by the dominant monad, but the *unity* of the corporeal substance that they

[24] Leibniz 1714a, sec. 62. See also Leibniz 1686, sec. 33.
[25] Leibniz 1989, 181.
[26] Leibniz 1686, sec. 28.
[27] Leibniz 1989, 289.

form the body of does depend on the dominant monad's distinct perception of the monads it dominates; and without that unity, there would be no corporeal substance. You will perhaps see why I said that Leibniz's notion of substance (whether simple or composite) is very different from the Aristotelians' notion of substance, even though he keeps their form/matter vocabulary.

Leibniz's and Berkeley's Notions of Substance Compared

We can now see both where Leibniz and Berkeley agree, in their notions of substance, and where they differ. On the one hand, for Leibniz, as for Berkeley, all simple substances are perceivers capable of action (according to Berkeley, "there is not any other substance than *spirit*, or that which perceives" and "a spirit is one, simple, undivided, active being").[28] On the other hand, there is nothing in Berkeley's ontology analogous to Leibniz's corporeal substances. Further, where for Berkeley the "ideas" our senses perceive are not representatives of something not an idea, for Leibniz the extended world our senses perceive is the way corporeal substances appear to us. But while Leibniz's notion of phenomena thus differs from Berkeley's, it also differs radically from that of thinkers like Hobbes, Gassendi, or Locke, since for Leibniz, the phenomena we perceive are not the appearances of *extended* substances having size, shape, and motion, but of unextended composite things made up of simple, perceiving substances.

For both Leibniz and Berkeley, God plays an indispensable role in this story, and here again we find both points of agreement and of difference. In places, Leibniz can sound closer to Berkeley than, I think, he was (at least in his mature period). For example, in an early text (1672), Leibniz wrote, "I seem to myself to have discovered that to Exist is nothing other than to be Sensed [*Sentiri*] – to be sensed, however, if not by us, then at least by the Author of things, to be sensed by whom is nothing other than to please him, or to be Harmonious."[29] But certainly Leibniz didn't think that the existence of monads *consists in* being sensed by God, although their existence does *depend on* God (for Berkeley, too, of course, the existence of spirits does not consist in being perceived by God or anyone, for their *esse* is not *percipi* but *percipere*). And on the other hand there are a few places where Leibniz sounds further from Berkeley than I think he

[28] P 7 and 27.

[29] Quoted in Adams 1994, 169, from Leibniz, *Sämtliche Schriften und Briefe* (Damstadt and Berlin: Berlin Academy, 1921-1923), series VI, vol. 3, 56.

was, for example in this late but unrepresentative passage from a draft of a letter to Des Bosses:

> The reality of bodies, of space, of motion, and of time seems to consist in the fact that they are phenomena of God, that is, the object of his knowledge by intuition [*scientia visionis*]. And the distinction between the appearance bodies have with respect to us and with respect to God is, in a certain way, like that between a drawing in perspective and a ground plan. For there are different drawings in perspective, depending upon the position of the viewer, while a ground plan or geometrical representation is unique. Indeed, God sees things exactly as they are in accordance with geometrical truth, although he also knows how everything appears to everything else, and so he eminently contains in himself all other appearances.[30]

Now the claim made here that God "knows how everything appears to everything else" undoubtedly does express a genuine Leibnizian doctrine, for God is the cause of the pre-established harmony among the perceptions of all monads and so must know how everything appears to them. In that sense it may be said that "he eminently contains in himself all other appearances." But since, at bottom, simple substances, with their perceptions and appetitions, are all that exist, there isn't anything else for God to know about the bodies in the *actual* world (he does of course also know all possible worlds) except how they appear to monads. That is, all there is for him to know (of those bodies that are actual) *is* "how everything appears to everything else." The suggestion that there is something *else* known by God – the unique "geometrical representation" of how bodies really are – seems inconsistent with Leibniz's central doctrine that nothing really exists apart from monads, with their perceptions and appetitions (unless by a unique "geometrical representation" of bodies we are to suppose that Leibniz merely means that, because God knows how things appear to *all* monads, he has knowledge of bodies that is complete in a way that no other being's knowledge of them is). But I do not think we need view this passage as expressing Leibniz's considered view – we've seen that there is reason to think that in his correspondence with Des Bosses Leibniz is not always expressing views he actually held, and in any case he omitted this passage from the letter as he sent it to Des Bosses.

A central point of agreement between Leibniz and Berkeley about God's relation to perceivers is that God must know what all perceivers perceive by the senses, for he is the cause of those perceptions. But here, too, there are notable differences. For one thing, Berkeley thinks that God

---

[30] Notes for Leibniz's letter of 5 February 1712 to Des Bosses, Leibniz 1989, 199.

is the immediate cause of our sensations; for Leibniz, God causes them because he has, in creating monads, programmed into them all the perceptions they will ever have. And for another, Leibniz holds that finite monads, taken collectively, perceive the whole monadic universe from every possible perspective it can be perceived from (this follows from his principle of plenitude), though no two monads ever perceive it from the same perspective (from his principle of the identity of indiscernibles).[31] Thus, for each possible point of view, there is some finite monad or other that actually perceives the universe from that point of view. Berkeley, on the other hand, although presumably believing that God knows how things *would* appear if they *were to be* perceived from any possible perspective (cf. *Principles* 3 and 58), never suggests that there are actual finite perceivers who perceive the world from every possible point of view.

Two further differences between Leibniz and Berkeley

When we consider the similarities and differences between the two men's views, it is unsurprising that Leibniz found himself in agreement with Berkeley that the only true substances are perceivers and that nothing would exist if there were no perceivers, yet could urge that Berkeley should progress beyond his denial of matter to the discovery of "an infinity of monads from which all things are constituted, and to their pre-established harmony." Such "progress" would, of course, have required many changes in Berkeley's views. I will note two of them.

First, he would have had to abandon his belief that perceivers themselves cannot be perceived. What we perceive, he says, are ideas; but ideas are "passive and inert," so cannot represent spirits (perceivers), which are active beings. "Such is the nature of *spirit*," he concludes, "that it cannot be of itself perceived." (P 27) When Leibniz objected that Berkeley "restricts ideas to images," one thing he may have had in mind was this denial that we have an idea or perception of spirit. For Leibniz, precisely what monads (perceivers) perceive, albeit confusedly, is the totality of other monads, although he never, I think, explained this claim as clearly as one might like, beyond saying that the perceptions of all perceivers are in harmony with each other and that each monad is a microcosm – a mirror, from its unique perspective, of the whole monadic universe (that is, the whole of reality).[32]

The other important change Berkeley would have to accept involves

---

[31] Leibniz 1686, secs. 9 and 14.

[32] Leibniz 1989, 177 and Leibniz 1714b, sec. 3.

the Leibnizian doctrine that there are perceptions so "minute" that one can have them and yet not be aware of having them. The notion of unconscious perception enters into Leibniz's monadology in the following way. Because he held that monads perceive the universe from every possible point of view, he concluded that there is an infinity of monads, which vary infinitely in how distinct or how confused their perceptions are – a variation that ranges from God's perfectly distinct perception of everything to the utterly confused, minute perceptions of monads that never have "apperception" or conscious knowledge of their perceptions.[33] By contrast, Berkeley thinks that what we perceive, we know perfectly – nothing in our perceptions can be hidden from us. "Colour, figure, motion, extension and the like, considered only as so many *sensations* in the mind, are perfectly known, there being nothing in them which is not perceived." (P 87) He would, therefore, reject the notion that we might perceive ideas and yet not know we are perceiving them. Leibniz would presumably reply that experience itself shows us that even we human beings, who have apperception, often have perceptions we are unaware of; thus those who live always beside a river may not notice the sound of the river flowing, though they are perceiving it, for were it suddenly to stop flowing, they might at once become aware of a difference in what they are perceiving.

This is a central difference in the two men's accounts of perception, a difference so great that it led the late Margaret Wilson to argue that those (including Leibniz himself) are mistaken who think that Leibniz and Berkeley agree, at least, in the belief that all true substances are perceivers. That agreement, according to Wilson, is only verbal, not real, for what Leibniz means by "perception" is "*utterly* different from what Berkeley means by 'perception'."[34] Hence when Leibniz says (as he does in his remarks about Berkeley) that true substances are perceivers, his meaning is completely different from what Berkeley means when he seems to say the same thing.

But that, I think, exaggerates the distance between the two thinkers. Even those, like Berkeley, who deny that there are perceptions the perceiver is unaware of can *understand* the claim that there are (though I grant that Berkeley himself might deny this) – can understand, say, what Leibniz means when he maintains that those who live beside a river can perceive the sound of it flowing (for they would notice a difference if it stopped), yet not be aware that they are perceiving it. Indeed, it is an empirical claim that images can be flashed so briefly on people's visual

[33] Leibniz 1714a, secs. 14 and 19-25.

[34] Wilson 1987, 7 (emphasis Wilson's).

fields that they are unaware of them and yet give evidence in their subsequent behavior that they have perceived them. There are ways that that claim might be tested, for example by comparing the frequency with which two groups of people buy a certain thing, where those in first group have had images of that thing flashed on their visual fields, and those in the second group have not. Whether such unconscious perceptions occur or not, I think we can understand the claim made by those who think they do occur. And that suggests that "perception" is not being used in an "utterly different" sense by those, like Berkeley, who hold that all perceptions are conscious and by those, like Leibniz, who think that some are not.

Margaret Wilson herself granted that there might be subliminal or unconscious perceptions but argued that we can make sense of them because they have "a role in a readily identified mental life, and [are] continuous with related conscious experiences."[35] But I think examples of putative unconscious perceptions provide a model that makes it at least intelligible to talk about the *possibility* of perceivers who may never be aware of their perceptions, at least in the sense that they are never able to reflect on the fact that they are now having such and such perceptions. For all I know, such perceptions as clams have may be exactly like that.

What Berkeley might have said to Leibniz

We are left to conjecture what Berkeley would say if asked to respond to Leibniz's theory of corporeal substance and the secondary matter that constitutes its body. I think we can get some notion of how he might respond by looking at what he actually did say about the conception of matter found in Nicolas Malebranche and the Occasionalists. For the Occasionalists, matter – that is, extension – is something known by God, who produces all the effects that extended substances ever undergo. Or, as Berkeley put it, "matter" in this sense is something "perceived by God, to whom it is the occasion of exciting ideas in our minds. ... That is to say, that there are certain permanent and distinct parcels of matter, corresponding to our ideas, which, though they do not excite them in our minds, or any ways immediately affect us ... are nevertheless to God, by whom they are perceived, as it were so many occasions to remind him when and what ideas to imprint on our minds."[36]

---

[35] Wilson 1987, 9.

[36] P 70. The story is actually more complex than how Berkeley here represents it, for according to Malebranche God does not, to speak strictly, actually perceive extended substances; rather he perceives "infinite intelligible extension," which is his archetypal idea of physical extension, and thereby he knows physical

About the Occasionalist notion of matter, Berkeley said two things. First, it is not a notion of matter that contradicts his central thesis that all that exists are spirits (that is, perceivers) and their ideas (that is, things perceived), since the "matter" of the Occasionalists is always being perceived by God, directing him to produce such and such effects, "much after the same manner as a musician is directed by the notes of music to produce that harmonious train and composition of sound, which is called a *tune*." So conceived, "it is in effect no objection against what we have advanced, to wit, that there is no senseless, unperceived substance," for *matter*, so conceived, is always being perceived by God. The second thing Berkeley says is that "this notion of matter seems too extravagant to deserve a confutation." (P 71)

I think Berkeley might well have said something similar about Leibniz's notion of "secondary matter" and the "corporeal substance" it is the "body" of. For to assert that "matter" or "body," so conceived, exists is not to assert something contrary to Berkeley's claim that the only things that exist are spirits (that is, perceivers) and ideas (that is, their perceptions). For, as we've seen, secondary matter consists of an aggregation of monads, *all* of which are perceivers; and such unity as that aggregation has is the result of its being perceived by the "soul" or dominant monad of a corporeal substance. So Berkeley might well say of Leibnizian matter that "it is in effect no objection against what we have advanced, to wit, that there is no senseless, unperceived substance."

We can only guess whether Berkeley would further say of Leibniz's corporeal substance and its secondary matter what he said of Malebranchean matter: "This notion of matter seems too extravagant to deserve a confutation." But I think it not hard to imagine that he might have said that. After all, Leibniz held that "there is nothing in the world except simple substances and, in them, perception and appetite." Why then should he proceed to conjure a world of composite or corporeal substances?--why do we need anything more than the world of simple, perceiving substances and their perceptions?

Were Berkeley to ask those questions, Leibniz would no doubt have replied that there must be a sufficient reason for everything that is the case, and that nothing is completely arbitrary.[37] So, there must be a sufficient reason for the appearances things present to us – they are not just ideas that God arbitrarily gives rise to in us, making eggs look oval instead of round and oranges round instead of oval. That things appear to us as

extension.

[37] 1714a, secs. 32 and 54.

extended and as having size, shape, motion, and so on, must find its sufficient reason in how things really are; and since the only ultimately real things are simple perceiving substances, the ground of the phenomena we perceive must be found in the kinds of perceptions monads have. In particular, it is the harmonious ordering of aggregations of perceiving monads that appear to us as extended things that have size, shape, motion, and place.

If Berkeley were to demand *why* these aggregations of simple substances should thus appear to us as extended things, Leibniz's answer seems to be that it is most consonant with God's wisdom that he create a universe with the greatest possible variety of things, obeying the simplest set of laws, which will be a universe that is perceived from every possible point of view. And that will require an infinity of perceivers whose perceptions range over an infinite series of degrees, from monads (perhaps angelic beings) whose perceptions most closely approach God's perfectly distinct perception of things down to monads whose perceptions are so minute and confused that those monads are never conscious of the perceptions they are now having nor do they remember those they have previously had.[38] The perceptions of finite monads always involve some degree of confusion and indistinctness, and when those confused, indistinct perceptions represent an aggregate of monads with similar perceptions, that aggregate will appear as some continuous, extended thing.[39] Thus extension is not an attribute of substance (as Spinoza thought), but instead "only a repetition of perceivings."[40] I think we can be pretty confident that Berkeley would not have found this a satisfactory reply to his question.

The "Idealisms" of Leibniz and Berkeley

At the end of the day, both Leibniz and Berkeley are idealists, if by that we mean those who believe that the only substances are minds or mind-like things – things that think or perceive – and that the extended, sensible world exists only because it is perceived by those minds or perceivers. Yet there is, in ways I've tried to indicate, a great difference between their idealisms. There is a further difference that I'll note in conclusion. Leibniz's world is composed not just of perceivers, but of living beings – that is, of organisms. For he holds that *every* monad, save only God,

[38] Leibniz 1686, sec. 35 and Leibniz 1714a, sec. 60.
[39] Leibniz 1989, 203.
[40] Leibniz 1989, 276; cf. Leibniz 1714a, sec, 60 and Leibniz 1714b, sec. 13.

always has a body – that is, an aggregation of other monads to which that monad is related as the soul or substantial form that unifies that aggregation. Since Leibniz believed in an infinity of monads, each monad in an aggregate dominated by a dominant monad can be, in its turn, the dominant monad of another aggregate, with each of the dominated members of *that* aggregate being in turn the dominant monad of yet other aggregates, and so on, *ad infinitum.*[41] Now a living thing or organism is simply the union of a soul (a dominant monad) and a body (an aggregation of dominated monads): so the whole universe is full of organisms, some of which appear to us as the living things – the plants and animals – that we perceive about us.[42]

This allows Leibniz to give an answer to a question that Berkeley seems to have avoided answering: What is the ontological status of non-human animals? For Berkeley, it seems, there are only two possible answers to that question: Either animals are perceivers or they are only collections of ideas – Berkeley, after all, has no other categories in his ontology. But neither answer may have been one Berkeley was eager to embrace. If animals are themselves perceivers, then they, like us, are spirits; for only spirits perceive. And if spirits, then they are immortal, according to *Principles* 137-141, a consequence the theologically-conservative Berkeley was probably disinclined to grant. (Samuel Johnson of Connecticut expressly asked Berkeley whether he thought animals were perceivers; and if he thought they were, how – given his argument for immortality – he could avoid concluding that animals too are immortal. Significantly, although Berkeley's letter of reply answered other questions Johnson had asked, it passed in silence over this question.[43])

On the other hand, if animals are only collections of ideas, then they don't really sense, feel, or perceive, which would amount to a view of animals as far removed from common sense as was Descartes' belief that animals are automata – something that Berkeley, always eager to show himself a friend of common sense, would probably not have welcomed. Leibniz here, I think, has a distinct advantage over Berkeley, for he has a definite answer to questions about the ontological status of the organisms we meet in the world: they are the appearances of composite substances that consist of a body and a soul – even if "body" and "soul," as here used, have a highly idiosyncratic meaning.

[41] Leibniz 1989, 168, and Leibniz 1714a, sec. 70.

[42] Leibniz 1714a, secs. 63 and 66.

[43] See Johnson's letter of Feb. 5, 1730, and Berkeley's reply of March 24, 1730, in Berkeley, *Works*, vol. 2, 284ff.

Bibliography

Adams, R. M. (1994), *Leibniz: Determinist, Theist, Idealist,* Oxford University Press, Oxford.

Berkeley, George. (1948-1957), *The Works of George Berkeley*, 9 vols, A. A. Luce and T. E. Jessop (eds), Nelson, London.

Broad, C. D. (1975), *Leibniz: An Introduction*, C. Lewy (ed.), Cambridge University Press, Cambridge.

Descartes, René. (1641), *Meditations on First Philosophy.*

Furth, M. (1972), "Monadology," in *Leibniz: A Collection of Critical Essays*, H. G. Frankfurt (ed.), Doubleday Anchor, Garden City.

Garber, D. (1985), "Leibniz and the Foundations of Physics," in *The Natural Philosophy of Leibniz*, K. Okruhlik and J. R. Brown (eds), Reidel, Dordrecht.

Hartz, G. A. (1992), "Leibniz's Phenomenalisms," *Philosophical Review* 101, pp. 511-549.

Jolley, N. (1986), "Leibniz and Phenomenalism," *Studia Leibnitiana* 18, pp. 38-51.

Kabitz, W. (1932), "Leibniz und Berkeley," *Sitzungsberichte der preußischen Akademie der Wissenschaften.* Philosophisch-historische Klasse 24, pp. 623-636.

Leibniz, G. W. (1686), *Discourse on Metaphysics.*

—. (1695), *A New System of Nature.*

—. (1714a), *Monadology.*

—. (1714b), *Principles of Nature and Grace.*

—. (1875-1890), *Die philosophischen Schriften von Gottfried Wilhelm Leibniz*, 7 vols, C. I. Gerhardt (ed.), Weidman, Berlin.

—. (1969), *Gottfried Wilhelm Leibniz: Philosophical Papers and Letters*, L. E. Loemker (ed.), Reidel, Dordrecht.

—. (1981), *New Essays on Human Understanding*, P. Remnant and J. Bennett (trs), Cambridge University Press, Cambridge.

—. (1989), *G. W. Leibniz: Philosophical Essays*, R. Ariew and D. Garber (eds), Hackett, Indianapolis.

Loeb, L. E. (1981), *From Descartes to Hume*, Cornell University Press, Ithaca.

MacIntosh, J. J. (1971), "Leibniz and Berkeley," *Proceedings of the Aristotelian Society* 71, pp. 147-163.

McCracken, C. J. and I. Tipton (eds.) (2000), *Berkeley's Principles and Dialogues: Background Source Materials*, Cambridge University Press, Cambridge.

Robinet, A. (1983), "Leibniz: Lecture du *Treatise* de Berkeley," *Les*

Etudes Philosophiques no 2, pp. 217-223.
Rutherford, D. (1994), "Leibniz and the Problem of Monadic Aggregation," *Archiv fűr Geschichte der Philosophie* 76, pp. 65-90.
—. (1995), *Leibniz and the Rational Order of Nature*, Cambridge University Press, Cambridge.
—. (2008), "Leibniz as Idealist," *Oxford Studies in Early Modern Philosophy* 4, pp. 141-190.
Sosa, E. (1987), *Essays on the Philosophy of George Berkeley*, Reidel, Dordrecht.
Wilson, M. D. (1987), "The Phenomenalisms of Leibniz and Berkeley," in Sosa (1987), p. 3-22.

PART FOUR:

BERKELEY'S METAPHYSICS

SHORT-SIGHTEDNESS AND LONG-SIGHTEDNESS IN BERKELEY

GENEVIÈVE BRYKMAN

Abstract

Berkeley mainly uses the terms "short-sightedness" and "long-sightedness" in a figurative sense: "short-sightedness" for a minute inspection of particular things, and "long-sightedness" for a divine perspective on the universe that is only partly available to human understanding. This distinction reflects the revolutionary use of optical instruments at that time. Galileo's telescope made it possible to take a large view on reality, allowing a rational explanation of planetary motions, and microscopes opened a new possibility of a minute examination of tiny objects. In 1707, George Berkeley applied an analytic approach to a minute examination of words and ideas. In his *Notebooks*, he sometimes calls himself "naturally short-sighted," a "defect" that made him able to look more closely at words and things than other people. My aim is to show how the tension between short-sightedness and long-sightedness underlies Berkeley's writings. Being present in his immaterialism as well as in his moral philosophy, it even produces a clash between Berkeley's own "freethinking" and his apologetic concern.

Distance not Immediately Perceived by Sight

In the *Theory of Vision*, Berkeley does not develop a "long-sighted" perspective. Instead he uses an analytic method to examine our ideas very closely. In this book he develops a strictly scientific approach to vision,[1] sharply distinguishing between descriptive and metaphorical usage, particularly when we speak of mind and its ideas.[2] At the outset, he announces the three topics he will consider with regard to vision:

---

[1] See Belfrage 1992 and Belfrage 2003.
[2] TV 49-51; 94; 111-112.

> My design [he says] is to show the manner wherein we perceive by sight the distance, magnitude, and situation of objects. Also to consider the difference there is betwixt the ideas of sight and touch, and whether there be any idea common to both senses. (TV 1)

As early as section 2, Berkeley states that: "it is agreed by all that distance of itself and immediately, cannot be seen." In section 3, about estimating the distance of remote objects, he mentions the opinion that an act of judgment is required when we perceive remote objects by sight; and this judgment is grounded on experience rather than on sense: (1) if I perceive a great number of intermediate objects, which experience has taught me take up a considerable space, I judge from that that the object I see beyond them is at a great distance; (2) if an object appears faint and small that I have often seen as "vigorous and large" when it was closer, I judge it to be of some considerable distance from me. Without these two means, we "should not have inferred anything concerning the distance of objects" (TV 3). Thus, our perception of remote objects by sight seems to be based on a long-lasting experience.

Our perception of objects placed at a *near distance* is more problematic. Here, Berkeley mentions "the speculative men" ("Descartes and some others"), according to whom there is a "remarkable difference" between the perception of *remote* objects and that of *near* objects by sight (TV 5). In the first case, everybody admits that distance is only mediately perceived; in the second case, the "optic writers" argue that we perceive distance by a *necessary connexion* between a small distance and a "vigorous and large" appearance, and that we can know this connexion without earlier experience, but Berkeley argues that visual perception cannot be explained by "geometrical optics":

> Those lines and angles [...], are themselves not at all perceived, nor are they in truth ever thought of by those unskilful in optics (TV 12). [... They] have no real existence in nature, being only an hypothesis framed by the mathematicians and by them introduced into optics, that they might treat of that science in a geometrical way. (TV 14)

So, even for near objects, Berkeley says, we don't have a purely visual experience of distance. We have a tangible sensation of the widening or narrowing the interval between our pupils; and it is only a customary connexion between such and such different tangible sensations and different degrees of distance that gives a means of having a steady experience of distances. Though distance cannot be immediately perceived by sight, Berkeley pays much attention to the perception of distance, at least up to section 51. Therefore, when we speak of *distance*, what *distance* are we speaking of?

Since distance is not immediately perceived by sight (TV 2), "the ideas of space, outness, and things placed at a distance are not, strictly speaking, the objects of sight; they are not otherwise perceived by the eye than by the ear" (TV 46). And Berkeley adds:

> Sitting in my study I hear a coach drive along the street; I look through the casement and see it; I walk out and enter into it; thus common speech would incline one to think I heard, saw, and touched the same thing, to wit, the coach. It is nevertheless certain, the ideas intromitted by each sense are widely different and distinct from each other; but having been observed constantly to go together, they are spoken of as one and the same thing. (TV 46)

Berkeley points out that, "common speech would incline one to think I heard, saw, and touched the same thing" (TV 46); though it be certain "a man no more sees and feels the same thing, than he hears and feels the same thing" (TV 47). But because we constantly experience regular connexions between tactual and visual ideas, we are more inclined to speak of them as "*one thing*," than we are to speak of a sound and a tactual feeling as one thing. Now a close and accurate view will make us admit that "that which is seen is one thing," and "that which is felt is another" (TV 49). In other words, it is necessary to keep in mind "that *there are two sorts of objects apprehended by the eye*, the one primarily and immediately [light in all its colours], the other secondarily and by the intervention of the former [tactual data]" (TV 50). Berkeley underlines that objects of the first sort (light and colours) are neither without the mind nor at any distance from us. They cannot come closer to us or go farther away. Therefore, we can better understand what we mean, strictly speaking, by *distance*:

> Whenever we say an object is at a *distance*, whenever we say it draws near, or goes farther off, we must always mean it of the latter sort, *which properly belong to the touch*, and are not so truly perceived as suggested by the eye in like manner as thoughts by the ear." (TV 50, italics mine)

Primacy of Tactual Experience and Necessity of Metaphors

The two sorts of objects are as closely united as the sounds of words in a familiar language are to the meaning they present to the mind: as soon as we hear the sounds, the meaning enters our mind. So likewise the second objects (tangible data) "are only suggested by sight"; but since they "do often more strongly affect us," they "are more regarded than the proper objects [of sight]." (NTV, §51) [3]

From what Berkeley discovers about our estimations of *distance* by sight, it seems obvious that everything else about the perception of space, magnitude and situation of objects will have *a main relation with our tactual experience*. Concerning tangible ideas, Berkeley went so far as to give to the term "idea" a very large meaning, including any sensation whatever:

> Note that when I speak of tangible ideas, I take the word 'idea' for any the immediate object of sense or understanding, in which large signification it is commonly used by the moderns. (TV 45)

Given this large meaning of the word *idea*, B. Belfrage emphasizes the complexity of the tactual data in Berkeley and observes several kinds of tactual experiences[4]: (1) three tactual *markers*: (i) sensations of *pleasure* and *pain*, (ii) the sensation of *gravitating downwards*, by which we decide what is *down*, *up*, *right* and *left*, (iii) *kinaesthetic experiences of moving our body*, by which we form our conception of space; and (2) other tactual ideas that may be termed *qualities*, such as *cold*, *warm*, *hot*, *soft*, *hard*; the sensation of *something hard* being the most basic of all tactual sensations.[5]

A new born child, a newly operated-on blind, and born-blind persons are guided by their tactual experience. In the *Theory of Vision* Berkeley emphasizes the vital importance of tactual ideas:

> We regard the objects that environ us *in proportion* as they are adapted to benefit or injure our own bodies, and thereby produce in our minds the sensation of pleasure or pain. Now bodies operating on our organs, by an immediate application, and the hurt or advantage arising there-from, depending altogether on the tangible, and not at all on the visible qualities of any object: this is a plain reason why those should be regarded by us much more than these. And for this end the visive sense seems to have been bestowed on animals, to wit, that by the perception of visible ideas [...] they may be able to foresee [...] the damage or benefit which is like to ensue, upon the application of their own bodies to this or that body which is at a distance. (TV 59; 109, 147, italics mine)

Visible ideas, which we seldom pay any attention to in themselves, form a

---

[3] See Brykman 1985.

[4] See Belfrage 2003 and Belfrage 2006.

[5] This sensation might have incited the high interest in the notion of *substance* among philosophers.

natural language by reference to the more important tactual ideas.[6] Thus, when we estimate distance by sight, this is by reference to tangible objects.[7]

Berkeley illustrates the priority of tactual data by "a man actually blind and who had continued so from his birth":

> Whatever judgments he makes concerning the situation of objects are confined to those only that are perceivable by touch. All those things that are intangible and of a spiritual nature, his thoughts and desires, his passions and in general all the modifications of the soul, to these he would never apply the terms *upper* and *lower* in a metaphorical sense." (TV 94)

As visual data are not without the mind, we cannot use use colours to describe our passions or desires either to a man born blind or to other people:

> We denominate an object of sight *high* or *low* in proportion as it is more or less distant from the visible earth. But to define the situation of visible things with relation to the distance they bear from any tangible thing, or *vice versa*, this were absurd and perfectly unintelligible. For all visible things are equally in the mind and take up no part of the external space. And consequently are equidistant from any tangible thing which exist without the mind. [...]
>
> Or rather, to speak truly, the proper objects of sight are at no distance, neither near, nor far, from any tangible thing. For, if we inquire narrowly into the matter we shall find that those things only are compared together in respect of distance which exist after the same manner, or appertain unto the same sense. (TV 111-112)

Objects which do not "exist after the same manner," can only be compared in a metaphorical sense. When we speak about intangible things, we are likely to use terms that literally refer to tactual and spatial data. Hence how

---

[6] TV 59-61, 73-74, 85-87, 109. Such settled lengths as *inches*, *feet*, etc., do not refer to visible lengths, "because a visible inch is, itself, no constant determinate magnitude" (TV 61), and cannot be used to mark out and measure objects. The judgments we make of the magnitude of objects by sight, are in reference to their tangible extension; "the visible though immediately perceived is little taken notice of" (*ibid.*). On natural language, see TV147, 152; TVV 38, 40, 43.

[7] TVV 67 : "We must not imagine that, in all cases, the apparent place or distance of an object must be suggested by the same means. And indeed it answers the ends of vision to suppose that the mind should have certain additional means or helps, for judging more accurately of the distance of those objects which are the nearest, and consequently most concern us."

are we to understand the meaning of "short-sightedness" and "long-sightedness"?

Relativity in Human Knowledge

Our knowledge by sight of the external world is ultimately based on *minima visibilia*, which are supposed to be "exactly equal in all beings that are endowed with the visive faculty" (TV 80),[8] but our visual field is always limited to an equal number of visible points:

> When my view is on all sides bounded by the walls of my study, I see just as many visible points as I could, in case that by the removal of my study-walls and all other obstructions, I had a full prospect of the circumjacent fields, mountains, sea, and open firmament: for so long as I am shut up within the walls, by their interposition every point of the external objects is covered from my view. [...] Whenever therefore we are said to have a greater prospect at one time than another, this must be understood with relation, not to the proper and immediate, but the secondary and mediate objects of vision, which, as hath been shewn, properly belong to the touch. (TV 82)

This seems to indicate an imperfection of the sense of sight: we are only aware of a limited number of visible points, and when we focus on one object the background appears dark and indistinct (TV 83). Now this imperfection cannot be rectified (1) by reference to higher intelligences that could take in a much greater number of visible points and be able to see them all at once with the utmost perfection, because we cannot know anything about how those higher intelligences perceive; or (2) by a microscopic inspection of objects, because microscopes bring us to another world, in which there is no connection between visible and tangible objects. This connection is however important to our preservation (by it we learn to predict what will happen if we approach an object that we see at a distance). Microscopes are useful instruments in science, but "microscopic eyes" could not guide us in real life.[9]

---

[8] TV 80: " No exquisite formation of the eye, no peculiar sharpness of sight, can make it less in one creature than in another; for it not being distinguishable into parts, nor in any wise consisting of them, it must necessarily be the same in all."

[9] Upon the whole, we should be satisfied with our nature as it was created: "If we consider the use and end of sight, together with the present state and circumstances of our being, we shall not find any great cause to complain of any defect or imperfection in it, or easily conceive how it could be mended. With such an admirable wisdom is that faculty contrived, both for the pleasure and convenience

It is from the background of his interest in optics and his minute examination of visible ideas (similar to Descartes' search for the *distinctness* of ideas)[10] that Berkeley emphasizes the importance of "short-sightedness" as a means of solving difficulties and scepticism in "several sects of philosophy" (PI 4) in the Introduction to the *Principles*:

> How difficult and discouraging soever this attempt may seem, when I consider how many great and extraordinary men have gone before me in the same designs: yet I am not without some hopes, upon the consideration that the largest views are not always the clearest, and that he who is short-sighted will be obliged to draw the object nearer, and may, perhaps, by a close and narrow survey, discern that which had escaped far better eyes. (PI 5)

For Berkeley a careful examination of ideas and words is the strongest means of destroying materialism and atheism. But a close inspection is a narrow view as well. Hence, at the end of the *Principles*, he asks the reader to take a large view on the world; such a "long-sighted" view is essential to comprehend that the whole universe is governed by a providential God and that any tiny event which may appear as evil is not so when connected with the general laws which display both the wisdom and goodness of God.[11]

> Our prospects are too narrow: we take, for instance, the idea of some particular pain into our thoughts, and account it *evil*; whereas, if we enlarge our view, so as to comprehend the various ends, connexions, and dependencies of things, on what occasions and in what proportions we are affected with pain and pleasure, the nature of human freedom, and the design with which we are put into the world; we shall be forced to acknowledge that those particular things, which considered in themselves appear to be evil, have the nature of *good*, when considered as linked with the whole system of beings. (P 153)

Practical Implications

The importance of combining a nearsighted and a long-sighted aspect is

---

of life" (TV 87). See Locke's *Essay* II 23, 12.

[10] Descartes, vol.1, p.33.

[11] P151-156. The panoramic view on the world is again widely described in *Alciphron*, and is a means of proving God's existence. Crito argues in Alc. IV 8-10, 14 : "The visual Language proves not a Creator merely but, a Provident Governor, actually and intimately present to all our interests and motions, who watches over our conduct, and takes care of our minutest actions and designs."

emphasized in *Passive Obedience*. God acts, on the one hand, according to certain fixed laws, which he will not transgress on account of accidental evils arising from them:

> Suppose a prince on whose life the welfare of his kingdom depends to fall down a precipice: we have no reason to think that the universal law of gravitation would be suspended in that case. The like may be said of all other laws of nature, which we do not find to admit of exceptions on particular accounts. Without such steadiness in nature we should soon, instead of this beautiful frame, see nothing but a disorderly and confused chaos [...].
>
> It is true, he who stands close to a palace can hardly make a right judgment of the architecture and symmetry of its several parts, the nearer ever appearing disproportionably great. And if we have a mind to take a fair prospect of the order and general well-being which the inflexible laws of nature and morality derive on the world, we must, if I may so say, go out of it, and imagine ourselves *to be distant spectators* of all that is transacted and contained in it; otherwise we are sure to be deceived by the too near view of the little present interests of ourselves, our friends, or our country. (PO 27-28, my italics)

Passive Obedience stresses how knowledge of human nature and of the general laws of nature is basic to act upright. Indeed, *self-love* is the most deeply rooted principle of action which ties every one to the present impressions. Nonetheless human beings are able to discover far greater goods than those which affect our senses and to have a long-sighted perspective of eternal pleasures for blessed souls in heaven. (PO 5).

Another instance of the need of combining the two perspectives is given in *Guardian* no. 70, where Berkeley imagines he is walking in St Paul's and develops the following analogy between the Cathedral and the Christian church:

> As [the Cathedral] consists of a great variety of parts united in the same regular design, according to the truest art, and most exact proportion; so [Christianity] contains a decent subordination of members, various sacred institutions, sublime doctrines, and solid precepts of morality digested into the same design and with an admirable concurrence tending to one view, the happiness and exaltation of human nature.
>
> In the midst of my contemplation, I beheld a fly upon one of the pillars; and it straightway came into my head that this same fly was a Freethinker. For it required *some comprehension in the eye of the spectator*, to take in at one view the various parts of the building [...]. But to the fly, whose prospect was confined to a little part of one of the stones of a single pillar, the joint beauty of the whole or the distinct use of its parts were inconspicuous, and nothing could appear but small inequalities

> in the surface of the hewn stone, which in the view of that insect seemed so many deformed rocks and precipices. [12]

In the same way as the fly's, "the thoughts of a freethinker are employed on certain minute particularities of religion, on the difficulty of a single text, or the unaccountableness of some step of Providence … to his narrow faculties," which are not able to comprehend the scope and design of Christianity.[13] This is part of Berkeley's endeavour to educate mankind:

> This raised in me some reflections on that frame or disposition which is called *largeness of mind*, its necessity towards forming a true judgment of things, and where the soul is not incurably stinted by nature, what are the likeliest methods to give it enlargement. (*ibid.,* italics mine)[14]

Philosophy and such sciences as astronomy serve purpose of enlarging the mind:

> In that science there are good reasons assigned to prove the sun an hundred thousand times bigger than our earth, and the distance of stars so prodigious, that a cannon-bullet continuing in its ordinary rapid motion, would not arrive from hence at the nearest of them in the space of an hundred and fifty thousand years. These ideas wonderfully dilate and expand the mind.[15]

However, "Christian religion enlarges the mind beyond any other profession." And Christianity alone is able to extend the mind "beyond the light of nature."[16] In the same essay in the *Guardian*:

> The mind of man seems to adapt itself to the different nature of its objects; it is contracted and debased by being conversant in little and low things, and feels *proportionable* enlargement arising from the contemplation of […] great and sublime ideas. (*ibid.*, italics mine)[17]

Now, when at the beginning of the *Principles* Berkeley decides to use a near-sighted method to clear up the difficulties that have blocked the way to knowledge, such a method is to be considered, as a provisional and

---

[12] *Works*, vol. 7, 206-209. This essay, (Monday, June 1713) was entitled by Luce "Minute Philosophers" (*italics mine*).
[13] *Ibidem.*
[14] On Berkeley's interest for education, see Laurent Jaffro 2010.
[15] *Works*, vol. VII, 208-209.
[16] *Ibid.*, 208.
[17] *Ibidem.*

relative method, the value of which depending on the end it serves.[18] The short-sighted method needs to be completed by a panoramic view of the laws of nature as connected by God; and such a large view is explicitly described as such at the end of the *Principles*. If not completed by a long-sighted perspective, short-sightedness is a defect in human beings.[19]

Nearsighted Method and Minute Philosophy

In *Alciphron*, the two libertine characters are described as counterfeit pedants wasting their time with trifles, though ready to compare themselves to acute eagles seeing many things at once from the highest point of view. When Euphranor observes that the name "free-thinker," as denoting "all those who think by themselves," is too general and further proposes to borrow the Cicero's term "*minute philosophers*," Crito at once agrees:

> Right [...], the modern free-thinkers are the very same with those Cicero called *minute philosophers* [...], they being a sort of sect which diminish all the most valuable things, the thoughts, views and hopes of men; all the knowledge, notions and theories of the mind they reduce to sense; human nature they contract and degrade to the narrow standard of animal life, and assign us only a small pittance of time instead of immortality. (Alc I 10)

Of such a description of freethinking, Alciphron gives an opposite interpretation, which has much to do with the short-sighted method set up at the beginning of the *Principles*:

> [Free-thinkers are] no more to blame for whatever defects they discover than a faithful glass for making the wrinkles which it only shows. As to what you observe ... of those we now call free-thinkers, having been anciently termed minute philosophers, it is my opinion this appellation might be derived from their considering things minutely, and not swallowing them in the gross, as other men are used to do. (*ibid.*)

---

[18] *Works*, VII, "Short-sightedness," 212- 213.

[19] *Works*, VII, *Sermons*, "On religious zeal," 18: "The peculiar aim and design of Christianity [is] to put away the narrowness of a party spirit and instead thereof to introduce a largeness of soul, a noble and diffused charity and unite the hearts of all men by the strictest bands of love and benevolence." "On the Will of God," 135: "In order to enlarge our views for the receiving of these notions and to inspire us with a zeal to live up to them, they have reminded us of the divine immortal part of our being, that was framed for nobler purposes, than merely to gratify [our] senses and passions." *Guardian*, *ibid.*, "Short-sightedness," 210-217; "Immortality," 222-223 ; "The Bond of Society," 225-228.

Berkeley's free-thinkers are bold enough to pretend they are able to avail themselves of both ways of knowledge: that is, a minute examination of things and a comprehensive view on the world and its future, even if this large view is rather an ideal or a dream. Thus Lysicles says:

> If wishing was to any purpose, I could wish for a telescope that might draw into my view things future in time, as well as distant in place. Oh that I could but look into the next age, and behold what it is that we are preparing to be, the glorious harvest of our principles! (Alc II 21-22)

Crito answers:

> Would it not be prudent to try the success of your principles on a small model in some remote corner? For instance, set up a colony of atheists in Monomotapa, and see how it prospers before you proceed any further at home? (*ibidem*)

To send these conceited men to a small, remote corner of the world is a good way to get rid of freethinking and atheism. If distance, by itself and immediately, is not perceived by sight, tangible distance is a good way to save your life (and, according to Crito, to win eternal life).

Conclusion

Berkeley's near-sighted method, as presented in the Introduction to the *Principles*, is a double edge sword: it is only a means that works well only if connected with its end.[20] The freethinkers sometimes present a sharp analysis of words, ideas and customs, sometimes they widen their view to embrace the entire universe, but their scepticism illustrate the finite nature of man. Crito on the other hand (Berkeley's spokesman in *Alciphron*) is convinced that "a man [can be] conscious that his will is inwardly conformed to the divine will" (Alc III 11). But this is a kind of blindness, because nobody knows what is meant by the "will of God." All of us are like the fly on St Paul's Cathedral, dreaming only about a cosmic perspective. So that short-sightedness and long-sightedness might be Berkeley's way to describe metaphorically, at his own risk, the give and take between reason and faith.

[20] *Supra*, note 18.

Bibliography

Belfrage, Bertil. (1992), "The Constructivism of Berkeley's *New Theory of Vision*," in Cummins and Zoeller (1992), pp. 167-186.

—. (2003), "Vers une nouvelle interprétation de la *Théorie de la vision* de Berkeley," in Berlioz (2003), pp. 159-211.

—. (2006), "The Scientific Background of George Berkeley's Idealism," in Gersh and Moran (2006), pp. 202-223.

Berlioz, Dominique (ed.) (2003), *Berkeley. Langage de la perception et art de voir*, Débat philosophiques. Presses Universitaires de France, Paris 2003.

Berman, David. (1985), *George Berkeley. Essays and Replies*, Irish Academic Press, Dublin.

Brykman, Geneviève. (1985), "Pleasure and pain versus ideas in Berkeley," in Berman 1985, pp. 127-137.

Cummins, Phillip D. and Guenter Zoeller (eds.) (1992), *Minds, Ideas, and Objects: Essays on the Theory of Representation in Modern Philosophy*, North American Kant Society Studies in Philosophy, vol. 2, Ridgeview *Publishing*, Atascadero, Cal.

Descartes, René. (1985), *The Philosophical Writings of Descartes*, 3 vols, J. Cottingham, R. Stoothoff, D. Murdoch, and A. Kenny (eds and trs), Cambridge University Press, Cambridge.

Gersh, Stephen and Dermot Noran, (eds.) (2006), *Eriugena, Berkeley, and the Idealist Tradition*, University of Notre Dame Press, Notre Dame, Indiana.

Jaffro, Laurent. (2010), "Éducation moderne et tradition antique selon Berkeley," in Jaffro, Brykman & Schwartz. 2010, pp. 277-286.

Jaffro, Laurent, Geneviève Brykman, and Claire Schwartz (eds.). (2010), *Berkeley's* Alciphron. *English Text and Essays in Interpretation*, Georg Olms Verlag, Hildesheim.

BERKELEY ON THE DIFFERENCE BETWEEN BRUTES AND MEN

MARC A. HIGHT

Abstract

I attempt to shed more light on Berkeley's theory of mind by analyzing what little he tells us about the nature of brutes and how they differ from men. I start by noting what Berkeley says about the distinction, namely that men have a free rational faculty whereas brutes are determined. I then argue that there are separate pressures within Berkeley's writings that led him to endorse both a form of compatibilism and libertarianism about the free will. These pressures lead to various difficulties that might make one question whether Berkeley's claims about the nature of brutes are consistent with the rest of his metaphysics. After exploring the various avenues available to him to preserve his stated distinction between brutes and men, I contend that Berkeley has some options that will preserve the coherence of his system, but none of them solve the deeper philosophical issues concerning the nature of the free will.

The Difference Between Brutes and Men

Like most of his contemporaries, George Berkeley maintains that there is a clean distinction between brutes and men, despite other superficial similarities. He recognized, however, that the distinction had to be motivated. He has Lysicles write in the *Alciphron*: "Have brutes instincts, senses, appetites, and passions, to steer and conduct them? So have men…." (Alc V 27). Given the superficial overlap, one should wonder how Berkeley thinks men and brutes differ and, furthermore, how he accommodates his theory of difference within his unique immaterialism.

In this paper I argue that Berkeley's views about the difference between men and brutes hide tensions with his conception of the mind, specifically with respect to his views about free will. Berkeley is forced either to embrace a form of libertarianism about the will, which I argue is a poor fit with some of his other philosophical claims, or else endorse a form of compatibilism that flirts with theological unorthodoxy and raises philosophical problems of its own. I do not see a happy resolution to the dilemma given the textual evidence we have. This paper is more a discussion of the conceptual territory surrounding Berkeley's insistence that man and beast are distinct kinds of beings rather than a criticism of his views, although I believe our explorations here will force us to rethink some portions of his system.

So what is the difference between brutes and men according to Berkeley? To start, he explicitly rejects one theory of the difference between men and brutes advanced by John Locke. He dismisses Locke's claim that men differ by their ability to form abstract ideas. Berkeley argues that humans cannot perform that feat either (PI 11) and continues by arguing that Locke's position depends on the observation that brutes do not use language or signs. The inability of animals to use language, however, is poor evidence for Locke's conclusion. There might be other reasons animals cannot use language, and language use by itself is no guarantee that an agent actually has abstract ideas, as Berkeley argues at length in the *Principles* and elsewhere.[1]

Positively, over his career Berkeley articulates a number of distinctions between men and other animals. Despite superficial disparities, they all ultimately may be brought into agreement in a single theory. Let's consider each briefly in turn. (1) Men differ by shape and language use, but only in degree. Thus Berkeley writes, "If you take away abstraction, how do men differ from Beasts. I answer by shape. By language rather by Degrees of more & less." (NB 594)[2] Elsewhere Berkeley argues that we have knowledge of other minds (souls) only by their *effects*. "From the speech and motion of a man we evidently infer the soul or spirit within him."[3] As a result, a natural way to understand Berkeley's distinction is that the minds of beasts differ from those of men because empirically we can perceive that brutes do not produce the same kinds of complicated effects as men. Brutes do not speak, nor act with the same kinds of sophisticated intentions as men. This characterization of the distinction is not enough, however, since it obviously parallels Locke's theory, which Berkeley has already rejected.

Elsewhere Berkeley narrows the point, pursuing a second theory of the

---

[1] The strategy here mirrors Berkeley's remark in the *Notebooks* (NB 746) where he notes that brutes do not have the ideas of unity or existence either. Thus his reason for rejecting the Lockean theory remains consistent in his writings.

[2] The passage is not "+" marked.

[3] See *Works*, vol. 7, 97 and P 145.

difference. (2) Men differ by possessing the ability to compose complex ideas and have notional knowledge, especially concerning God. Thus he wonders in the *Notebooks*:

> Qu: whether Composition of Ideas be not that faculty which chiefly serves to discriminate us from Brutes. I question whether a Brute does or can imagine a Blue Horse or Chimera. (NB 753)[4]

The ability of men to know extends beyond ideas, however. Berkeley on a few occasions extends this point to include knowledge of God. "Man alone of all animals hath understanding to know his God." (Alc V 28) Part of what enables us to rise above mere brutes is that we are capable of contemplating our immortality.[5] As I shall subsequently argue, this point holds special importance for Berkeley. Beasts do not have this power of contemplation, or at least do not demonstrate any power to do so.

Most often, however, Berkeley joins the first two distinctions in a more general formulation. What enables us to use language and compose complex ideas and contemplate God is that we are free, rational agents. Thus, the most fitting theory of the difference between men and brutes as displayed by Berkeley is the general claim (3): Men differ from brutes insofar as they possess a free rational faculty. This faculty enables men to have a conscience, be moral agents, engage complex ideas, use language, and rise above their own animal natures associated with the senses and passions:

> It is evident there are two parts in the composition of man: The mind which is pure and spiritual, which is made in the image of God, and which we have in common with angels: and the corporeal part containing the senses and passions which we have in common with brute beasts.[6]

Brutes are consistently associated with the senses and passions (only),[7] whereas men, similarly burdened with these animal features, are distinct in virtue of their ability to regulate these desires through the use of reason. The more we suppress our appetites, the more Godly and angelic we are.[8] When Euphranor (one of Berkeley's spokespersons) engages Alciphron about the brutish nature of man, he admits that men are creatures with senses, passions, and appetites that do not always display their rational

---

[4] The passage is not "+" marked.
[5] *Works*, vol. 7, 222. Guardian Essay XI "Immortality."
[6] *Works*, vol. 7, 88. Sermon VI "On the Mystery of Godliness."
[7] Compare Alc I 12.
[8] See Alc I 13.

nature. That said, he defends the nature of man as being rational even if not all men consistently demonstrate that quality.[9] Thus, what ultimately distinguishes man from beast is that the former is rational.

The theme of rationality is a common one in the history of western thought, and Berkeley tows the line. "The same faculty of reason and understanding, which placeth us above the brute part of creation, doth also subject our minds to greater and more manifold disquiets than creatures of an inferior rank are sensible of."[10] As we should expect from the foregoing passages, typically Berkeley presents the difference in rationality as a matter of degree. Men have a greater degree of rational power than beasts. "But as the human mind is dignified by a more comprehensive faculty than can be found in the inferior animals…."[11] But if the difference is of degree, how are we to capture this difference in a manner that explains the distinction between men and brutes? Merely saying that men are more rational and complicated than beasts does not immediately enable Berkeley to separate human persons from the occasionally odious rules of the natural world that free-thinkers want to extend to men. Thus Euphranor complains, "What motives, what grounds, can there be for bringing down man, in whom are all these things, to a level with such a creature? What merit, what ambition, in the minute philosopher to make such an animal a guide or rule for human life?" (Alc II 14) Berkeley clearly wants to draw a clean line between the rational capabilities of men and those of our animal brethren.

As Lysicles notes immediately following the aforementioned speech, Euphranor is the one who admits "freedom of thought." Thus the key to separating men from brutes is that only the former will *freely*. That is, there is a difference only of degree between men and brutes in terms of *being* rational, but there is a difference in kind in terms of *how* men are able to will and exercise their reason. Crito expresses Berkeley's position best later in the *Alciphron*:

> Besides, other animals are, by the law of their nature, determined to one certain end or kind of being, without inclination or means either to deviate or go beyond it. But man hath in him a will and higher principle; by virtue whereof he may pursue different or even contrary ends; and either fall short of or exceed the perfection natural to his species in this world; as he is capable, either by giving up the reins to his sensual appetites, of

---

[9] See Alc I 14.

[10] *Works*, vol. 7, 223. Guardian Essay XI "Immortality."

[11] *Works*, vol. 7, 214. Guardian Essay IX "Happiness."

> degrading himself into the condition of brutes, or else, by well ordering and improving his mind, of being transformed into the similitude of angels. (Alc V 28)

Thus Berkeley provides us with one of the clearest examples of how he conceives of the difference between man and brute. Although we share a base nature, human persons have a key feature that lofts them above other animals. Men are *freely* rational and not determined to any one end.

Berkeley on Human Freedom

As anyone with even a passing familiarity with the literature in the metaphysics of freedom knows, much hinges on what one *means* by 'free' in these discussions. Furthermore, the issue is sufficiently dense and difficult that we ought not be surprised to find entanglements in the thoughts of even first rate philosophers. I assert that such might be the case here. Berkeley typically defends a Lockean-style compatibilist theory of human free action, but he also makes claims that appear to require a libertarian conception of the free will. I am not interested in the metaphysical merits of any particular position; rather, I am interested in Berkeley's metaphysical commitments given his clear allegiance to the claim that men and brutes differ in virtue of the nature of their rational wills. So I turn first to examine Berkeley's views concerning the freedom of men and their wills.

Late in the *Alciphron* Berkeley advances a theory of free action that is partly reminiscent of Locke's own theory as outlined in Book II Chapter 21 of his *Essay Concerning Human Understanding*. Berkeley's primary spokesman Euphranor provides an explicit definition when the topic of whether man is free arises:

> Euphranor: In my opinion, a man is said to be free so far forth as he can do what he will. Is this so, or is it not?
> Alciphron: It seems so.
> Euphranor: Man, therefore, acting according to his will, is to be accounted free. (Alc VII 19)

If I will to raise to my hand and can do so, Berkeley thinks I am freely acting. Only when I am precluded from executing my will may I be said to not be free. Like Locke's famous prisoner, if I voluntarily will to be (or stay) in a locked room, then I am a free man.[12] When Alciphron challenges

---

[12] See Winkler 1989, 131-132, who has a similar analysis of Berkeley's views in

him on the point and asks whether a man is free to will, Euphranor dismisses the point as idle. "That is, whether he can will as he wills? …it is not doubted that man is accountable, that he acts, and is self-determined." (Alc VII 19) Following Locke, Berkeley does not at this point seem to have a theory of the freedom of the *will*, a position he thinks apparently is nonsensical. It only makes sense to speak of *acts* that are free, and his analysis mirrors that of Locke.

Unfortunately, there are strong reasons to think that Berkeley was not a consistent advocate of a Lockean-style compatibilism. In order to more cleanly engage the issues, I want first to isolate and sketch a particular libertarian theory of the will that I think resonates with Berkeley's thinking. In particular, we require a theory that accommodates a robust conception of moral accountability, which is dear to him. Once we have completed this sketch, we can turn to see whether it lurks within Berkeley's thinking.

Perhaps the most simple libertarian theory is that genuinely free actions of the will must satisfy two criteria. First, the action must be the agent's action and no other's. If an action is performed by my body because another has somehow taken control of it, the action is not genuinely mine and hence not free. Second, the metaphysical foundation for the principle of alternative possibilities (PAP) must be true. The principle, as formulated famously by Harry Frankfurt, indicates that "a person is morally responsible for what he has done only if he could have done otherwise."[13] The metaphysical ground for the principle is the physical possibility of agents acting otherwise given the exact same conditions. I am not morally responsible for actions that are in fact unavoidable, and the very possibility of moral responsibility thus requires the physical possibility of having been able to have done otherwise. Note that I am not defending the merits of this theory and I recognize that there are many important subtleties and variants to libertarian accounts. It is a convenient tool that will enable me to demonstrate the libertarian strands in Berkeley's thinking. With this loose conception in mind, we can turn to investigate more of what Berkeley says about our freedom.

When discussing the nature of the will, I believe that Berkeley retained the standard early modern view inherited from René Descartes that the will is always free.[14] Like Descartes, Berkeley seems to think that the

---

the different context of God's foreknowledge.

[13] Frankfurt 2003, 167.

[14] See *The Passions of the Soul*, I, Article 41, where Descartes writes "But the will is by its nature so free that it can never be constrained." Descartes 1985, vol. I, 343.

faculty of the will is identical with freedom of choice. He delights in continually attacking Locke's theory of uneasiness as the determinant of the will.[15] Unease and indeed anything ideational cannot possibly determine the will, since both are passive whereas the will is active. To my knowledge, Berkeley at no time ever mentions *anything* that determines the will. Similarly, Paul Olscamp identifies four separate lines of argument aimed by Berkeley against determinism, noting in particular that Berkeley holds the will to be undetermined.[16] Thus, when Berkeley ridicules Alciphron for asking whether the will is free (by recasting the question as whether a man can will as he wills), perhaps Berkeley ought not be thought of as endorsing a form of compatibilism. Instead, his position, at least here, may well be closer to that of libertarianism. Consider another speech by Euphranor later in the *Alciphron*:

> Euphranor: It is no less evident that man is a free agent: and though, by abstracted reasonings, you should puzzle me, and seem to prove the contrary, yet, so long as I am conscious of my own actions, this inward evidence of plain fact will bear me up against all your reasonings, however subtle and refined. (Alc VII 18)

When it comes to separating men from brutes, the difference is not that men can act according to their wills whereas brutes do not. Instead, the difference is that men have wills that may *deviate* from their natural desires; there are *multiple* physically possible options for men. Furthermore, we know this by introspection. An appeal to everyday commonsense experience reveals that our wills are not determined; hence they are not.[17] This passage is strikingly reminiscent of the strategy Descartes uses to defend the freedom of the will in the fifth set of replies:

> You may be unfree, if you wish; but I am certainly very pleased with my freedom since I experience it within myself.... I affirm what I have experienced and what anyone else can experience for himself, whereas your denial seems merely to be based on your own apparent failure to have appropriate experience; so my own view is probably entitled to receive more widespread acceptance.[18]

If we just carefully *look* into our own minds we can experience our own freedom. Such claims strongly suggest that Berkeley would endorse

---

[15] See "On Immortality," *Works*, vol. 7, 11 and NB 653. See also NB 611, 611a.
[16] Olscamp 1970, 91-2.
[17] Olscamp has a similar analysis. Olscamp 1970, 97.
[18] Descartes 1985, vol. II, 259-60.

something like the principle of alternative possibilities.

One might object at this point that Berkeley is aware of the issue and rejects my claim. Consider entry 616 from the *Notebooks*: "To ask whether a man can will either side is an absurd question. for the word can presupposes volition." This particular entry, however, does not undercut the ground for the principle of alternative possibilities; rather, if anything the entry reinforces it. The presupposed volition is itself non-determined. To ask whether we can will otherwise is absurd first because it is asking to treat the volition as an object of thought. But as they are actions, we can have no ideas of volitions. Second, since Berkeley believes that volitions are undetermined, positing a case where a volition determines an outcome with options begs the question about the nature of volitions and whether they are determined in the first place. In any event, a more positive case can be made for the presence of a libertarian strand in Berkeley's thinking.

In *Principles* 28 Berkeley asserts that he can "excite ideas in my mind at pleasure." Now what does this mean? It might mean (a) I can will when I choose to will. That is, when I am determined to will, I do and the willing is mine. That is a compatibilist reading. The problem, of course, is that such a reading is perfectly consistent with what brutes do as well. When my dog is determined to will, he does and the willing is his. No difference betwixt man and beast is to be found there. The more likely option, I believe, is that Berkeley believed it to mean (b): I can will without having my ideas determined by something else.[19] I admit that Berkeley never explicitly endorses libertarianism, and in fact in general does not say as much on the issue as one would prefer, promising instead to discuss the topic of human freedom at the start of the mysteriously missing second part of the *Principles*.[20] Nevertheless, at times he does say things that imply a fairly straightforward endorsement of libertarianism.

In addition to the *Principles* 28 passage, he also thinks that a key difference between men and brutes is that the former have a conscience and are morally accountable for their actions. Berkeley does explicitly link moral accountability to human freedom in the *Notebooks*[21] and he even asserts that morality consists in volition chiefly. (NB 669) But if the volition be determined, one might wonder whether moral accountability is

[19] Now one has to worry about the coherence of this claim, since if *nothing* determines the will then, in particular, the *agent* does not determine the will. One is then hard pressed to maintain the claim that the willing is *his*. That, however, is a standard worry with libertarian conceptions of the will, especially the Cartesian form, so I will lay aside that worry for present purposes.

[20] See NB 508.

[21] NB 508. Compare Clark 2005, 370

really appropriate in such cases.[22] The intuitive pull of PAP is operative. Berkeley nonetheless seems to think that one is responsible for one's willings (and their effects) independent of their nature as determined or otherwise. "And if man be free, he is plainly accountable." (Alc VII 18) The foundation of morality (and religion) for Berkeley is the ability of rational agents to freely will in a manner that makes them responsible agents. The claim is obvious to Berkeley because he cannot think of anything that *could* determine or constrain the will beyond the agent him or her self. "I know I act, and what I act I am accountable for." (Alc VII 19) The emphasis here is that the actions in question are *owned* by the individual agent. Berkeley would not argue that should someone physically force me to pull a trigger on a weapon that I would own that act (and hence be morally culpable for the effects of said act). This conception of freedom falls squarely in the tradition of the one that defines free actions as those that satisfy the above mentioned two criteria. The action is the action of the agent, and it is physically possible for the agent to have acted otherwise.

Another reason to think Berkeley has some implicit commitment to a libertarian conception of the will comes from his response to the problem of evil. In the *Three Dialogues* Philonous responds to Hylas' concern that God might be responsible for all evil in the world if He is the author of everything in nature.

> It is true, I have denied there are any other agents beside spirits: but this is very consistent with allowing to thinking rational beings, in the production of motions, the use of limited powers, ultimately indeed derived from God, but immediately under the direction of their wills, which is sufficient to entitle them to all the guilt of their actions. (3D 237)

Berkeley has a problem he does not seem to fully recognize. Just previous to that speech, Philonous says that God is "represented [in the Holy Scriptures] as the sole and immediate Author of all those effects, which some heathens and philosophers are wont to ascribe to Nature, matter, fate, or the like unthinking principle." (3D 236) The assertion here appears inconsistent with Berkeley's claim in the prior passage, where the finite agent is the immediate actor, and God is only "ultimately" responsible for the action. In order to *freely will* it must not be the case that the will is determined, even ultimately, by God. If God controls the hand of a puppeteer which in turn controls the strings of the marionette, evil actions

---

[22] Thus Galen Strawson argues that it is a consequence of there being no libertarian freedom of the will that no agent can be moral. Strawson 1994, 5-24.

performed by the marionette do not absolve God even if the puppeteer is required to pull the strings. All of this analysis, of course, is completely consistent with Berkeley's Cartesian denial that the will is determined by anything. Tom Stoneham argues that a form of compatibilism can escape the problem, but I am somewhat skeptical.[23] Given that Berkeley so openly pursues a free-will theodicy in response to the problem of evil, I am again drawn to the conclusion that he has a libertarian conception of the free will in mind. On this point I am not alone. Olscamp concludes, "In all of these arguments, Berkeley's own views are constant. Free will, spontaneously free will, is a necessary condition for moral behavior; determinism of whatever variety is false."[24]

If Berkeley did hold a libertarian theory of the free will, then one benefit immediately arises: he can maintain that men differ from brutes in virtue of the fact that the rational wills of men are free and undetermined. Thus, although humans are tied to their senses as we find in brutes[25] and humans are subject to passions just as are other animals, (Alc V 28) human minds are "dignified by a more comprehensive faculty."[26] As a result, men can act contrary their natures because their free faculty of reason includes a conscience. Animals are determined in their behaviors and in what they will, whereas men recognize their animal natures yet can freely choose otherwise. In that distinction we can see why men are moral agents and animals are not.

The Implications of Freedom

Having established that Berkeley (at least at times) believed that the key difference between man and beast is that the former possesses a free rational will, does this theory square with the rest of Berkeley's philosophical system? A series of problems arise almost immediately on the supposition that human persons have robustly (i.e. libertarian) free wills. I will limit my discussion here to two concerns before exploring the rival alternative of trying to preserve compatibilism in his system.

The first problem concerns the sovereignty of Nature and God. If we are agents that freely will, then since volitions are paired with ideas (as their effects), as a consequence we are at least in part responsible for the ideas other minds perceive. Now we have a classic problem. If the natural world is

---

[23] Stoneham 2002, 207ff.

[24] Olscamp 1970, 98.

[25] See, for example, Alc I 12 and *Works*, vol. 7, 95.

[26] *Works*, vol. 7, 214. Guardian Essay IX "Happiness."

determined in terms of the ordering of ideas we perceive, then we are *not* really free in terms of what we will *if* our willings are a part of nature. Berkeley is quite adamant in the *Principles* that the effects we perceive as the Laws of Nature are constant and necessary. "… [I]t being visible, that the aforesaid methods of Nature are absolutely necessary, in order to working by the most simple and general rules, and after a steady and consistent manner; which argues both the *wisdom* and *goodness* of God."[27] Thus, if we will freely and every volition has an attendant idea, then we ought to expect that we will not find *necessary* connections in what we perceive. Berkeley is thus committed to the presence of necessary connections in nature (the laws of nature) and a view that entails that some events in nature will not be necessary (the effects of our free actions).

To make matters worse, Berkeley also famously argues that every willing depends entirely on the will of God:

> For it is evident that in affecting other persons, the will of man hath no other object, than barely the motion of the limbs of his body; but that such a motion should be attended by, or excite any idea in the mind of another, depends wholly on the will of the Creator. (P 147)

Not only is there a problem with the necessary order of Nature, we also have to reconcile the utter dependence of human wills on God. Stoneham argues that the *Principles* 147 passage is "a bit of an exaggeration,"[28] and there is some reason to think he might be right, since in the *Alciphron* Berkeley argues that it is logically possible for God to know the actions of free agents. That said, no analysis is provided about the mechanics of this solution. There is room for serious concern here and I have no ready answer on Berkeley's behalf.

The second problem concerns Berkeley's theory of mind. Eventually Berkeley developed the position that minds are collections of active willings or volitions.[29] Spirit is entirely active, but is not to be identified with a particular idea or volition. Instead, the mind involves the ordering of volition-idea pairings. Spirit is a principle distinct from its ideas and volitions. Thus Berkeley writes in the *Notebooks*, "The Spirit, the Mind, is neither a Volition nor an Idea." (NB 849) The key is to not think of the mind as a bundle of distinct volitions (Berkeley considers but rejects a bundle theory of the mind) and instead recognize that the mind involves a kind of ordering. "A spirit is one simple, undivided, active being: as it

---

[27] P 151. See also P 62, 31.

[28] Stoneham 2002, 187.

[29] I follow in part George Pitcher's analysis in what follows. Pitcher 1977, 184ff.

perceived ideas, it is called the *understanding*, and as it produces or otherwise operates about them, it is called the *will*." (P 27) According to Berkeley spirits should be construed in part as active principles. They are still substances which endure as independent (from all except God) atemporal beings, but they are not substances in the sense of some *perceivable* object. Philonous helps clarify matters in the *Three Dialogues*:

> How often must I repeat, that I know or am conscious of my own being; and that I myself am not my ideas, but somewhat else, a thinking active principle that perceives, knows, wills, and operates about ideas. I know that I, one and the same self, perceive both colours and sounds.... Farther, I know what I mean, when I affirm that there is a spiritual substance or support of ideas, that is, that a spirit knows and perceives ideas. (3D 233-234)

Whether the mind is a traditional substance or not, we know that the nature of the mind involves a principled ordering of idea-volition pairings.[30] If just this rough portion of Berkeley's theory of mind is correct, then invoking the freedom of men to distinguish them from brutes runs into trouble. What is the difference between an ordering of activities like volitions and a "free" ordering of the same? It is not clear there is one. Berkeley tells us that we cannot separate volitions one from another except by their effects, namely the ideas with which they are paired.[31] But there is no reason to suspect that the ideas paired with "free" volitions will differ from those paired with unfree ones. There might be differences in what I *infer* from a perceived idea based on whether or not I judge the attendant volition to be free or not (about whether I hold an agent morally accountable or not, for instance), but that is of no help to us in determining an antecedent distinction. In short, Berkeley has no resources with his professed theory of the mind to explain how free willings differ from determined ones. As a result, from the foregoing analysis Berkeley has no way to distinguish between men and brutes if the will is free.

Perhaps, however, we have erred by relying too heavily on the libertarian strands that appear in Berkeley's thinking. Might Berkeley be able to maintain the distinction between men and brutes in some other fashion while adhering to compatibilism more strictly? Let us explore. If

---

[30] For a non-traditional understanding of the nature of mental substances and minds in Berkeley see Daniel (2001b), esp. 61 and Daniel (2008b).

[31] NB 788: "We see no variety or difference betwixt the Volitions, only between their effects." Compare P 27, where Berkeley notes that souls are also only detectable by their effects.

the difference between man and beast is not in the freedom of the will, then given what Berkeley says there are two other initially promising options. The first fails. The second, although flirting with some theological difficulties, might be a defensible option Berkeley could have endorsed.

We might first suppose that men and brutes differ because the former have minds while the latter do not. Although Berkeley only obliquely suggests this possibility once, it is worth briefly exploring.[32] Brutes would then be akin to Cartesian automata, collections of ideas that behave like creatures with minds but in fact only imitate the behaviors of genuine agents. Unfortunately, Berkeley is not in a good position to defend this kind of distinction (even if true), primarily because he claims that volitions are differentiated only by their effects (i.e. the ideas with which they are paired). (NB 788) Thus, if *we* (qua minds) can only learn of the existence of other minds in virtue of the effects they produce, then there is no way to *know* whether brutes have minds or not. But Berkeley does not actually say that brutes lack minds, nor should he. Berkeley has no resources to conclude that brutes in fact do lack minds; he can only say that brutes behave in ways that do not suggest that they have minds. Such a view is equally as compatible with brutes having minds with lesser capabilities as with brutes being automata. Given that he wants the distinction to be clearly demonstrable, Berkeley cannot plausibly argue that the difference between men and brutes depends on the mere possession of a mind or soul.

Most commonly Berkeley writes as if brutes do have minds. Yet if we instead opt to claim that brutes have minds, but lack the mental sophistication we associate with rational faculties, then a new set of complications arises. If, as Berkeley does sometimes suggest, animals differ from humans only by degree (in language use and the ability to manipulate complex ideas), then Berkeley's system is threatened with a loss of theological orthodoxy regarding the special status of human persons. In particular, there initially does not appear to be any compelling reason to suppose that animals are not immortal like humans.

As a theist, Berkeley could draw on ready responses from theologians with which he was familiar. The challenge, however, is to reconcile the standard theological moves that separate human and beast with Berkeley's own professed theory of the difference as being grounded in our rational faculties. As an Anglican, Berkeley adopted the traditional reading of Genesis that gives animals "the breath of life" (1:30) but not souls per se, which are reserved for humans created in the image of God (Genesis

[32] See *Works*, vol. 7, 88.

1:26). When Berkeley claims that every living thing has a soul,[33] the language is loose but not an uncommon shorthand for the breath of life as opposed to an immortal soul. That he sometimes thinks that there is a distinction between souls and the animating principles of other animals is *suggested* occasionally by his discussion of natural immortality:

> It must not be supposed, that they who assert the natural immortality of the soul are of opinion, that it is absolutely incapable of annihilation even by the infinite power of the Creator who first gave it being: but only that it is not liable to be broken or dissolved by the ordinary Laws of Nature or motion. They indeed, who hold the soul of man to be only a thin vital flame, or system of animal spirits, make it perishing and corruptible as the body, since there is nothing more easily dissipated than such a being, which it is naturally impossible should survive the ruin of the tabernacle, wherein it is enclosed.... We have shewn that the soul is indivisible, incorporeal, unextended, and it is consequently incorruptible. Nothing can be plainer, than that the motions, changes, decays, and dissolutions which we hourly see befall natural bodies (and which is what we mean by the *course of Nature*) cannot possibly affect an active, simple, uncompounded substance: such a being therefore is indissoluble by the force of Nature, that is to say, *the soul of man is naturally immortal.* (P 141)

Here Berkeley draws a distinction between the substantial soul, which is naturally immortal, and other conceptions of the soul (as a vital flame or animal spirits[34]) which are not. One might think that mere animal souls differ by not being naturally immortal. The "second rate" souls of brutes dissolve upon their bodily death. Unfortunately, Berkeley never actually says as much, which is why I was careful to note that this passage at best is only suggestive. There is no principled bit of philosophy in Berkeley's system that admits for a distinction amongst kinds of immaterial souls in this way. We have, in short, no compelling reason to suppose that the souls of beasts are not immaterial substances similar in kind to those of human persons. Again, the best we have are Berkeley's repeated claims that somehow the rational faculties of the soul do all the work. Given his metaphysic and his claims about animals differing only by degree from us, positing "second rate" souls appears *ad hoc*.

Perhaps Berkeley has a better solution available to him that might

---

[33] *Works*, vol. 7, 219.

[34] The reference might be slightly misleading in this context. "Animal spirits" here is most likely a reference to the Cartesian doctrine of animal spirits operative in explanations of mind-body causal interaction and *not* to a special kind of soul or spirit possessed by beasts.

preserve the simplicity of his ontology. The difference between brutes and men, both of whom have souls, is not simply their rationality, but their rational awareness. What distinguishes us is that only the minds of men are sufficiently advanced to *understand* that they as selves are in fact immortal. Thus Berkeley writes that "If it were not for this thought [of immortality], I had rather be an oyster than a man, the most stupid and senseless of animals than a reasonable mind tortured with an extreme innate desire of that perfection which it despairs to obtain."[35] Every living thing has a soul in a minimal sense, but a *self* consists in a conscious, rational faculty aware of its own immortality. In this feature – which may be construed as either a distinction of kind or degree – Berkeley can draw a firm line between animals that display rational behavior and those that are conscious of their own immortality. The latter are men and have souls capable of salvation.

The oyster passage, unfortunately, is hardly a clear indication that Berkeley thinks that there is a principled division between brutes and humans based on reflective knowledge of our own immortality. I thus advance this interpretative possibility with some caution, since the textual evidence is thin. Even so, if this reading of the distinction is right, then Berkeley has an option available to him which need not invoke a libertarian account of the free will. The wills of men are determined, but have special capabilities that differ in kind from those possessed by brutes. We at least have found a reasonable way to accommodate Berkeley's claims about our rational faculties with a form of compatibilism about the nature of human freedom.

The problem, of course, is that availing ourselves of this option leaves Berkeley without explicit resources to answer the problem of evil or explain moral accountability. Furthermore, there are now textual problems to resolve concerning Berkeley's apparent commitment to a libertarian theory of the free will elsewhere. In Berkeley's defense, I suggest it is reasonable to observe that he did not think carefully about the implications of his claims about brutes, instead relying to some degree on the standard views of his day (recall his apparent imitation of Descartes' views about freedom).

At the end of our exploration, we find that Berkeley appears to have available two options to explain the difference between man and beast. Neither of them is particularly attractive. On the one hand, he might ground the difference in our libertarian freedom of the will. The wills of men are not determined while the wills of brutes are. Selecting that theory

[35] *Works*, vol. 7, 222. Guardian Essay IX, "Immortality."

creates problems with respect to the sovereignty of God and Berkeley's metaphysics of mind. On the other hand, he might retain compatibilism and argue that men and beasts differ by the fact that men were created with the reflective ability to understand their own immortality. In that case, however, Berkeley owes us an account of genuine moral agency and we need to find some way to reconcile his libertarian claims about his response to the problem of evil and the undetermined nature of the will. Aside from seriously re-thinking some of Berkeley's other core metaphysical positions, I have no happy solution.

Bibliography

Berkeley, George. (1948-1957), *The Works of George Berkeley*, 9 vols, A. A. Luce and T. E. Jessop, Nelson, London.

Clark, Stephen. (2005), "Berkeley on Religion," in Winkler (2005), pp. 396-404.

Daniel, Stephen. (2001b), "Edwards, Berkeley, and Ramist Logic," *Idealistic Studies* 31, pp. 55-72.

—. (2008b), "Berkeley's Stoic Notion of Spiritual Substance," in Daniel 2008), pp. 203-230.

—. (ed.) (2008a), *New Interpretations of Berkeley's Thought*, Humanity Books, Amherst, NY.

Descartes, René. (1985), *The Philosophical Writings of Descartes*, 3 vols, J. Cottingham, R. Stoothoff, D. Murdoch, and A. Kenny (eds and trs), Cambridge University Press, Cambridge.

Frankfurt, Harry. (2003), "Alternate Possibilities and Moral Responsibility," in Watson (2003), pp. 167-176.

Locke, John. (1975), *An Essay Concerning Human Understanding*, ed. Peter Nidditch, Oxford University Press, New York.

Olscamp, Paul. (1970), *The Moral Philosophy of George Berkeley*, Martinus Nijhoff, The Hague.

Pitcher, George. (1977), *Berkeley*, Routledge & Kegan Paul, Boston.

Stoneham, Tom. (2002), *Berkeley's World*, Oxford University Press, Oxford.

Strawson, Galen. (1994), "The Impossibility of Moral Responsibility," *Philosophical Studies* 75, pp. 5-24.

Watson, Gary (ed.) (2003), *Free Will*, Oxford University Press, New York.

Winkler, Kenneth (ed.) (2005), *The Cambridge Companion to Berkeley*, Cambridge University Press, New York.

—. (1989), *Berkeley: An Interpretation*, Oxford University Press, New York.

MARVELLOUS EMPTINESS: BERKELEY ON CONSCIOUSNESS AND SELF-CONSCIOUSNESS[1]

KENNETH P. WINKLER

> Tis not to be imagin'd wt a marvellous emptiness & Scarcity of Ideas that man shall descry who will lay aside all use of Words in his Meditations.
> —NB 600

Abstract

Berkeley's philosophy of mind strikes even sympathetic readers as the weakest part of his immaterialism. It seems to many of them, as it seemed to Hylas, that "to act consistently," Berkeley "must either admit matter or reject spirit." The present paper is a limited defense of the scant philosophy of mind that Berkeley left us. I call attention to what Berkeley saw as the "marvellous emptiness" of mind. Berkeleyan self-consciousness, I suggest, is not consciousness of an object. In its clearest and most unmistakable form, it is the experience of free acts of will: acts that are, inevitably, directed towards objects, though they themselves can never be objectified. This view seems plausible to me, but I do offer some criticisms. What is most admirable in Berkeley's philosophy of mind is its denials, and some of his deepest assumptions may stand in the way of its positive development.

Introduction

In 1710, when George Berkeley's *Treatise concerning the Principles of Knowledge* first saw the light of day, it included a general "Introduction" of twenty-five numbered paragraphs, followed by the 156 paragraphs of "Part I." In the second edition of 1734, the last to appear in Berkeley's lifetime,

---

[1] The paper was delivered to the NYU Mind and Language Seminar in February 2006 and presented at the Helsinki Berkeley Conference in August 2007.

the "Part I" label remained, but no further part was ever published. Berkeley was certainly planning on Part II in 1713, when he announced to readers of the *Three Dialogues between Hylas and Philonous* that "the business" of that book was to "treat more clearly and fully of certain principles laid down" in Part I of the *Principles*, "before I proceed to publish the Second Part" (P 167-168). He may have held to the plan as late as 1725, when the preface making this announcement was republished. But by 1729, when Samuel Johnson told Berkeley how keenly he was awaiting the publication of Part II (*Works*, vol. 2, 277), the plan had been abandoned. "I had made considerable progress in it," Berkeley told his friend, "but the manuscript was lost about fourteen years ago, during my travels in Italy, and I never had leisure since to do so disagreeable a thing as writing twice on the same subject" (*Works*, vol. 2, 282).

Part II was to cover some of what we now call the philosophy of mind, as the following entries, from the private notebooks Berkeley kept between 1706 and 1708, testify:

> Mo. The 2 great Principles of Morality. the Being of a God & the Freedom of Man: these to be handled in the beginning of the Second Book. (NB 508)
> M. Extension tho it exist only in the Mind, yet is no Property of the Mind, The Mind can exist without it tho it cannot without the Mind. But in Book 2 I shall at large shew the difference there is betwixt the Soul & Body or Extended being. (NB 878)

Berkeley's philosophy of mind strikes even sympathetic readers as the weakest part of his immaterialism. It seems to many of them, as it seemed to Hylas, that repudiating material substance while insisting on spiritual substance is not "fair dealing" – that "to act consistently," Berkeley "must either admit matter or reject spirit" (3D 232). This very natural reaction may give rise to a suspicion: was Berkeley really too busy, as he breezily suggests, to write twice on the same subject, or did he recognize, however dimly, that his first draft wasn't worthy of recovery, and that the safest course was to let the subject lie?[2] The present paper, a limited defense of the scant philosophy of mind that Berkeley left us, is an effort to allay that suspicion. I'll concentrate, as my title suggests, on what Berkeley saw as the "emptiness" of consciousness, by which I mean its relative emptiness of content or objects. The passage from Berkeley's notebooks that I've taken as a motto is one of many, published and unpublished, warning against the assumption that every meaningful word stands for an object of

---

[2] See the final paragraph of McCracken 1986, 602.

consciousness (or what Berkeley calls an *idea*). Because of that assumption, “a great number of dark and ambiguous terms presumed to stand for abstract notions, have been introduced into metaphysics and morality, and from these have grown infinite distractions and disputes amongst the learned.” (P 143). This is especially true of the sciences “particularly conversant about spiritual things.” (P 143). Berkeley’s aim is to promote a very different (and, he hopes, radically simplifying) way of thinking. If consciousness is consciousness of objects, then “self-consciousness” – knowledge of one’s own mind, and of its acts and operations – is not, for Berkeley, a form of consciousness at all. Berkeleyan self-consciousness is knowledge based on experience (or on what we might call “phenomenological fact”), but it is not (insofar as it is *self*-consciousness) object-involving. In its clearest and most unmistakable form, it is the experience of free acts of will: acts that are, inevitably, directed towards objects, though they themselves can never be made into objects. Berkeley’s view is close to one defended in our own day by Brian O’Shaughnessy, who writes that “our fundamental relation to our own actions” (which for him include “mental actions” such as visualizing, even though he is mainly concerned with bodily actions) “is non-observational.”[3] This view seems correct to me. I have, nonetheless, some criticisms to make of Berkeley. What is most admirable in his philosophy of mind is its denials, and there may be central Berkeleyan assumptions standing in the way of its positive development.

The Emptiness of Mind

To provide some sense of the pressures to which Berkeley was responding, I will begin by examining an interesting thread in his notebooks, in which he questions whether knowledge of the mind is even possible. This discouraging possibility is empathically denied in Berkeley’s published writings, as I will later document.

The thread begins with an entry explaining why many suppose we do not know the soul:

> S. We think we know not the Soul because we have no imaginable or sensible Idea annex’d to that sound. This the Effect of prejudice. (NB 576)

The entries in Berkeley’s notebooks, which have been numbered by his editors, were generally entered on the right-hand (or “recto”) side of its folios. Second thoughts, marked by the letter “a,” were entered on the left-

---

[3] 1980, 2:1.

hand (or "verso") side, and keyed to the entry that prompted them. (Letters in the left margin classify entries by topic: according to Berkeley's own index, "S" stands for *spirit*, "M" for *matter*, "G" for *God*.) Here is Berkeley's surprising comment on 576; the italics are my own:

> S. *Certainly we do not know it.* This will be plain if we examine wt we mean by the Word knowlege. Neither doth this argue any defect in Our knowlege no more than our not knowing a contradiction. (NB 576a)

The thread continues with a series of entries on the will, or on spirit insofar as it is active:

> S. If by Idea you mean object of the Understanding.
> Then certainly the Will is no Idea, or we have no idea annext to the word Will. (NB 665)
> M.S. The Substance of Body we know, the Substance of Spirit we do not know it not being knowable. it being purus Actus [pure act]. (NB 701)
> S. The Will is purus actus or rather pure Spirit not imaginable, not sensible, not intelligible. in no wise the object of ye Understanding. no wise perceivable. (NB 828)
> S. Substance of a Spirit is that it acts, causes, wills, operates, or if you please (to avoid the quibble yt may be made on ye word it) to act, cause, will, operate it's substance is not knowable not being an Idea. (NB 829)

Berkeley's notebooks are, of course, full of trials and experiments. I am not suggesting that the unknowability of mind or spirit was ever his settled opinion. But as the notebooks come to a close, the question raised by these entries continues to haunt him. There these entries are suggestively connected to others, which I will examine later, about freedom of the will. One such entry asks:

> S.G. Qu: whether the Will can be the object of Praescience or any knowlege. (NB 875)

The entries I've quoted contemplate two claims: (i) spirit is not (and cannot come to be) an object of the understanding; and (ii) spirit (or its substance) is not (and cannot be) known. We can only guess at the reasoning behind them. Of the two, (i) seems to be more basic: if spirit is not (and cannot come to be) an object of the understanding, it follows, on the assumption that the understanding is the faculty by which we know, that spirit is not (and cannot come to be) something known. Entry 576 tells us that the truth of claim (ii) will be plain if we examine what we mean by knowledge. If Berkeley is working, at this point in the notebooks, with a Lockean understanding of knowledge as the perception of the agreement or disagreement of ideas (perhaps a reasonable assumption in view of entry 522: "All knowlege onely about ideas. V. Locke B. 4 c. 1."), (ii) will follow from (i), given what we (that is, we Lockeans) mean by knowledge. (i) itself might be defended on phenomenological grounds, or on the basis of ambitious further claims about the understanding (for example, that its object must be passive).

Whatever Berkeley's reasoning was, by the time he published the *Principles*, claim (ii) at least had been decisively rejected. The evidence for this is worth reviewing. The main theme of the closing sections of the *Principles* is our knowledge of spirits. Berkeley introduces these sections with the following words:

> Having dispatched what we intended to say concerning the knowledge of *ideas*, the method we proposed leads us, in the next place, to treat of *spirits*: with regard to which, perhaps human knowledge is not so deficient as is vulgarly imagined. (P 135)

"The great reason that is assigned for our being thought ignorant of the nature of spirits," he continues, "is, our not having an idea of it. But surely it ought not to be looked on as a defect in a human understanding, that it does not perceive the idea of *spirit*, if it is manifestly impossible there should be any such *idea*. And this, if I mistake not, has been demonstrated in Sect. 27." It seems that Berkeley intends to reject claim (ii) while retaining claim (i). Given what he identifies (in his 1709 *Theory of Vision*) as a prevailing modern understanding of *idea* ("any the immediate object of sense or understanding" [§ 45]), (i) is equivalent to the contention that we have no idea of spirit.

As the sections on spirit continue, the evidence for Berkeley's optimism regarding knowledge of spirit only mounts. "From the opinion that spirits are to be known after the manner of an idea or sensation," he explains, "have risen many absurd and heterodox tenets, and much scepticism about the nature of the soul" (P 137). The opinion he is condemning is not that spirits are known, but that they are known in a certain fashion. According to *Principles* 140, "we know other spirits by means of our own soul." "After what hath been said, it is I suppose plain," he writes two sections later, "that our souls are not be known in the same manner as senseless inactive objects." To say they are not known in the same manner as ideas is not to say they are unknown or unknowable, but to imply that they *are* known, though in a different way. The *Three Dialogues* is, if anything, more clear: "My own mind and my own ideas," Philonous tells Hylas, "I have an immediate knowledge of" (3D 232). "How often must I repeat," he says a bit later on, "that I know or am conscious of my own being; and that I myself am not my ideas, but somewhat else, a thinking active principle that perceives, knows, wills, and operates about ideas" (3D 233).

Although there is, in my view, no question that Berkeley wants to deny (ii), there is a passage later in the *Principles* that does confuse the picture. The theme of the passage is the vast difference between spirit and idea:

> *Spirits* and *ideas* are things so wholly different, that when we say, *they exist, they are known*, or the like, these words must not be thought to signify anything common to both natures. There is nothing alike or common in them: and to expect that by any multiplication or enlargement of our faculties, we may be enabled to know a spirit as we do a triangle seems as absurd as if we should hope to *see a sound*. (P 142)

If the two kinds of "knowledge" have only the name in common (if they are, to borrow an example from Spinoza, no more alike than a dog and the dog star), then it looks as if spirits are not known, if ideas are. There is an ancestor of this passage in the *Notebooks*:

> S. The grand Cause of perplexity & darkness in treating of the Will, is that we Imagine it to be an object of thought (to speak wth the vulgar), we think we may perceive, contemplate & view it like any of our Ideas whereas in truth 'tis no idea. Nor is there any Idea of it. tis toto coelo different from the Understanding i.e. from all our Ideas. If you say the will or rather a Volition is something I answer there is an Homonymy in the word thing wn apply'd to Ideas & volitions & understanding & will. all ideas are passive, volitions active. (NB 643)

I want to save Berkeley from the claims he seems to be making in this entry and in the published passage descending from it because they make nonsense of his optimism in the closing sections of the *Principles*. If our knowledge of spirit really has no more than a name in common with our knowledge of ideas, then he might as well speak of it as ignorance. His bold hope, announced on the title page of the *Dialogues*, "plainly to demonstrate the reality and perfection of human knowledge," will be crushed. In supposing that he has to conduct his thinking in terms of the notion of homonymy, Berkeley makes conspicuously poor use of what the tradition passed on to him. What he needs but ignores is the honorable ancient notion of *paronymy*.[4] This is the notion that enabled Aristotle to say that a healthy body and a healthy diet have more in common than a

---

[4] Bettcher (2007, 55-62) intriguingly suggests that P 142 rests on the doctrine of analogy.

name.[5] If, as entry 429 of the *Notebooks* tells us, "Existere is percipi or percipere," then "exists" in application to spirit is not a homonym of "exists" in application to idea, but a paronym. A very similar (but somewhat more complex) point can be made about "is known." If we adopt Bertrand Russell's distinction between knowledge of things and knowledge of truths,[6] the passages I have quoted leave us with no choice but to say that Berkeley takes us to have knowledge of truths about spirits, just as he takes us to have knowledge of truths about ideas. (Note that *Principles* 142 says nothing about knowledge of truths; it speaks only of knowledge of two kinds of *things*, spirits and ideas.) It also seems clear that for each domain, Berkeley takes our propositional knowledge to derive from our knowledge of (that is, our acquaintance with) the associated things. This means that *spirits are known* and *ideas are known* have more in common than a name: however much the underlying cognitive relations differ, they serve in each case to make propositional knowledge possible. Thus "is known" in application to spirit is not a homonym of "is known" in application to idea, but (at least) a paronym.

Berkeley makes another unfortunate appeal to homonymy earlier in the *Principles*, but the surrounding material makes the appeal less troubling. The passage is *Principles* 89, where Berkeley writes that "*thing* or *being* is the most general name of all, it comprehends under it two kinds entirely distinct and heterogeneous, and which have nothing common but the name, to wit, *spirits* and *ideas*." This appeal is less troubling than the one in *Principles* 142 because the present passage, in the second edition, goes on to indicate that they do have something vital in common, because both are known. (In the second edition of the *Principles*, Berkeley adds several new passages saying that we have a "notion" of spirit, even though we have no idea of it. As he writes in a passage added to *Principles* 27 in the second edition, "it must be owned ... that we have some notion of soul, spirit, and the operations of the mind, such as willing, loving, hating, in as much as we know or understand the meaning of those words." Commentators agree that this is a change in vocabulary, rather than in doctrine.)

> We comprehend our own existence of inward feeling or reflexion, and that of other spirits by reason. We may be said to have some knowledge of or

---

[5] Aristotle, *Categories* 1. Technically, paronyms have different endings, but I put aside that complication here. I understand "paronymy" broadly, so that it embraces what is known as "focal meaning" or "*pros hen* equivocity." Ross helpfully discusses paronymy and related phenomena in Ross 1981.

[6] See for example Russell 1912, 44.

> notion of our own minds, of spirits and active beings, whereof in a strict sense we have not ideas. In like manner we know and have a notion of relations between things or ideas, which relations are distinct from the ideas or things related, inasmuch as the latter may be perceived by us without our perceiving the former. To me it seems that ideas, spirits and relations are all in their respective kinds, the object of human knowledge and subject of discourse: and that the term idea would be improperly extended to signify everything we know or have any notion of. (P 89)

Berkeley alludes to this passage in the closing line of *Principles* 142, also added in the second edition: "But if in the modern way the word *idea* is extended to spirits, and relations, and acts; this is after all an affair of verbal concern."

If Berkeley in his published works rejects claim (ii) – if he holds, despite what he says in the notebooks, that we have knowledge of spirit – we are left to ask what form he thinks that knowledge takes. My view is that he continues to accept claim (i), and that our knowledge of spirit, if we choose to speak of it as consciousness, is not *object*-consciousness but *subject*-consciousness. The acts and operations of the mind are not known insofar as we contemplate and view them; they are known insofar as we enact or perform them. The mind itself is also not an object that we contemplate and view, but a thing known through acting, operating, or performing. Berkeley writes in the notebooks that the substance of spirit is "to act, cause, will, [and] operate" (NB 829). I am proposing that to know spirit is to experience oneself as acting, willing, and operating – to experience oneself as the subject of acts, rather than as an object. That is why consciousness, seen as it really is, and not as the doctrine of abstract ideas tells us it should be, is empty – empty of the objects a prejudiced mind would expect to find there.[7]

All this is, I have to grant, far from explicit in the texts. Berkeley's constructive remarks on self-consciousness are crude and formulaic.[8] In

---

[7] Adams 1973 defends a similar view. Adams speaks of "two modes of awareness" (48): one of ideas "as of objects distinct from us, over against us" (50); and one of spirits and their acts. In much the same spirit, Bettcher speaks of Berkeley as "an originator of the theme that the subject cannot be an object" (2007, 2; for further discussion see 41, 46-7, and especially 117-132).

[8] Berkeley's formulaic pronouncements leave many questions unanswered. Does every act of mind, for example, carry awareness of itself along with it, or does such awareness require a separate reflex act? If separate reflex "acts" are required, are they active or passive? Berkeley's allusions to doctrines of inner sense suggest that they might in some way be passive, another indication (see the final paragraph of the paper) that the Berkeleyan mind may be more passive than he is willing to

the *Principles*, he says that "we comprehend our own existence by inward feeling or reflexion" (P 89).[9] In the *Dialogues*, Philonous tells Hylas that we perceive ourselves by a "reflex act" (3D 232). "I do not perceive [spirit] as an idea or by means of an idea," Philonous says later, "but know it by reflexion" (3D 233). In *De Motu* (1721), Berkeley writes that we know souls or thinking things by "a certain internal consciousness" [*conscientia quadam interna*]" (DM 21). These remarks do not take us past the terms of art that figure in them: *reflexion*, *reflex act*, and *conscientia*. All of these terms are borrowed by Berkeley from his predecessors. Reflection (of which "reflexion" is simply a variant spelling, more revealing of the word's etymology) is John Locke's label for our experience of our own selves. Locke speaks of a "reflex act" at Essay II xxvii 13, where he predicts that "till we know what kind of action it is that cannot be done without a reflex act of perception accompanying it, and how performed by thinking substances, who cannot think without being conscious of it," we cannot determine whether "the consciousness of past action can be transferred from one thinking substance to another" (Locke 1975). Gerard De Vries, in his *Diatribe de ideis rerum innatis* (1695), to which Berkeley refers in the last two entries of his notebooks, uses *conscientia* as a label for inner sense.[10] Its French cognate, *conscience* (standardly translated as "consciousness"), is very prominent in the writings of Nicolas Malebranche, who also calls it "inner sensation." *Conscience* is, according to Malebranche, our only source of knowledge concerning the soul, of which we have no purely intellectual representations (or "ideas," in Malebranche's carefully circumscribed sense of that expression).[11] Berkeley takes up these views of Malebranche in entries 230 and 888 of the Notebooks.

Berkeley's sources do tell us something about self-consciousness as Berkeley understands it: it is not a purely intellectual operation, but a form of experience, a variety of inner sense. This is confirmed by Berkeley's use of the more everyday expression "inward feeling," which serves in *Alciphron* (Dialogue 3, section 5) as an alternative for "passion," as well as by *De Motu* 30, where Berkeley says that "a thinking, active thing is given which we experience as the principle of motion within ourselves."

---

admit.

[9] This passage is emphasized by Gueroult 1956, who speaks of Berkeleyan self-knowledge as "sentiment intérieur" (92). He goes on to compare Berkeley's view to Malebranche's (93).

[10] See Luce's notes on 328-329 of Berkeley 1976.

[11] See especially Malebranche 1980, Book 3, part 2, chapter 6, section 4, "How we know our own soul," 237-239.

Our only other certainty about Berkeleyan self-consciousness is that it is not idea-involving, as Berkeley repeatedly emphasizes:

> A spirit is one simple, undivided, active being: as it perceives ideas, it is called the *understanding*, and as it produces or otherwise operates about them, it is called the *will*. Hence there can be no idea formed of a soul or spirit: for all ideas whatever, being passive and inert, *vide Sect.* 25, they cannot represent unto us, by way of image or likeness, that which acts. A little attention will make it plain to anyone, that to have an idea which shall be like that active principle of motion and change of ideas, is absolutely impossible. Such is that nature of *spirit* or that which acts, that it cannot be of itself perceived, but only by the effects which it produceth. ... [T]he words *will*, *soul*, *spirit*, do not stand for different ideas, or in truth, for any idea at all, but for something which is very different from ideas, and which being an agent cannot be like unto, or represented by, any idea whatsoever. Though it must be owned at the same time, that we have some notion of soul, spirit, and the operations of the mind, such as willing, loving, hating, in as much as we know or understand the meaning of those words. (P 27)

> We may be said to have some knowledge or notion of our own minds, of spirits and active beings, whereof in a strict sense we have not ideas. (P 89)

> A spirit has been shown to be the only substance or support, wherein the unthinking beings or ideas can exist: but that this *substance* which supports or perceives ideas should itself be an *idea* or like an *idea*, is evidently absurd. (P 135)

> By the word *spirit* we mean only that which thinks, wills, and perceives; this, and this alone, constitutes the signification of that term. If therefore it is impossible that any degree of those powers should be represented in an idea, it is evident there can be no idea of a spirit. (P 138; see also 139 and 142.)

My proposal – that Berkeleyan self-consciousness is subject-consciousness, an awareness of acts and operations presenting themselves not as objects before the mind, but as the mind's own undertakings – is consistent with all that Berkeley says, but goes beyond it in supposing that ideas are the mind's only "objects," and that acts and operations that cannot be known as objects (because they cannot be known as ideas) must instead be known from within, as the mind's own performances. I think this is, in view of the role of claim (i) in the *Notebooks*, a plausible elaboration, but I must admit it is a guess.[12] It has, however, interesting implications that Berkeley

[12] I see no basis for Bennett's report that there are "indications that [Berkeley] thinks that his own existence is inferred from ideas which are immediately given,

seems to accept, and this may lend it some measure of confirmation. But before turning to those implications I should consider two objections.

My proposal has it that in his published writings, Berkeley in effect identifies *idea* with *object of the mind*. This is plausible in view of Locke's definition of *idea* as "whatsoever is the object of the understanding when a man thinks" (*Essay* I i 8, Locke 1975), as well as passages in Berkeley's published writings (for example TV 45, already quoted) where *object* and *idea* are, if not identified, very closely linked. The problem is that there are passages prying them apart. In *Principles* 142, for example, a passage I've already considered in another context, "ideas, spirits and relations" are all classified as "the *object* of human knowledge and subject of discourse" (my emphasis). The most interesting passage along these lines is the opening section of Part I of the *Principles*:

> It is evident to anyone who takes a survey of the objects of human knowledge, that they are either ideas actually imprinted on the senses, or else such as are perceived by attending to the passions and operations of the mind, or lastly ideas formed by help of memory of imagination, either compounding, dividing, or barely representing those originally perceived in the aforesaid ways. (P 1)

The grammar of this sentence has occasioned a great deal of commentary. If the antecedent of "such as are perceived" is the closest appropriate noun, it looks as if Berkeley is saying that the passions and operations of the mind are ideas, but as we've seen, this is (according to Berkeley) just what they are not. Michael Ayers and David Berman have both proposed that in *Principles* 1, Berkeley is, for strategic reasons, temporarily portraying himself as more of a Lockean than he is really is.[13] I myself think it is at least as likely, as G. A. Johnston and T. E. Jessop long ago suggested, that Berkeley wants "such" to pick up *objects* rather than *ideas*.[14] But on either reading, the passage treats passions and operations

---

through the principle that there cannot be unowned ideas" (2001, 156). Nor do I agree that "this is what he ought to think, given his insistence that he has no idea of himself."

[13] Ayers 2005, 47-48, and Berman, 2005, 22-23. Ayers seems to take a somewhat different view in his edition of Berkeley 1992, 77.

[14] See Jessop's footnote to the passage in vol. 2 of Berkeley's *Works*, 41. For further discussion, critical of Jessop's suggestion, see Furlong 1960. There is another, less ambiguous Lockean survival in P 25: "But whoever shall attend to his ideas, whether of sense or reflexion, will not perceive in them any power or activity." I suppose it is possible that Berkeley is thinking specifically of pleasure and pain, which according to Locke are ideas of both sensation and reflection

of the mind as objects, which seems to undercut my suggestion that a commitment to claim (i) carries over from Berkeley's notebooks to his published writings.

I think this objection can be met by distinguishing two senses of "object." In one sense, an object is simply a subject of discourse, or a thing with which we are somehow acquainted (and concerning which we can therefore have propositional knowledge). Insofar as spirits and their acts are known and meaningfully discussed, they qualify as objects in this undemanding sense.[15] But they are not objects in a second, phenomenological sense: they are not present to the mind in the way (for example) sensory images are. As Robert M. Adams very helpfully puts it, we are not aware of them "as of objects distinct from us, over against us" (Adams 1973, 50). Objects in the first sense are the concern of what I earlier called object-consciousness; objects in the second sense (and not the first) are the concern of what I called subject-consciousness. I hope the distinction between two kinds of objects (and two kinds of awareness or consciousness) is clear enough to leave me free to say that for Berkeley, the mind is emptier of objects than we might at first expect.

A second objection to my proposal is based on *Principles* 27, where Berkeley writes that "such is the nature of *spirit* or that which acts, that it cannot be of it self perceived, but only by the effects which it produceth." If to say that spirit cannot itself be "perceived" is to say that it cannot itself be experienced, my proposal must be on the wrong track. But *Principles* 27, so understood, is flatly incompatible with Berkeley's repeated declarations to the contrary (and with the otherwise puzzling P1, where Berkeley speaks of the objects "perceived by attending to the passions and operations of the mind"). I think it is all but certain that in *Principles* 27, "perceived" is being used in a sense that goes hand in hand with "idea." In that sense, only ideas can be perceived, as Philonous for example asserts in the Third Dialogue (3D 234). The main burden of *Principles* 27 is to argue that there can be no idea of soul or spirit. This is not to deny that it can be experienced or known in a way ideas are not.

Personal Identity

I turn now to the first of the implications of my proposal that Berkeley

---

(*Essay* II vii 1 and 2 and II xx 1 and15). It isn't obvious to me that Berkeley shouldn't interpret internal pains and pleasures just as he interprets external ones: as ideas, rather than as acts or operations of the mind.

[15] Because this sense of "object" is available, I do not follow Bettcher in saying that for Berkeley, spirits are not objects of knowledge (2007, 41).

seems to accept: personal identity cannot be a matter of ideas – a matter, that is, of object-consciousness. Berkeley (through his representative Euphranor) makes the point in *Alciphron* (1732), by means of an example that became better known (in a somewhat different form) as Thomas Reid's "brave officer" objection:

> Let us then suppose that a person hath ideas and is conscious during a certain space of time, which we will divide into three equal parts, whereof the later terms are marked by the letters A, B, C. In the first part of time, the person gets a certain number of ideas, which are retained in A: during the second part of the time, he retains one half of his old ideas, and loseth the other half, in place of which he acquires as many new ones: so that in B his ideas are half old and half new. And in the third part, we suppose him to lose the remainder of the ideas acquired in the first, and to get new ones in their stead, which are retained in C, together with those acquired in the second part of time. (Dialogue 7, section 8)

If this is possible, Euphranor contends, he can "demonstrate that personal identity doth not consist in consciousness." For A and B will be the same, "being conscious of common ideas," as will B and C, for the same reason. From this it follows that A is C. "But the person in C hath no idea in common with the person in A. Therefore personal identity doth not consist in consciousness" – that is, object-consciousness.

I don't think it can be doubted that Berkeley is positioning Euphranor to address Locke. Euphranor opens the discussion with the amnesia objection entertained by Locke in Essay II xxvii 20, to which Alciphron replies by making the same distinction between *man* and *person* made by Locke in his own reply. Yet the example of the ABC man may be unfair, because Locke's account is not clearly framed in terms of object-consciousness. What makes me the same as an earlier person, in Locke's view, is not (say) my consciousness of the overflowing Thames, but my consciousness of having observed it (*Essay* II xxvii 16) – that is, my consciousness of *my* having observed it (Locke 1975). This seems to be a matter of subject-consciousness, not object-consciousness. I wonder, though, whether Berkeley states the Lockean view as he does because he suspects Locke is unentitled to this distinction. Because Locke treats every immediate object of thought (in the broad sense of "object") as an idea (or object in the narrow sense), Berkeley may think, my consciousness of having observed the overflowing Thames threatens to become, if not simply an idea of the overflowing Thames, an idea of its observed overflowing, rather than a consciousness of my having observed it. There doesn't seem to be anything in a Lockean idea, even a Lockean idea of reflection, that marks it as my own.[16]

Berkeley's concern seems to me to be reasonable, and a brief look at David Hume's search for the relations among perceptions that induce belief in personal identity may help to establish its force (*Treatise* 1.4.6, Hume 2000). Hume thinks there are two such relations, resemblance and causation, and that causation is by far the more important. Consider, though, what he says about resemblance. "What is the memory," he asks, "but a faculty, by which we raise up the images of past perceptions? And as an image necessarily resembles its object, must not the frequent placing of these resembling perceptions in the chain of thought, convey the imagination more easily from one link to another, and make the whole seem like the continuance of one object?" (*Treatise* 1.4.6.18) The qualitative similarity of perceptions is something to be assessed by what I've called object-consciousness. A high degree of it might well incline me to view a succession of perceptions as one object (as in Hume's account of our belief in the identity of body at *Treatise* 1.4.2), but why should it lead me to view that one object as *myself*? It seems that qualitative similarity, like any other feature of perceptions or ideas that we contemplate or view, isn't fit for the task Hume assigns to it. Berkeley comments on qualitative similarity and personal identity in a notebook entry eerily consonant with what he says a quarter-century later in *Alciphron*: "No identity other than perfect likeness in any individuals besides persons" (192). A deleted later comment (192a in the Thomas edition: "When there is no difference intrinsecal or extrinsecal of moment") makes it clear that by "perfect likeness" Berkeley means exact qualitative similarity. He goes on to ask, in entry 194a, "Whether Identity of Person consists not in the Will." Berkeley's point here may be that qualitative similarity, even when exact or perfect, is insufficient for the numerical identity that persons (perhaps

[16] Here it's worth taking note of the impersonality in Locke's accounts of ideas of reflection. Consider for example *Essay* II vi 1-2. There Locke makes what Berkeley would view as a promising beginning. The mind, he writes in § 1, "turns its views inward upon it self" and "observes its own Actions" concerning the ideas received by sense. But the "other *Ideas*" it "takes" from these are, in § 2, impersonally characterized. In §1 Locke insists that ideas of reflection "are as capable to the Objects of [the mind's] Contemplation, as any of those it received from foreign things," but it's hard to see how any "objective" feature of an idea – any feature we contemplate or view – can be the source of our consciousness of it as our own. Berkeley takes issue with impersonal conceptions of mental acts and operations in P 143: "Men have imagined they could frame abstract notions of the powers and acts of the mind, and consider them prescinded, as well from the mind or spirit it self, as from their respective objects and effects."

uniquely) enjoy. He therefore wonders whether it resides in the will, an "object" of subject-consciousness concerning which questions of qualitative similarity cannot be raised, because a will is not the sort of thing whose qualities can be contemplated and compared to the qualities of other things.

Even if we allow that Locke can appeal to subject-consciousness, the objection in *Alciphron*, suitably revised, remains telling. Suppose B is conscious of his having performed an action of A. And suppose C is conscious of his having performed an action of B. C will then be B and B will be A, entailing that C is A. Suppose further, though, that C is not conscious of his having performed any action of A. It follows that C is not A. (Revised in this way, Berkeley's objection coincides exactly with Reid's.) Berkeley's own view is that personal identity does not consist in consciousness, but in sameness of substance. (Berkeley's commitment to spiritual substance will be taken up below.) I assume it is his view, though, that it can be ascertained by subject-consciousness. This epistemological outlook is, however, not open to the revised version of Berkeley's ABC objection. B can know he is the same as A because he is conscious of having performed some thought or deed of A, and C can know he is the same as B because he is conscious of having performed some thought or deed of B. This perhaps entails that C can know (or have good reason to believe, say on the basis of testimony left by B) that he is A. But C's failure to recall performing any thought or deed of A does not mean C is not A, that C has no reason to believe he is A, or even that C does not know he is A, so there is no contradiction.

Before leaving the topic of personal identity I want to take note of some other entries in the notebooks that are critical of Locke's account and consonant with my proposed interpretation of Berkeleyan self-consciousness. In *Notebooks* 200, Berkeley asks "wherein consists identity of Person." He answers: "not in actual consciousness, for then I'm not the same person I was this day twelvemonth, but while I think of wt I then did. Not in potential for then all persons may be the same for ought to know." Two entries later he writes, "two sorts of Potential consciousness Natural & praeternatural in the last § but one I mean the latter" (NB 202). In entry 200, in contrast to *Alciphron*, Berkeley seems to be thinking of subject-consciousness ("I think of wt I then did"). His objection is that personal identity cannot consist in actual subject-consciousness, unless we're willing to repudiate many ordinary judgments of self-identity. But if it consists in potential consciousness it is unknowable. Entry 202 suggests a way around the latter point: perhaps personal identity consists in naturally potential consciousness. But if we do not know where the limits of *naturally* potential consciousness lie, Berkeley's objection may still stand.

The Bundle View of Mind or Spirit

A second implication of my interpretive proposal (and one that is, like the first, accepted by Berkeley) is that we can easily look within ourselves and fail to discover everything we should, because we wrongly confine our attention to the objects of consciousness, narrowly understood. "For my part," Hume writes in the *Treatise* "when I enter most intimately into what I call *myself*, I always stumble on some particular perception or other, of heat or cold, light or shade, love or hatred, pain or pleasure. I never can catch *myself* at any time without a perception, and never can observe any thing but the perception. When my perceptions are remov'd for any time, as by sound sleep; so long am I insensible of *myself*, and may truly be said not to exist. And were all my perceptions remov'd by death, and cou'd I neither think, nor feel, nor see, not love, nor hate after the dissolution of my body, I shou'd be entirely annihilated, nor do I conceive what is farther requisite to make me a perfect non-entity" (1.4.6.3). I am, he concludes, "nothing but a bundle or collection of different perceptions, which succeed each other with an inconceivable rapidity, and are in a perpetual flux and movement." (1.4.6.4) (Hume 2000)

Berkeley would certainly object that Hume should have cast his net more widely. He entertains a view like Hume's in the notebooks:[17]

> + Consult, ransack yr Understanding wt find you there besides several perceptions or thoughts. Wt mean you by the word mind you must mean something that you perceive or yt you do not perceive. a thing not perceived is a contradiction. to mean (also) a thing you do not perceive is a contradiction. We are in all this matter strangely abused by words. (NB 579)
>
> + Mind is a congeries of Perceptions. Take away Perceptions & you take away the mind put the Perceptions & you put the mind. (NB 580)

The plus sign marking these entries indicates material Berkeley (for whatever reason) decided not to use. In this case we can safely conclude that Berkeley took the bundle view of the self to be mistaken. Hylas imputes the view to Philonous, who decisively rejects it:

> HYLAS. Notwithstanding all you have said, to me it seems, that according to your own way of thinking, and in consequence of your own principles, it should follow that you are only a system of floating ideas, without any

[17] See also NB 587, 614, and 615.

> substance to support them. Words are not to be used without a meaning. And as there is no more meaning in spiritual substance than in material substance, the one is to be exploded as well as the other.
> PHILONOUS. How often must I repeat, that I know or am conscious of my own being; and that I myself am not my ideas, but somewhat else, a thinking active principle that perceives, knows, wills, and operates about ideas. I know that I, one and the same self, perceive both colours and sounds: that a colour cannot perceive a sound, nor a sound a colour: that I am therefore one individual principle, distinct from colour and sound; and, for the same reason, from all other sensible things and inert ideas. (3D 233-334)

Some readers of Hume have suggested that Humean perceptions are not objects of perception but acts. If they are right, it may seem wrong to say that Hume illicitly restricts his introspective awareness to object-consciousness. But even if we grant that Humean perceptions are acts, his awareness of them, as he describes it, falls short of subject-consciousness as Berkeley understands it. For Berkeley, immediate awareness of an act of mind is, as Philonous indicates, awareness that I am warm, or cold, or in love, or full of hatred. When Hume looks within he may never "stumble" across himself, but in Berkeley's view that self is there nonetheless, and it is known in or through every perception, whether act or object.

Substance

Berkeley does not simply deny the bundle view of self or spirit; he confidently affirms that spirits are substances – indeed, the only substances (for example *Principles* 7).[18] The present section is a speculative attempt to determine how robust an ontology of substance we can eke out of Berkeleyan subject-consciousness. (Berkeley's ontology of substance may in part depend on other considerations, but in this paper I put them to one side.)

Berkeley describes our knowledge of our own selves as immediate (3D 232).[19] I think Adams is right when he suggests that for Berkeley, the

---

[18] His sincerity in this has been doubted, for example by Muehlmann 1992 in chapter 6. For a convincing effort to put such doubts to rest see Cummins 2005, 209-218.

[19] It is curious, though, that at *Principles* 144, where, having said in *Principles* 140 that "we know other spirits by means of our own soul, which in that sense is an image or likeness of them," Berkeley chooses to contrast our knowledge of other minds, which he describes as "not immediate," with knowledge of our own

immediacy of self-knowledge, like the immediacy of our knowledge of ideas, confers infallibility (Adams 1973, 56). If, then, I am conscious of my perceiving both a color and a sound, I can conclude that both color and sound are united in my consciousness (as in the Third Dialogue, 3D 233-234, quoted just above). More significantly, if I am now conscious of a gently flowing Thames, and I recall being conscious of the river when it overtopped its banks, I can conclude that I've existed at different times, between which I underwent a change.[20] One traditional mark of substance is that it is an enduring subject of change. It is, as Aristotle put it, able to receive contraries.

The same considerations establish that a spirit has hidden potential: it is, characteristically, always more than it has so far become. In an idea, by contrast, everything is manifest or open to view: part of the reason Berkeley deems ideas "visibly inactive" (P 25) is that they cannot vary from the ways in which they appear at any moment to be. Change *of* ideas is possible, but change *in* ideas is not. The point might also be put by saying that ideas are nothing but surface: they have no inner depths. Although I find this very hard to spell out, I think the inner depth of a spirit, when compared to an idea's lack of depth, has something to do with its (comparatively greater) independence – independence being another traditional mark of substance. As ideas come and go, I remain the same. What Berkeley calls the "fleeting" character of ideas (P 89 and the Second Dialogue (3D 216), where in each case it is linked with dependence)[21] is a sign of their diminished purchase on reality. I do not think the deliverances of consciousness can show by themselves that ideas are dependent on spirit. But they may give us a reason to judge that an idea is unable to support the existence of anything other than itself. An idea cannot support another thing covertly, because nothing about the idea is hidden. But it seems no better able to do so openly, because "*x* supports *y*" can be true only if *x*'s absence would entail the absence of *y*, and no such power of cancellation can be found in *x*.[22] We cannot be sure, as I've granted, that

ideas, rather than with knowledge of our selves.

[20] I am assuming, perhaps controversially, that Berkeley can take subject-consciousness of the past to be infallible.

[21] In the first edition version of *Principles* 89, Berkeley contrasts "*indivisible, incorruptible substances*" with "*inert, fleeting perishable passions*, or *dependent beings*." The "or" may be one of apposition or alternation, but if so, Berkeley does not reveal the reasoning behind it.

[22] Could the relevant power exist in *y*? Not if *y* is an idea. But if y is a non-idea that has the power, I wonder whether its presence in *y* (as opposed to *x*) would undercut any reason we might have for thinking that *y* depends on *x*. *y*'s dependence on *x*

spirits support the existence of ideas, but their hidden depths at least hold out that possibility.

Perhaps, then, Berkeley can eke out of an infallible subject-consciousness both the capacity of spirit to endure through change and the bare possibility that spirit supports ideas. Some of the other marks of substance for which Berkeley seems to be reaching – simplicity, activity, and stronger forms of independence – cannot so easily be had. I want to say something in particular about at least some of these marks, but in his attempts to gain hold of them Berkeley encounters a common problem. Precisely because spirit has hidden depths, subject-consciousness cannot assure us that spirit does not have parts, that its changes (or the changes it triggers) have their source within spirit itself, or that its apparent independence isn't compromised by a hidden dependence on something else. Earlier I advised that we follow Adams in treating Berkeleyan subject-consciousness as infallible. I took this to mean that anything disclosed by subject-consciousness is present there. But it cannot follow from this that spirit is *transparent* to the mind: that everything present there is disclosed (or even disclosable) by subject-consciousness.[23]

Let me conclude this section with some particular remarks about simplicity and activity. The deliverances of subject-consciousness do seem to be partly responsible for Berkeley's conviction that spirit is simple. In two late notebook entries, he voices his sense that what differentiates one state of mind from another is not spirit or anything internal to spirit, but the objects or upshots of those states:

> S. We see no variety or difference betwixt the Volitions, only between their effects. Tis One ill one Act distinguish'd by the effects. This will, this Act is the Spirit, operative, Principle, Soul etc. (NB 788)
> S. Will, Understanding, desire, Hatred etc so far forth as they are acts or active differ not, all their difference consists in their objects, circumstances, etc. (NB 854)

---

would in such a case be the upshot of *y*'s nature alone, making it a very unusual sort of dependence.

[23] The distinction between infallibility and transparency makes intuitive sense, but unless some control is exerted over what it is that can be known, the distinction is in danger of collapse. Suppose I am infallible, and claim to detect that spirit is not-*F*. Then it seems that being *F* cannot be hidden in its depths, which suggests that my infallibility has more bearing on spirit's transparency than it should have. A natural first step would be to stipulate that the objects of infallible knowledge be positive. But how are positive objects to be distinguished from negative ones? "Independence" nicely illustrates the difficulty: it is, like "infinite," negative in form, but arguably positive in meaning.

Something like the view expressed in these entries nearly found its way into Berkeley's published writings, but not quite. The closing sentences of Principles138, in the first edition of 1710, read as follows. (Words omitted in the 1734 edition are bracketed.)

> For by the word *spirit* we mean only that which thinks, wills, and perceives; this, and this alone, constitutes the signification of that term. If therefore it is impossible that any degree of those powers should be represented in an idea [or notion], it is evident there can be no idea [or notion] of a spirit.

Berkeley's manuscript version of *Principles* 138 (from a manuscript spanning from section 85 through the opening sentence of 145) continues with these words:

> Again the soul is without composition of parts, one pure simple undivided being. Whatever distinction of faculties or parts we may conceive in it arises only from its various acts or operations about ideas. Hence it is repugnant that it should be known or represented in some parts and not in others, or that there should be an idea, which incompletely resembles it. (P 104)

The thought expressed here resembles the thought expressed in the notebook entries, but the match is not exact: the entries say that spirit is diversified by its objects or effects, while the manuscript says it is diversified by its own acts or operations. An obvious objection to the notebook view, however true it may be to some of our experience, is that the difference between a volition and a perception is internal. (Descartes speaks of the difference as one of "form." It is not only a matter of "objective reality" or worldly effect.) Although the deleted manuscript lines deftly avoid this objection, Berkeley elected not to use them. Why?

I believe his decision had to do with an internal intellectual struggle that had not come to an end even by the time Berkeley published the *Principles*. I will say more about the details of that struggle in the next (and final) section of my paper; here I hope it is enough to say that the struggle left Berkeley uneasy about even the slightest suggestion that understanding and will are distinct. His official view is that "understanding" and "will" are labels for the same simple thing. "A spirit," he announces in *Principles* 27, "is one simple, undivided, active being: as it perceives ideas, it is called the *understanding*, and as it produces or otherwise operates about them, it is called the *will*." He goes on to deny that we have "ideas of two principal powers, marked by the names *will* and *understanding*, distinct from each other." By acknowledging a "distinction" between the "various acts or operations" of the mind, the manuscript lines convey the very impression Berkeley hopes to avoid. In the following very late notebook entry, it is almost as if he has the manuscript lines in mind:

> S. I must not Mention the Understanding as a faculty or part of the Mind, I must include Understanding & Will etc in the word Spirit by wch I mean all that is active. I must not say that the Understanding differs not from the particular ideas, or the Will from particular Volitions. (NB 848)

When Berkeley writes in *Principles* 27 that a spirit is "one simple, undivided, active being," he very strongly suggests that it is active in every one of its aspects – in perceiving no less than in willing. As we'll see in the next section, the notebooks conclude that the spirit is active even insofar as it understands (NB 871). When, earlier in the notebooks, Berkeley first persuaded himself of the thoroughgoing activity of spirit, he described it as "pure act" (701), but in entry 871 he cautions himself against using that expression:

> S. I must not give the Soul or Mind the Scholastique Name pure act, but rather pure Spirit or active Being. (NB 870)

He was wise not to use it in print, because strictly speaking "pure act" applies solely to God, the only being who is fully perfected and without unrealized potential. Samuel Johnson brings out the dangers when he explains to Berkeley that "the Schoolmen, it is true, call the soul *actus* [act] and God *Actus purus* [pure act]; but I confess I never could well understand their meaning, perhaps because I never had the opportunity to be much versed in their writing" (*Works*, vol. 2, 288). Berkeley responds by assuring him he has "no doubt" that "the soul of man is passive as well as active" (*Works*, vol. 2, 293). I take this to be a deliverance of Berkeley's subject-consciousness. As he says at *Principles*, the ideas he perceives by sense are not dependent on his will:

> When in broad day-light I open my eyes, it is not in my power to choose whether I shall see or no, or to determine what particular objects shall present themselves to my view; and so likewise as to the hearing and other senses, the ideas imprinted on them are not creatures of my will. (P 29)

It follows that subject-consciousness does not unequivocally support the simplicity of spirit. Experience testifies that we are passive (in sense-perception) and active (in willing), and to the extent we follow its lead, it seems we should conclude that spirit is complex rather than simple.

I turn now to activity. Berkeley portrays spirit as essentially active and ideas (or things) as essentially passive. Along with the dualism of finite and infinite, this is probably the most fundamental dualism in his thinking, and in the next section I will explore a difficulty to which this gives rise. My present goal is to understand more fully why it is that subject-consciousness cannot reliably disclose the activity of spirit. Consider the traditional distinction between active and passive power, made for example by Locke (at various points in *Essay* II xxi).[24] In the seventeenth and eighteenth centuries, the distinction was often illustrated by the contrast between the active bodily power of *originating* motion and the passive bodily power of *transferring* it. Inertia was viewed as a merely passive power, capable of explaining why a body moves when another body collides with it, and why the body set in motion can move another body in turn. The active power of originating motion was ascribed by everyone (or virtually everyone) to God rather than to body, and by most (Locke, for example, but not occasionalists such as Malebranche) to finite minds. If Berkeleyan subject-consciousness is to disclose a similarly active power in spirit, it must show that spirit can *originate* change among ideas, just as a Lockean mind can originate bodily motion. But to assure us that the change we seem to originate truly has its source in spirit, subject-consciousness has to rule out the existence of any more ultimate cause from which our power to bring about change has been transferred. Even if subject-consciousness is infallible, though, it is very far from being able to rule out all such causes. I suppose it could be objected to this argument that we have no clear conception of how it is that that the power to cause change among ideas could be transferred from something else to our own selves. I would be the last to claim to have such a conception, but the effect of this concession may not be to save the belief that finite spirit can originate change among ideas, but to cast doubt on our very ability to investigate the question fruitfully. In this connection it may be worth recalling that many early modern philosophers, Locke among them, found even the transfer of motion very puzzling. The difficulties they encountered would not have persuaded them that the distinction between origination and transfer could not be sustained.

Spirit's activity, conceived as originating change, is, for Berkeley, closely related to its freedom, a topic examined at length in the seventh and final dialogue of *Alciphron*, where Berkeley's spokesman, the farmer-

---

[24] Scholastic treatments of this distinction, which (to judge from the notebooks) may have influenced Berkeley, are extremely complicated. For helpful discussion see Gracia 1982, 178-179, 238-239, and Pasnau 2002, 146-151.

philosopher Euphranor, claims to have "inward evidence" of freedom that can withstand Alciphron's elaborate arguments for what we now call hard determinism. There have been philosophers, Euphanor observes, who try to prove that there is no such thing as motion. "Walking before them," he says, "was thought the proper way to confute" them. "It is," he then adds, "no less evident that man is a free agent":

> So long as I am conscious of my own actions, this inward evidence of plain fact will bear me up against all your reasonings, however subtle and refined. ... It is evident to me, in the gross and concrete, that I am a free agent. ... I am conscious that I am an active being, who can and do determine myself. (Alc VII 18)

For reasons akin to those I've already stated, the deliverances of subject-consciousness cannot prove I am an uncaused cause of change.[25] Later, Euphranor attempts another defense of freedom, but it seems to involve a different conception of the notion:

> EUPHRANOR. To determine [the] question, ought we not first to determine what is meant by the word *free*?
> ALCIPHRON. We ought.
> EUPHRANOR. In my opinion, a man is said to be free so far forth as he can do what he will. Is this is so, or is it not?
> ALCIPHRON. It seem so.
> EUPHRANOR. Man, therefore, acting according to his will, is to be accounted free. (Alc VII 19)

Alciphron admits the conclusion in a "vulgar sense," but insists that a philosopher "goes higher." Euphranor mocks this suggestion, but his own earlier appeal to self-determination or agent-causation conveys the same basic thought.[26] In the notebooks, whose reflections on freedom seem closely linked to Berkeley's emerging conception of the self as active, the kind of compatibilist freedom at work in Euphranor's exchange with Alciphron is, at one point at least, condemned as superficial:

---

[25] The context of Euphranor's appeals to inward evidence suggests that Berkeley may see them as components of a wider attempt to show that belief in our freedom is (as we now say) "properly basic." But he frames that attempt very sketchily.

[26] For further evidence of a change in heart between the notebooks and *Alciphron*, compare entry 797 ("Hobbs in his object. 3. ridicules those expressions of the Scholastiques the Will wills etc so does Locke. I am of another Mind") with *Alciphron* VII 19 ("Whether he can will as he wills? I know not how philosophical it may be to ask this question, but it seems very idle").

> + In moral matters Men think (tis true) that they are free but this freedom is only the freedom of doing as they please, wch freedom is consecutive to the Will, respecting onely the operative faculties. (NB 156)

Throughout the notebooks Berkeley seems to be seeking a freedom internal to the will, rather than consecutive to it. Entries such as the following suggest that the will itself is determined by nothing but itself:

> S. Folly to enquire wt determines the Will. Uneasiness etc are Ideas, therefore unactive, therefore can do nothing therefore cannot determine the Will. (NB 653)

In view of his commitment to spirit's activity such self-determination (implying determination by nothing else) is just the kind of freedom he should be seeking, but it seems clear that it cannot be secured by bare appeals to subject-consciousness.

Is the Understanding Active or Passive?

In the *Notebooks*, as we have seen, Berkeley concludes that the mind is active in understanding, but in the *Principles* he seems to be of two minds about the point, sometimes denying it (as at P 29) and sometimes hinting at its truth (as at P 27). He struggles long and hard with the question in the notebooks. Early on, in entry 286, he says that the mind is passive in sensation or perception. In later entries, perhaps unhappy with the suggestion that the mind can in any way be passive, he identifies the whole mind or spirit with the will:

> S. The soul is the will properly speaking & as it is distinct from Ideas. (NB 478)
>
> S The Spirit the Active thing that wch is Soul & God is the Will alone The Ideas are effects impotent things. (NB 712)

Elsewhere he acknowledges that there is more to spirit than will, but suggests that whenever we perceive by sense, the active will collaborates:

> S. While I exist or have any Idea I am eternally, constantly
> willing, my acquiescing in the present State is willing. (NB 791)
>
> S. It seems there can be no perception, no Idea without Will, being there are no Ideas so indifferent but one had rather Have them than annihilation, or annihilation than them. or if there be such an equall Ballance there must be an equal mixture of pleasure & pain to cause it. there being No ideas perfectly void of all pain & uneasiness But wt are preferable to annihilation. (NB 833)

In an especially interesting entry, he suggests that whenever there is certainty, "We must not be altogether Passive, there must be a disposition to act, there must be assent, wch is active, nay wt do I talk There must be Actual Volition." In still other entries the activity of understanding is simply asserted, without supporting argument (NB 808, for example).[27]

Although Berkeley's take on the activity (or passivity) of the understanding was not entirely settled by the time he wrote the *Principles*, the passivity of sense perception is emphatically reasserted in a long and puzzling exchange in the First Dialogue.[28] The exchange raises a challenge to the interpretation of subject-consciousness I have put forward in this paper.

As the exchange begins, Hylas proposes a distinction between object and sensation (3D 194). "If I take you right," Philonous says, "you distinguish in every perception two things, the one an action of the mind, the other not." The exchange then runs as follows:

> PHILONOUS. When is the mind said to be active?
> HYLAS. When it produces, puts an end to, or changes any thing.
> PHILONOUS. Can the mind produce, discontinue, or change any thing but by an act of the will?
> HYLAS. It cannot.
> PHILONOUS. The mind therefore is to be accounted active in its perceptions, so far forth as volition is included in them.
> HYLAS. It is.
> PHILONOUS. In plucking this flower, I am active, because I do it by the motion of my hand, which was consequent upon my volition; so likewise in applying it to my nose. But is either of these smelling?
> HYLAS. No.
> PHILONOUS. I act too in drawing the air through my nose; because my breathing so rather than otherwise, is the effect of my volition. But neither can this be called smelling: for if it were, I should smell every time I breathed in that manner.
> HYLAS. True.
> PHILONOUS. Smelling then is somewhat consequent to all this.
> HYLAS. It is.
> PHILONOUS. But I do not find my will concerned any further. Whatever more there is, as that I perceive such a particular smell or any smell at all, this is independent of my will, and therein I am altogether passive. Do you

---

27 For an especially helpful survey of the early Berkeley's developing thoughts on spirit, see McCracken 1986.

28 McKim 1989 defends the view that the Berkeleyan mind is active in sense-perception.

> find it otherwise with you, Hylas?
> HYLAS. No, the very same.
> PHILONOUS. Then as to seeing, is it not in your power to open your eyes, or keep them shut; to turn them this or that way?
> HYLAS. Without doubt.
> PHILONOUS. But doth it in like manner depend on your will, that in looking on this flower, you perceive white rather than any other colour? Or directing your open eyes towards yonder part of the heaven, can you avoid seeing the sun? Or is light or darkness the effect of your volition?
> HYLAS. No, certainly.
> PHILONOUS. You are then in these respects altogether passive.
> HYLAS. I am.
> PHILONOUS. Tell me now, whether seeing consists in perceiving light and colours, or in opening and turning the eyes?
> HYLAS. Without doubt, in the former.
> PHILONOUS. Since therefore you are in the very perception of light and colours altogether passive, what is become of that action you were speaking of, as an ingredient in every sensation? (3D 196-197)

What troubles me about this passage is not that Philonous denies that sense-perception is an act, but that he (and through him Berkeley) seems to have no use for the distinction between the object of perception and the state (however construed) of the mind perceiving it. In the absence of such a distinction, my distinction between object-consciousness and subject-consciousness cannot (in the case of sense-perception) acquire a foothold. One quick way out of the difficulty is to say that Philonous is not rejecting every distinction between object and sensation, but only the particular distinction made by Hylas, [29] but I do not find this entirely satisfying. Hylas puts forward the distinction for a very simple reason: he is trying to create room for saying that although a sensation may be unable to exist "without the mind," the same needn't be true of its object (3D 194). If Philonous manages to defeat this maneuver only by treating the sensation as a full-fledged action, rather than as the actualization of a (possibly passive) capacity, he hasn't really addressed Hylas's underlying concern. Yet I do have to grant that at times in the *Dialogues*, Philonous seems more interesting in scoring debater's points than in advancing his interlocutor's understanding. This may be another of those times.[30]

---

[29] This is McKim's way of dealing with the passage (1989, 340-341).

[30] So much is actually suggested by the lines that immediately follow the exchange as I have quoted it. There Philonous finishes off the argument in a very odd way, apparently in order to saddle Hylas with a contradiction. Although I haven't looked into the matter closely, my feeling is that the *Dialogues* is deliberately shaped by the theory and practice of academic disputation.

The passivity of the Berkelyan mind is, in any case, more widespread than either the *Principles* or the *Dialogues* acknowledges. It is passive not only in sensation, but when undergoing suggestion or association, the mechanism at the heart of Berkeley's theory of vision.[31] Phenomenologically, an expectation seems no less distinct from the idea that is its object than an act of will is from the idea that it excites "at pleasure" (P 28). My concern is that in the exchange from the First Dialogue, Berkeley papers over a distinction that inward experience should incline him to recognize, and that accords with his dualism of spirit and idea.[32] It is a distinction that supports what is most vital and compelling in Berkeley's philosophy of mind.

Bibliography

Adams, Robert M. (1973), "Berkeley's 'Notion' of Spiritual Substance," *Archiv für Geschichte der Philosophie* 55, pp. 47-69.

Aristotle, *Categories*.

Ayers, Michael. (2005), "Was Berkeley an Empiricist or a Rationalist?," in Winkler (2005), pp. 34-62.

Bennett, Jonathan. (2001), *Learning from Six Philosophers*, vol. 2, Oxford University Press, Oxford.

Berkeley, George. (1976), *Philosophical Commentaries*, George H. Thomas (ed.), Mt. Union College, Alliance, Ohio.

—. (1948-1957), *The Works of George Berkeley*, 9 vols, A. A. Luce and T. E. Jessop (eds), Nelson, London.

Berman, David. (2005), "Berkeley's Life and Works," in Winkler (2005), pp. 13-33.

Bettcher, Talia Mae. (2007), *Berkeley's Philosophy of Spirit: Consciousness, Ontology, and the Elusive Subject*, Continuum, London.

Cummins, Phillip D. (2005), "Berkeley's Philosophy of Mind and Agency," in Winkler (2005), pp. 190-229.

Furlong, E. J. (1960), "An Ambiguity in Berkeley's *Principles*,"

[31] I see no reason why "internal" passions cannot be as passive as external ones. If an intense heat is also a pain, as Philonous contends in the First Dialogue, why can't intense loneliness also be a pain, and a pain no less passive than the other?

[32] As McKim for example astutely recognizes, to the extent that the Berkeleyan mind is passive, it seems that there could after all be an idea of it (1989, 337). He later observes that "if the mind is entirely passive in sense-perception, then Berkeley's crucial distinction between minds and ideas risks erosion, and his close association, if not outright identification, of the existence of a spirit with its perceiving is undermined" (343).

Hermathena 94, pp. 84-102.

Gracia, Jorge J. E. (ed.) (1982), *Suarez on Individuation*, Marquette University Press, Milwaukee.

Gueroult, Martial. (1956), *Berkeley: Quatre études sur la perception et sur dieu*, Aubier, Paris.

Hume, David. (2000), *A Treatise of Human Nature*, D. F. Norton and M. J. Norton (eds), Oxford University Press, Oxford.

Locke, John. (1975), *An Essay concerning Human Understanding*, P. H. Nidditch (ed), Clarendon Press, Oxford.

McKim, Robert. (1989), "Berkeley's Active Mind," *Archiv für Geschichte der Philosophie* 71, pp. 335-343.

Malebranche, Nicolas. (1980), *The Search after Truth*, T. M. Lennon and P. J. Olscamp (trs), Ohio State University Press, Columbus.

McCracken, Charles J. (1986), "Berkeley's Notion of Spirit," *History of European Ideas* 7, pp. 597-602.

Muehlmann, Robert. (1992), *Berkeley's Ontology*, Hackett, Indianapolis.

O'Shaughnessy, Brian. (1980), *The Will: A Dual Aspect Theory*, 2 vols, Cambridge University Press, Cambridge.

Pasnau, Robert. (2002), *Thomas Aquinas on Human Nature*, Cambridge University Press, Cambridge.

Ross, James F. (1981), *Portraying Analogy*, Cambridge University Press, Cambridge.

Russell, Bertrand. (1912), *The Problems of Philosophy*, Oxford University Press, Oxford.

Winkler, Kenneth P. (ed.) (2005), *The Cambridge Companion to Berkeley*, Cambridge University Press, Cambridge.

BELIEF AND ITS OBJECTS IN BERKELEY'S SYSTEM

MARTHA BRANDT BOLTON

Abstract

Berkeley maintains that when we immediately perceive a sensible thing, we certainly know the existence and nature of that thing. Knowledge, of the relevant anti-skeptical sort, implies assent to a propositional content, a content that is true or false. Yet Berkeley maintains that the immediate and proper objects of perception are colors, figures, tastes, and other sensible things which are not intrinsically propositional. At least they lack the complex structure that distinguishes propositions from their simple terms, ideas which represent sensible things (inter alia) in traditional logic. The paper aims to determine Berkeley's view of the intentional objects of perceptual knowledge and assent. Since the texts are nearly silent on this issue, the method of inquiry is to situate his view in context of theories of his near-contemporaries especially Locke and Hume.

Introduction

George Berkeley is nearly silent on two issues inevitably raised by theories of perception and knowledge. In present day terminology, the issues are: what are the intentional objects of belief and what are the sources of belief? Berkeley's silence is by no means typical of 17th and early 18th century philosophers of mind and metaphysicians. Early modern thinkers inherit these questions from their scholastic and humanist predecessors, and do not, in general, fail to address them. English language authors seldom use the word "belief" to signify the relevant mental state or attitude, roughly one which contrasts with doubt and suspense of judgment;[1] instead, they use "assent ," or "affirmation" and "denial." A quick survey may suffice to

[1] John Locke is unusual because he uses the term "belief"; he restricts it to assent to propositions that one takes to be probably true; see Locke 1975, 4.16.9.

indicate the currency of the two issues. Different accounts of the origin of assent (as I will call it) are implied by epistemic debate over the principles or standards by which assent is properly regulated. Among early moderns, some maintain that assent is the exclusive function of the sensory faculty, whereas others argue that it is the exclusive prerogative of the faculty of intellect.[2] René Descartes maintains that assent is an act of will in response to a propositional content presented to the will by intellect, sense or imagination;[3] others deny that assent is voluntary. Nor is the status of the things to which we assent neglected by Berkeley's immediate predecessors. In general, the intentional contents of affirmation, denial, knowledge, doubt, and the like are called "propositions" or "judgments."[4]

Logic manuals of the period typically devote a section to propositions – entities said to have a complex semantic structure in virtue of which they are either true of false.[5] The metaphysical status of these entities is problematic, and notoriously difficult. Crudely speaking, one might say that opinions range over the following alternatives. A proposition is either a mental act of a finite (or infinite) mind considered as a sign or representation; or a mental act of conceiving (or perceiving) considered with regard to its intentional object, which may depend for its existence on the acting mind or exist independently; or one or more sentences in a language, or a particular utterance of one or more sentences.[6]

Although the two issues in view are topical in Berkeley's time, it may not be surprising that he has little to say about them. After all, he wrote no systematic treatise on human understanding, nor any logic text. Yet the immaterialist philosophy he advocates, which consists largely of a theory of sense perception and sensible objects, is claimed to have important epistemic consequences. *The Principles of Human Knowledge* is one of his major works; it boasts that immaterialism withstands skepticism unlike its

---

[2] E.g. Cudworth 1996, 57-62 takes the Platonic view that the sensory faculty apprehends sensations prompted by the physical state of the sensory organs, but only the essentially active faculty of intellect is capable of forming propositions and capable of assent; also Malebranche 1980, 34; Leibniz 1981, 50-51, 143. Thomas Hobbes and Locke, by contrast, recognize no cognitive faculty distinct from the faculty of sense perception.

[3] Descartes 1984, 40.

[4] Propositions, or judgments, were seldom distinguished from mental acts of affirming or denying them; as a result, it is unclear that early modern philosophers recognized the possibility of entertaining a proposition without assent. See e.g. Arnauld and Nicole 1970, 156-159.

[5] E.g. Arnauld and Nicole 1970, 159.

[6] For one view of main scholastic doctrines and early modern views on these logico-semantic issues, see Nuchelmans 1983.

materialist competitor; experience is said to be a language in which God informs us about the world. All of this unmistakably implies that we form beliefs, that is we assent to something-or-other capable of being true or false. It is hardly to be supposed that Berkeley has no implicit positions, or at least assumptions, on the disputed questions concerning assent and its intentional objects. In the absence of some account of these matters, we cannot hope fully to grasp his notion of immediate perception or his anti-skeptical account of our knowledge and certainty of the existence of things we immediately perceive. The aim of this paper is to reconstruct an account of these assumptions of Berkeley on the basis of views explicitly held by his near contemporaries. The contextual evidence is drawn mainly from John Locke's *Essay concerning Human Understanding*, which greatly influenced the young Berkeley. The next section of the paper reviews Locke's position on the objects and sources of assent and suggests that Berkeley's views are very similar in some respects. The following section turns to the more difficult question of his views about the intentional objects of assent, arguing that Berkeley's view is very different from that of Locke. The final section considers the prospects for finding an account of the truth evaluable objects of knowledge and assent that would be congenial to Berkeley.

The Sources of Assent: Locke and a Surmise about Berkeley

According to Locke, knowing is nothing other than a sort of perceiving. As he defines it, "Knowledge ... [is] nothing but *the perception of the connexion and agreement, or disagreement and repugnancy of any of our Ideas*. In this alone it consists." (Locke 1975 IV.i.2). This formulation alludes to his theory of propositions, or the intentional objects of knowledge, in general, so let's begin with that. The most complete account of a proposition is embedded in his theory of truth:

> *Truth* then seems to me, in the proper import of the Word, to signify nothing but the *joining or separating of Signs, as the Things signified by them, do agree or disagree one with another*. The *joining or separating* of signs here meant is what by another name, we called Proposition. So that Truth properly belongs only to Propositions ... (Locke 1975, 4.5.2)

Signs are either mental signs, i.e. ideas, of which we are immediately aware, or words in a language; and ideas are the more fundamental of the two. A proposition is, then, composed of two mental signs "joined" or "separated" by a mental act; they are joined if the proposition is affirmative and separated, if negative.[7] A proposition is true provided it joins (separates) ideas as the things those ideas represent agree (disagree). Now the ideas themselves are said to "agree" ("disagree"), if they manifestly show that the things they signify are as they are represented to be – hence, the definition of knowledge.

The passage just quoted goes on to say there are verbal, as well as mental, propositions. For purposes of comparison with Berkeley, it is useful to have in view a rough sketch of Locke's theory of linguistic signification. On this account, words are conventionally assigned to ideas from which words inherit their signification.[8] Verbal propositions mirror mental ones. This is, roughly, because words and phrases other than "particles ," as Locke calls them, immediately signify ideas; ideas naturally signify other things, and the verbal signs are, thereby, signs of these things. Particles, moreover, immediately signify mental acts by which two or more ideas are combined, such as the acts of joining or separating signs that result in propositions; "is" and "is not" immediately signify acts of this sort.[9] On this theory, then, the meaning of a verbal proposition is determined by a corresponding mental proposition, and the former is true just in case the latter is. In general, Locke insists that propositions, alone, are properly true or false.[10] We just saw that propositions are complex signs which truly or falsely represent the things their constituents stand for.

Further, we saw that knowledge, for Locke, is perception of the manifest truth of a propositional representation. It hardly needs to be said that a person who knows a proposition assents to it. Indeed, Locke mentions it rarely, and only when using the verb "to know" would get in the way of his meaning. For instance, in arguing against innate knowledge, he grants that once we have acquired ideas "wherein the Agreement or Disagreement we can perceive in [those] Ideas, when put together, is expressed, we at first hearing assent." (Locke 1975, 1.2.23; 60: 35-61:1). Again, in connection with demonstrative knowledge: "This Knowledge by intervening Proofs, though it be certain, yet the evidence of it is not altogether so clear and bright, nor the assent so ready, as in intuitive Knowledge." (Locke 1975, 4.2.4)

In everyday affairs we often assent to, and act upon, assumptions

---

[7] This is very close to the account given in Arnauld and Nicole 1970, 156. The logic manual follows a prominent scholastic treatment; see Ashworth 1974, 26-32.

[8] For detailed accounts of Locke's theory of linguistic signification, see Ashworth 1981; Losonsky 1994.

[9] There are four ways in which ideas may be joined or separated; see Locke 1975, 4.1.2.

[10] Also Locke 1975, 2.32.1, 4.

which we do not strictly know in any way.[11] The *Essay* recognizes two different assent-producing operations:

> ... the Mind has two Faculties, conversant about Truth and Falshood.
> *First, Knowledge,* whereby it certainly perceives, and is undoubtedly satisfied of the Agreement or Disagreement of any Ideas.
> Secondly, Judgment, which is the putting Ideas together, or separating them from one another in the Mind, when their certain Agreement or Disagreement is not perceived, but presumed to be so. (Locke 1975, 4.14.4)

It is plain that knowledge consists in an act of assent intrinsic to an act of perceiving the manifest truth of a proposition; the causes of such perceptions are, at the same time, causes of assent. Judgment, by contrast, is assent to a proposition in the absence of perception of its truth.[12] In this case, Locke explains, "that which makes me believe is something extraneous to the thing I believe; something not ... manifestly showing the Agreement or Disagreement of those *Ideas*, that are under consideration" (Locke 1975, 4.15.3). In particular, a person's belief is caused by the "grounds of probability" of which she is apprised. There are two such grounds: the testimony she has received and her past experience.[13] To put it roughly, a person's having heard testimony or having relevant experiences causes it to seem to her that the proposition is more or less likely to be true. This appearance is the presumption of truth which constitutes judgment, or assent without certainty, as Locke has it. If the grounds of probability one has are strong enough to make the proposition nearly certain, assent is unhesitating.[14] If the grounds are weaker, however, one may withhold assent and choose to seek further evidence for and against the presumed truth. Many of us are able to exert some voluntary control over whether or not to seek further evidence, suspending judgment for the time being. But the press of circumstances often precludes this choice, and some of us have

---

[11] As mentioned above, "assent" is used in this paper as a synonym for what we know call "belief." The *Essay* often uses the term is this way; see e.g. Locke 1975, 1.2.4, 5, 17; 4.1.8; 4.6.1, 6, 9; 4.17.14; 4.20.15. But in 4.15 and 16, "assent" is explicitly restricted to the entertaining of propositions to which we have a range of attitudes including judging, guessing, doubting, and disbelieving; see 4.15.3 and 4.16 *passim*. It seems that the context imposes this restriction on the use of "assent," rather than Locke's understanding of its central meaning.

[12] For detailed discussion, see Owen 2007.

[13] Locke 1975, 4.15. These are also said to be "Foundations on which our *Assent* is built" (4.16.1), which suggests that judgment is the result of inference.

[14] Locke 1975, 4.16.

mental habits which make unbiased review of evidence psychologically impossible at least at the moment of judging. In context of the Cartesian theory of assent, the crucial point is that if judgment, or assent, takes place at all, it is caused by nothing but apprehension of the grounds of probability accessible to the person who judges. Volition may govern suspense of assent, "But that a Man should afford his Assent to that side, on which the less Probability appears to him, seems to me utterly impracticable, and as impossible, as it is to believe the same thing probable and improbable at the same time" (Locke 1975, 4.15.5). For Locke, then, a person's assent to the probable truth of a proposition, if she does assent, is included in the appearance of its probability caused by her apprehension of grounds of its probability.

Studying the *Essay*, Berkeley could have found the following doctrines: (1) Knowledge is intrinsic to perception of a certain sort of intentional content (namely, the agreement or disagreement of the ideas comprised in a proposition); perception of this sort is necessary and entirely sufficient for knowledge of what is so perceived. (2) Knowledge includes assent, and so does probable judgment. From these two doctrines, we can infer: (3) Assent is intrinsic to perception of a certain sort of intentional content (as above). More generally, a person's assent to a proposition is included in her awareness of either its manifest or evident truth or its probable truth. (4) Assent is given to nothing but intentional contents that are true or false and nothing is true or false but a proposition. Now as we will see, Berkeley cannot consistently agree with Locke's doctrine (4). But I want to suggest that he tacitly assumes (1) through (3). To be more exact, he assumes versions of these doctrines that omit the parts in parentheses which have reference to Locke's theory of propositions.

This may suffice to explain the fact that Berkeley typically says nothing about assent, or belief, in texts that speak of immediate perception, knowledge and certainty of the existence of the things we perceive by sense. It is likely that he just takes the first two Lockean doctrines for granted. Consider the following passages:[15]

> Wood, stones, fire, water, flesh, iron, and the like things, which I name and discourse of, are things that I know. And I should not have known them but that I perceived them by sense ... (3D 230)
>
> I see this cherry, I feel it, I taste it: and I am sure nothing cannot be seen, or felt, or tasted; it is therefore real . . .. Hence, when I see, and feel, and taste, in sundry manners, I am sure the cherry exists, or is real; its reality being in my opinion nothing abstracted from those sensations ... (3D 249)

[15] See 3D 224, 230, 237, 238, 249; P 40, 44, 88; TVV 20.

The first passage would seem to say that we know things such as wood and stones only if, and because, we perceive them by sense; so perception of a certain sort is at least necessary for knowledge, and perhaps sufficient. According to the second passage, seeing, feeling, or tasting in such-and-such a way is clearly sufficient for knowledge that a cherry presently exists. Taken together the two passages accord well with doctrine (1) expunged of allusions to Lockean propositions, even though no doctrine to this effect is explicitly stated by Berkeley, as far as I can see. The second passage plainly takes the intentional object of knowledge to be a content that is true rather than false. This would seem to imply that knowledge, and thus seeing, feeling, and the like, comprise assent. Although, here again, the texts seem to take this for granted, it is licensed by doctrines (2) and (3). To be sure, for Locke, knowledge consists in perception of something evidently, manifestly true; but then according to Berkeley, ideas and (parts of) sensible objects perceived by sense are evident, or manifest to the perceiver's awareness, for their being is to be perceived. My suggestion is that Berkeley tacitly adopts the view that a certain sort of perception is a sort of knowledge and, as such, intrinsically includes assent to what is perceived. This serves him in lieu of any explicit consideration of the origin of belief or assent. It is nothing other than a certain sort of perception.

Berkeley on the Intentional Objects of Assent

What are the intentional objects of perception, knowledge, and assent in Berkeley's view? To be sure, we can be said to know, or have some sort of acquaintance with, things that are not evaluable for truth or falsity at all.[16] Knowledge of this sort is not Berkeley's concern in passages like those above. If it were, then it would make no sense for him to pit his account of sense perception against skepticism. Skepticism is endemic to materialism, he contends, but forestalled by immaterialism. Skepticism is doubt raised by the apparent lack of evidence for and lack of evidence against the truth of that to which one might assent.[17] By claiming that immaterialism withstands skeptical doubt, Berkeley plainly indicates his concern with knowledge of the sort directed to something susceptible of being true or false.

---

[16] Although it is controversial that knowing-how is different in kind from knowing-that, there is also knowledge by acquaintance, e.g. knowing the taste of a pineapple.

[17] See e.g., 3D 173.

In the logical tradition, propositions, alone, are said to have the semantic properties and complex structure capable of truth and its opposite. Locke follows scholastic logic here. In this paper, unless otherwise indicated, "proposition" is used to mean a Lockean proposition, that is, a complex representation comprising two signs connected by a mental act that can be expressed by verbs such as the copula. Now according to Locke, an act of sense perception produces a semantic structure evaluable for truth and falsity; but this is a path Berkeley declines to follow.

Locke is in a position to say that ideas, in general, are signs. This is not just true of those ideas that represent actual or possible things in thought when one is not at the moment perceiving them by sense or reflection; the sensory ideas that are constituents of sense perceptions are also signs. For Locke, we perceive by sense only if we receive one or more sensory ideas caused by bodies operating on our sensory organs. Further, we perceive by sense only if we take the received ideas to be signs of the presence of external objects. We use the ideas as marks by which to distinguish things around us for purposes of acting.[18] Whether sense perception alone provides propositions of the sort that are the intentional contents of sensitive knowledge, according to Locke, is debatable.[19] Still sense perception intrinsically involves a sign referred to an external object which is, thereby, supposed to exist. A supposition to the effect that a certain sort of object presently exists is suitable for assent.[20] The structure of sense perception contains something propositional, for Locke. This is just to say perception has a representative structure, and this is just what Berkeley denies. He contends that the ideas we properly and immediately perceive are not representations of sensible objects without the mind, but rather sensible things themselves – colors, tastes, cherries, stones, and the like. In themselves, Berkeley's sensory ideas involve no signs, representations, or suppositions which might be true or false.[21]

Locke's traditionally minded doctrine that truth and falsity belong to propositions alone poses a challenge for such a view. Berkeley claims we know the existence and nature of things we immediately perceive by

---

[18] Locke 1975, 2.30.2; 2.23.1.

[19] Doubt about this is due more to Locke's account of knowledge than his view of propositions. It is very difficult to square the doctrine that knowledge is perception of a certain relation *between ideas* and the theory that "receiving *Ideas* from without" makes us know the present existence of particular things without us (Locke 1975, 4.11.3).

[20] Locke 1975, 2.32.4, 13-15, also 2.30.2.

[21] I refer here to a person's initial and basic objects of perception; the signification bestowed on such ideas by suggestion is discussed below in section 3.

sense; knowledge of the intended sort must be directed to something susceptible of truth and falsity, otherwise skepticism is not kept at bay. He faces a choice with regard to these truth-evaluable objects of knowledge – either retain the Lockean doctrine that propositions alone are capable of truth and falsity or reject it. Either choice has its price. If he follows tradition, he is forced to say that the propositions known directly through sense perception are extrinsic to immediate perception itself; that is, they describe or record what is currently perceived. In this case, propositional knowledge is directed to reports of what one perceives, because the objects of perception – figures, aromas, apples and the like – lack the semantic character and structure of propositions. We perceive sweet tastes and cherries, not that tastes and cherries exist. The second alternative is to deny that propositions alone are capable of truth and falsity. This would allow that present perception, in itself, contains a non-propositional structure which nevertheless has a truth value. On this view, the existence and natures of objects presently perceived is presented to awareness in a truth-evaluable way without involving Lockean representation. That is we perceive that a sweet red cherry exists without perceiving a Lockean proposition. This would clear the way for Berkeley to take from Locke the theory that perception comprises assent to, and knowledge of, this truth-evaluable content. But then it remains to explicate the truth-evaluable structure comprised in non-propositional objects of sense perception.

The second alternative is puzzling, to my mind; but there are two reasons to think Berkeley opts for it. One comes from the *Notebooks*, which contain several entries that endorse non-propositional truths. Of course interpreting these notes is risky; even if I am right that non-propositional objects of perceptual knowledge are envisaged there, Berkeley may reject them later on. The second reason in support of the non-propositional view comes from reviewing the resources for framing propositions available to Berkeley. This makes it highly implausible that immediate perceptual knowledge is directed to propositions, as Berkeley sees it, or so I will argue.

Berkeley's *Notebooks* contain an entry expressing doubt that all truths are Lockean propositions: "I approve not of that which Locke says viz truth consists in the joining or separating of signs" (NB 554). This shows, at least, a willingness to entertain the possibility that truth pertains to something in addition to representations constructed from mental or verbal signs.

Moreover, the notebooks uncouple linguistic propositions and mental ones. Berkeley has several ways of prying them apart, but one is especially pertinent for us.[22] The wedge is driven by the formal properties openly displayed by verbal propositions, and it is motivated by Locke's doctrine of trifling propositions.[23] The earlier philosopher belittles identical propositions, such as those expressed by "The soul is the soul" and "A law is a law"; he calls them "trifling." Although certainly true, they are uninstructive, useless, "merely verbal certainties." Locke means to debunk the widely held theory that the law of identity is a main foundation of human knowledge. Still he is committed to saying that verbal identities correspond to mental identities, for otherwise they would be neither significant nor true.

Berkeley, by contrast, ascribes identical form exclusively to verbal propositions. And verbal identities are "nonsensical," he says; I take him to mean that they do, indeed, signify nothing.[24] It seems he agrees with Locke that a linguistic formula means nothing unless it gets its meaning from a mental counterpart, but apparently he thinks mental representations cannot be formally regimented.[25] *Notebooks* contains several entries to this effect: "Homo est homo etc comes at last to Petrus est Petrus etc Now if these identical Propositions are sought after in the Mind they will not be found. There are no identical mental Propositions tis all about sounds & terms." (NB 728).[26] Still a series of comments records Berkeley's fascination with propositions that have the form of identities. Kenneth Winkler plausibly suggests that during this period, he explores the view that all demonstrable necessary truths are true in virtue of tautologous form.[27] Demonstration would then consist in displaying formal relations among combinations of words regarded as definitions.

This helps explain the following entry, which is especially revealing

---

[22] See e.g. Nuchelmans 1983 for one account of Berkeley's departure from Lockean theory.

[23] NB 771 mentions this doctrine of Locke.

[24] "A stone is a stone. This is a nonsensical Proposition & such as a Solitary Man would never think on Nor do I believe he would ever think on this viz that a whole is greater than its parts, etc." (NB 592).

[25] Charles McCracken plausibly suggested to me that Berkeley denies formal mental identities for the same reason Hume does (Hume 2000, 1.4.2). As I understand the point, two ideas co-present in a mind represent two objects, on Hume's theory of representation, and two objects are not one. See Baxter 2008, 48-67.

[26] Also: "Cogito ergo sum, tautology, no mental Proposition answering thereto." NB 738; "There are four sorts of Propositions Gold is a Metall, Gold is yellow; Gold is fixt, Λ Gold is not a stone. Of which 1st 2nd & 3rd are merely Nominal and have no mental propositions answering them." NB 793; also 592.

[27] Winkler 1989, 82-95.

for our purpose. Here Berkeley is so struck by the certainty of the truth of formally identical verbal propositions that he momentarily questions whether he is certain of anything else:

> We may have certainty and knowledge without Ideas Λ. (NB 730)
> Λ i.e. without other Ideas than the Words & their standing for one idea i.e. their being to be used indifferently. (NB 730a)
> It seems to me that we have no certainty about ideas. But only about words. Tis improper to say I am certain I see, I feel etc. there are no Mental propositions form'd answering to these Words & in simple perception tis allowed by all there is no affirmation or negation & consequently no certainty. (NB 731)
> This seems wrong certainty real certainty is of sensible ideas pro hic & nunc. I may be certain w/o affirmation or negation. (NB 731a)

The first comment (NB 730) states a hypothesis; the next to last entry (NB 731) reaches a conclusion drawn from the initial comment; the final remark (NB 731a) repudiates the hypothesis.[28] According to the hypothesis, certainty pertains only to words, or verbal propositions. Berkeley notes that if this is correct, we cannot be certain with regard to what we see, feel, or otherwise perceive by sense – if I utter a sentence such as "I see a cat," its truth is uncertain. Clearly this sentence is not true in virtue of tautologous form. The note offers two more particular reasons to say that such utterances are uncertain. First, they do not inherit certainty from corresponding mental propositions, because there are no matching mental propositions, or so the entry states. This is not explained, but we might speculate it is because Berkeley thinks we have no idea of the referent of "I"; or perhaps, the sentence implies an act-object division which is not present in the perceptual situation, as he sees it (see NB 578, 585). The second reason the verbal perceptual report is uncertain is that simple perception lacks the complexity of what can be affirmed or denied; I take this to be a reference to the distinctive complexity of propositions. Summing up, the hypothesis implies that we cannot be certain about the existence of things perceived by sense, and so far this is confirmed. But Berkeley cannot accept the conclusion and pronounces against the hypothesis. He is then driven to say that simple perception gives us certainty without affirmation or denial; that is, without assent to something with the complex structure of a proposition. Berkeley apparently arrives at a view on which we are certain of something evaluable for truth and falsity that is not a Lockean proposition. This unorthodox position may be

---

[28] *Ibid.*, p. 96 notes that NB 731a is written on the back of the page with 731 on the front.

momentarily tolerated here, but is it retained in published work?

Many passages proclaim that we have knowledge or certainty of the existence of things we perceive by sense. Two are quoted above; here are two more: "I can as well doubt my own being, as of the being of those things which I actually perceive by sense: it being a manifest contradiction, that any sensible object should be immediately perceived by sight or touch, and at the same time have no existence in Nature, since the very existence of an unthinking being consists in *being perceived*" (P 88). He also writes:

> . . .it is my opinion that the real things are those very things I see and feel, and perceive by my senses. These I know and finding they answer all the necessities and purposes of life, have no reason to be solicitous about any other unknown beings . . .. It is likewise my opinion that colours and other sensible qualities are on the objects. I cannot for my life help thinking that snow is white, and fire hot ... (3D 230)

When I know or cannot doubt the existence of something I perceive, what sort of intentional object is known or indubitable? We have two candidates before us: a propositional representation that describes or reports the things perceived and a non-propositional content contained in immediate perception of things, as envisaged in Notebooks.

The first view is favored by some astute interpreters of Berkeley. In a careful consideration of texts, to which I cannot do justice here, Kenneth Winkler notes that immediate perception is of sensible qualities and objects that are non-propositional. He takes this to show that, although perception is sensory awareness, it is not so far knowledge-involving. Yet immediate perception is epistemic for Berkeley, Winkler observes. In view of this, he suggests, Berkeley is best interpreted as follows: "Immediate perception is, at the very least, a form of non-propositional awareness, and as it occurs in human beings belief tends to follow in its train. In Berkelean seeing there is, characteristically, epistemic or doxastic involvement."[29] In other words, belief is not comprised in sense perception itself, but belief generally follows immediately after perception in human beings. Winkler does not elaborate, but it is natural to assume that on this interpretation, belief is directed to a proposition which records what was just perceived. George Pappas argues carefully and in great detail for an account similar in that immediate perception, as such, is said to be "fully non-epistemic."[30] That is, the fact that one immediately perceives

[29] *Ibid.*, 156.

[30] Pappas 2000, 168.

something does not, in itself, imply that one gains knowledge or even belief.[31] But, in a person who has acquired the requisite concepts, immediate perception is typically attended by a proposition which describes the object perceived. Such propositional reports are in some way, which Pappas does not explain here, justified by perception, on this interpretation.[32] To be sure, the view that non-propositional perceptual content justifies propositional belief is of considerable theoretical interest in its own right. But what recommends it as an interpretation of Berkeley is mainly that it avoids non-propositional objects of *knowledge*, or non-propositional entities evaluable for truth and falsity. To put it differently, such interpretations preserve the traditional doctrine that the objects of knowledge are Lockean propositions.

If this is right, Berkeley adheres to Locke's doctrine (4). This conflicts with his subscribing to doctrines (1) through (3); they state that knowledge and assent are contained in perceptions of a certain sort and the intentional content of perception is non-propositional, according to Berkeley. So perhaps the earlier suggestion that he tacitly assumes (1) through (3) is mistaken. In fact, however, the sort of interpretation we are considering is problematic in view of the resources for framing propositions available in Berkeley's philosophy. This is because, to begin with, propositions are either verbal or mental. Verbal propositions are clearly not the primary objects known on the basis of sense perception, for Berkeley. On the contrary, he urges that words are a distraction and source of error in matters pertaining to the existence and nature of sensible things.[33]

As for mental propositions, they are composed of mental representations or signs. In Berkeley's theory of mind, there is one, and only one, type of ideas that are, in their own right, signs or representations, namely, ideas of imagination, which are copied from, resemble, and said to represent things immediately perceived by sense.[34] Abstract general ideas are also signs, but they reduce to particular ideas of imagination and a certain mental disposition.[35] Ideas of imagination, copied as they are from sensory

---

[31] Pappas 2000, 164-167.

[32] Pappas 2000, 252.

[33] PI 25; P 54.

[34] See P 30, 33; 3D 235.

[35] In *Manuscript Introduction to the Principles* (MI) (Belfrage 1987) Berkeley says that a general abstract idea is a particular idea which the mind uses to stand for all other particular ideas similar to it (in a selected respect), whereas PI merely says the particular idea stands for other ideas in the same kind (selected by attention). But because a particular idea cannot stand for things in a kind that the particular idea does not exemplify, it represents on the same basis all images do, namely,

presentations, are images. The problem is that propositions formed from nothing but images are images themselves. If a person who sees and tastes an apple frames a mental proposition describing what she perceives, the proposition is nothing but a complex visual and gustatory image similar to the apple she perceived. To ascribe to Berkeley the view that sense perception of an object is regularly attended by an image of this object is already implausible. Sense experience rarely exhibits this sort of duplication, and none of the texts suggest it does.

A more theoretical difficulty is that an image cannot do the work a propositional representation is meant to do; it cannot serve as the intentional object when we know the existence of things we perceive by sense. There is no image of the existence of a thing, as David Hume was shortly to point out. To elaborate briefly: an image is true of an object in virtue of resembling it; it is typically thought that an image is arbitrarily divisible into parts, each of which represents a corresponding part of the object. What an image conveys about a thing is a function of the parts the image comprises and their mutual order. For instance, it signifies that a man wears a hat only if it contains a part that images a man suitably related to a part that images a hat. There is no image of existence to combine with other images in the effort to represent the existence of such a man. A view on which we assent to Lockean propositions has the advantage that we assent to structures that represent perceptual objects and their existence. But for Berkeley, perceptual content lacks this sort of structure; for that reason, so do the ideas that copy perceptual content. Berkelian images can represent the sensible features of sensible things, but cannot represent their existence. His imagistic theory of representation will not support a theory on which knowledge of the existence of things perceived by sense is directed to Lockean propositions.

So far, however, I have neglected the fact that there is representational structure contained in mediate perception, according to Berkeley. This is the sort of perception introduced in his treatise on vision. The objects proper to vision alone are light, colors, and nothing more; in themselves, Berkeley contends, the proper objects of sight signify nothing with regard to the distances, figures, or situations of objects in the line of sight. When we first begin to use our eyes, we can *see* nothing but light and color. However, entirely as a result of experience, we come to regard different colors and patterns of light (plus attendant cues) as signs of the spatial properties of tangible objects. As a result, we acquire the ability to have *mediate* perception of tangible objects by sight. For us, the point is that

---

resemblance.

mediated visual perception, unlike non-mediated perception of the proper objects of sight, comprises signs, or representations, of tangible objects. The following passage from the treatise on vision, *Theory of Vision*, conveys the theory:

> ... having of a long time experienced certain ideas, perceivable by touch, as distance, tangible figure, and solidity, to have been connected with certain ideas of sight, I do upon perceiving these ideas of sight forthwith conclude what tangible ideas are, by the wonted course of Nature like to follow. Looking at an object I perceive a certain visible figure and colour, with some degree of faintness and other circumstances, which from what I have formerly observed, determine me to think that if I advance forward so many paces or miles, I shall be affected with such and such ideas of touch. (TV 45)

Berkeley often calls this sign function "suggestion."[36] In subsequent works, suggestion is extended to all sense modalities:

> ... when I hear a coach drive along the streets, immediately I perceive only the sound; but from the experience I have had that such a sound is connected with a coach, I am said to hear the coach. It is nevertheless evident, that in truth and strictness, nothing can be *heard* but *sound*: and the coach is not then properly perceived by sense, but suggested from experience. So likewise when we are said to see a red-hot bar of iron; the solidity and heat of the iron are not the objects of sight, but suggested to the imagination by the colour and figure, which are properly perceived by sight. (3D 204)

This is fortunate for us, because, as it is put in the *Principles*, it "gives us a sort of foresight, which enables us to regulate our actions for the benefit of life." (P 31)

If hearing a sound suggests a coach to me, then it causes my imagination to form ideas that represent the purported coach.[37] Because such ideas are images, hence intrinsically representative, they may be evaluated for truth, that is, for correctly representing a portion of the sensible world. I will call this sort of truth-evaluable representation an "image based proposition" to distinguish it from a Lockean proposition. The latter contains mental acts expressed by "is" and "is not ," and is capable of representing that an object exists. In fact, Berkeley's theory of suggestion requires that such image based propositions express subjunctive

---

[36] P 43; TV 16, 17, 25; TVV 39, 58, 60.

[37] On the point that the ideas formed are representative ideas of imagination, as opposed to ideas perceived by sense, see Glauser 2003.

conditional predictions to the effect that if I were to have such-and-such tactile-motor sensations, then I would feel such-such tangible object.[38] Now we might well ask how a complex image can represent the conditional form and subjunctive mood of this prediction, but images are at least representations. Let us grant, for the sake of argument, that a theory of image based propositions supports Berkeley's view of the intentional content *suggested* by sensible objects proper to sight, hearing, touch, and so on. We are trying to discover the truth evaluable objects of sense perception and knowledge, according to Berkeley. It might seem that the predictive proposition included in an act of mediate perception provides the intentional content we seek. But it is important to understand that the coach that is suggested is distinct from the sound that suggests it. The properly auditory perception is the cause, and the image of a purported coach is the habitual effect. The former is the sign; the latter represents the thing signified. A person needs to perceive the sign in order to think of what it stands for.

Still sensory awareness sometimes fuses the sign and the object it signifies, mixes them so inextricably that we are unable to disentangle them.[39] The image of a tangible and visible coach may be so indiscernibly mixed with the sound that caused imagination to form it, that we seem literally to hear the tangible vehicle. It might then seem that the image based proposition describing the coach is the only available object of knowledge and assent. This cannot be right. The image based propositions suggested to a perceiver cannot be the *only* truth-evaluable components of what she perceives. Assent to the *present* existence of the sign, for instance the sound, is what inclines one to assent to the prediction, in this instance that a coach is about to come into view. Berkeley insists on the difference between perceived objects of these two sorts; consider the following passage on a different instance of mediated perception:

> Thus in the case of the oar, what he immediately perceives by sight is certainly crooked; and so far he is in the right. But if he thence conclude, that upon taking the oar out of the water he shall perceive the same crookedness; or that it would affect his touch, as crooked things are wont to do: in that he is mistaken ... But his mistake lies not in what he perceives immediately and at present (it being a manifest contradiction to suppose he should err in respect of that) but in the wrong judgment he makes concerning the ideas he apprehends to be connected with those immediately perceived: or concerning the ideas that, from what he

[38] See e.g. TV 45.

[39] TV 144-145; TVV 52. Atherton 2008 stresses this point in connection with the constitution of sensible objects.

> perceives at present, he imagines would be perceived in other circumstances ... (3D 238)

The proper object of sight, the object the man perceives by using sight alone, is something bent[40]; by virtue of an acquired habit, it signifies to him a tangible oar and this particular man judges that he would feel a bent oar if he were to reach out his hand. He is right with regard to the first; indeed error is impossible here.[41] But he can, and actually does, err with regard to the second. The man assents to two distinctly different truth-evaluable contents. Moreover, the content perceived by sight alone involves no image based proposition, whereas belief in the predicted object of touch is directed to the intentional object of such a proposition. Perhaps the man is scarcely aware of the properly visible oar; nevertheless, were it not for the fact that he assents to its existence, he would make no judgment about how the oar would feel.[42] Anyone with the right breadth of experience has perceptions involving signs and image based propositions, but this does nothing to relieve the systematic need for non-propositional objects of perception, knowledge, and assent.

Prospects for Resolving the Question

We found that Berkeley assumes objects perceived, as opposed to suggested, by sense have a truth evaluable structure that is neither a Lockean nor an image-based proposition. Yet this thesis about the intentional objects of sense perception is never explicitly mentioned in the texts, and Berkeley has no occasion to explicate the structure that renders it susceptible of truth. Still, as we saw, he is not afraid to challenge the accepted doctrine that Lockean propositions are the only objects of knowledge and certainty, hence assent. Even though no alternative is proposed in the texts, we can make a few surmises about how he thinks of the intentional objects of perceptual knowledge.

---

[40] The "proper" objects of a sense modality are objects of the sort perceived by that modality alone; by the same token, perception of such objects is due to that one sensory faculty alone. By speaking of the "proper" object or the object perceived by use of a "single faculty," rather than the object of "immediate perception," I intend to avoid taking a stand on the controversial question whether the things we immediately perceive include sensible objects, i.e. collections of ideas, or are instead restricted to ideas currently presented to the perceiver's sensory awareness. See, e.g., the paper by George Pappas in this volume and Atherton 2008.

[41] Also 3D 230; P 88.

[42] TV 3; TVV 27.

The earlier suggestion that Berkeley tacitly accepts the three Lockean theses mentioned earlier has borne out so far. Moreover, his commitment to a theory of sense perception without representations of the objects perceived is unfailing. It is the materialists who think sense perception comprises awareness of sensory ideas which supposedly represent objects that exist "without the mind," cherries, stones, and the like. For Berkeley, we perceive a stone provided that the stone is presented to sensory awareness. To be sure, a sensible object, such as a stone, is a vast collections of ideas (P 1), but for Berkeley, it seems that a person's present sensory awareness of just one, or more, of the ideas contained in a collection of ideas that compose an actual stone counts as her perceiving a stone by sense.[43] All of this points to a *de re* theory of perception, i.e. a theory on which we perceive objects rather than objects as represented by a propositional content. On this account, if I perceive an object *x*, and *x* is identical to *y*, then I perceive *y*.[44] I do not perceive *x* as *F*, and perceive that an *F* exists; instead, no way of characterizing the object is implied by the intentional content I perceive. Given the Lockean doctrines Berkeley seems to accept, this implies a *de re* notion of knowledge and assent, as well. By this I mean, a notion on which we know an object and affirm (or deny) something of the object, as opposed to the object under some representation.

This may find some confirmation in passages, some quoted above, where Berkeley claims to know the things he perceives. *De re* locutions are typical: we know cherries, stones, and houses; we are certain of the existence of cherries, and so on.[45] More important, consider this passage (quoted above):

> I can as well doubt my own being, as of the being of those things which I actually perceive by sense: it being a manifest contradiction, that any sensible object should be immediately perceived by sight or touch, and at the same time have no existence in Nature ... (P 88; also 3D 230)

---

[43] As we saw, perception of one or more ideas by a single sensory faculty typically suggests a proposition to the perceiver. The relevance of this to the question whether the person perceives a sensible object deserves more attention than I can give it here.

[44] See also Pappas 2000, 157-158.

[45] E.g. 3D 224, 237, 249; P 40. I do not place a great deal of weight on the grammatical fact that "perception" takes a noun, rather than a "that" clause, in Berkeley's usage. Still, although Locke sometimes speaks of knowing the existence of things of some kind, e.g. something black and white, a piece of paper, a man, he seems to think this is the same as knowing that a thing of this kind exists; Locke 1975, 4.11.1-3.

What is the argument Berkeley intends to make? It is, indeed, a contradiction to suppose that I perceive a stone that does not exist, but this remark hardly seems apt. In an anti-skeptical defense of perceptual knowledge, we do not expect a premise claiming that we actually perceive a stone. To take for granted that a stone is perceived makes things altogether too easy. But the passage can be seen to contain more by way of argument, if it is read in terms of a *de re* notion of perception and knowledge. On this account, we perceive a stone and know its existence; this contrasts with perceiving an object as a stone and knowing that a stone presently exists. The *de re* reading yields an argument along the following lines. *De re* existential affirmations, unlike assent to propositions of the sort just illustrated, are guaranteed to be true if they have any truth value at all. It is impossible that I affirm existence of an object that does not exist. So my affirmations of the existence of things I perceive *de re* cannot be false. Of course, the anti-skeptical force of this point is debatable. For although affirmations of the sort in question cannot be false, they need not be true. Perhaps Berkeley means to stress the pragmatics of the situation: if we merely succeed in affirming existence of something, we are assured of knowing its existence. In any case, I am inclined to think the passage trades on a *de re* theory of perception, affirmation, and knowledge.

But even if this is right, two crucial matters remain to be explained: how we apprehend the existence of an object of perception and how this apprehension combines with the object perceived to form an intentional content suitable for assent, or capable of being true. In fact, Berkeley sees no need to explain either matter. As we said at the start, the metaphysical status of things capable of truth and falsity was a long-established *topos* in Berkeley's time; many early modern philosophers address it. To Berkeley's mind, however, philosophers are benighted on any number of issues; he took no interest in their disputes. We might, then, attribute his lack of concern to his tendency to ally with the mob against the philosophers.[46]

But although Berkeley wrote no essay of the sort in which such philosophical issues were typically discussed, it was not long before one was composed by Hume. *A Treatise of Human Nature* is an empirical investigation of the workings of the human mind; as such, it is not completely silent on the issues we have in view. This is relevant to our topic because Hume shares with his predecessor an image theory of mental representation. We might, then, glean from the later philosopher's account

[46] I am grateful to Ken Winkler for suggesting to me that Berkeley may have thought there is no need to posit things capable of truth and falsity.

of human cognition a model suitable to fill out Berkeley's theory of perceptual knowledge.

It is well known that Hume reserves the term "idea" for perceptions that serve to represent, or direct thought to, things which we are not presently experiencing, e.g. we form an idea of the sun when thinking of it at night. In effect, Hume's ideas function as ideas of imagination do for Berkeley. In Hume's terminology, sense perceptions are called "impressions." Both authors maintain that sense perceptions are like mosaics in that they have no structure other than minimal parts and the wholes they compose. For Locke, on the contrary, sense perception is articulated by one or more ideas of sensible qualities, which the perceiver refers to a common object in which they are supposed to inhere. We saw that for Berkeley, ideas of imagination copy and represent sensory ideas. Hume's theory is similar. According to his Copy Principle, every idea either copies and represents a simple impression or is composed of ideas that do so. Ideas are, then, nothing but images with no means of representation other than resemblance to the objects they represent. In short, Hume's resources for truth evaluable representation are similar to his predecessor's.

Most of *Treatise*, Book I is devoted to explaining the causes of various natural human beliefs.[47] Beliefs are true or false; they are directed to propositions, according to Hume, and he does not neglect the semantic structure distinctive of propositions. The traditional model, two signs united by a mental act corresponding to the copula, hardly suits a theory on which signs of things are nothing but images of those things. As we said, images represent by virtue of their qualitative and mereological features; images have no resources for representing the existence of things they are images of. It is only to be expected that Hume is critical of the logicians' theory of propositions.

Existential propositions are his main case in point. On the traditional account, we have an idea of existence, which is available to combine with the idea of an object to form an existential proposition.[48] If we have such an idea, Hume contends, it is copied from an impression of existence. But it is plain that we have no impression of existence distinct from the impression of something that exists. As he concludes, "The idea of existence, then, is the very same with the idea of what we conceive to be existent." (Hume 2000, 1.2.6) This grounds his case against the logical doctrine:

---

[47] As is well known, Hume uses "belief" more or less as we do nowadays.

[48] See Locke 1975, 2.7.1.

> For ... 'tis far from being true, that in every judgment, which we form, we unite two different ideas; since in that proposition, God is, or indeed any other, which regards existence, the idea of existence is no distinct idea, which we unite with that of the objects, and which is capable of forming a compound idea by the union. (Hume 2000, 1.3.7, n. 1)

According to Hume, propositions are "nothing but particular ways of conceiving our objects." Applying this to existential propositions:

> . . .tho' every impression and idea we remember be consider'd as existent, the idea of existence is not deriv'd from any particular impression. The idea of existence, then, is the very same with the idea of what we conceive to be existent. To reflect on any thing simply, and to reflect on it as existent, are nothing different from one another. ... Whatever we conceive, we conceive to be existent. Any idea we please to form is the idea of a being; and the idea of a being is any idea we please to form. (Hume 2000, 1.2.6)

A proposition is a way of conceiving an object, and any object we perceive is conceived as an existent. We might hope to find in this a suitable answer to the questions Berkeley's texts leave unanswered.

The rough idea would be that any object we perceive by sense is thereby conceived as existent. This way of conceiving the object might seem to provide the truth evaluable structure included in the intentional object of perception. This is one of the points, mentioned earlier, which needs to be explained. The other point to be explicated is how we apprehend the existence of objects we perceive by sense. Hume's account of the idea of the existence of a thing might prove helpful with this as well. Yet the way to this is not smooth. Hume seems to think that it is only when we remember or reflect upon an impression or idea that we conceive it as existing. At the moment of perceiving an impression of sense we do not conceive it this way; it is only afterward, when we reflect on just having the impression that we conceive it as a being. Again, Hume does not say that the idea of an object and the idea of its existence are precisely the same idea; rather, "the idea of existence ... is the same with the idea of what we conceive to be existent."

It seems we must consider a thing, conceive it as existing, in order to form an idea of its existence. Applying these theories to Berkeley's account of perceptual knowledge would require some adjustments. Most glaring, in view of our discussion, it would complicate the *de re* theory of perception and knowledge that Berkeley favors. That is, inserting Hume's theory, that an existential proposition is the conception of an object as existing, into Berkeley's Lockean doctrine, that perceiving an object by sense includes knowing the existence of the object, would require that the intentional object of perception include a sort of representation; namely, a conception of the object perceived as existing. Sense perception would then have a *de re* component and a *de dicto*, or representational, component, the former not evaluable for truth and the latter assured of being true.[49] As for the representational constituent, Berkeley recognizes no mental act comparable to Hume's notion of considering an idea; it is not clear how the act of conceiving something as existing could be accommodated in his philosophy. Nevertheless, the basic theory that propositions are ways of conceiving our objects conjoined with Hume's account of existential propositions might be bent to Berkeley's purposes. It would be an error to read it back into the earlier philosopher's texts, but we might at least surmise that reading his predecessor's work called Hume's attention to the peculiarity of existential beliefs.

Bibliography

Arnauld, Antoine and Pierre Nicole. (1970), *La Logique, ou L'art de Penser* (5th ed., 1683), Louis Marin (ed.), Flammarion, Paris.

Ashworth, E. J. (1974), *Language and Logic in the Post-Medieval Period*, Reidel, Dordrecht.

—. (1981), "'Do Words Signify Ideas or Things?' The Scholastic Sources of Locke's Theory of Signification," *Vivarium* 14, 299-326

Atherton, Margaret. (2007), "The Objects of Immediate Perception," in Daniel (2007), pp. 107-120.

—. (2008). "'The Books Are in the Study as Before: Berkeley's Claims about Real Physical Objects," *British Journal of the History of Philosophy*, 16, pp. 85-100.

Baxter, Don. (2008). *Hume's Difficult*, Routledge, London.

Belfrage, Bertil. (1987), *George Berkeley's Manuscript Introduction: An Edition Diplomatica Transcribed and Edited with Introduction and Commentary by Bertil Belfrage*, Doxa, Oxford.

Berkeley, George. (1948-1957), *The Works of George Berkeley*, 9 vols, A. A. Luce and T. E. Jessop (eds), Nelson, London.

Berlioz, Dominque (ed.) (2003), *Berkeley. Langage de la perception et art de voir*, Presses Universitaires de France, Paris.

Cudworth, Ralph. (1996). *Treatise concerning Eternal and Immutable*

[49] Berkeley also claims to know the natures of the objects he perceives. It is not clear how Hume's doctrines could be used to explicate the truth evaluable structure that implies.

Morality, S. Hutton (ed.), Cambridge University Press, Cambridge.
Daniel, Stephen H. (ed.) (2007), *New Interpretations of Berkeley's Thought*, Humanity Books, Amherst, NY.
Descartes, René. (1984). *Philosophical Writings of Descartes*, vol. 2, J. Cottingham, R. Stoothoff, and D. Murdoch (trs), Cambridge University Press, Cambridge.
Glauser, Richard. (2003), "La structure de la perception médiate dans la théorie berkeleyenne de la vision," in Berlioz (2003), pp. 103-133.
Hume, David. (2000), *A Treatise of Human Nature*, D. F.Norton and M. J. Norton (eds.), Oxford University Press, Oxford.
Leibniz, G. W. (1981), *New Essays*, P. Remnant and J. Bennett (trs), Cambridge University Press, Cambridge.
Locke, John. (1975), *An Essay concerning Human Understanding*, P. H. Nidditch (ed.), Clarendon Press, Oxford.
Losonsky, Michael. (1994) "Locke on Meaning and Signification" in Rogers (1994), pp. 123-141.
Newman, Lex (ed.). (2007), *Cambridge Companion to Locke's Essay concerning Human Understanding*, Cambridge University Press, Cambridge.
Malebranche, Nicholas. (1980), *Search After Truth*, T. M. Lennon and P. J. Olscamp (trs), Ohio State University Press, Columbus.
Nuchelmans, Gabriel. (1983), *Judgement and Proposition from Descartes to Kant*, North Holland, Amsterdam.
Owen, David. (2007), "Locke on Judgment ," in Newman (2007), pp. 406-435.
Pappas, George. (2000), *Berkeley's Thought*, Cornell University Press, Ithaca.
Rogers, G. A. J. (ed.). (1994), *Locke's Philosophy: Content and Context*, Clarendon Press, Oxford.
Winkler, Kenneth. (1989), *Berkeley: An Interpretation*, Oxford University Press, Oxford.

CERTAINTY AND KNOWLEDGE OF OBJECTS IN BERKELEY

GEORGE S. PAPPAS

Abstract

Berkeley contends, both in the *Notebooks* and in his later published works, that in his philosophy there is intuitive knowledge of ordinary physical objects. Berkeley also says that such intuitive knowledge is not claimed by other philosophers to whom he is opposed, and hints that these philosophers cannot claim intuitive knowledge of objects. His idea seems to be that relative to this issue, his philosophical position is superior. The same sorts of comments are made about certainty. Berkeley claims that on his philosophy we have certain knowledge of objects, while on rival systems this is not so. Berkeley counts this very fact as a mark of the superiority of his philosophical position over those he opposes.

I consider what Berkeley may have meant with his claims about intuitive and certain knowledge of objects, and I raise the question of whether his claims have merit. With regard to certain knowledge of objects, I argue that Berkeley is wrong if he means to say that he has certain knowledge of objects in a sense of certainty that would allow for Cartesian certainty in beliefs about objects. Berkeley is right, however, that certain knowledge of objects is an attainable goal given the concept of certainty that he deploys. He may have failed to see, though, that with this weaker, Berkeleyan concept of certainty, nothing stands in the way of Locke or even Descartes claiming that we have certain knowledge of objects. With regard to intuitive knowledge, Berkeley is on safer ground so long as he means just that we have non-inferential knowledge of objects. This he may plausibly claim independently of whether his view is that perception of objects is immediate or mediate. Berkeley does not seem to have noticed, however, that this same option is also open to Locke.

George Berkeley contends, both in the Notebooks and in his later published works, that he has intuitive knowledge of ordinary physical objects. He means, I take it, that on his philosophy there is intuitive knowledge of objects. Berkeley also says that such intuitive knowledge is not claimed by other philosophers to whom he is philosophically opposed, and hints that these philosophers are in no position to claim intuitive knowledge of objects. His idea seems to be that relative to this issue, his philosophical position is superior. Very much the same sorts of comments are made about the notion of certainty. Berkeley claims that on his philosophy we have certain knowledge of objects, while on rival systems this is not so. Again, Berkeley seems to count this very fact, assuming it to be one, as a mark of the superiority of his philosophical position over those he opposes.

In this paper I consider what Berkeley may have meant with his claims about intuitive and certain knowledge of objects, and I also raise the question of whether his claim have merit. With regard to certain knowledge of objects, I argue that Berkeley is wrong if he means to say that he has certain knowledge of objects in a sense of certainty that would have been of interest to and used by his opponents. Neither Berkeley nor John Locke has that sort of certainty in beliefs about objects. Berkeley is right, however, that certain knowledge of objects is an attainable goal given the concept of certainty that he deploys. He may have failed to see, though, that with this weaker, Berkeleyan concept of certainty, nothing stands in the way of Locke or even Rene Descartes claiming, plausibly, that we have certain knowledge of objects.

Strictly speaking, I argue, Berkeley is in no position to maintain that we have intuitive knowledge of objects. I suggest that he more likely means that we have non-inferential knowledge of objects, and his grounds for this point seem to be solid. Two sticking points stand in the way, however. First, Berkeley may be committed to holding that we only mediately perceive objects, and this might commit him to the thesis that any knowledge we have of objects is inferential. Moreover, Berkeley's official statement about knowledge of objects is bound up with his talk of predictions, and these seem to be conclusions reached via inference from more basic premises. That, too, would tend to show that knowledge of objects, for Berkeley, is inferential.

I do not try to decide the question of whether object perception for Berkeley is immediate or mediate. I focus, instead, on the question of whether mediate perception of objects allows for at best inferential knowledge, and on this issue I argue that the answer is negative. Mediate perception of objects is perfectly compatible with non-inferential knowledge of those objects. But this fact does not help to establish the superiority of Berkeley's philosophy over that of Locke, relative to knowledge of objects. This is because Locke's account of perception also allows for non-inferential knowledge of objects. Thus, on the two epistemic points at issue – certainty and non-inferential knowledge of objects – Berkeley is only partly right. He is correct in thinking that his philosophy allows for both, especially when certainty is given its Berkeleyan reading. But he is wrong to claim any advantage for his own philosophical position relative to these points.

Intuitive knowledge, of course, is a topic we associate with John Locke, and so it is natural to assume that, in his comments about intuitive knowledge Berkeley has Locke in mind. I will make this assumption in what follows, both about intuitive knowledge and about certainty, though with the concession that it remains an issue for scholarly attention as to just who Berkeley's targets were.

Intuitive Knowledge

In the *Notebooks*, Berkeley first relates intuitive knowledge to skepticism:

> We have an intuitive Knowledge of the Existence of other things besides our selves & even praecedaneous to the Knowledge of our own Existence. in that we must have Ideas or else we cannot think. (NB 547)

Here the term "other things" may be referring solely to sensible ideas and not to objects. However Berkeley returns to the same point at entry 563:

> I am the farthest from Scepticism of any man. I know with an intuitive knowledge the existence of other things as well as my own Soul. This is wt Locke nor scarce any other Thinking Philosopher will pretend to. (NB 70)

Since Berkeley is here contrasting his view with Locke's, he must mean to refer to objects and not merely ideas by the term "other things." After all, Locke would allow that we have intuitive knowledge of ideas, but hardly agree that we have such knowledge of objects. Thus, in these comments Berkeley is telling us that on his philosophy we gain something, namely intuitive knowledge of objects, that is not merely unacceptable to Locke, but is also something that Locke's philosophy lacks the resources to accommodate.

Locke explicates intuitive knowledge by means of three characteristics, each of which seems to function as a necessary condition and which, taken jointly, seem to be sufficient for intuitive knowledge. That is, for Locke intuitive knowledge is irresistible, non-inferential, and certain. Regarding non-inferentiality, Locke says:

> … sometimes the Mind perceives the Agreement or Disagreement of two *Ideas* Immediately by themselves, without the intervention of any other: And this, I think, we may call *Intuitive Knowledge*. (E, IV, II, 1; emphases Locke's)[1]
>
> Of truths such as that white is not black, Locke says: Such kind of Truths, the Mind perceives at the first sight of the *Ideas* together, by bare *Intuition*, without the intervention of any other *Idea*; and this kind of Knowledge is the clearest, and most certain, that humane Frailty is capable of. This part of Knowledge is irresistible, and like the bright Sunshine, forces it self immediately to be perceived. (*Ibid.*)

The certainty attending intuitive knowledge, Locke says:

> … which Certainty, every one finds to be so great, that he cannot imagine,and therefore not require a greater: for a Man cannot conceive himself capable of a greater Certainty, than to know that any *Idea* in his Mind is such, as he perceives it to be … (*Ibid.*)

Locke also characterizes certainty, as found in intuitive knowledge, in terms of the highest probability. He says that "…the highest Probability, amounts not to Certainty; without which there can be no true Knowledge." (E, IV, III, 14)

The highest probability, of course, is unity; so, on one reading of this last passage Locke would be saying that even a probability of one would not amount to certainty. On another reading, he would be using the term "probability" to mean any number in the interval zero to one, but neither of these end points. Then, however close the fraction would be to unity, that high probability would not amount to certainty, and the proposition to which that probability attached would not qualify as knowledge. I think Locke intends the latter idea, which would make the relevant notion of

---

[1] Nidditch 1975. Further references to Locke are given in the text. This passage makes it seem as though Locke regards non-inferentiality as equivalent to and definitive of intuitive knowledge. If this were so, it would obviate some of what I say below about Berkeley's claim to have intuitive knowledge of objects. But I think non-inferentiality is not all there is to intuitive knowledge. Sensitive knowledge, for Locke, is also non-inferential, I would argue, but it is sharply contrasted with intuitive knowledge. That point would militate against the view that non-inferentiality makes up all there is to intuitive knowledge. See Pappas 2010.

probability connected to intuitive knowledge equal to unity. Support for this reading of Locke's point comes from other passages in which he equates certainty with infallibility. In *Draft A* of the *Essay*, Locke speaks of certainty in terms of infallibility, or the impossibility of mistaken belief. For example he says: "That a man may have a certaine infallible knowledg of universal affirmative Identicall propositions (viz wherein any of his Ideas is affirmed of its self) and of all propositions depending there upon."[2]

Here Locke is speaking of single ideas presently before the mind. If one is presently immediately aware of an idea of red color, then one cannot be mistaken in believing that one is then immediately aware of red color. He extends the point to some pluralities of current ideas: "That a man may have a certain infallible knowledg of universal negative propositions wherein one of his simple Ideas is denyed of an other and all subsequent propositions depending there on."(*Ibid.*)

Locke's examples in this sort of case include situations when one has two visual ideas, one of red and another of yellow, about which he says: "when he hath in his understanding ... the Idea of yellow and Idea of red he cannot but certainly know. ... the Idea of red is the Idea of red and not the Idea of yellow." (*Ibid.*)

Locke's comments about infallibility are stated in the form of rules, but in the remarks he makes just before the rules he says the following:

> All which certainty arises only from that cleare evident distinct knowledge our understanding hath of those simple Ideas it hath received from the operations of our own minds..., which perception and knowledge of its own Ideas that are in it cannot erre about them. (*Op. cit.*, 52)

We thus see that Locke understands the notion of infallibility to mean the impossibility of mistaken belief. In turn, this notion implies that of having a probability of one; the probability that p is true, given that one believes that p, is equal to one, because the proposition that one has that belief entails the believed proposition. This, then, is the sort of certainty, what will here be called "strong certainty," that Locke thinks attaches to intuitively known propositions about ideas.

If all three of these characteristics (non-inferentiality, irresistibility, and certainty in Locke's strong sense) are ingredient in the concept of intuitive knowledge, then one way to understand Berkeley's claims to have intuitive knowledge of bodies would be as the claim that our beliefs

---

[2] Locke 1936, 53. Further citations in the text are to this book. The spelling is as Locke gave it.

about bodies are at least often non-inferentially known, certain, and irresistible. We can consider, in turn, the notions of non-inferentiality and certainty, and leave aside that of irresistibility since that is a concept that Berkeley never considers in an epistemic context. It will be enough if Berkeley has grounds to hold that beliefs about bodies are non-inferentially known and strongly certain.

Berkeley sometimes speaks of this strong notion of certainty, and in an endorsing manner. For example, he says:

> So long as I confine my thoughts to my own ideas divested of words, I do not see how I can easily be mistaken. The objects I consider, I clearly and adequately know. I cannot be deceived in thinking I have an idea which I have not. It is not possible for me to imagine, that any of my own ideas are alike or unlike, that are not truly so. (PI 22, 39)

We should notice, however, that Berkeley is here speaking of ideas and idea pairs, and not about objects. And, indeed, it would be just a mistake for Berkeley to think otherwise, for it is plain that no beliefs about objects are certain in the strong sense found in Locke.

More exactly, no beliefs in contingent propositions about objects are strongly certain. If we consider a case of clear perception of an object with a resulting belief that it is an object of a specific sort or with some quality, it is still possible that the belief is mistaken, however clear the perception. The perception can be as clear as we please and still be illusory, resulting in mistaken belief. Necessary truths about objects are a different matter. One's belief in such a proposition cannot be mistaken, and that belief would count as strongly certain even though it is a belief about objects. Nevertheless, it is not the sort of belief about objects that is of concern to Berkeley.

In the *Three Dialogues*, Berkeley speaks of a weaker notion of certainty: "Let me be represented as one who trusts his senses, who thinks he knows the things he sees and feels, and entertains no doubts of their existence. (3D 237). This line of thought is presaged in the *Notebooks*: "I am certain there is a God, tho I do not perceive him have no intuition of him. This not difficult if we rightly understand wt is meant by certainty." (NB, 813). At NB 776 Berkeley speaks of other religious statements that are "Agreeable to my Doctrine of Certainty." And at NB 800, Berkeley says, "Malbranch in his Illustration differs widely from me. He doubts of the Existence of Bodies I doubt not in the least of this."

The idea behind these several comments is that certainty is nothing more than the complete absence of doubt. This is a far weaker notion of certainty than that found in Locke's account of intuitive knowledge. We can see at once that, armed with this weak concept of certainty, Berkeley is entirely right to maintain that on his philosophy he is certain that there are bodies. Nothing stands in the way of this concept of certainty having genuine application.

There is a cost to utilization of this weak concept of certainty, however, namely the superiority that Berkeley claims for his philosophy relative to Locke's is lost. Even if Locke is best interpreted as a representative realist, as Berkeley would have it, beliefs about bodies would easily count as certain in this weak Berkeleyan sense of that term. In effect, then, Berkeley would confront a dilemma with respect to this component of intuitive knowledge. If he uses the strong notion of certainty, then it would just be a mistake for Berkeley to claim that we have intuitive knowledge of bodies, since that would demand that we have strongly certain beliefs about bodies, which of course we do not. On the other hand, if, much more likely, Berkeley utilizes his own weak notion of certainty, then while he would be correct to hold that beliefs about bodies qualify as certain, the touted superiority of Berkeley's philosophy over Locke's vanishes, at least with regard to this aspect of the concept of intuitive knowledge.

It is possible and even likely that in his comments on "his doctrine of certainty," Berkeley's main point was to stress that strong certainty is simply too demanding, and that Berkeleyan weak certainty is all that is needed or to be expected in epistemic contexts, at least as regards beliefs about objects. Read in this way, Berkeley can be seen as an innovator in matters epistemic even if the point about superiority cannot be sustained.

Non-Inferential Knowledge

In his comments on intuitive knowledge with which we began, Berkeley may have meant to stress only non-inferential knowledge and not the full complement of features ingredient in Locke's concept of intuitive knowledge. Recall that we noticed above that Berkeley never brings up Locke's notion of irresistibility. That notion aside, we might then suppose that Berkeley is on safe ground, inasmuch as he sometimes stresses that ordinary objects are typically immediately perceived, and this immediate perception paves the way for non-inferential, or immediate knowledge, of those same objects. In a letter to the American philosopher Samuel Johnson Berkeley wrote:

> I see no difficulty in conceiving a change of state, such as is vulgarly called Death, as well without as with material substance. It is sufficient for that purpose that we allow sensible bodies, i.e., such as are immediately

> perceived by sight and touch. (*Works*, vol. 2, 282)

This passage shows that Berkeley accepted, and even stressed, the point about the immediate perception of objects. A second passage goes some way towards showing that he also thought that by immediate perception of objects we also gain non-inferential knowledge of them:

> Wood, stones, fire, water, flesh, iron, and the like things, which I name and discourse of, are things that I know. And I should not have known them, but that I perceived them by my senses; and things perceived by the senses are immediately perceived. (*Works*, vol. 2, 230)

This latter passage does not say that the knowledge of objects gained through immediate perception of them is non-inferential. But when this passage is read in the light of Berkeley's many statements about our having intuitive knowledge of objects, given his philosophical position, it is hard to read the passage about wood and stones in any other way.

Nonetheless, both of these points are open to challenge. Regarding perception, there are many places where Berkeley says that the only objects that are immediately perceived are ideas, and where the context seems to make it clear that he means only ideas. Here is a good example from the first dialogue as illustration:

> Philonous: This point then is agreed between us, that *sensible things are those only which are immediately perceived by sense.* You will farther inform me, whether we immediately perceive by sight any thing beside light, and colours, and figures: or by hearing, any thing but sounds: by the palate, any thing beside tastes: by the smell, beside odours: or by the touch, more than tangible qualities. (3D 175)

This passage, which is representative of others in the same vein, certainly seems to carry with it the result that objects, when perceived, are always mediately perceived.

Moreover, if this is Berkeley's all-things-considered position, then, one might argue, he would have to give up the claim that we have non-inferential knowledge of objects. Mediate, or indirect, perception of objects would imply that any knowledge we gain about such objects, through mediate perception of them, would always be inferential. Moreover, there is some textual evidence that Berkeley's mature position is that knowledge of objects is inferential. For at *Principles* 59 he says:

> We may, from the experience we have had of the train and succession of ideas in our minds, often make, I will not say uncertain conjectures, but

> sure and well-grounded predictions, concerning the ideas we shall be affected with, pursuant to a great train of actions, and be enabled to pass a right judgment of what would have appeared to us, in case we were placed in circumstances very different from those we are in at present. Herein consists the knowledge of Nature… (P 59)

The first part of this passage concerns predictions to which ideas one will experience, having just experienced some others. But in saying that these predictions are bound up with knowledge of nature Berkeley certainly appears to be saying that in order to have this knowledge, we must make inferences from the experiences of ideas to beliefs about objects (or nature). Knowledge of nature, in other words, would be inferential.

The first challenge contains both a textual component and a philosophical one. I will not address the textual thesis – that all perception of objects, for Berkeley, is mediate perception – but will consider, instead, the philosophical issue of whether mediate perception of objects implies at best inferential knowledge of objects.[3] In the end, I will argue, the textual issue of immediate versus mediate perception of objects has no bearing on the philosophical question.

To assess the philosophical challenge we need to be clear about the concept of mediate perception in Berkeley. As this concept is worked out in the *Theory of Vision*, mediate perception of an object O is dependent on some other perception of a different object X, and the perception of X somehow suggests O. We see the dependence claim at work in comments Berkeley makes about immediate perception:

> It is evident that when the mind perceives any idea, not immediately and of itself, it must be by the means of some other idea. Thus, for instance, the passions which are in the mind of another are of themselves to me invisible. I may nevertheless perceive them by sight, though not immediately, yet by means of the colours they produce in the countenance. (TV 9)

In this example, the passions are perceived mediately by sight, and this experience depends upon the visual perception of the person's face. When Berkeley then moves to explicate how it is that the passions are perceived by sight he brings in the concept of suggestion: the passions are said to be suggested by sight of something else (the person's face).

To see that mediate perception of objects, thus understood, is perfectly compatible with non-inferential perceptual knowledge of objects we can

---

[3] I discuss this point about perception in *Berkeley's Thought* (Pappas 2000, Chapter 6.).

consider a simple reliable process theory of knowledge, a counterpart to a reliabilist theory of warrant. Reliable processes, in such a theory, are belief-forming and belief-sustaining processes such as visual perception and memory, respectively. Following Goldman's early statement of this theory as it applies to epistemic justification,[4] two sorts of reliable belief-forming processes can be distinguished: those that take as causal inputs only non-doxastic items such as sensory states, and those that contain doxastic items among the causal inputs. A belief-forming process that takes only non-doxastic items as causal inputs, and which produces or would produce over time a preponderance of true beliefs as opposed to false ones, is said to be unconditionally reliable. If a belief is formed by a process that is unconditionally reliable in this manner then Goldman counts this belief as epistemically justified. A belief-forming process is said to be conditionally reliable when a preponderance of its output beliefs are true, and when the processes that formed the input beliefs were themselves unconditionally reliable. Using Goldman's theory as a model we could state a reliable process theory of knowledge: a belief counts as knowledge just in case it is true, and it is either produced or sustained by a process that is either unconditionally or conditionally reliable.[5]

The application of these points to the matter of mediate perception of objects is straightforward. If a person immediately experiences an idea, and this event suggests another item O which is said to be experienced mediately and about which a belief is formed, then neither the immediately experienced idea nor the mediate perception of O count as doxastic inputs to the process that generates the belief about O. Hence, provided that the belief about O is true, and the process which generates it is reliable, the belief would count as knowledge, having been produced by an unconditionally reliable process. As the inputs that generate this belief are not doxastic items, they do not function evidentially on the basis of which an inference might be made. We can thus say that such a belief qualifies as non-inferential knowledge. Thus it is not true that mediate perception of objects, as Berkeley understands mediate perception, forces him, logically, to accept the result that perceptual knowledge of objects is always inferential.[6] Further, if the foregoing argument succeeds for mediate

[4] Pappas 1979.

[5] We cannot attribute this theory of knowledge to Goldman, because he has defended only a reliable process theory of justified belief.

[6] How we understand this point overall will depend on whether we construe mediate perception as itself a doxastic item. I have here assumed that neither the immediate perception of the idea, nor the mediate perception reached via suggestion are themselves beliefs or inclusive of beliefs. But one might hold that

perception, then it is clear it will work as well in case Berkeley's real view is that objects are immediately perceived. The fact that this argument works in either context, assuming that it does, is the reason that the textual issue of immediate versus mediate perception of objects, in Berkeley, could be by-passed.

The really important textual issue for present purposes arises with the discussion of predictions in *Principles* (P 59), for there Berkeley seems to claim that our knowledge of Nature is inferential, and this would conflict with those passages, quoted earlier, where he says that our knowledge of bodies is intuitive. One possible interpretation of this passage would be that knowledge of nature amounts to theoretical, scientific knowledge, rather than knowledge of ordinary bodies such as chairs and tables. The former, one might say, is all Berkeley is claiming to be inferential, and he is making no mention of ordinary bodies. However, I think this interpretation is not plausible; in an earlier part of the *Principles* (P 31) Berkeley spoke similarly about regularities in ideas, and in that passage he speaks about knowledge that food nourishes, and that sleep refreshes as examples, and those items surely count as instances of knowledge of ordinary objects. A more promising line of interpretation is to understand Berkeley's talk of predictions not as inferences from some evidence base, itself restricted to experiences of ideas, but rather in terms of reliable indicators. Experiences of certain ideas are reliable indicators of the truth of certain beliefs, in the sense that the objective probability of the beliefs, given the occurrences of those experiences of ideas, is quite high. Experiences of such-and-such ideas, in other words, would be said to "track the truth" of the resulting beliefs. When those beliefs are also true, they count as knowledge of bodies, but these beliefs are not evidentially based upon or inferred from beliefs about experienced ideas. Understood in this way, Berkeley does accept something like a reliability account of knowledge of bodies, but it is of the reliable indicator, or tracking variety, rather than the reliable process version.[7]

---

the event of mediately perceiving object O just is a belief-forming event, and so be moved to think that all knowledge resulting from mediate perception is inferential. However, there is reason to think that Berkeley does not think of mediate perception in this manner. In his *Theory of Vision Vindicated* he says: "To perceive is one thing, to judge is another. So likewise to be suggested is one thing, and to be inferred is another. Things are suggested and perceived by sense. We make judgments and inferences by the understanding." (TVV 42)

[7] Two comments about this attribution of a reliable indicator theory to Berkeley are worth noting. First, he may understand the tracking in a manner stronger than high objective probability, for he affirms the truth of certain subjunctive conditionals (of

If this is the right way to understand Berkeley's talk of predictions and laws of nature in connection with knowledge of bodies, as I think is plausible, then he would be on safe ground to claim that our perceptual knowledge of bodies is non-inferential. That, it seems to me, is what he is really claiming when he says that our knowledge of bodies is intuitive and, all things considered, he would be right.[8]

Bibliography

Aaron, Richard. (1936) (ed.), *An Early Draft of Locke's Essay*, Clarendon Press, Oxford.

Daniel, Stephen. H. (ed.) (2007), *Reexamining Berkeley's Philosophy*. University of Toronto Press, Toronto.

Goldman, Alvin. (1979), "What Is Justified Belief?" in Pappas (1979), pp. 1-23.

Locke, John. (1975), *Essay Concerning Human Understanding*, P. Nidditch (ed.), Clarendon Press, Oxford.

—. (1936), *An Early Draft of Locke's Essay*, R. Aaron (ed.), Clarendon Press, Oxford.

Campbell, J. K., M. O'Rourke, and H. S. Silverstein (eds), (2010), *Knowledge and Scepticism: Topics in Contemporary Philosophy*, MIT Press, Cambridege, Ma.

Pappas, George. (ed.) (1979), *Justification and Knowledge*, Reidel, Dordrecht.

—. (2000), *Berkeley's Thought*, Cornell University Press, Ithaca.

—. (2007), "Berkeley's Assessment of Locke's Epistemology," in S. Daniel (2007), pp. 229-249.

—. (2010), "Locke's Account of Sensitive Knowledge," in Campbell, O'Rourke, and Silverstein (2010), pp. 165-179.

---

the form "If I were to experience ideas of type A, then if I were to take such-and-such action, I would experience ideas of type B") and also makes reference to laws of nature. In that case, tracking would have to be understood as a nomological relation. Moreover, if the tracking theory is understood in terms of high probability, it would face the lottery paradox, and so additional refinements would be required, though none of these refinements are taken notice of by Berkeley.

[8] What about the claim of superiority already investigated with regard to certainty? Can that be sustained with respect to non-inferential knowledge of bodies? I believe that Berkeley mistakenly thought that it could, at least about Locke. Elsewhere I have tried to show that Locke's version of indirect realism is perfectly compatible with non-inferential sensitive knowledge of bodies. See Pappas 2010 and also Pappas 2007.

NON-CONSCIOUS AGENCY AND BERKELEY'S THEORY OF SIGNS

RICHARD BROOK

Abstract

My interest concerns the causal origin of conscious mental states such as expectations, fears, and the like, occasioned by association. Assuming Berkeley thinks all mental states have efficient causes, the question concerns the locus of such causation. One possibility is that God causes in me, for example, an expectation of B on the occasion of A after I've often witnessed their juxtaposition. Berkeley never considers this possibility, and it has, I argue, serious difficulties. Another approach is to consider psychological association an activity of mind albeit subconscious; a form of "blind agency," something, however, that Berkeley often rejects. I consider, though, whether such a conception can be made consistent with Berkeley's general views about mind and causality and argue it cannot.

Introduction

Although this paper concerns Berkeley's conception of "learn[ing] by experience" I begin with some remarks John Locke makes about memory. He writes of 'retention' as "The Power to revive again in our Minds those Ideas, which after imprinting have disappeared, or, as it were, laid out of Sight: And thus we do, when we conceive Heat or Light, Yellow or Sweet, the object being removed."[1]

[1] Locke 1700, 151.

Locke recognizes two kinds of memory. We might recall an idea after intentionally searching for it. (The mind "turns, as it were, the eye of the Soul upon it.") [2] Sometimes, however, memories come unbidden, "they start up," Locke says, "in our Minds of their own accord and offer themselves to the Understanding," [3] It's the second kind of memory that interests me, a conscious state that is (1) the result of psychological association, and (2) not apparently caused by volition. Conscious memories are just one example. Emotions and expectations resulting from psychological association often have this character, i.e., conscious states that occur without our consciously choosing to have them. – Berkeley writes:

> Now the set rules or established methods wherein the mind we depend on excites in us the ideas of sense are called "The Laws of Nature"; and these we learn by experience, which teaches us that such and such ideas are attended with such and such other ideas in the ordinary course of things. (P 30)

Phillip Cummins, illustrating Berkeley's notion of mediate perception, gives a good example:

> Even if I can train myself not to do so, it still seems that my attributing heat to what I see when I see a vivid red poker just removed from the fire, is an instance of mental activity. My attribution is, indeed, a result of experience, but still it is an anticipation of experience – tactile experience – and as such exhibits a mind that is more than passive.[4]

It's certainly tempting to agree with Cummins that this attribution of heat to the poker signifies the mind active. Just as expecting rain when the sky darkens after witnessing a number of times certain cloud formations followed by rain. But it's important to note again that my expectation of rain, or attribution of heat to the poker, although conscious states, are not in any obvious sense willed by me to occur. Cummins puts it this way:

> If one just considers how an ordinary thought is of its object, as when a cloud reminds me of my brother's profile, neither causation nor voli-tion is invoked to account for how it is of him, though one may offer a causal explanation of why the cloud provoked my thought.[5]

---

[2] *Ibid*, 152.
[3] *Ibid*. 2.10.30,152.
[4] Cummins 2005, 220.
[5] *Ibid*, 229, fn 21.

It's not clear what Cummins means by a "causal explanation" here, but he's certainly right that in this case volition isn't invoked as a reason for the connection. In fact, as Cummins notes about the poker, it can be quite difficult or impossible to nullify an association. The power of habit is witness often to the powerlessness of will.[6] The question then, as I see it, is whether Berkeley's conception of mind or spirit allows either non-volitional mental activity, or perhaps volitional activity beneath the level of consciousness. We can think of this as a puzzle about efficient causality, particularly given Berkeley's apparent view that the only strict or efficient cause is volition. [7] The question is this: what strictly causes the conscious anticipation of a token of B, upon witnessing a token of A after a number of joint occurrences of A and B, where A and B may have, as Berkeley notes, no "relation of similitude or causality, nor any necessary connection." He notes:

> two things by their mere coexistence, or two ideas, merely being perceived together, may suggest or signify one the other, their connection being all the while arbitrary; for it is the connection only, as such, that causes this effect. (TV 39)

Later David Hume, after introducing his spare taxonomy of types of association; resemblance, contiguity and cause and effect, notes its power:

> These are therefore the principles of union or cohesion among our simple ideas, and in the imagination supply the place of that inseparable connexion by which they are united in our memory. Here is a kind of Attraction, which in the mental world will be found to have as extraordinary effects as in the natural, and to shew itself in as many and as various forms.[8]

Certainly materialist explanations of association were widespread in the seventeenth and eighteenth centuries. John W. Yolton, and more recently Richard C. Allen, gives a good account of these. [9] With some over simplification we can contrast accounts that viewed nerves as hollow tubes that conveyed the 'animal spirits' from sense organs, to the brain and then

---

[6] Richard Brook 1995, 15-31.

[7] See for example NB 49. It might be best to say that for Berkeley volition is a power of mind rather than say, as suggested by some comments in the *Notebooks*, that the mind is identical with will or volition. The issue is controversial and one I don't deal with.

[8] Hume 1739, 14.

[9] John W. Yolton 1983, Richard C. Allen 1999.

to the mind, from accounts that founded both sensation and association on nerve vibrations in a medium often modeled on Newton's speculations in the Optics (1717) about an all pervading ether. Locke, although not committed to any particular materialist theory, comments as follows about the cause of perception:

> If then external Objects be not united to our Minds, when they produce Ideas in it; and yet we perceive these *original* Qualities in such of them As singly fall under our Senses, 'tis evident, that some motion must be thence Continued by our Nerves or animal Spirits, by some parts of our Bodies, to the Brains or the seat of Sensation, there to *produce in our Minds the Particular* Ideas *we have of them.*[10]

About association he writes:

> Custom settles habits of Thinking in the understanding as well as Determining in the Will, and motions of the Body; all of which seems to be but Trains of Motion in the Animal Spirits, which once set a going continue on the same steps they have been used to, which by often treading are worn into a smooth path, and the motion in it becomes easy and as it were Natural.[11]

Hume, though not denying that our associative abilities have materialist underpinnings, is prudently skeptical about the existing materialist theories of association. He comments:

> Twou'd have been easy to have made an imaginary dissection of the brain, and have shewn why, upon our conception of any idea, the animal spirits run into all the contiguous traces, and rouze up the other ideas, that are related to it."[12]

Although Yolton apparently takes the passage seriously, [13] Hume is simply noting here that's there's insufficient evidence for an acceptable materialist theory of association. In the sentence preceding the above he writes "that we must in the end rest contented with experience, than for want of something specious and plausible, which I might have display'd on that subject" [14]

The amount of speculation about the physiology of the brain was

---

[10] Locke, 136.
[11] Locke, 396.
[12] Reprinted in Yolton, 176.
[13] *Ibid.*
[14] *Ibid.*

perhaps inversely proportional to how much was known about it. In any case for Berkeley there would be at least two obvious problems with these materialist explanations. The first – the traditional mind/body problem – was that no matter how ethereal you made the stuff that ultimately propagated physical stimuli from sense organs to the mind, you had the issue of how matter, however thin and vibratory, produced mental states. The second, particularly germane to his immaterialism, was that whatever account you gave of the 'material' correlates of immediate perception, or of mediate perception through association, you could not, given his view of causality, attribute efficient causality to brain states.

In the *Three Dialogues*, Berkeley has Hylas give a fair summary of the materialist theories of the day:

> It is supposed the soul makes her residence in some part of the brain, from which the nerves take their rise, and are thence extended to all parts of the body; and that outward objects, by the different impressions they make on the organs of sense, communicate certain vibrative motions to the nerves, and these being filled with spirits, propagate them to the brain or seat of the soul, which according to the various impressions or traces thereby made in the brain, is variously affected with ideas. (3D 208-209)

Berkeley (as Philonous) responds, with perhaps feigned frustration, to the effect that

> they've gone over these things before and agreed that sensible things are composed of ideas, and ideas are passive. Therefore since the brain is a sensible thing it couldn't strictly be the cause of our perceptions.

Philonous puts it this way: "If you do [conceive of the brain] then you talk of ideas imprinted in an idea causing that same idea, [i.e., of the brain] which is absurd."[15] This echoes the earlier claim in the *Notebooks* (NB 435) "The absurd account of Memory by the Brain etc., makes for me." And later in the *Dialogues*, discussing whether God feels pain, Philonous says:

> We are chained to a body; that is to say, our perceptions are connected with corporeal motions. By the law of our nature we are affected upon every alteration in the nervous parts of our sensible body; which sensible body, rightly considered is nothing but a complexion of such qualities or ideas as have no existence distinct from being perceived by a mind; so that this connection of sensations with corporeal motions means no more than a

[15] 3D 210. Strictly speaking for Berkeley the brain, as any physical object, is a bundle or collection of ideas, not itself an idea.

> correspondence in the order of nature between two sets of ideas or things immediately perceivable. (3D 241)

Since God isn't 'chained to a body,' he in some manner knows pain without feeling it, just as he knows objects of sense without literally sensing them. Whatever we think of that claim, Berkeley's clear point is that although we can make correlations between brain states and mental states, the first, being passive, can't in principle, strictly or efficiently cause the second.

But this can't be the whole story, particularly with respect to mental states occasioned by signs. With regard to those I am again often as passive as I am to the taste of chocolate when I eat it, or to the color of the walls of my room when I open my eyes. I once speculated Berkeley might require attributing strict causality to sense data in their role of signs, for example, using the case at the beginning, that after witnessing the temporal juxtaposition of certain cloud formations and rain a certain number of times those formations later gain a strict causal property, that of suggesting or being a sign of rain. [16] After all Berkeley uses what we would normally consider causal verbs to suggest the relation of sign to what's signified. He writes, for example, in *Theory of Vision Vindicated*: (TV 39) "And as sounds suggest other things, so characters suggest those sounds. And in general all signs suggest the things signified." And unlike mechanics where Berkeley, particularly in *De Motu*, (38) explicitly interprets terms in dynamics such as impressed force in an instrumental way, he makes no comparable attempt to interpret dynamical terms like suggest, signify, or evoke in his comments about association. Moreover, it's quite possible that that can't be accomplished without already assuming in the interpretation, human powers of association.

However, attributing strict causal powers to sensible objects as signs, though perhaps worth considering at another time, is not an issue I take up here. Such a view would seriously undermine Berkeley's quite fundamental position that ideas are passive and only spirit or mind is active. Yet there remains the question of what does, in a strict sense, causally account for those conscious states, e.g., emotions, beliefs, expectations and the like, which both are occasioned by association, and about which we are as passive as, using his own example, we are to the smell of a flower when I bring my nose to it. For Berkeley the conscious consequences of association must have strict or efficient causes, since presumably every mental state has an efficient cause. Aside, then, from taking sense data qua

[16] Brook, 15-31.

signs as the strict cause of conscious mental states they occasion, the only other candidates are divine or human agency. I now turn to these possibilities.

Divine Agency and Psychological Association

In *Siris*, Berkeley's late major work, there is the following interesting passage:

> It must be owned, we are not conscious of the systole and diastole of the heart, or the motion of the diaphragm. It may not nevertheless be thence inferred that unknowing nature can act regularly, as well as ourselves. The true inference is that the self-thinking individual, or human person, is not the real author of those natural motions . . The same may be said of the fingers of a musician, which some object to be moved by habit which understand not; it being evident that what is done by rule must proceed from something that understands the rule; therefore, if not from the musician himself, from some other active intelligence, the same perhaps which governs bees and spiders and move the limbs of those who walk in their sleep. (*Siris* 122)

This is a heterogeneous group of behaviors, including autonomic motions, the innate, goal directed, and perhaps non-conscious behaviors of insects, and, in the musician case, what might best be described as blind agency. About music Locke uses a comparable example:

> A Musician used to any Tune will find that let it be once in his Head, the Ideas of the several Notes of it will follow one another orderly in his Understanding without any care or attention, as regularly as his Fingers move over the Keys of the Organ to play out the Tune he has begun though his unattentive thoughts be elsewhere a wandering. [17]

In a similar vein, Rene Descartes, responding to Antoine Arnauld concerning the question whether animals ("brutes") have souls (a view Descartes rejects) notes not only that motions "within us" like "heart beat digestion and respiration" do not depend on the mind, but, as he says, "waking actions," such as walking, singing and the like when these occur without the mind attending to them."[18]

Berkeley notably rejects the possibility of blind agency, (see e.g. NB 812) but his opposition might be based on an implicit but assumed

[17] Locke, 396.

[18] Descartes 1984, 161.

distinction between (1) simply voluntary behavior, and (2) human action where the agent needs to conceive what she aims for. Volition in action is sighted in the sense that if I consciously will something to occur, I must entertain a concept of what I wish to bring about. Examples of (2) by definition can't be blind, since to intend to do X requires having a concept of X, but that might not be true of instances of (1).

In any case, what links the examples in the Siris passage is not only that they exhibit regularity or 'rule following,' but that they are non-conscious. Similarly, as mentioned above, the linkages established by psychological association are often for Berkeley if not invariably non-conscious. The argument for this is simple. Say that after witnessing on three occasions certain cloud formations followed by rain that it's only after the fourth cloud appearance that I consciously anticipate rain. The actual associating of A and B, must begin the first time I witness their joint occurrence. Otherwise my prior witnessing their juxtaposition is needless with respect to explaining my later expecting rain after witnessing a similar cloud formation. At some point the association emerges into a conscious anticipation. Conditioning or learning by experience has this character. The mind's associating two kinds of items generally (though not invariably) must happen at least once before a token of one may later serve as a sign for consciously expecting a token of the other.

It's true that considering the behavior of ourselves and others we learn by observation that association, conceived as simply witnessing some juxtapositions of items, conditions much of what we do. We develop informal regularities, or more rigorous 'laws' based on experimental setups using operant conditioning, between association and certain mental states; emotions, ocurrent beliefs, conscious expectations and the like.[19] I call these 'C-laws,' those whose antecedent clause requires essential reference to conditioning.

C-laws are a special subset of the laws or regularities of nature. The other subset, which I call "N-laws," are those, for example, like the law of gravity, that don't require essential reference in their antecedents to conditioning. We can think of both subsets as those regularities instituted by God for our benefit. God's benevolent interest in our welfare coupled with our powers of association, explains, for example, the existence of natural regularities. As he writes in the *Principles*:

> That food nourishes, sleep refreshes, and fire warms us: that to sow in the

[19] I thank Bertil Belfrage for his helpful comments on this section, and on the paper in general.

> seedtime is the way to reap in the harvest; and in general to obtain such or such ends, such or such means are conducive – all this we know, not by discovering any necessary connection between our ideas, but only by observation of the settled laws of nature, without which we should all be in uncertainty and confusion. . . (P 31)

And of course C-laws are themselves useful in a variety of ways, for example developing successful learning strategies, whether, for instance, to offer carrots or sticks, or some combination to change behavior. However, the existence of C-laws can't be explained simply by that kind of usefulness, since that usefulness, in fact, depends on their existence. The same is true if we were to look inwards, so to speak, to the brain. We might observe what happens in the brain of other beings (or ourselves) being conditioned. We might witness, for instance, the gradually changing brain states of a mouse as it learns to navigate a maze under positive reinforcement. These psycho-physical correlations are useful if we wish to modify perception or behavior. However, as Philonous pointed out to Hylas (quoted above) the connection between brain states and sensory states is simply a correlation between sets of ideas. We make use of those correlations since we already possess associative abilities.

However, there is still the question how divine causality could explain instances of conscious states (like an expectation of rain at a certain time) occasioned by signs? To put it briefly and bluntly, how does the expectation get to consciousness? Which is another way of asking what is the efficient cause of that particular mental state. As I might ask what is the strict cause of that flower's smell when I bend towards it. Again I don't will either the smell or the expectation to occur. In the first case of course God, for Berkeley, is the strict or efficient cause of the smell as he is for any object of sense.

Perhaps – to continue the analogy – after witnessing the juxtaposition of certain cloud formations and rain three times, God produces in me an expectation of rain when the formation appears a fourth time. And, *pace* Cummins's example, touching a hot poker once, or just feeling the heat, may be sufficient for God to produce in me an anticipation of heat when I next see it glowing. In fact, under this speculation, all mediate perception might involve God in this way. We would have occasionalism on the plane of *ideas*. Put abstractly, when I've associated (X) and (Y) N number of times, *God* induces in me a conscious anticipation of Y on my (N+1)th perception of X. Mediate perception, then, (again under this hypothesis) would require two simultaneously causal activities of God. Take the following examples: (1) Constitutive of my experience as I walk along a road, are conscious expectations of tactile experience if I take certain actions, say walking up a hill, or touching a wall. (2) Listening to music, my conscious expectation of a cadence at a place in the melody has its roots in past experience of harmonic patterns. Under the above hypothesis, God, when presenting me with temporally new (immediate) sense data causes at the same time my consciousness anticipation of that which I had previously associated with that data; that the wall feels smooth, or that a cadence occurs at a certain point in the piece.

There are at least two objections to this conception of God's role in signification. In the first place there is nothing in the texts to suggest that Berkeley entertained this hypothesis to explain conscious states like expectations occasioned by sense data as signs. And that makes sense. It's unlikely he would endorse the view that, taking just the second example, God, at the precise moment I would expect a cadence, puts that expectation in my mind. Psychological association is bedrock for Berkeley; it accounts for the usefulness of all natural regularities including C-laws. Natural regularities, whether expressed as rules of thumb, the mathematical laws of motion, or C-laws, again require for their usefulness the associative abilities of finite minds.

A second problem with this theory of divine causality is that it seems superfluous for God to induce a conscious anticipation of a token of B on the occasion of a token of A when an agent has witnessed the juxtaposition of A and B, say four times, rather than three. Why not after one time? Isn't it more efficient and beneficent for God to induce fears of glowing pokers before first having to touch one? In general one might think human foresight more efficacious if God induced agents to expect B on the occasion of A before having to first witness their temporal and/or spatial juxtaposition.[20]

Of course it's difficult to speculate about what a world would be like if successful foresight didn't require past association. That's not our world; moreover, it's a speculation Berkeley doesn't engage in. Association for him, as I mentioned, is basic; the mind, as it were, cements types of objects of sense or reflection so that a later instance of one usefully leads us to anticipate an instance of the other. More plausibly finite minds strictly cause those conscious expectations, emotions desires, and the like occasioned by association. This I think is Cummins point and one that seems quite natural.

[20] In the music example there is in reality no discrete A and B to be associated. My past experience of the melody and my expectation of a cadence are inextricably bound in how, from a phenomenological point of view, I actually hear the passage. I hear it leading to the cadence.

Human agency, and psychological association.

The thesis to be considered is that for Berkeley finite minds have a strict albeit non-conscious causal power to bring about conscious states like expectations occasioned by signs. Locke, in discussing the formation of complex *ideas*, writes:

> As simple Ideas are observed to exist in several Combinations united together, so the Mind has a power to consider several of them united together, as one Idea; and that not only as they are united in external Objects, but *as it itself has join'd them.*[21]

Though controversial, I take it that that for Locke the "power" of the mind to consider "several ideas as one," ("as it itself has join'd them") perhaps like the power (secondary quality) of the primary qualities to produce sensible ideas in us, or the power (tertiary quality) of the sun to melt wax, expresses a causal relation in a strict, rather than simply occasionalist sense of cause.[22]

Is there anything similar in Berkeley that suggests psychological association exhibits a non-conscious power of mind? He writes:

> A spirit is one simple, undivided, active being: as it perceives ideas it is called the understanding, and as it produces or *otherwise operates* about them, it is called the will. (P 27, my emphasis)

Perhaps we can we include among the other ways mind "operates about [ideas]" that it induces conscious states occasioned by association? Interestingly in *Principles* 1 Berkeley includes both "memory and "imagination" as aids to forming ideas. With respect to imagination Berkeley mostly takes it to be productive faculty controlled by volition:

> I find I can excite ideas in my mind at pleasure, and vary and shift the scene as oft as I think fit. It is no more than willing, and straightaway this or that idea arises in my fancy, and by the same power it is obliterated and makes way for another. This making and unmaking of ideas does properly denominate the mind active. (P 28)

Ordinary imagination, as Berkeley often conceives it requires willing; voluntarily bringing to mind the image of a rose, a face, a triangle, a

---

[21] Locke 64, my emphasis.

[22] On Locke's view of causality see Lowe 2005, 136-138.

unicorn. This is sighted rather than non-conscious agency, the intended "making and unmaking of ideas." However, in the *Theory of Vision Vindicated* Berkeley writes that what is associated with sense data as signs are "things only *suggested by the imagination*, and originally belonging to some other sense or faculty." (TVV 9, my emphasis). For example, the smooth feeling of the wall presumably enters my imagination from haptic experience, and later, when I look at the wall, visual sense data evoke anticipations of what I should feel if I touched it. However, there's not really enough in the text here to grasp precisely what Berkeley means; for example would he count "suggestion by the imagination" as an example of efficient albeit non-conscious causality?

As for memories, successful recall, say, of a formerly forgotten name is, as Locke noted, (see above) sometimes causally related to volition; e.g., the conscious search for the name that's on the 'tip of the tongue.' However, as he also remarked, volitional memory is one type of recall; some memories of places or activities arise unsought for. Independent of volition, we are again passive with respect to their occurrence as we are to the immediate ideas of sense that elicit them. Thus we still have the problem of how something gets from what we'll roughly call here "memory or imagination banks" to consciousness. The importance of memory and imagination to signification introduces a certain density to finite minds in two ways; the non-conscious binding of items witnessed in juxtaposition, and the equally non-conscious eliciting of a conscious expectation that one item will occur on the occasion of the other.

Conclusion

If we think conscious states like expectations occasioned by association require an efficient cause, Berkeley's philosophy raises serious difficulties as to how that works. Our finite minds, he claims, have powers, but they often appear to be just productive powers; to create, destroy, and manipulate images, and to move our limbs. We don't consciously will conscious expectations, fears, desires and the like occasioned by signs. I suggested earlier a possible Berkeleian solution; that after an agent witnesses the juxtaposition of ideas a certain number of times God induces a particular conscious state; an anticipation of the signified item on the occasion of the sign.[23] Aside from Berkeley not entertaining this hypothesis,

[23] One might object that God simply creates minds that have *powers* of association but doesn't himself causally induce a particular conscious expectation of B on the occasion of an instance of A. Of course that commits Berkeley to the belief that

there are, as discussed above, serious problems with it. If, on the other hand, the efficient cause of association based mental states are finite minds, it must be non-conscious causality. We might rightly call this blind agency. Whether Berkeley's view of mind permits this is a real question.

Bibliography

Allen, Richard C. (1999), *David Hartley on Human Nature*, SUNY Press, Albany.

Berkeley, George. (1948-1957), *The Works of George Berkeley*, 9 vols, A. A. Luce and T. E. Jessop (eds), Nelson, London.

Brook, Richard. (1995) "Berkeley, Causality and Signification," *International Studies in Philosophy* 27, pp. 15-31.

Cummins, Phillip D. (2005), "Berkeley on Minds and Agency," *Cambridge Companion to Berkeley*, K. Winkler (ed.), Cambridge University Press, Cambridge, pp. 190-230.

Descartes, Rene. (1984) *Philosophical Writings of Descartes*, vol. II, 4th Set of Replies, J. Cottingham, R. Stroothoff, and D. Murdoch (eds), Cambridge University Press, Cambridge.

Hume, David. (1739/1967) *A Treatise of Human Nature*, L. A. Selby-Bigge (ed.), Clarendon Press, Oxford.

Locke, John. (1700/1975) *An Essay Concerning Human Understanding*, P. H. Nidditch (ed.), OUP, Oxford.

Lowe, E. J. (2005), *Locke*, Routledge, New York.

Yolton, John W. (1983), *Thinking Matter*, University of Minnesota Press, Minneapolis.

---

finite minds exercise non-conscious efficient causality when bringing to consciousness a certain propositional attitude, e.g., an expectation that it will rain when the sky darkens.

BIBLIOGRAPHY

Works by George Berkeley

Arithmetica absque Algebra aut Euclide Demonstrata. Cui accesserunt, Cogitata Nonnulla de Radicibus Surdis, de Æstu Aeris, de Ludo Algebraico, &c. (London 1707).

An Essay Towards a New Theory of Vision (Dublin. 1709).

A Treatise Concerning the Principles of Human Knowledge. Part I. Wherein the chief Causes of Error and Difficulty in the Sciences, *with the Grounds of* Scepticism, Atheism, *and* Irreligion, *are inquir'd into.* (Dublin, 1710).

Passive Obedience. Or the Christian Doctrine of Not Resisting the Supreme Power, Proved and Vindicated upon the Principles of the Law of Nature (London and Dublin, 1712).

Three Dialogues between Hylas and Philonous. The Design of which is plainly to demonstrate the Reality and Perfection of Human Knowledge, the Incorporeal Nature of the Soul, and the Immediate Providence of a Deity: In Opposition to Sceptics and Atheists. Also, To open a Method for rendering the Sciences more easy, useful, and compendious (London, 1713).

Advice to the Tories Who have Taken the Oaths (London, 1715).

De Motu; sive, De Motus Principio & Natura, & de Causa Communicationis Motuum (London, 1721).

An Essay Towards Preventing the Ruin of Great Britain (London 1721).

A Proposal For the better Supplying of Churches in our Foreign Plantations, and for Converting the Savage Americans to Christianity (London 1724).

Alciphron: or, the Minute Philosopher. In Seven Dialogues. Containing an Apology for the Christian Religion, against those who are called Free-thinkers (London and Dublin, 1732).

The Theory of Vision, or Visual Language, showing The Immediate Presence and Providence of a Deity, Vindicated and Explained (London, 1733).

*The Analyst; or, a Discourse Addressed to an Infidel Mathematician. Wherein it is examined whether the Object, Principles, and Inferences of the modern Analysis are more distinctly conceived, or more *evidently deduced, than Religious Mysteries and Points of Faith* (London and Dublin, 1734).

The Querist, containing Several Queries, Proposed to the Consideration of the Public (1735-1737).

A Discourse addressed to Magistrates and Men in Authority. Occasioned By the enormous Licence, and Irreligion of the Times (Dublin, London and Cork 1738).

Siris: A Chain of Philosophical Reflexions and Inquiries Concerning the Virtues of Tar Water, And divers other Subjects connected together and arising one from another (London and Dublin, 1744).

A Word to the Wise: or, the Bishop of Cloyne's Exhortation to the Roman Catholic Clergy of Ireland (Dublin 1749).

A Miscellany, containing Several Tracts on Various Subjects (Dublin and London 1752).

Secondary Sources

Aaron, Richard. (1936) (ed.), *An Early Draft of Locke's Essay*, Clarendon Press, Oxford.

Adams, Robert M. (1973), "Berkeley's 'Notion' of Spiritual Substance," *Archiv für Geschichte der Philosophie* 55, pp. 47-69.

Adams, R. M. (1994), *Leibniz: Determinist, Theist, Idealist*, Oxford University Press, Oxford.

Airaksinen, Timo. (2006), "The Chain and the Animal: Idealism in Berkeley's *Siris*," in Gersh and Moran (2006), pp. 224-243.

—. (2008), "The Path of Fire: The Meaning and Interpretation of Berkeley's *Siris*," in Daniel (2008), pp. 261-281.

—. (2010), "Berkeley and Newton on Gravity in *Siris*," in Parigi (2010) (forthcoming).

Algra, K., J. Barnes, J. Mansfeld, and M. Schofield (eds.) (1999), *The Cambridge History of Hellenistic Philosophy*, Cambridge University Press, Cambridge.

Allen, Richard C. (1999), *David Hartley on Human Nature*, SUNY Press, Albany.

Annas, Julia. (1992), *Hellenistic Philosophy of Mind*, University of California Press, Berkeley.

Aquinas, Thomas. (1947-1948), *Summa Theologica*, Fathers of the English Dominican Province (tr.), rev. ed., Benziger Brothers, New York.

Ariew, Roger and Daniel Garber (eds.) (1989), *G. W. Leibniz: Philosophical Essays*, Hackett, Indianapolis.

Aristotle. (1963) *Aristotle's Categories and De Interpretatione*, J. L.

Ackrill (tr.), Clarendon Press, Oxford.

—. (1984), *The Complete Works of Aristotle*, W. D. Ross (ed.), 12 vols, Oxford, 1938-1952, revised by J. Barnes, 2 vols, Princeton University Press, Princeton.

Arnauld, Antoine and Pierre Nicole. (1970), *La Logique, ou L'art de Penser* (5th ed., 1683), Louis Marin (ed.), Flammarion, Paris.

Arnauld, Antoine and Nicole, Pierre. (1996), *Logic or the Art of Thinking*, J. V. Buroker (tr.), Cambridge Texts in the History of Philosophy, Cambridge University Press, Cambridge.

Atherton, Margaret. (1990), *Berkeley's Revolution in Vision*, Cornell University Press, Ithaca.

—. (2003), "Apprendre à voir: les enseignements de la *Défense de la Théorie de la Vision*," in Berlioz (2003), pp. 135-157.

—. (2007), "The Objects of Immediate Perception," in Daniel (2007), pp. 107-120.

—. (2008). "'The Books are in the Study as Before: Berkeley's Claims about Real Physical Objects ," *British Journal of the History of Philosophy*, 16, pp. 85-100.

Ashworth, E. J. (1974), *Language and Logic in the Post-Medieval Period*, Reidel, Dordrecht.

—. (1981), "'Do Words Signify Ideas or Things?' The Scholastic Sources of Locke's Theory of Signification," *Vivarium* 14, 299-326

Austin, John L. (1962), "Discussion," *Cahiers de Royaumont*, pp. 282-304.

Ayers, Michael. (1984), "Berkeley and Hume: A Question of Influence," in Rorty *et al.* (1984), pp. 303-327.

—. (2005), "Was Berkeley an Empiricist or a Rationalist?," in Winkler (2005), pp. 34-62.

Barnouw, Jeffrey. (2008), "The Two Motives Behind Berkeley's Expressly Unmotivated Signs: Sure Preception and Personal Providence," in Daniel (2008a), pp. 145-177.

Baxter, Don. (2008). *Hume's Difficult*, Routledge, London.

Belfrage, Bertil. (1992), "The Constructivism of Berkeley's *New Theory of Vision*," in Cummins and Zoeller (1992), pp. 167-186.

—. (2003), "Vers une nouvelle interprétation de la *Théorie de la vision* de Berkeley," in Berlioz (2003), pp. 159-211.

—. (2006), "The Scientific Background of George Berkeley's Idealism," in Gersh and Moran (2006), pp. 202-223.

—. (2007), "Berkeley's Four Concepts of the Soul," in Daniel (2007), pp. 172-187.

—. (ed.) (1987), *George Berkeley's Manuscript Introduction*. An editio diplomatica transcribed and edited with introduction and commentary by Bertil Belfrage. Doxa (Oxford), Oxford.

Bennett, Jonathan. (2001), *Learning from Six Philosophers*, Vo. 2, Oxford University Press, Oxford.

Berman, David. (1985), *George Berkeley. Essays and Replies*, Irish Academic Press, Dublin.

—. (2005), "Berkeley's Life and Works," in Winkler (2005), pp. 13-33.

Berlioz, Dominique (ed.) (2003), *Berkeley. Langage de la perception et art de voir*, Débat philosophiques. Presses Universitaires de France, Paris 2003.

Bettcher, Talia Mae. (2007), *Berkeley's Philosophy of Spirit: Consciousness, Ontology, and the Elusive Subject*, Continuum Press, London.

Bobzien, Susanne. (2003), "Logic" in Inwood (2003), pp. 85-123.

Boyle, Robert. (1979), *Selected Philosophical Papers of Robert Boyle*, M. A. Stuart (ed.), Philosophical Classics, Manchester University Press, Manchester.

Bracken, Harry M. (1974), *Berkeley*, St. Martin's Press, New York.

Broad, C. D. (1947), "Professor Marc-Wogau's *Theorie der Sinnesdaten*," *Mind* 56, pp. 120-124.

—. (1975), *Leibniz: An Introduction*, C. Lewy (ed.), Cambridge University Press, Cambridge.

Brook, Richard. (1995) "Berkeley, Causality and Signification," *International Studies in Philosophy* 27, pp. 15-31.

Brown, S. and P. Phemister (eds.) (2007), *Leibniz and the English-Speaking World*, Springer, Dordrecht.

Brykman, Geneviève. (1985), "Pleasure and pain versus ideas in Berkeley" in Berman 1985, pp. 127-137.

—. (2008), "On Human Liberty in Berkeley's *Alciphron* VII," in Daniel (2008a), pp. 231-246.

Caffentzis, C. G. (1996), "The Scottish Origin of Civilization," in Federici (1996), pp. 13-36.

—. (2000), *Exciting the Industry of Mankind: George Berkeley's Philosophy of Money*, Kluwer, Dordecht.

—. (2001), "Hume, Money, and Civilization; or, Why was Hume a Metallist?," *Hume Studies* 27, pp. 301-335.

—. (2005), "Civilizing the Highlands: Hume, Money and the Annexing Act," *Historical Reflections* 31, pp. 169-194.

—. (2008), "Fiction or Counterfeit? David Hume's Interpretations of Paper and Metallic Money," in Wennerlind and Schabas (2008), pp. 146-167.

Cajetan, Thomas de Vio. (1959), *The Analogy of Names and The Concept of Being*, 2nd ed., Edward A. Bushinski with Henry J. Koren (trs), Duquesne University, Pittsburgh.

Campbell, J. K., M. O'Rourke and H. S. Silverstein (eds), (2010), *Knowledge and Scepticism: Topics in Contemporary Philosophy*, MIT Press, Cambridege, Ma.

Carrier, L. S. (1969), "The Time-Gap Argument, " *Australasian Journal of Philosophy*, 47, pp. 263-272.

Charles, Sébastien (ed.) (2004), *Science et épistémologie selon Berkeley*, Presses de l'Université Laval, Quebec.

Clark, Stephen. (2005), "Berkeley on Religion," in Winkler (2005), pp. 396-404.

Cléret, Nathalie. (1999), "Paracelse, l'alchimie et les stoïciens: Quelques aspects des conceptions stoïciens et paracelsienne du feu," in Moreau (1999a), pp. 65-76.

Conroy, Grapham P. (1969), "Did Hume Really Follow Berkeley?," *Philosophy* 44, pp. 238-242.

Cornman, James. (1971), *Materialism and Sensation*, Yale University Press, New Haven and London.

—. (1975), *Perception, Common Sense, and Science*, Yale University Press, New Haven and London.

Cudworth, Ralph. (1996). *Treatise concerning Eternal and Immutable Morality*, S. Hutton (ed.), Cambridge University Press, Cambridge.

Cullen, L. M. (1972), *The Economic History of Ireland Since 1660*, Batesford, London.

Cummins, Phillip D. (2005), "Berkeley's Philosophy of Mind and Agency," in Winkler (2005), pp. 190-229.

Cummins, Phillip D. and Zoeller, Guenter (eds.) (1992), *Minds, Ideas, and Objects: Essays on the Theory of Representation in Modern Philosophy*, North American Kant Society Studies in Philosophy, vol. 2, Ridgeview Publishing, Atascadero, Cal.

Dancy, Jonathan. (1987), *Berkeley: An Introduction*, Blackwell, Oxford.

Daniel, Stephen H. (1990), *Myth and Modern Philosophy*, Temple University Press, Philadelphia.

—. (2001a), "Berkeley's Christian Neoplatonism, Archetypes, and Divine Ideas," *Journal of the History of Philosophy* 39, pp. 239-258.

Daniel, Stephen. (2001b), "Edwards, Berkeley, and Ramist Logic," *Idealistic Studies* 31, pp. 55-72.

Daniel, Stephen H. (2004), "Les limites de la philosophie naturelle de Berkeley," in Charles (2004), pp. 163-170.

—. (ed.) (2007a), *Reexamining Berkeley's Philosophy*, University of Toronto Press, Toronto.

—. (2007b), "The Harmony of the Leibniz-Berkeley Juxtaposition," in Brown and Phemister (2007), pp. 163-180.

—. (ed.) (2008a), *New Interpretations of Berkeley's Thought*, Humanity Books, Amherst, NY.

—. (2008b), "Berkeley's Stoic Notion of Spiritual Substance," in Daniel (2008a), 203-230.

Davie, G. E. (1965), "Berkeley's Impact on Scottish Philosophers," *Philosophy* 40, pp. 222-234.

Deleuze, Gilles. (1990), *The Logic of Sense*, C. V. Boundas (ed.), M. Lester and C. Stivale (trs), Columbia University Press, New York.

Democritus. (1968), in W. Capelle, (tr. and ed.), *Die Vorsokratiker: Die Fragmente und Quellenberichte*, Alfred Kröner Verlag, Stuttgart.

Derrida, Jacques. (1980), *The Archeology of the Frivolous: Reading Condillac*, J. P. Leavey, Jr. (tr.), Duquesne University Press, Pittsburgh.

Descartes, René. (1952), *The Geometry of René Descartes*, D. E. Smith and M. L, Latham (trs.), Open Court, La Salle, IL.

—. (1985), *The Philosophical Writings of Descartes*, 3 vols, J. Cottingham, R. Stoothoff, D. Murdoch, and A. Kenny (eds and trs), Cambridge University Press, Cambridge.

Downing, Lisa. (2005), "Berkeley's Philosophy of Science," in Winkler (2005), pp. 230-265.

Ebert, Theodor. (1987), "The Origin of the Stoic Theory of Signs in Sextus Empiricus," *Oxford Studies in Ancient Philosophy* 5, pp. 83-126.

Einstein, Albert. (1922), "Ether and the Theory of Relativity," in his *Sidelights on Relativity*, Methuen, London.

—. (1934), "The Problem of Space, Ether, and the Field in Physics," in his *The World As I See It*, Covici-Friede, New York.

Federici, Silvia (ed.) (1996), *Enduring Western Civilization*, Praeger, Westport, CT.

Ficino, Marsilio. (2006), *Platonic Theology*, vol. 6, M. J. Allen (tr.), Harvard University Press, Cambridge, MA.

Flage, Daniel E. (1987), *Berkeley's Doctrine of Notions: A Reconstruction based on His Theory of Meaning*, Croom Helm, London.

Flage, Daniel E. and Bonnen, Clarence A. (1999), *Descartes and Method: A Search for Method in Meditations*, Routledge, London.

Flage, Daniel E. (2006), "Berkeley's Ideas of Reflection," *Berkeley Newsletter* 17, pp. 7-13.

—. (2009), "Berkeley's Contingent Necessities," *Philosophia* 37, pp. 361-372.

Fogelin, Robert J. (2001), *Berkeley and the Principles of Human Knowledge*, Routledge, London and New York.

Fontenelle, Bernard le Bovier de. (1732), "Préface sur l'utilité des mathématiques," in *Histoire de l'Académie Royale des Sciences année M.DC.XCIC avec les Mémoires de Mathématiques et de Physique pour la même Année*, Paris.

—. (1741), "Eloge de Malebranche," in *Histoire de l'Académie Royale des Sciences année M.DCC.XV avec les Mémoires de Mathématiques et de Physique pour la même Année*, Paris.

Foster, John. (1982). *The Case for Idealism*, Routledge, London.

Forman, David. (2008), "Free Will and the Freedom of the Sage in Leibniz and the Stoics," *History of Philosophy Quarterly* 25, pp. 203-219.

Frankfurt, Harry. (2003), "Alternate Possibilities and Moral Responsibility," in Watson (2003), pp. 167-176.

Frede, Michael. (1999), "Stoic epistemology," in Algra et al. (1999), pp. 295-322.

Furlong, E. J. (1964), "An Ambiguity in Berkeley's Principles," *Philosophical Quarterly* 14, pp. 334-44.

Furth, M. (1972), "Monadology," in *Leibniz: A Collection of Critical Essays*, H. G. Frankfurt (ed.), Doubleday Anchor, Garden City.

Galilei, Galileo. (1967), *Dialogue Concerning the Two Chief World Systems*, S. Drake (ed.), 2nd revised edition, University of California Press, Berkeley.

Garber, D. (1985), "Leibniz and the Foundations of Physics," in *The Natural Philosophy of Leibniz*, K. Okruhlik and J. R. Brown (eds), Reidel, Dordrecht.

Gaukroger, Stephen (ed.) (1991), *The Uses of Antiquity: The Scientific Revolution and the Classical Tradition*, Kluwer, Boston.

Gersh, Stephen and Dermot Noran (eds.) (2006), *Eriugena, Berkeley, and the Idealist Tradition*, University of Notre Dame Press, Notre Dame, Indiana.

Goldman, Alvin. (1979), "What Is Justified Belief?" in Pappas (1979), pp. 1-23.

Gould, Josiah B. (1970), *The Philosophy of Chrysippus*, State University of New York Press, Albany.

Glauser, Richard. (2003), "La structure de la perception médiate dans la théories berkeleyenne de la vision," in Berlioz (2003), pp. 103-133.

Graeser, Andreas. (1978), "The Stoic Theory of Meaning," in Rist (1978), pp. 77-100.

Gracia, Jorge J. E. (ed.) (1982), *Suarez on Individuation*, Marquette University Press, Milwaukee.

Grafton, Anthony. (1997), *The Footnote: A Curious History*, Harvard University Press, Cambridge, Ma.

Grayling, A. C. (1986), *Berkeley: The Central Arguments*. Open Court, La Salle, Illinois.

Gueroult, Martial. (1956), *Berkeley: Quatre études sur la perception et sur dieu*, Aubier, Paris.

Hahm, David E. (1977), *The Origins of Stoic Cosmology*, Ohio State University Press, Columbus.

Hall, Roland. (1970), "Yes, Hume Did Use Berkeley," *Philosophy* 45, pp. 152-153.

Hamou, Philippe. (2003) "Sens et fonction du modèle linguistique dans la Nouvelle Théorie de la Vision," in Berlioz (2003), pp. 47-78.

Hartz, G. A. (1992), "Leibniz's Phenomenalisms," *Philosophical Review* 101, pp. 511-549.

Hegel, Georg Wilhelm. (1975), *Hegel's Logic: Being Part One of the Encyclopaedia of the Philosophical Sciences*, tr. William Wallace, foreword J. N. Findlay, Clarendon Press, Oxford.

Hintikka, Jaakko. (1978), "A Discourse on Descartes' Method," in Hooker (1978), pp. 74-88.

Hintikka, Jaakko and Remes, Unto. (1974), *The Method of Analysis: Its Geometrical Origin and Its General Significance*, Boston Studies in the Philosophy of Science, vol. 25, Reidel, Dordrecht.

Hobbes, Thomas. (1656), *The Questions concerning Liberty, Necessity, and Chance*, in Molesworth (1839-1845), vol. 5.

Hooker, Michael (ed.) (1978), *Descartes: Critical and Interpretive Essays*, Johns Hopkins University Press, Baltimore.

Hont, Istvan. (1983), "The 'Rich Country-Poor Country' Debate in Scottish Classical Political Economy," in Hont and Ignatieff (1983), pp. 271-315.

Hont, I. and M. Ignatieff (eds.) (1983), *Wealth and Virtue: The Shaping of Politcal Economy in the Scottish Enlightenment*, Cambridge University Press, Cambridge.

Hume, David. (1987), *Essays Moral, Political, and Literary*, Revised Edition, E. F. Miller (ed.), Liberty Fund, Indianapolis.

—. (2000), *A Treatise of Human Nature*, D. F. Norton and M. J. Norton (eds), Oxford University Press, Oxford.

Hunter, Michael. (1989), *Establishing the New Science: The Experience of the Early Royal Society*, Boydell Press, Woolbridge.

Hutcheson, Francis. (2006), *Logic, Metaphysics, and the Sociability of Mankind*, James Moore and Michael Silverthorne (eds.), Liberty Fund, Indianapolis.

Hutchison, Keith. (1982), "What Happened to Occult Qualities in the Scientific Revolution?" ISIS 73, pp. 233-253.

Hutchison, Terence. (1988), *Before Adam Smith: The Emergence of Political Economy, 1662-1776*, Basil Blackwell, Oxford

Imbert, Claude (1980), "Stoic Logic and Alexandrian Poetics," in Schofield *et al.* (1980), pp. 182-216.

Inwood, Brad (ed.) (2003), *The Cambridge Companion to the Stoics*, Cambridge University Press, New York.

Jacob, Alexander. (1991), "The Neoplatonic Conception of Nature, in More, Cudworth, and Berkeley," in Gaukroger (1991), pp. 101-122.

Jaffro, Laurent. (2010), "Éducation moderne et tradition antique selon Berkeley," in Jaffro *et al.* (2010), pp. 277-286.

Jaffro, Laurent, Geneviève Brykman, and Claire Schwartz (eds.). (2010), *Berkeley's* Alciphron. *English Text and Essays in Interpretation*, Georg Olms Verlag, Hildesheim.

James, Susan. (1993), "Spinoza the Stoic," in Sorrell (1993), pp. 289-316.

Jesseph, Douglas M. (1993), *Berkeley's Philosophy of Mathematics*, Chicago University Press, Chicago, 1993.

Johnston, G. A. (1923), *The Development of Berkeley's Philosophy*, Macmillan, London.

Johnston, Joseph. (1970), *Bishop Berkeley's Querist in Historical Perspective*, Dundalgan Press, Dundalk.

Jolley, N. (1986), "Leibniz and Phenomenalism," *Studia Leibnitiana* 18, pp. 38-51.

Kabitz, W. (1932), "Leibniz und Berkeley," *Sitzungsberichte der preußischen Akademie der Wissenschaften*. Philosophisch-historische Klasse 24, pp. 623-636.

Kant, Immanuel. (1974), *Logic*, R. Hartman and W. Schwartz (trs), Library of Liberal Arts, Bobbs-Merrill, Indianapolis.

—. (1977), *Prolegomena to Any Future Metaphysics*, Paul Carus revised J. W. Ellington (tr.), Hackett, Indianapolis.

Kassler, Jamie C. (1991), "The Paradox of Power: Hobbes and Stoic Naturalism," in Gaukroger (1991), pp. 53-78.

Klemmt, Alfred. (1957), "Anmerkungen," in *George Berkeley; Eine Abhandlung über die Prinzipien der menschlichen Erkenntnis*, Felix Meiner, Hamburg.

Kneale, William C. and Martha Kneale. (1962), *The Development of Logic*, Clarendon Press, Oxford.

Kremer, Elmar J. and M. J. Latzer (eds.) (2001), *The Problem of Evil in Early Modern Philosophy*, University of Toronto Press, Toronto.

Kristeller, Paul O. (1984), "Stoic and Neoplatonic Sources of Spinoza's

Ethics," *History of European Ideas* 5, pp. 1-15.

Lapidge, Michael. (1978), "Stoic Cosmology," in Rist (1978), pp. 161-185.

Leduc-Fayette, Denise. (1997), "Qu'est que 'parler aux yeux'? Berkeley et le 'langage optique'," *Revue philosophique de la France et l'étranger* 122, pp. 409-427.

Leibniz, G. W. (1677-80), "Two Sects of Naturalists," in Ariew and Garber (1989), pp. 281-284.

—. (1686), *Discourse on Metaphysics.*

—. (1695), *A New System of Nature.*

—. (1714a), *Monadology.*

—. (1714b), *Principles of Nature and Grace.*

—. (1875-1890), *Die philosophischen Schriften von Gottfried Wilhelm Leibniz,* 7 vols, C. I. Gerhardt (ed.), Weidman, Berlin.

—. (1969), *Gottfried Wilhelm Leibniz: Philosophical Papers and Letters,* L. E. Loemker (ed.), Reidel, Dordrecht.

—. (1981), *New Essays on Human Understanding*, P. Remnant and J. Bennett (trs), Cambridge University Press, Cambridge.

—. (1989), *G. W. Leibniz: Philosophical Essays*, R. Ariew and D. Garber (eds), Hackett, Indianapolis.

Linden, D. E. J. et al. (1999), "The Myth of Upright Vision: A Psychophysical and Functional Imaging Study of Adaptation to Inverting Spectacles," *Perception* 28, pp. 469-491.

Lipton, Peter. (1991), *Inference to the Best Explanation*, Routledge, London.

Lloyd, A. C. (1978), "Emotion and Decision in Stoic Psychology," in Rist (1978), pp. 233-246.

Locke, John. (1936), *An Early Draft of Locke's Essay*, R. Aaron (ed.), Clarendon Press, Oxford.

—. (1975), *An Essay concerning Human Understanding*, P. H. Nidditch (ed.), Clarendon Press, Oxford.

Loeb, L. E. (1981), *From Descartes to Hume*, Cornell University Press, Ithaca.

Long, A. A. (ed.) (1971a), *Problems in* Stoicism, Athlone Press, London.

—. (1971b), "Language and Thought in Stoicism," in Long (1971a), pp. 75-113.

—. (1974), *Hellenistic Philosophy: Stoics, Epicureans, Sceptics*, Charles Scribner's Sons, New York.

—. (2003), "Stoicism in the Philosophical Tradition: Spinoza, Lipsius, Butler," in Miller and Inwood (2003), pp. 7-29.

Losonsky, Michael. (1994) "Locke on Meaning and Signification," in

Rogers (1994), pp. 123-141.
Lowe, E. J. (2005), *Locke*, Routledge, New York.
Luce, A. A. (1945), *Berkeley's Immaterialism*, Nelson, London.
Lüthy, C., J. E. Murdoch, and W. R. Newman (eds). (2001), *Late Medieval and Early Modern Corpuscular Matter Theories*, Brill, Leiden.
MacIntosh, J. J. (1971), "Leibniz and Berkeley," *Proceedings of the Aristotelian Society* 71, pp. 147-163.
Mackie, J. L. (1976), *Problems from Locke*, Oxford University Press, Oxford.
Malebranche, Nicholas. (1980), *The Search After Truth*, T. Lennon and P. J. Olscamp (trs), and *Elucidations of the Search After Truth*, T. Lennon (tr.), Ohio State University Press, Columbus.
Mates, Benson. (1961), *Stoic Logic*, University of California Press, Berkeley.
Mazauric, Simone. (2007), *Fontenelle et l'invention de l'histoire des sciences à l'aube des Lumières*, Fayard, Paris.
McCracken, Charles J. (1986), "Berkeley's Notion of Spirit," *History of European Ideas* 7, pp. 597-602.
McCracken, C. J. and Tipton, I. (eds.) (2000), *Berkeley's Principles and Dialogues: Background Source Materials*, Cambridge University Press, Cambridge.
McKim, Robert (1989), "Berkeley's Active Mind," *Archiv für Geschichte der Philosophie* 71, pp. 335-343.
Miller, Jon. (2003), "Stoics, Grotius, and Spinoza on Moral Deliberation," in Miller and Inwood (2003), pp. 116-140.
Miller, Jon and Brad Inwood (eds.) (2003), *Hellenistic and Early Modern Philosophy*, Cambridge University Press, New York.
Mitsis, Phillip. (2003), "Locke's Offices," in Miller and Inwood (2003), pp. 45-61.
Moked, Gabriel. (1988), *Particles and Ideas: Bishop Berkeley's Corpuscular Philosophy*, Clarendon Press, Oxford.
Molesworth, William (ed.) (1839-1945), *The English Works of Thomas Hobbes*, 11 vols, John Bohn, London.
Molyneux, William. (1692), *Dioptrica Nova*, Benj. Tooke, London.
Moreau, Pierre-François (ed.) (1999a), *Le Stoïcisme au XVIe et au XVIIe Siècle: Le retour des philosophies antiques à l'Age classique*, Albin Michel, Paris.
—. (1999b), "Les trois étapes du stoïcisme moderne," in Moreau (1999a), pp. 11-27.
Morrisroe Jr., Michael. (1973), "Did Hume Read Berkeley? A Conclusive Answer," *Philological Quarterly* 52, pp. 310-315.

Mossner, Ernest Campbell. (1948), "Hume's Early Memoranda, 1729-1740: The Complete Text," *Journal of the History of Ideas* 9, pp. 492-518.

Mossner, E. C. (1959), "Did Hume Ever Read Berkeley? A Rejoiner to Professor Popkin," *Journal of Philosophy* 56, pp. 992-95.

—. (1980), *The Life of David Hume*, 2nd Edition, Oxford University Press, Oxford.

Muehlmann, Robert. (1992), *Berkeley's Ontology*, Hackett, Indianapolis.

Neuchelmans, Gabriel. (1980), *Late-Scholastic and Humanist Theories of the Proposition*, North Holland, Amsterdam.

Newman, Lex (ed.) (2007), *Cambridge Companion to Locke's "Essay concerning Human Understanding,"* Cambridge University Press, Cambridge.

Newton, Isaac. (1952), *Optics, or A Treatise of the Reflections, Refractions, Inflections & Colours of Light*, based on the 4th edition London [1730], Dover, New York.

—. (1966), *Mathematical Principles: Of Natural Philosophy and His System of the World*, 2 volumes, A. Mott (tr.), revised F. Cajori, University of California Press, Berkeley.

Norton, David Fate and Mary J. Norton. (1996), *The David Hume Library*, Edinburgh Bibliographical Society, Edinburgh.

Nuchelmans, Gabriel. (1983), *Judgement and Proposition from Descartes to Kant*, North Holland, Amsterdam.

Olscamp, Paul. (1970), *The Moral Philosophy of George Berkeley*, Martinus Nijhoff, The Hague.

O'Shaughnessy, Brian. (1980), *The Will: A Dual Aspect Theory*, 2 vols, Cambridge University Press, Cambridge.

Osler, Margaret J. (ed.) (1991), *Atoms,* Pneuma*, and Tranquility: Epicurean and Stoic Themes in European Thought*, Cambridge University Press, New York.

Ott, Walter. (1997), "Locke and the Scholastics on Theological Discourse," *Locke Newsletter* 28, pp. 51-66.

Owen. G. E. L. (1965), "Inherence," *Phronesis* 10, pp. 97-105.

Owen, David. (2007), "Locke on Judgment ," in Newman (2007).

Pappas, George. (ed.) (1979), *Justification and Knowledge*, Reidel, Dordrecht.

Pappas, George S. (1983), "Adversary Metaphysics," *Philosophy Research Archives* 9, pp. 571-585.

Pappas, George. (2000), *Berkeley's Thought*, Cornell University Press, Ithaca.

—. (2007), "Berkeley's Assessment of Locke's Epistemology," in S.

Daniel (2007), pp. 229-249.
—. (2010), "Locke's Account of Sensitive Knowledge," in Campbell, O'Rourke, and Silverstein (2010), pp. 165-179.
Parigi S. (ed.). (2010), *George Berkeley: Religion and Science in the Age of Enlightenment*, International Archives of the History of Ideas, Springer, Berlin (forthcoming).
Pasnau, Robert. (2002), *Thomas Aquinas on Human Nature*, Cambridge University Press, Cambridge.
Peirce, Charles Sanders. (1940), *Philosophical Writings of Peirce*, Justus Buchler (ed.), Dover, New York.
Peterschmitt, Luc. (2005), *Sciences de la nature et philosophie dans la pensée de George Berkeley*, Atelier National de Reproduction des Thèses, Lille (see also http://documents.univ-lille3.fr/files/pub/www/recherche/theses/PETERSCHIMITT_LUC/html/these.html).
Pitcher, George. (1977), *Berkeley*, Routledge & Kegan Paul, Boston.
Popkin, Richard H. (1959), "Did Hume Ever Read Berkeley?," *The Journal of Philosophy* 56, pp. 535-545.
—. (1964), "So, Hume did Read Berkeley," *The Journal of Philosophy* 61, pp. 773-778.
Principe, L. M. (2001), "Wilhelm Homberg: Chymical Corpuscularianism and Chrysopoeia in the Early Eighteen Century," in Lüthy, Murdoch, and Newman (2001), pp. 535-556.
Randall, John Hermann. (1940), "The Development of Scientific Method in the School of Padua," *Journal of the History of Ideas* 1, pp. 177-206.
Rashid, Salim. (1990), "Adam Smith's Acknowledgments: Neo-Plagiarism and the Wealth of Nations," *The Journal of Libertarian Studies* IX, pp. 1-24.
Reid, Thomas. (1969), *Essays on the Intellectual Powers of Man*, Introduction B. A. Brody, M.I.T. Press, Cambridge.
Rist, John M. (ed.) (1978), *The Stoics*, University of California Press, Berkeley.
Robinet, A. (1983), "Leibniz: Lecture du *Treatise* de Berkeley," Les Etudes Philosophiques no 2, pp. 217-223.
Robinson, Howard. (1994), *Perception*, Routledge, London and New York.
Rogers, G. A. J. (ed.). (1994), *Locke's Philosophy: Content and Context*, Clarendon Press, Oxford.
Rorty, Richard, J. B. Schneewind, and Q. Skinner (eds.) (1984), *Philosophy in History: Essays in the Historiography of Philosophy*, Cambridge University Press, Cambridge.

Ross, James F. (1981), *Portraying Analogy*, Cambridge University Press, Cambridge.

Russell, Bertrand. (1912), *The Problems of Philosophy*, Oxford University Press, Oxford.

—. (1927), *An Outline of Philosophy*, W. W. Norton, New York.

—. (1948), *Human Knowledge: Its Scope and Limits*, Simon and Schuster, New York.

Rutherford, D. (1994), "Leibniz and the Problem of Monadic Aggregation," *Archiv fűr Geschichte der Philosophie* 76, pp. 65-90.

—. (1995), *Leibniz and the Rational Order of Nature*, Cambridge University Press, Cambridge.

Rutherford, Donald. (2001), "Leibniz and the Stoics: The Consolations of Theodicy," in Kremer and Latzer (2001), pp. 138-164.

—. (2003), "*Patience sans Espérance*: Leibniz's Critique of Stoicism," in Miller and Inwood (2003), pp. 62-89.

—. (2004), "On the Happy Life: Descartes vis-à-vis Seneca," in Strange and Zupko (2004), pp. 177-197.

Rutherford, D. (2008), "Leibniz as Idealist," *Oxford Studies in Early Modern Philosophy* 4, pp. 141-190.

Rynasiewicz, Robert. (1996), "Absolute versus Relational Space-Time: An Outmoded Debate?," *Journal of Philosophy* 93, 279-306.

Sargent, Rose-Mary. (1995), The Diffident Naturalist. *Robert Boyle and the Philosophy of Experiment*, The University of Chicago Press, Chicago and London.

Schofield, M., M. Burnyeat, and J. Barnes (eds.) (1980), Doubt and Dogmatism, Clarendon Press, Oxford.

Simon, Gérard. (1996), "Kepler ou les leçons d'un contre-exemple en épistémologie," in *Sciences et savoirs aux XVIe et XVIIe siècles*, Presses Universitaires du Septentrion, Villeneuve d'Ascq.

Smith, A. D. (2002), *The Problem of Perception*, Harvard University Press, Cambridge, Mass.

Sorrell, Tom (ed.) (1993), *The Rise of Modern Philosophy*, Clarendon Press, Oxford.

Sosa, E. (1987), *Essays on the Philosophy of George Berkeley*, Reidel, Dordrecht.

Sprat, Thomas. (1958), *History of the Royal Society* [1667], ed. with critical apparatus by J. I. Cope and H. W. Jones, Washington Universities Studies, Saint-Louis, Miss.

Steven K. Strange, K. Steven, and J. Zupko (eds.) (2004), *Stoicism: Traditions and Transformations*, Cambridge University Press, New York.

Stoneham, Tom. (2002), *Berkeley's World: An Examination of the Three Dialogues*, Oxford University Press, Oxford.

Strawson, Galen. (1994), "The Impossibility of Moral Responsibility," *Philosophical Studies* 75, pp. 5-24.

Timmermann, A., N. Jardine, and D. Banham (eds). (2006), *The Body as Instrument*, Latin Therapy Group, HPS Department, Cambridge: "The World on a String" and "Kepler and the Earthly Soul Detector."

Todorov, Tzvetan. (1982), *Theories of the Symbol*, Catherine Porter (tr.), Cornell University Press, Ithaca, NY.

Turbayne, Colin, M. (1970), *The Myth of Metaphor*, University of South Carolina Press, Columbia.

—. (1982), "Lending a Hand to Philonous: The Berkeley, Plato, Aristotle Connection," in Turbayne (1982), pp. 295-310.

—. (ed.) (1982), *Berkeley: Critical and Interpretive Essays*, University of Minnesota Press, Minneaopolis.

Valberg, J. J. (1992), *The Puzzle of Experience*, Clarendon Press, Oxford.

Van Cleve, James. (2008), "Berkeley vs. Reid on Three Puzzles of Vision" (International Berkeley Conference, Newport RI, June 2008).

Verbeke, Gerard. (1991), "Ethics and Logic in Stoicism," in Osler (1991), pp. 11-24.

Walmsley, P. (2001), *The Rhetoric of Berkeley's Philosophy*, Cambridge University Press, Cambridge.

Watson, Gerard. (1966), *The Stoic Theory of Knowledge*, Queen's University Press, Belfast.

Watson, Gary (ed.) (2003), *Free Will*, Oxford University Press, New York.

Watts, Isaac. (1996), *Logic, or The Right Use of Reason in the Inquiry After Truth with a Variety of Rules to Guard Against Error in the Affairs of Religion and Human Life, as well as the Sciences* [1724], Soli Deo Gloria Publications, Morgan, PA.

Weiner, Philip. (1959), "Did Hume Ever Read Berkeley?," *Journal of Philosophy* 56, pp. 533-535.

Wennerlind, Carl and M. Schabas (eds.) (2008) *David Hume's Political Economy*, Routledge, London.

White, Michael J. (2003), "Stoic Natural Philosophy (Physics and Cosmology)," in Inwood (2003), pp. 124-152.

Wilson, M. D. (1987), "The Phenomenalisms of Leibniz and Berkeley," in Sosa (1987), p. 3-22.

Winkler, Kenneth P. (1989), *Berkeley: An Interpretation*, Oxford University Press, Oxford.

Winkler, K. P. (ed.) (2005), *The Cambridge Companion to Berkeley*, Cambridge University Press, Cambridge.

Yolton, John W. (1983), *Thinking Matter*, University of Minnesota Press, Minneapolis.

CONTRIBUTORS

Timo Airaksinen is Professor of Philosophy, University of Helsinki, and the Vice-President of the International Berkeley Society and the Philosophical Society of Finland, author of several papers on Berkeley's *Siris*.

Bertil Belfrage is Research Fellow in the History of Ideas and Sciences, Lund University, author of numerous papers on Berkeley, editor of *George Berkeley's Manuscript Introduction* (1987).

Talia Mae Bettcher is an Associate Professor of Philosophy at California State University, Los Angeles, author of Berkeley's *Philosophy of Spirit: Consciousness, Ontology, and the Elusive Subject* (2007).

Martha Bolton, Professor of Philosophy at Rutgers University, is author of numerous papers on Berkeley.

Richard Brook, Professor Emeritus of Philosophy, Bloomsburg University, author of *Berkeley's Philosophy of Science* (1973).

Geneviève Brykman, Professor Emerita of Philosophy, Université Paris X, Nanterre, author of *Berkeley, philosophie et apologétique* (1982) and *Berkeley et le voile des mots* (1993).

Constantine George Caffentzis, Professor of Philosophy, University of Southern Maine, Portland, Maine, author of *Exciting the Industry of Mankind: George Berkeley's Philosophy of Money* (2000).

Stephen H. Daniel, Professor of Philosophy, Texas A&M University, editor of *New Interpretations of Berkeley's Thought* and *Reexamining Berkeley's Philosophy* (2007).

Mykolas Drunga, Lecturer at the Public Communications Department and Research Associate at the Lithuanian Studies Center, Vytautas Magnus University, Kaunas, Lithuania.

Daniel Flage, Professor of Philosophy at James Madison University, author of *Berkeley's Doctrine of Notions: A Reconstructions Based on His Theory of Meaning* (1987).

Marc Hight is Associate Professor of Philosophy at Hampden-Sydney College and author of *Idea and Ontology* (2008).

Charles McCracken, Professor Emeritus of Philosophy at Michigan State University, author of *Malebranche and British Philosophy* (1983) and co-editor (with Ian C. Tipton) of *Berkeley's Principles and Dialogues: Background Source Materials* (2000).

George Pappas is Professor Emeritus of Philosophy, at Ohio State University, author of *Berkeley's Thought* (2000).

Luc Peterschmitt, Associate Professor, Lycee Diderot, Carvin, author of *Sciences de la nature et philosophie dans la pensée de George Berkeley* (2007).

Howard Robinson is University Professor in Philosophy at Central European University, Budapest and Honorary Visiting Professor in Philosophy at York. He is editor of the Oxford World's Classics edition of Berkeley's *Principles* and *Three Dialogues* and co-editor (with John Foster) of *Essays on Berkeley* (1985).

Kenneth P. Winkler, Professor of Philosophy at Yale University, author of *Berkeley: An Interpretation* (1989) and editor of *The Cambridge Companion to Berkeley* (2005).

INDEX